The Best Book
of

Paradox 3

The Best Book of WordPerfect® 5.1
Vincent Alfieri,
Revised by Ralph Blodgett

The Best Book of: WordStar® (Features Release 5.0)
Vincent Alfieri

The Best Book of Microsoft® Word 5
Kate Miller Barnes

The First Book of WordPerfect® 5.1
Kate Barnes

The Best Book of: dBASE IV™
Joseph-David Carrabis

The Best Book of: OS/2™ Database Manager
Edward Jones

dBASE IV™ Programmer's Reference Guide
Edward Jones

The First Book of Paradox® 3
Jonathan Kamin

The First Book of PC Tools® Deluxe
Gordon McComb

The First Book of Quicken
Gordon McComb

Understanding dBASE IV™
Judd Robbins

Understanding dBASE IV™ Programming
Judd Robbins

The Best Book of: DOS
Alan Simpson

The Best Book of: Lotus® 1-2-3®, Third Edition, Release 2.2
Alan Simpson

The First Book of Lotus® 1-2-3® Release 2.2
Alan Simpson and Paul Lichtman

The Best Book of Microsoft® Works 2.0 for the PC, Second Edition
Ruth K. Witkin
(forthcoming)

For the retailer nearest you, or to order directly from the publisher, call 800-257-5755. International orders telephone 609-461-6500.

The Best Book of

Celeste Robinson

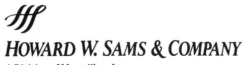

HOWARD W. SAMS & COMPANY

A Division of Macmillan, Inc.
11711 North College, Suite 141, Carmel, IN 46032 USA

FIRST EDITION
FIRST PRINTING–1990

International Standard Book Number: 0-672-22704-5
Library of Congress Catalog Card Number: 89-64073

Acquisitions Editor: *Richard K. Swadley*
Development Editor: *Marie Butler-Knight*
Manuscript Editor: *Martin E. Brown*
Production Editor: *Marj Hopper*
Production Coordinator: *Becky Imel*
Illustrator: *Don Clemons*
Indexer: *Hilary Adams*
Cover Art: *DGS&D Advertising, Inc.*
Cover Photography: *Cassell Productions, Inc.*
Compositor: *Cromer Graphics*
Production: *Dan Armstrong, Bill Basham, Claudia Bell, Brad Chinn, Don Clemons, Sally Copenhaver, Tom Emrick, Dennis Hager, Corinne Harmon, Tami Hughes, Bill Hurley, Jodi Jensen, David Kline, Larry Lynch, Lori A. Lyons, Jennifer Matthews, Cindy L. Phipps, Joe Ramon, Dennis Sheehan, Louise Shinault, Bruce Steed, Mary Beth Wakefield, Jenny Watson, Nora Westlake*

Printed in the United States of America

To Ray, Ray, Coco, and DD

Overview

Contents

Foreward xxix

Preface xxx

Introduction xxxv

PART One

Using Paradox Interactively 1

***1.* Paradox Basics** 3

Paradox Modes 3

Paradox Commands 4

The Paradox Main Menu 4

P A R T

Using Scripts and PAL 321

P A R T

Getting the Most Out of Paradox 411

Foreword

Finally—a book for Paradox users that teaches the fundamentals of building your own database applications. As easy to read as Paradox is easy to use, this comprehensive guide not only explains the concepts and commands, but also shows you how to "glue" them together to create useful applications.

The Best Book of Paradox 3 is written by a lady who knows her stuff—as well she ought to, having spent two years serving on and managing the Paradox customer support team. When it comes to users' questions, Celeste Robinson has heard 'em all, from the fine points of posing multi-table queries to practical advice for the lovelorn. Her wealth of experience in explaining Paradox to users at all levels of sophistication is quite evident in this book. In addition to clear explanations of the fundamentals, Ms. Robinson offers a gold mine of tips and tricks that manuals (usually written before anyone has had much experience with the product) never cover.

Among the chief design goals of Paradox was to make databases fun, rather than scary; to make building an application more like playing a game than like real work. Ms. Robinson has ably contributed to that aim with a hit that will take you well beyond first base in using Paradox.

ROB SHOSTAK

Preface

Paradox's name is fitting because it is easy to use, yet rich in features that make it suitable for a wide variety of applications. Paradox is unusual in that it can be used effectively by different levels of computer users. It is popular with first-time database users as well as with programmers who use it to create their own software.

Paradox evolved from the work of Richard Schwartz and Robert Shostak, two computer scientists who worked together at SRI in Menlo Park, California. Their goal was to use QBE technology in a database program that would make it easy for all types of personal computer users to retrieve and analyze their data. QBE stands for Query-By-Example, a technique for extracting data from a database. Until recently, Paradox was the only PC database manager that utilized true QBE capabilities.

Paradox's QBE capabilities are really the heart of the software and what make the software special. The Paradox implementation of QBE enables you to ask questions about your data without having to learn any special command language. This means you have easy access to your information once it is in Paradox format. Some of the other features which Paradox includes are:

- "What you see is what you get" form and report generators
- Graphing
- Instant script recording
- PAL, the Paradox Application Language
- Multiuser capabilities

There is also an inexpensive Runtime version available and special versions of Paradox for 386 computers and OS/2. From the list above, you can see that Paradox is a very complete product. It is user-friendly, but there is so much available that sometimes it is difficult to know just where to start.

The intention of this book is not just to summarize the information available in the Paradox manuals, but to assist you in getting Paradox to be truly useful in managing your information. For many people, there is a place for using Paradox somewhere between poking through the menus to do ad hoc tasks and programming a ready-to-use application. This book is designed for the Paradox user in that place.

A lot of your success in using Paradox depends on your willingness to sit down and actually try things for yourself. Paradox offers you the possibility of doing many tasks in several different ways. When this first becomes obvious, it can be confusing. With a little practice, though, Paradox becomes a joy to use. Hopefully this book will assist in getting you to that point. Good luck in your "Paradoxing!"

Acknowledgments

The biggest thank you goes to my family—my husband Ray, Mom, Dad, Monique, Madonna, Veronica and my children Ray, Coco and Deirdre. They all helped create the time for me to write. Thanks also to Steve King who had the idea for this book and to Bill Gladstone for arranging for it to be published. To the people at Sams who I worked with—Marie Butler Knight, Jim Rounds and Richard Swadley—thank you for your help and encouragement. Thanks to Marty Brown for his thoughtful changes to the text. And thanks to Jonathan Kamin, author of *The First Book of Paradox*, for his advice on the mechanics of writing a book and to Dr. Scott Starrett for the use of his color monitor. Also, many of the pictures in Appendix I were contributed by Corinne Cottle—thank you, Corinne.

Trademarks

CompuServe is a trademark of CompuServe Information Service.

dBASE II, dBASE III, dBASE III Plus, and dBASE IV are trademarks of Ashton-Tate, Inc.

Desktop for Paradox is copyrighted by Kallista, Inc.

Disk Optimizer is a trademark of SoftLogic Solutions.

Hayes is a registered trademark of Hayes Microcomputer Products, Inc.

Hercules Graphics Card is a trademark of Hercules Computer Technology.

Hewlett-Packard, HP, and HP LaserJet are registered trademarks of Hewlett-Packard Corporation.

IBM OS/2 Extended Edition 1.1 Database Manager is a trademark of International Business Machines Corp.

IBM PC-XT 286 and PC-AT are trademarks of International Business Machines Corp.

IBM PS/2 Models 50, 60, and 80 are trademarks of International Business Machines Corp.

InSet is a registered trademark of Inset Systems, Inc.

Lotus 1-2-3 is a registered trademark of Lotus Development Corporation.

Microsoft SQL Server is a trademark of Microsoft Corporation.

Norton Utilities is a trademark of Peter Norton Computing.

Novell and Novell Advanced Netware are registered trademarks of Novell, Inc.

ORACLE SQL Server is a trademark of Oracle Corporation.

PAL-Edit is a trademark of Kallista, Inc.

Paradox 2.0 and Paradox 3.0 are registered trademarks of Borland International, Inc.

Paradox 386 is a registered trademark of Borland International Inc.

Paradox Network Pack (2.0) and Paradox LAN Pack (3.0) are registered trademarks of Borland International, Inc.

Paradox OS/2 and Paradox SQL are registered trademarks of Borland International, Inc.

Paralex is copyrighted by Zenreich Systems.

ParaTrack is a registered trademark of Financial Modeling Specialists.

P-Dial is copyrighted by Kallista, Inc.

PFS is a trademark of Software Publishing Corporation.

PlayRight is a trademark of the Burgiss Group.

Postscript, Encapsulated Postscript File are registered trademarks of Adobe Systems, Inc.

pTools is a trademark of Compumethods.

QEMM (Quarterdeck Expanded Memory Manager) is a trademark of Quarterdeck Office Systems.

Quattro and Reflex are registered trademarks of Borland International, Inc.

Symphony is a registered trademark of Lotus Development Corporation.

3Com and 3Com 3Plus are trademarks of AT&T.

Torus and Tapestry Network are registered trademarks of Torus Systems, Inc.

VINES is a registered trademark of Banyan Corporation.

VisiCalc is a trademark of Visi-Corp.

X-TAB is a registered trademark of Financial Modeling Specialists.

XTree and XTree Pro are trademarks of Executive Systems, Inc.

Introduction

What Is Paradox?

Paradox is a relational database management system. In a relational database, information is stored in files called *tables* which can be linked using common information. A group of tables which are used together is referred to as a *database*.

Paradox lets you link information in separate files called tables.

Paradox provides the means to create tables and to use them together in many ways. You can link tables to create new tables, update tables against each other, create graphs and reports, and accomplish other information-management tasks. The benefits of Paradox's relational capabilities will become clear as you read through this book.

What This Book Covers

This book is written for interactive Paradox users who want to make the most of their system. It contains information about how to design and create Paradox tables which can be used together in a relational database system. It also outlines how to create custom forms, reports, and graphs from your tables. These are the basic building blocks of your Paradox system.

Mastering queries lets you maximize what Paradox can do for you.

Another important part of your Paradox system is queries. Queries can be used to do much of the work involved in managing a database.

The query portion of Paradox is described in detail, with many examples of various types of queries.

Information on how to use scripts and PAL, the Paradox Application (programming) Language, is covered. An introduction to PAL will get you started using PAL. Advanced PAL techniques will not be described, but there are some notes about using procedure libraries and the Runtime version of Paradox.

This book also offers tips on performance, customizing your Paradox system, networking with Paradox, and troubleshooting. This reference information can help you get the most out of your Paradox system.

How This Book Is Organized

This book is *not* organized according to the Paradox menu structure. That is because looking at the Main Menu does not really give you an idea of what to do first. We'll set up a Paradox system for a fictitious children's clothing company, The Raspberry Patch, and in the process, see how Paradox commands work.

There are three sections to this book as outlined below.

Part One: Using Paradox Interactively

Outline your database needs before you get started using Paradox.

The first part of this book offers information on how to plan and set up a Paradox database. Chapter 1 covers basics such as the menus, what you see on the Paradox screen, and definitions. If you are already familiar with Paradox, you may want to forgo reading the first chapter and just review the items highlighted with icons in the margins.

Chapters 2 through 8 show you how to use the Create, Form, Modify, Ask, Report, and Graph Menus. Descriptions of the commands on each menu are included as well as step-by-step instructions on how to use them for specific tasks for The Raspberry Patch.

Chapter 9 contains information on how to keep your Paradox database organized once it is set up.

Part Two: Using Scripts and PAL

One of the nicest things about Paradox is that it is relatively easy for a non-programmer to automate repetitive tasks. This section of the book shows you how to automate your Paradox system, making the most of your computer's timesaving capabilities. How to use the Paradox Scripts feature is explained along with an introduction to PAL. Examples are given which illustrate how to use PAL for utility functions as well.

Information is included on the Personal Programmer, another part of Paradox. There are suggestions about when to use the Personal Programmer, and when to avoid using it. The last chapter in that section contains information about using procedure libraries, Runtime, and the PAL Debugger.

Part Three: Getting the Most Out of Paradox

The last part of this book offers tips on customizing your Paradox system, networking, troubleshooting, and performance tips. Once you have set up your Paradox system, those chapters may prove the most useful to you.

The Appendices

There are several appendices which cover general information on system requirements and installation procedures, add-on products, command summaries, and a condensed reference of useful PAL commands and functions.

Notes on the Format Used in This Book

Icons

Icons are used in the margins of this book to indicate points which should not be missed. Here is a legend of the areas which they highlight:

 indicates a key point in understanding how Paradox works.

 points out timesaving tips.

 highlights performance tips.

shows where you may run into problems.

 is used for helpful tips.

Paradox Commands

Menu Commands

Most commands can be invoked through Paradox's menu system. Strings of Paradox menu commands are shown in this format: **T**ools/**I**nfo/**I**nventory/CUSTOMER. **T**ools, **I**nfo, and **I**nventory represent menu choices from successive menus. *CUSTOMER* is used to represent the name of a typical Paradox table. All references to Paradox table names are shown in uppercase letters.

Function Key Commands

There are function key shortcuts for many menu commands.

Function key commands are noted as *Fx* where *x* is the number of the function key to be pressed. Many menu commands can be invoked by pressing a function key. These shortcuts are listed in Appendix B.

Other Key Combinations

Paradox also has commands which are invoked by holding down the Alt or Ctrl key and then pressing a letter or function key. These commands are shown as *Alt-F7* and *Ctrl-U*, for example. All of these commands are listed in Appendix B.

Planning Your Paradox System

Here is a general guideline which can be used to set up your Paradox system. Some suggestions may not be clear until the corresponding section of the book has been reviewed. All of the steps will be illustrated by setting up sample Paradox tasks for The Raspberry Patch.

Design and Create Your Tables

Although Paradox's ease-of-use makes it tempting to sit down at the computer and start typing, spending some time considering the best design for your database can save you much effort in the long run. Analyze your information and decide into what logical groups the information falls. This step is the most important of all your Paradox tasks. Each group of information will become a table in Paradox.

It makes sense to be familiar with how Paradox links tables, both in queries and multitable forms and reports, before you actually create your tables. There are certain rules for linking tables which affect how a table should be structured. These rules will be explained in Chapter 2, along with the instructions about how to create tables.

To import fixed length ASCII files, use the Flimport utility included with Paradox.

If your information is already in one of the many file formats which Paradox can "import," you may be able to eliminate the table-creation step altogether. The Tools/ExportImport/Import commands are used to access Paradox's data import feature. However, if you import tables which will be used together, you may need to restructure them to make sure that the proper linking fields are in place. How to restructure tables also will be covered in Chapter 2.

When you create tables, either manually or by importing information, be sure to save them in a directory which is separate from the Paradox system files. It is a good idea to keep all tables for a related set of tasks in their own directory.

See What Is Possible with Paradox Forms, Queries, and Reports

Taking the time to understand how to do tasks in Paradox will shorten the overall process of getting your system to work. Even if you have been using a spreadsheet program, or another database program, it may not be immediately obvious how to best use Paradox to manage your information. Consider the following points before you start setting up your forms, queries, and reports:

- You can use forms to view and update more than one table at a time without first doing queries.

Tables can be linked using forms or reports as well as queries.

- The query mechanism is quite powerful. It can be used for many functions other than to just search for data.

- You can use reports to perform calculations and to summarize information.

By following through the examples in this book, you probably will see ways to use Paradox which you had not considered.

Create Forms

Create any custom forms needed to view, enter, or update your information. Use the Paradox Image command to customize your table views, if desired, and to set default formats for displaying your information. Chapter 3 will show you how to do this.

Choose a Method for Updating Tables

Decide on the best way to update your tables. Paradox has Edit, Coedit, DataEntry and MultiEntry modes which are used to update tables. These modes will be described in Chapter 4. Each mode has its own unique features which you may want to take advantage of.

You can also update tables using queries. Chapter 5 will explain how to use a query to update tables, as well as to search for information. For many applications, Paradox queries can be used to do most of the work.

Create Reports and Graphs

Think about any reports which you will want to create from your tables. If you will be reporting just on one table, you can use the Report Generator to create the custom reports you need. Remember that the Report Generator can perform calculations and provide other summary information, as well. If you don't need to save your calculations or summaries permanently, you may be able to simplify things by including these steps in your reports.

See Chapter 6 for the rules on linking tables with reports.

If you need to report on more than one table at a time, determine whether you can use the Report Generator's "lookup" feature to include the information you need. You can also create a query or queries to link your tables and then report on the resulting ANSWER table. Chapter 6 is devoted to Paradox reports. Chapter 8 will explain how to create graphs.

Customize Your Paradox System

Be sure to check the Blank = 0 setting with the Custom script if you do calculations with blank values.

Customize your copy of Paradox by using the Custom script and an .INIT file if desired. This can be a real time-saver. You may want to look at doing this early-on in your project. There are many options which you can change with the Custom script. You may want to change these right away. For example, you can define a default working directory and create custom set-up strings for your printer. A full explanation of all options which can be set with the Custom script is included in Chapter 13.

Tune Your Paradox System

Look at ways to optimize your Paradox system for better performance. You can change the way Paradox uses your computer's memory, table structures, directory organization, and make other such modifications. See Chapter 14 for suggestions.

Automate Your Paradox Tasks

Create the scripts necessary to automate any functions which must be done repeatedly. You can do this simply by recording scripts, or you can use PAL to write scripts, and optionally, proceduralize them for even better performance and memory utilization. Chapters 10 through 12 explain this process.

Getting Started

It is easy to change table structures, forms, reports, and even queries, in Paradox, so don't try to figure out the best way to do things before you even begin. Part of the fun in using Paradox is seeing how you can make it work more simply, or more quickly, than you originally thought possible. Paradox is quite complex. All of its extensive capabilities will not be obvious immediately. Only through using Paradox will you appreciate everything it can do for you. Hopefully, this book will help you get to that point more quickly!

Using Paradox
Interactively

Paradox Basics

Before you start creating your tables and working with them, it is important to understand how Paradox, itself, is organized. This chapter will show you how to use the Paradox menus and covers other Paradox basics. If you are already familiar with Paradox, you may want to skip this chapter and just look over the areas indicated by the icons for information which might be useful.

Paradox Modes

Paradox indicates the current mode in the upper-right corner of the screen.

Paradox is actually several programs in one. The main portion of the program allows you to look at your information and to ask questions about it, using queries. This part of Paradox is called Main mode. When you first load Paradox, you are in Main mode by default.

There are 11 other Paradox modes:

- *Create* is used to create Paradox tables.
- *Coedit* allows you and other users to edit tables concurrently.
- *DataEntry* is used to add records to a table using a separate ENTRY table.
- *Edit* is the basic mode for changing table information.
- *Form* allows you to design and change forms for viewing tables.
- *Graph* gives you access to Paradox's powerful Graph subsystem.
- *Report* is used to create, change, and generate reports used to print information in tables.

- *Restructure* is the way to change a table's structure.
- *Password* is the mode used to protect Paradox objects.
- *Script* lets you create and play scripts.
- *Sort* is used to sort Paradox tables.

Paradox Commands

Most Paradox commands can be invoked through the Paradox menu system. Each mode has its own set of menus.

The Paradox Main Menu

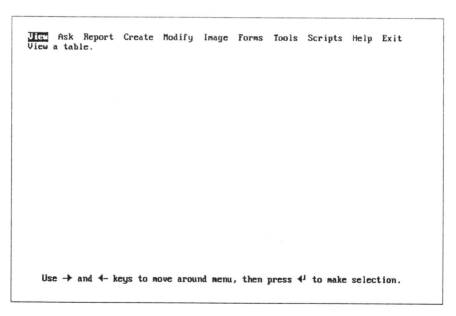

Figure 1.1. Paradox Main Menu

The Paradox Main Menu, shown in Figure 1.1, is brought up by pressing F10 when you are in Main mode. Menu choices can be selected by using the right- or left-arrow keys to highlight a menu choice and then pressing Enter. Home moves the cursor to the first menu choice. End goes to the last menu choice. You can also simply press the key of the first letter of the desired menu choice. This is a quick way for experienced users to navigate through menu trees. As you move the cursor through the menu choices, you will notice that a description for each menu choice is displayed on the second line of the screen.

The other Paradox modes are accessed through one or more commands on the Main Menu. For example, you can reach Edit mode by choosing Modify on the Main Menu and Edit on the next menu. Similarly, to enter Graph mode, choose Image/Graph from the Main Menu. We'll refer to a series of menu choices such as this in the following way: Modify/Edit. There are also some shortcuts, using the function keys, for entering some modes. Those commands will be pointed out in the text and are summarized in Appendix B.

Modes other than Main mode can be accessed only from Main mode. To change modes, therefore, you must first be in Main mode. In most cases, you do this by pressing F2 to "DO-IT!" or by canceling the current operation by choosing Cancel from that mode's menu.

Other Menus

F10 is the menu key in every mode.

Each mode has its own set of menus which are available by pressing F10. For example, while you are in Edit mode, you will get only the Edit Menu when you press F10. The Edit mode Menu is shown in Figure 1.2.

```
Image  Undo  ValCheck  Help  DO-IT!  Cancel                    Edit
Resize or reformat an image; move to a field, record, or value; pick a form.
ORDERS   Order #        Date      Customer # Salesperson
     1
```

Figure 1.2. Edit mode Menu

See Appendix A for a listing of the menus in each mode. A common mistake is trying to figure out how to do something which is available only in a mode other than the current one. For example, to perform a query on a table which you are editing, you must press F2 or choose DO-IT! from the Edit Menu to exit from Edit mode first. This will return you to Main mode. You can then press F10 and choose Ask on the Main Menu.

The current mode is displayed in the upper-right corner of the screen, unless it is overwritten by a menu or a prompt.

You can see this in Figure 1.3 where Main is displayed in reverse video in the upper-right corner of the screen.

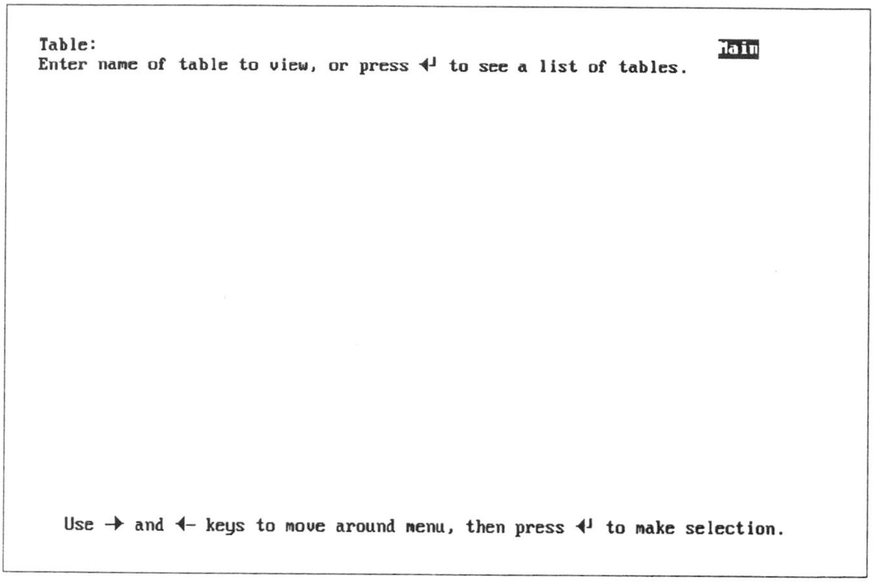

```
Table:                                                          Main
Enter name of table to view, or press ↵ to see a list of tables.




















Use → and ← keys to move around menu, then press ↵ to make selection.
```

Figure 1.3. Main displayed in upper-right corner of the screen

Special Command Keys in Paradox

Many Paradox commands (or a series of commands) can be invoked with a single keystroke or a combination of keystrokes. Instead of using **R**eport/**O**utput/TABLE/**R** to produce the standard report for *TABLE*, you can simply press Alt-F7 while viewing TABLE in Main mode. Similarly, you can get into Edit mode by pressing F9 while viewing a table in Main mode. The most frequently used command keys are listed below:

- *F1* gives you access to the context-sensitive help system.
- *F2* is used to "DO-IT!" and return to Main mode.
- *F3*, "Up Image," moves the cursor up one image on the screen.
- *F4* is the "Down Image" key.
- *F5* is used to place example elements in queries.
- *F6* Checkmarks fields in queries.
- *Alt-F7* produces an "Instant Report."
- *F8* clears an image from the workspace.
- *F9* takes you into Edit mode.
- *F10* brings up the menu for the current mode.

See Appendix B for other command shortcuts.

Some terms, such as *image* or *workspace*, may not be clear yet. They will be defined later in this chapter. The important thing to note is that you can use the function keys to invoke many Paradox commands, including some not available through the menus.

Paradox Tables

Paradox keeps database information in files which are called *tables*. Tables are simply rows and columns of information. A Paradox table, as it is displayed on the screen, is shown in Figure 1.4. This table, called *CUSTOMER*, is used to store customer-related information for The Raspberry Patch.

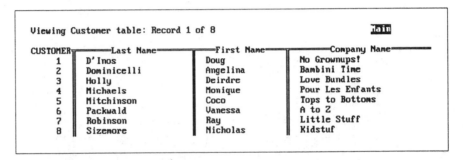

Figure 1.4. Paradox table as shown on the screen

Records

Although you can have records up to 4,000 characters, you will get better performance and memory utilization with shorter records.

Each row in a table is called a *record*. A record is simply a group of related pieces of information. In the CUSTOMER table, shown in Figure 1.4, there is one record for each Raspberry Patch customer. Notice that each record has the same layout.

Fields

Fields are individual pieces of information such as a name, a number or a date, which make up a record. The longest field you can have is 255 characters. You can have a total of 255 fields in a record, but the total record length cannot exceed 4,000 characters. For a "keyed table," this limit is 1,350 characters. (*Keyed tables* are tables which have a *primary index*. How to set up primary indexes, and when to use them, will be explained in Chapter 2.)

There are five different Paradox *field types*: Alphanumeric, Number, Short number, Currency and Date. Field types will be described, in detail, in Chapter 2.

The information which is stored in a field is called the *field value*. Paradox uses field values to relate, or link, tables in queries and other operations.

Temporary Tables

During operations such as queries and sorts, Paradox creates *temporary tables*. Some temporary tables are deleted by Paradox as soon as the current operation has been completed. Other temporary tables are deleted when you exit from Paradox, or the next time Paradox performs a similar task. An example of this a temporary table the ANSWER table which Paradox sometimes creates as the result of a query. You must not use the names of Paradox's temporary tables for your own tables unless you want your table to be deleted when you exit from Paradox. A complete list of temporary table names is included in Chapter 2.

Queries

Mastering the use of queries for different tasks will make you a power Paradox user.

A query is usually thought of as being a question. In Paradox, though, a query can be much more than that. Queries are created with the `Ask` command. They can be used to perform many varied tasks. The simplest queries are used to ask questions about a table such as:

- Which of my customers live in New York?
- How many pairs of jeans did The Raspberry Patch sell last month?
- Which bills are outstanding this month?

For queries which ask questions, Paradox will create an ANSWER table which contains records which meet the query criteria. An ANSWER table is a temporary table.

Queries also can be used to do calculations, update one table against another, insert or delete information from tables, find specific records, make global changes, and perform analyses of information in a table using "Set" operations. Each of these functions can be done selectively using "selection criteria" in queries.

Queries will be covered in detail in Chapter 5.

How Paradox "Links" Tables

As a relational database, Paradox can use more than one table at a time. It does this by a process called *linking*. Paradox "links" tables by looking for matching values in specified fields. In queries, you do this by using "placemarkers," called *example elements*, to indicate linking fields among tables.

For multi-table forms, Paradox will ask you to specify linking fields when you embed the form from one table into the form for a related table. *Lookup tables* in reports are handled similarly. Details on these linking operations will be included in the chapters on queries, forms, and reports.

It is important to remember that Paradox is flexible in the way it uses tables together. It is not necessary to define explicit relationships between tables when they are created. Table relationships are created "on-the-fly" when you tell Paradox to link tables using specific fields in forms, queries, and reports.

Families in Paradox

All Paradox objects, such as forms or reports, which are associated with a table are part of that table's *family*. The first part of a family member's filename has the same name as the table to which it belongs. The file extension indicates the type of family member it is. The different family members, and their file extensions, are listed in Table 1.1.

Table 1.1 Paradox Family Members

Extension	Type of Object
.DB	Table
.F or .Fxx	Form
.R or .Rxx	Report
.SET	Settings
.VAL	Validity Checks
.PX	Primary Index
.Xxx	Secondary Index
.Yxx	Secondary Index
.G	Graph

For *.Fxx* and *.Rxx* files, xx is a number corresponding to the number of the form or report for that table. For *.Xxx* and *.Yxx* files, xx is a hexadecimal number which indicates the number of the secondary index field. Each secondary index is comprised of an *.Xxx* file and a *.Yxx* file.

Paradox keeps track of family members so there are certain restrictions on moving them around. You must be careful when copying them and doing other tasks. These issues will be described in Chapter 9, "Managing Your Paradox Objects."

You can get a quick inventory of a table's family by using the menu commands **Tools/Info/Family/TABLE**, where *TABLE* is the name of the table being inquired about. The family members will be listed in a Paradox temporary table called *FAMILY* as shown in Figure 1.5. This is an example of how Paradox uses one of its own tables during an operation.

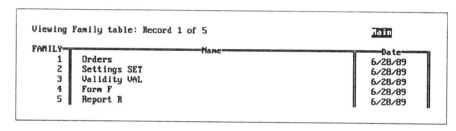

Figure 1.5. FAMILY listing created using **Tools/Info/Family** commands

What You See on the Screen

The Paradox Workspace

Paradox's Virtual Memory Management System lets you use tables larger than the workspace.

The workspace is an area in your computer's memory where Paradox keeps the tables which are in use and works with them. Because tables can be much larger than the RAM (Random Access Memory) available in most computers, a subset of each table is often all that is kept on the workspace. Any tables which are in use are said to be "on the workspace."

When you use Paradox interactively, every table or query image which is in use can be viewed on the screen. When you use Paradox under the control of a script or PAL procedure, the screen may not reflect the true state of the workspace. What you see on the screen in that case is the *PAL canvas*. A discussion of the workspace and the PAL canvas is included in the "PAL" section of this book.

Table Images

When you place a table on the workspace, using `View` or another command, it is represented by a *table image*. If more than one table is on the workspace at the same time, multiple table images are displayed. Figure 1.6 shows an example of this. As new tables are put into use, Paradox will add new table images below the last image on the screen. Images will scroll off the top of the screen if space is needed to display a new image.

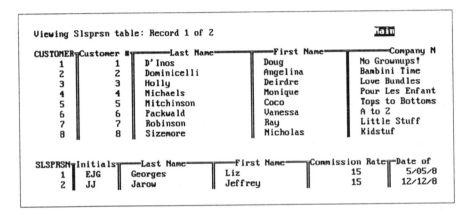

Figure 1.6. Multiple table images on the screen

In general, the more conventional memory or EMS you have available, the better the performance you will get from Paradox.

Although Paradox does not limit the number of tables which you can use at one time, you are limited by how much computer memory you have available. Regardless of how much memory your computer has, it is important not to "clutter up" the workspace. For performance reasons, and for the sake of good housekeeping, you should clear images from the workspace if you no longer need them. Images are cleared from the workspace using F8, the "Clear Image" key, to remove one image, or using Alt-F8, "Clear All," to clear the entire workspace.

Table View

The tables shown in Figure 1.6 are in *table view*. Table view is the default way Paradox displays a table. Any time you place a table on the workspace, by using commands such as `View` or **Modify/Edit**, the table will be shown in table view.

When you page down through a table, the last record on one screen will be the first record on the next screen.

In table view, each record in a table is represented by a screen row. Records can be scrolled through using the up- and down-arrow keys, PgUp, PgDn, Home, and End keys. For tables which are wider than the screen, the right- and left-arrow keys can be used to scroll through the fields. Pressing the Ctrl key with the right- or left-arrow key will move the cursor one screen width at a time. The Quick Reference Card lists all commands for moving through a table.

Paradox will display as many records from a table as can fit onto the screen, in groups of up to 22 at a time. You can use the `Image` command to adjust the number of records which are displayed. The `Image` command also can be used to control the width, and order of, columns in table view, as well as the format of Numeric fields. Using the `Image` command will be discussed, in detail, in Chapter 3, "Viewing Your Paradox Tables."

Form View

You cannot print a table using a form. Use a report instead.

Paradox tables may also be viewed in *form view*. Pressing F7, "Form Toggle," or using the **Image/PickForm** commands, will cause a table which is currently in table view to be shown in form view.

The Standard Form

Paradox will generate a "standard form" for a table the first time you press F7 while viewing the table or after the form has been deleted. The standard form looks like the form shown in Figure 1.7. It lists all table fields vertically.

You can use the `Forms` command to create up to 15 custom forms for viewing your information. Each form can have up to 15 pages of information, enabling you to view records from wide tables by using just one form.

Multi-table and Multi-record Forms

See Chapter 3 for restrictions on linking tables with forms.

Forms can be used to display one record at a time from one table, or they can be used to display multiple records and/or information from several tables at once. To create a multi-table form, you design a form for a master table and then use the **Multi/Table/Place** commands on the Form Menu to embed a form from another table into the master table's form. It is possible for tables on a multi-table form to be linked or unlinked. If they are linked, Paradox uses matching values in linking fields to relate records. The process for creating multi-table forms will be discussed in Chapter 3, "Looking at Your Tables."

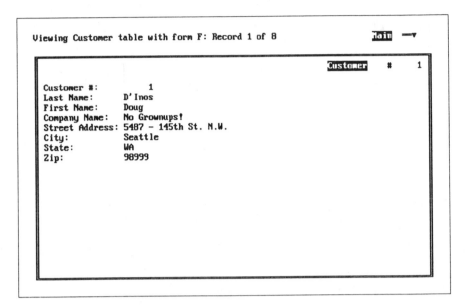

Figure 1.7. Form displayed on the Paradox workspace

Query Images

When you use the Ask command to query a table, Paradox puts a *query image* for that table onto the workspace. A query image, before you enter anything into it, looks like the table view of a table with no records. Figure 1.8 shows a query image for the CUSTOMER table which was shown in Figure 1.4. Special commands are used in query images to tell Paradox what type of query to perform. These commands will be covered in detail in Chapter 5.

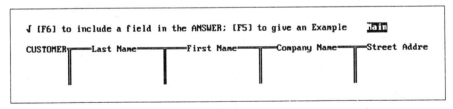

Figure 1.8. Query image on the Paradox workspace

When you want to create a query which requires more than one table, you use the Ask command for each table and specify the name of each table to be used. Paradox places a separate query image for each table on the screen.

Using the Paradox Workspace

As mentioned before, what you see on the screen does not always represent everything that is on the workspace. The screen can be thought of as a moving window onto the workspace, allowing you to view many more records and/or images than can fit onto one screen. The upward- and downward-pointing triangles in the upper-right corner of the screen indicate whether there are more images on the workspace than those currently displayed.

Moving Between Images on the Workspace

You move between images on the workspace by using the F3 ("Up Image"), and F4 ("Down Image"), keys. If you move to an image which is not currently on the screen, other images will scroll off the screen to make sure that the current image can be displayed.

The Current Image

The current image is an important concept in Paradox. It is the image which the cursor is in. The record and field which the cursor is in are similarly referred to as the *current record* and the *current field*, respectively.

Paradox keeps track of the current record and current field for each image on the workspace. As you move between tables, Paradox will always return the cursor to the spot it was in when it left a table. (This is important to remember when using PAL. If you understand exactly where the cursor is on the workspace, you can take advantage of this fact and avoid writing unnecessary code.) Even if you are not using PAL, this Paradox feature can save time if you jump back-and-forth between tables.

Reports

Reports are used to send information from tables to a printer, the screen, or to a file. Reports can be used simply to generate listings of each record in a table or to create complicated reports which may involve calculations and other summary information. There are two types of reports which you can create: Tabular and Free-form.

Tabular Reports

Paradox automatically prints a Standard Report, a tabular listing of all records in a table, when you press Alt-F7 while viewing a table. The Standard Report for the CUSTOMER table is shown in Figure 1.9. It has been modified slightly to present all fields on one pagewidth.

```
                              Test Title


Last Name          First Name      Company Name           Street Address             City                  State  Zip
-----------------  --------------  ---------------------  -------------------------  -------------------   -----  -----
D'Inos             Doug            No Grownups!           5487 - 145th St. N.W.      Seattle                WA    98999
Dominicelli        Angelina        Bambini Time           525 Cambridge Street       Los Angeles            CA    90299
Holly              Deirdre         Love Bundles           45 Thornhill Ave.          Venice                 CA    90291
Michaels           Monique         Pour Les Enfants       1775 Terrace Drive         Belmont                CA    94002
Mitchinson         Coco            Tops to Bottoms        999 Golden Lane            San Francisco          CA    94999
Packwald           Vanessa         A to Z                 927 Iris Ave.              Redwood City           CA    94061
Robinson           Ray             Little Stuff           200 W. 90th Street         New York               NY    10024
Sizemore           Nick            Kidstuff               1 June Way                 Marysville             WA    98270
Gaines             Gloria          PlayGear               580 Skokie Ave.            Highland Park          IL    60035
Tanner             Madonna         PlayGear               10050 Pacific Avenue       Beachtown              CA    90001
August             Ana Marie       Pour Les Enfants       1021 Summertime Lane       Rock Island            NY    10099
Dominicelli        Angelina        Pour Les Enfants       999 Main Street            Santa Monica           CA    90200
Michaels           Monique         Bambini Time           15 El Camino Real          San Mateo              CA    94409
Dominicelli        Angelina        Brown Berries          5757 Ocean Drive           Malibu                 CA    90555
August             Ana Marie       Bambini Time           9001 Broadway              New York               NY    10024
Pasquesi           Dominic         Grandpa's Place        720 Pieve Way              Chicago                IL    60000
Goldberg           Agnes           Grandpa's Other Place  131 High Way               Evanston               IL    60024
```

Figure 1.9. Standard Report for the CUSTOMER table

It is easy to create custom reports by using the `Report` command. Up to 15 custom reports can be created for each table. The default Tabular report lists all records in a table in the same format as they appear in default table view. Using the Report Generator, you can modify the standard Tabular report to include summary and calculated information.

Free-Form Reports

The default Free-form report lists all fields in a table vertically. It is similar to the format of the standard form. Free-form reports can be modified to create a wide variety of documents such as labels, checks, invoices, and letters. The Report menus used in designing a Free-form report are slightly different from the menus which are seen during Tabular report design. A few additional features are available to give you more flexibility in creating your report specification.

How Reports Work

Reports are designed around one table. While a certain amount of lookup information from other tables can be included, this feature is limited. Also worth noting is that Paradox will always report on all records in a table. This may sound trivial, but it is key. If you want to report on a subset of records from a table, you must first create a table with the records on which you want to report. This is done through the **Ask** command. A full explanation of the steps necessary to extract records for a report is included in Chapter 6, "Using The Report Generator."

Directories in Paradox

The Working Directory

You can also use different DOS batch files to start Paradox from different directories, as long as PARADOX3 is on your path.

When you load Paradox, the current DOS directory will be your working directory unless you have specified another directory by using the Custom script or an *Init* script. (How to use these options to customize your Paradox system will be explained in Chapter 13, "Customizing Your Paradox System.") By placing the directory in which your Paradox files are located on the DOS path, you will be able to start Paradox from any directory. It is a good idea to keep your tables and their families, scripts, and procedure libraries in directories other than in the Paradox directory. That way you can keep your files organized more easily.

You can also specify objects on other drives by typing d: \ dir \ table where d is the drive letter and dir is the subdirectory name.

Your working directory is where, unless otherwise specified, Paradox looks for all tables and scripts. It is possible to use Paradox objects which are in directories other than your working directory by giving an object's full pathname. For example, to view a table called *TODOLIST* in the directory \ PROJECTS, type **\ PROJECTS \ TODOLIST** after choosing **View** from Paradox's Main Menu. If you type just a directory name, such as **\ PROJECTS** and press Enter, Paradox will display a list of all tables which it finds in that directory.

Your working directory can be changed using the commands, **Tools/More/Directory**. Paradox will prompt for a new directory name. When you change directories, the workspace is always cleared. Any Paradox temporary tables in that directory will be deleted, so make sure that you rename these tables using the **Tool/Rename/Table** command before making the directory switch.

Private Directories in Paradox

 Paradox's temporary tables are placed into your *private directory*. On a standalone system, the location of that directory is not too important, assuming you have enough disk space on the drive the private directory is on. Also, it should be on a hard drive for performance reasons. (Paradox needs two to three times the size of any tables in use at one time available in free disk for most queries, sorts, and so on.)

 When you work on a network, private directories require more attention. The location of a private directory affects performance. Placing a private directory on a local drive will result in better performance because Paradox will not have to go to the file server to access its temporary files.

It is critical that private directories are separate from shared directories. Paradox places special lock files in private directories which deny access to other Paradox users. This is to protect one network user's temporary files from those of another user. Paradox uses the same names for temporary tables for all users. Using separate private directories for these tables ensures that the files are not mixed up.

How to set up private directories on a network will be covered in Chapter 15, "Networking With Paradox."

Scripts

A script is an ASCII text file which contains Paradox commands. Scripts are created, and played, using the `Scripts` command. There are several ways you can create scripts: you can record your keystrokes using the **S**cripts/**B**eginRecord command, Alt-F3 can be used to start recording an "Instant" script, or you can type commands into a file using the PAL editor or another text editor. A simple script is listed in Figure 1.10.

Paradox "Tools"

One choice on the Main Menu is `Tools`. There are many useful commands in this part of Paradox to save you time and help you to keep your Paradox system organized. They only can work for you, though, if you know what's available. Before you create tables, forms, queries, and reports, you might want to review Chapter 9, "Managing Your Paradox Objects," to see what is available through `Tools`. Using `Tools`, you can:

```
CLEAR
CLEARALL

VIEW "Customer"
FORMKEY
EDITKEY
END
DOWN

WAIT TABLE
     PROMPT "Press Esc to quit, F2 to save."
UNTIL "F2", "Esc"

IF Retval = "Esc"
     THEN CANCELEDIT
     ELSE DO_IT!
ENDIF

MESSAGE "Editing Session Over!"
SLEEP 2000
```

Figure 1.10. Simple Paradox script listing

- Import files into Paradox tables
- Copy, rename, or delete tables and other objects
- Get an inventory list of Paradox objects or other files
- Temporarily go to DOS
- Check the structure of a table
- List a table's family members
- Find out who, on a network, is using Paradox and what locks they have placed on individual tables
- Change your working or private directory
- Explicitly lock and unlock tables
- Change your network username and refresh interval
- Add, subtract, and empty tables
- Create secondary indexes
- Enter Password mode and use passwords to limit access to Paradox objects

You can see that the list is quite extensive. Using the `Tools` commands effectively is just as important as using queries and reports in putting Paradox to work. Throughout this book, you will see references to the `Tools` commands as we step through the examples.

The Paradox Configuration File

Paradox keeps configuration information in a file called PARA-DOX3.CFG. You can change the contents of this file using a special Paradox script called *Custom*. With Custom, you can set options such as:

- Display type and color settings
- Default report settings for page layout, setup strings, and group repeats
- Default graph settings, including device specifications
- Working and private directories
- Whether Paradox should use blanks as 0s in calculations
- The field order of ANSWER tables
- Expanded memory allocation
- Number and Date formats
- Network Username and AutoRefresh intervals
- Using an editor other than the Paradox Script Editor
- Delimited ASCII file characteristics

Chapter 13, "Customizing Your Paradox System," will show you how to use the Custom script to change these options and save them in the PARADOX3.CFG file.

Summary

Paradox is a relational database management system which you can use easily to manage large volumes of information. Here are the basic Paradox concepts with which you need to be familiar:

- Paradox is organized into separate areas called *modes*. When you load Paradox, you are in Main mode. Other modes are accessed only through Main mode.

- Each mode has its own set of menus which you access by pressing F10. You can select menu choices by moving the cursor to the desired choice and pressing Enter. To save time, you can press the first letter of the desired menu selection.

- Paradox keeps information in files called *tables*. Tables can be used together if they have common fields on which Paradox can link. Paradox links tables by looking for matching values in linking fields. You can link tables using queries, forms, and reports.

- The Ask command is used to create queries. Queries can be used to search for records using selection criteria. Paradox places selected records in a special ANSWER table.

- Queries are used for more than searching. You can create calculated fields with queries. There are also queries which change, add, or delete records. Set queries can be used to compare groups of records.

- You can create custom forms and reports for tables. Forms and reports belong only to one table. These files, along with index files and other special objects, are referred to as a table's *family*.

- Paradox works with table information in an area of your computer's memory called the "workspace." The size of the workspace depends upon how much memory is available when you load Paradox. Part of this memory is used for Paradox system files and memory management. What is left is allocated for the workspace.

- Paradox keeps an "image" on the workspace for each table or query in use. You see these images when you work interactively with Paradox.

- Table images can appear in table view or in form view. In table view, each record is shown as a row, and each field is shown as a column. Form views can be designed to show records in many different ways. You can have multi-record and multi-table forms. Up to 15 custom forms can be created for each table.

- You can place tables on the workspace using the View or Modify commands on the Main Menu. There can be more than one table at a time on the workspace. You can move between images on the workspace using F3, "Up Image," and F4, "Down Image."

- The current mode applies to all tables on the workspace. You can move between tables freely while editing. It is not possible to place tables onto the workspace except in Main mode.

- You can print a Standard Report by pressing Alt-F7, "Instant Report," while you are viewing a table. Using Report mode, you can design up to 15 custom reports for each table. You can link lookup tables to a report table.

- Paradox looks for all tables and other objects in the working directory (the current directory). You can access objects in other directories by giving their full pathnames.

- Paradox creates special *temporary tables*, during some of its operations. These tables are kept in your private directory. Paradox deletes these tables when you exit from Paradox, change directories, or perform another operation which creates the same table. Be careful not to use the names of temporary tables for your own tables, unless you do so on purpose.

- *Scripts* are files which contain Paradox commands. There are several ways to create scripts in Paradox. You can record your keystrokes, or write scripts using PAL, the Paradox Application Language.

- Paradox has many useful utility commands which are accessed through the `Tools` command on the Main Menu. Be sure to check the list of tasks for which you can use `Tools` to be familiar with these timesaving commands.

- You can customize your Paradox system by using the Custom script. Custom lets you change options in the PARADOX3.CFG file, the file in which Paradox stores your configuration information.

Designing and Creating Tables

Designing Tables for The Raspberry Patch

Deciding how to organize your information and set up your tables is the most important part of getting Paradox to work effectively for you. The successful use of Paradox's relational capabilities depends upon careful table design.

This book will not cover the theory of database design. There are many books available devoted exclusively to that subject. For theoretical information on setting up optimal data relationships, you may want to refer to these other sources. If you are setting up a database which involves many tables with complex relationships, it may be worthwhile to do some self-study on this topic or to hire a database consultant who can give professional advice about designing your system. Although this may seem an expensive investment of time and money, it can save you hours of time redesigning tables, forms, and reports which were built on a faulty plan.

For most projects, careful consideration of what you want to do with your information is enough before you start designing your tables. We will look at two projects for our fictitious company, The Raspberry Patch, to illustrate this.

A One-Table Project

First, let's look at setting up a table which can be later used to create mailing labels for The Raspberry Patch. Make a list of the information which you need to have on each label:

- Name
- Company
- Street Address
- City
- State
- Zip Code

This is a very simple list. There are no complicated relationships between list elements. There is a one-to-one relationship between all of the elements. Each label has one customer name, one company name, and one address. (The number of lines in the address might vary in real life. For simplicity's sake, we will use just one line for the Street Address. Regardless of the number of lines used, though, there is still only one address per customer per label.) Because of this, one Paradox table can be used to store all information needed to create labels. We will call this table, *CUSTOMER*.

Deciding Which Fields to Use

Before we actually create the CUSTOMER table, we need to decide which fields to use. Each piece of information in a record corresponds to a field in the table. When you create your table, you give Paradox a list of the fields which determine the table structure. You also need to specify a *field type* for each field.

There are five Paradox field types:

- Alphanumeric
- Number
- Short number (integer)
- Currency
- Date

You can change the default format for Currency and Date fields using the Custom script.

Choosing a field type is usually straightforward; you look at the type of information which will be in the field and make the most logical choice. In a few cases, you may want to use Alphanumeric fields, instead of Number fields, even if you will have only numbers as field values. This may be because you want your values sorted by character, rather than by numeric value. More detailed information on field types is included in the section, "Creating Tables," in this chapter.

Using the information needed for each label, we can create a list of fields, and corresponding field types, to use for CUSTOMER as shown in Table 2.1.

Table 2.1 Fields For CUSTOMER Table

Field	Field Type
Name	Alphanumeric
Company	Alphanumeric
Street Address	Alphanumeric
City	Alphanumeric
State	Alphanumeric
Zip Code	Alphanumeric

All fields used here, even Zip Code, are Alphanumeric. Zip Code must be Alphanumeric because it may include leading zeros. (Paradox does not allow leading zeros in Number fields.) Using an Alphanumeric field also accommodates the use of longer Zip Codes in the form, *#####-####*. In this case, you need an Alphanumeric field because a Number field cannot have dashes or characters other than period or comma separators. When we actually create the table, we must specify a length for Alphanumeric fields, as well. (The other field types have fixed field lengths which cannot be changed.)

Separating information into fields usually follows the obvious organization of the information. In some cases, it is useful to break down the information further, though. The structure you should choose depends upon how much flexibility you need for tasks such as sorting, and searching for, information.

While you can tell Paradox on which field, or fields, in a table to sort, you have no control over the positions in a field which are used for sorting. Paradox sorts an Alphanumeric value on the first character in the field, then on the second character, and so on. If the CUSTOMER table is created with the fields listed above, there will be only one field for Name. Unless you typed the Last Name first, the table would look like Figure 2.1 after being sorted on the Name field:

Customer information is usually sorted, or searched through, by Last Name. To do this in the above table structure, the Last Name would have to be typed as the first part of the Name field. Remembering to type the Last Name first would be awkward. In this case, then, it makes sense to divide the Name field into First Name and Last Name fields. By

entering the name into two separate fields, you allow Paradox to sort the
CUSTOMER table on the Last Name field first, and then on the First
Name field, as shown in Figure 2.2.

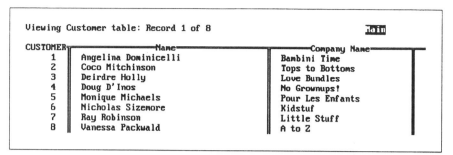

Figure 2.1 CUSTOMER table sorted on Name field

```
Viewing Customer table: Record 1 of 8                                    Main

CUSTOMER        First Name            Last Name              Company Name
    1     Doug               D'Inos                  No Grownups!
    2     Angelina           Dominicelli             Bambini Time
    3     Deirdre            Holly                   Love Bundles
    4     Monique            Michaels                Pour Les Enfants
    5     Coco               Mitchinson              Tops to Bottoms
    6     Vanessa            Packwald                A to Z
    7     Ray                Robinson                Little Stuff
    8     Nicholas           Sizemore                Kidstuf
```

Figure 2.2 CUSTOMER table sorted on Last Name, then on First Name

When deciding which fields to use, remember that Paradox cannot
link tables on substrings of field values. A field is the smallest unit
which Paradox can work within these operations.

Deciding on Key Fields

A keyed table must be sorted to a new table if you want to change the record order.

Paradox uses special fields, called *key fields* to create *primary indexes*.
A primary index keeps a table sorted in "key" order and provides a
performance benefit when doing queries, or other operations, which
involve searching for specific key values. It may seem early to think
about key fields and primary indexes, before we even have created a
table, but key fields are an important part of table design.

If you choose to use key fields, it impacts the table structure. Key
fields must be consecutive, and must start with the first field in a table.
How to specify key fields in your table structure will be covered later in
this chapter. More information about the benefits of indexing a table is
included in Chapter 14, "Performance Tips." For now, just note that if

you want to key a table, field order is important when determining your table structure.

Paradox can create an index from one or more fields in a table. There are two rules for setting up your key fields:

1. The "key" for each record in a table must be unique. The "key" is taken from the value in the key field or fields. To ensure a unique key value for each record, it may be necessary to key a table on more than one field. If there is more than one key field, Paradox concatenates (adds together) the values from all the key fields in a record to form the "key."

2. Key fields must start with the first field in a table and must be consecutive.

For the CUSTOMER table, this means that the Last Name field should be the first field in the table if the table is to be keyed on Last Name. Also, since the Last Name may not be unique, we need to key the First Name field as well. We will assume that the combination of Last Name and First Name will be unique for each Raspberry Patch customer, eliminating the need for more key fields or for a unique customer identifier which may be added later if necessary. For now, the field layout shown below should work for CUSTOMER:

- Last Name (key field)
- First Name (key field)
- Address
- City
- State
- Zip Code

We will use this design later in this chapter when creating the table with the `Create` command.

Using Related Tables

The next example illustrates how to design tables which allow use of Paradox's relational capabilities. Let's design the tables necessary to enter orders for The Raspberry Patch. A sample order form is shown in Figure 2.3.

```
┌─────────────────────────────────────────────────────────────────┐
│                                                                   │
│                      THE RASPBERRY PATCH                          │
│                                                                   │
│                         Order Form                                │
│                                                                   │
│        Order #:     1                                             │
│        Date:        6/10/89                                       │
│        Customer #:  3                                             │
│        Salesperson: JJ                                            │
│                                                                   │
│        First Name:       Deirdre                                  │
│        Last Name:        Holly                                    │
│        Company Name:     Love Bundles                             │
│        Street Address:   45 Thornhill Ave.                        │
│        City:             Venice           State: CA  Zip:  90291  │
│                                                                   │
│        Item #  Description      Quantity  Price   Extended Price  │
│        ------  --------------------  --------  -------  -------------- │
│           707  Black Jeans           10      7.50        75.00    │
│                                                                   │
│           708  Black Jeans           10      7.50        75.00    │
│                                                                   │
│                Total:                20               150.00      │
│                                                                   │
└─────────────────────────────────────────────────────────────────┘
```

Figure 2.3 Order Form for The Raspberry Patch

There are two main characteristics which make order information different from label information. The first is that order information falls into several groups.

Order Header Information

Order #

Date

Customer #

Salesperson

Customer Information

Name

Company Name

Address

Order Detail Information

Part #

Description

Quantity

Price

Summary Information

Extended Prices

Shipping, Taxes, and other costs

Total Cost

The second difference is that, while there always will be one customer and one salesperson for each Raspberry Patch order, the number of detail lines for each order will vary. It would be difficult to design a table for ORDERS with one order per record. Paradox uses a *fixed file* format. This means that you have a finite number of fields for each record. It is impossible to accommodate a variable number of line items in a fixed format record.

You can also display a non-related table on a form to use for reference information or some other purpose.

Paradox's relational capabilities, along with its multi-table form capability, offer a solution for this problem. You can use separate tables for the header information and for the detail information for each order. This gives flexibility for how many detail items can be entered for each order. It also makes better use of disk space. You do not have to create extra fields in the ORDERS table to allow for the possibility of multiple-line items in an order.

You can use Paradox's multi-table form feature to view fields from all necessary tables on one order form. After the information has been entered, you can use the Ask command to link the tables, as needed, to print orders. Remember, printing must be done through reports. You can't print from the forms which you create.

Rules for Designing Tables to Be Used Together

There are rules for designing tables which will be used together.

1. Tables which will be linked, using queries or multi-table forms, must have at least one field in common.
2. The linking field does not have to have the same name in both tables; the field type, however, must be the same.
3. You can link tables on more than one field at the same time.

Additional rules apply if you will be linking the tables through a multi-table form. If you are using tables in a linked multi-table form, one table is the *master* table. The tables whose forms are embedded in the master table form are called the *detail* tables.

1. The embedded tables must be keyed.
2. The linking field(s) in the detail table must begin with the first field and must be consecutive.

3. If you want Paradox to enforce *referential integrity*, the master table must be keyed and the linking fields must consist of the entire master table key.

"Referential integrity" is the way Paradox updates records in linked tables based on changes to master table records. This process will be fully described in Chapter 4, "Modifying Your Paradox Tables," in the section, "Editing Multi-table Forms."

A Multi-table Design for The Raspberry Patch Orders

Let's keep the above points in mind as we design tables to track orders for The Raspberry Patch. The first table we need to design is ORDERS. ORDERS will hold the header information for each order. It needs fields for each item listed in "Order Header Information." ORDERS will be keyed on the Order # field. In addition to ORDERS, we need separate tables for customer and for detail information.

The CUSTOMER table can have the same structure as the table used to create labels, with the addition of a field for Customer #. To link the CUSTOMER table to the ORDERS table using queries and multi-table forms, they must have a common field. Customer # will be that field. This field must be the first field in CUSTOMER, and it must be keyed, because of Paradox's rules for using multi-table forms.

The DETAIL table will need fields for the information listed in "Order Detail Information." Again, there must be a field common to both DETAIL and ORDERS so that the tables can be linked using queries and a multi-table form. The linking field here will be Order #. Order # must be the first field in DETAIL and it must be keyed. Because there may be more than one record in DETAIL for each order, DETAIL needs an additional key field. It makes sense to key the Part # field since this will be unique for each line-item within an order. (The Part # will incorporate size numbers so there is no need for a separate field for size.)

The structure of each table used for The Raspberry Patch's orders is shown in Figure 2.4. The relationships among the tables are indicated. Remember that the relationships are based only on common fields. If you change the field type, or the position of the linking fields, you will have problems later. Asterisks (*) indicate key fields. Note that the linking fields in the detail tables, CUSTOMER and DETAIL, are keyed and are, therefore, the first fields in the tables.

Although Paradox field types have not yet been discussed in detail, they are included in the above illustration. The field types in the illustration are shown as follows:

- **An** is for Alphanumeric fields where *n* is the field length.
- **S** is for Short number, or integer, fields.

- **N** is for Number fields.
- **$** is for Currency fields.
- **D** is for Date fields.

These field types will be described more fully later in this chapter. Field types are usually easy to choose based on the information which is to be included. **S** is used for the Order # and Customer # fields. It assumes that there will not be more than 32,767 individual customers or orders. Because there is no need to keep track of decimal values, integers will work fine. **N** is used for the Quantity field in an attempt to be optimistic. Decimal places are not needed (who ever bought half of a Bikini or a half a pair of pants), but who knows... The Raspberry Patch may have some orders for more than 32,767 of an individual item. The choice of **$**, **D** and **An** for the rest of the fields is self-explanatory.

Creating Paradox Tables

Once you have determined which tables you need, and what their structures should be, you are ready to start. Creating a Paradox table is quite simple. Let's create the CUSTOMER table designed above.

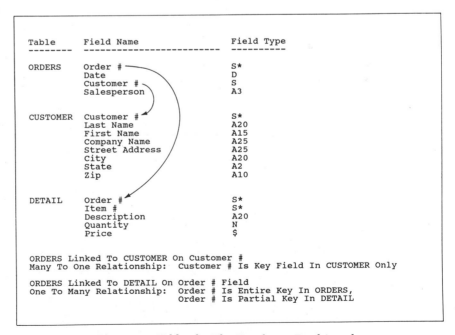

Figure 2.4 Tables for The Raspberry Patch's orders

1. Choose `Create` on the Main Menu.

2. Type **CUSTOMER** at the prompt for a table name and press Enter.

To move a field, type the same field name on another line. Use Ins or Del to add or delete lines.

3. Paradox is now in Create mode. Enter the field names and field types for CUSTOMER into the STRUCT table which is displayed. Figure 2.5 shows how STRUCT should look after it is filled in. All fields in CUSTOMER are Alphanumeric. Alphanumeric fields are indicated by an *A* followed by a number for the maximum field length.

4. If you haven't already done so, be sure to put asterisks after the field types for Last Name and for First Name. The asterisks tell Paradox to build a primary index for CUSTOMER using these two key fields.

5. Press F2 to tell Paradox to "DO-IT!" and save the table.

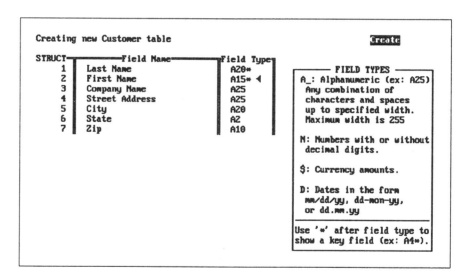

Figure 2.5 Creating the CUSTOMER table

Remaining Tables for The Raspberry Patch

Additional tables are needed for The Raspberry Patch. So far, we have designed the structures for CUSTOMER, ORDERS, and DETAIL. To create the remaining two tables, follow the above steps, using the table structures shown in Figure 2.4. Later in this book, other tables will be referred to in examples. We will not go through the `Create` process for each table because the steps are the same.

More Information About Tables!

Other information with which you should be familiar regarding tables is outlined below:

Naming Paradox Tables

Here are the rules you must observe when naming a table:

- The name can be up to eight characters long. You don't type the extension. (Paradox automatically adds the extension .DB.)
- You can use letters, numbers and special characters, such as $ and __, as long as you keep to DOS rules for file names.
- Spaces cannot be used.
- Characters from the IBM Extended Character Set cannot be used.

Be careful not to use DOS reserved words such as *CON* or *PRN*. Paradox will accept them, but doing so will cause serious problems later. Also, avoid using table names which are the same as subdirectory names at the same level. Because of the way Paradox searches for objects, it will not find tables in directories with subdirectories which have the same name as the table.

Paradox Temporary Table Names

You should not use names which Paradox uses for its temporary tables, unless you are purposely doing this and understand all the repercussions of doing so. There are several operations in which Paradox creates temporary tables. These tables are automatically overwritten the next time that same operation is performed. They are deleted when you change private directories, using **Tools/Net/SetPrivate**, and when you exit from Paradox. All temporary tables are created and kept in your private directory, whether or not you are working on a network. A list of these tables, and how they are created, is shown in Table 2.2.

Table 2.2 Paradox Temporary Tables

Name	Created By Operation
ANSWER	Ask
CHANGED	Ask (Changeto query) Tools/**More**/**Add** Tools/**More**/**MultiAdd**

(continued)

Table 2.2 *(continued)*

Name	Created By Operation
CROSSTAB	Image/Graph (CrossTab)
DELETED	Ask (Delete query)
ENTRY	Modify/**DataEntry** Modify/**MultiEntry**
FAMILY	Tools/**Info**/**Family**
INSERTED	Ask (Insert query)
KEYVIOL	Modify/**Restructure** Modify/**DataEntry** Modify/**MultiEntry** Tools/**More**/**Add** Tools/**More**/**MultiAdd**
LIST	Tools/**Info**/**Inventory** Tools/**Info**/**Who** Tools/**Info**/**Lock**
PASSWORD	Tools/**More**/**Protect**/**Password**/TABLE
PROBLEMS	Modify/**Restructure** Tools/**ExportImport**/**Import**
STRUCT	Tools/**Info**/**Structure**

Using the Name of an Existing Table

If you type the name of an existing table, Paradox will give you the opportunity of canceling the operation or replacing the existing table with the table which you are about to create. This confirmation request is shown in Figure 2.6. All DOS rules for file maintenance apply while you are in Paradox. If you use an existing table name for that of a new or copied table, the existing table will be deleted.

When you delete a table, by reusing its name or otherwise, that table's entire family of reports, forms, and other Paradox objects, is also deleted. To create a new table with the name of an existing table, but keep the existing table's family, you must first rename the existing table. This will prevent the existing table, and its family members, from being deleted. You can then use the Tools/Copy/JustFamily command to copy the family from the old table to the new table. More information on this process is covered in Chapter 9, "Managing Your Paradox Objects."

Using Create Mode

After typing a name, an empty table, called STRUCT, will be displayed. This is where you define your table's structure by entering field names and field types. STRUCT can be edited in the same way as any other

Paradox table. The Quick Reference Card has a listing of all commands which you can use to move around the table to change entries. You access the Create Menu by pressing F10 in Create mode. (See Figure 2.7.)

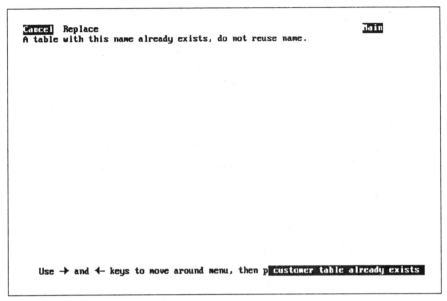

Figure 2.6 Paradox `Cancel` or `Replace` menu during table creation

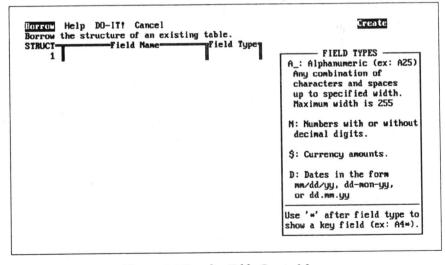

Figure 2.7 Paradox Table Create Menu

It is possible to "borrow" another table's structure, and create a table with exactly the same structure, by choosing `Borrow`, typing the desired table's name, and then pressing F2. The `Borrow` menu choice is also useful to create a table whose structure will be similar to that of an existing table. Choose `Borrow` to bring up the desired table's structure and edit the STRUCT table as necessary. Using `Borrow` can be a real time-saver.

Paradox Field Names

When you type field names, you must abide by the following rules:

Paradox reserves # for the name of the record number field.

- Field names can be up to 25 characters in length.
- A field name cannot begin with a space but it can include spaces.
- Do not use ", [ ], { }, ( ), → in field names, or use # by itself.
- Field names must be unique for each field in a table.

Paradox Field Types

After you type a field name, you must indicate which field type is to be used. There are five Paradox field types: Alphanumeric, Number, Short number, Currency, and Date. Each field type has a corresponding abbreviation: A, N, S, $, and D. The abbreviations are used in the Field Type field of the STRUCT table to indicate the type of data which the field will contain. All field types, except the Short number type, are described on the right side of the screen during the Create process. You can see this in Figure 2.7.

Alphanumeric Fields

Paradox will concatenate alphanumeric values that are added in an expression.

Alphanumeric fields should be used if a field will contain values other than numbers, currency amounts, or dates. Paradox will not allow you to enter values which are inconsistent with the field type. When typing the field type for an Alphanumeric field, type **A** and the maximum number of characters you want the field to contain, for example, *A2* or *A40*. The maximum number of characters an Alphanumeric field can hold is 255. There are cases when an Alphanumeric field is used for a field which will contain only Numeric data. For example, if you want a numeric value to be stored with leading zeros, you *must* define the field as Alphanumeric. (Paradox trims leading zeros from Numeric values.) Or, if you want Paradox to sort strings of numbers by first character, then second character, and so on, rather than by numeric value, you should use an Alphanumeric field type. Arithmetic cannot be done on Alphanumeric fields, though, even if the field contains only numbers.

Number Fields

Number fields are used to store numeric values. Paradox can store numbers with up to 15 significant digits. If you type a number which has more than 15 significant digits, Paradox will round the number and store it in scientific notation. Although you can change the way a number is displayed, using the Image/Format menu choices, a number is always stored the same way within the computer.

Short Number Fields

Short number fields can be used to hold whole numbers ranging from −32,767 to 32,767. The only advantage of using Short numbers is that S-type fields take up less disk space. If you are creating a large table with many numeric fields, this may be a significant consideration.

Currency Fields

Currency fields are used to store currency amounts. The currency indicator, $, is not automatically displayed or stored with the field values. It cannot be typed into the field, either. The main differences between Number and Currency fields are that a Currency field always displays two decimal places, uses whole-number separators, and puts parentheses around negative numbers. The whole-number separators can be changed to an International format using the Custom script. (See Chapter 13.)

Date Fields

Several types of validity checks are used to further limit what can be typed into a field.

Date-type fields can be used only to store dates. The default date format can be set using the Custom script. The format which is typed also can be controlled using a Paradox *picture* validity check. (See the section in Chapter 4 on "Validity Checks.")

Indexing Paradox Tables

Primary indexes are also necessary for tables linked using reports and forms.

Another important point to consider during the table creation process is whether or not you want to have a primary index for your table. Primary indexes usually are created to improve performance. Without an index, Paradox has to search through every record in a table until it locates the record for which it is looking. With an index, Paradox goes to the index file first and finds a "pointer" to the location of a record within a table.

Queries, and other operations on indexed tables, run significantly faster than do similar operations on non-indexed tables. This is particularly important when working with large tables.

Although you may not be concerned with performance now, there are other issues relative to primary indexes which you should be aware of in case you later choose to use them.

Restrictions Related to Using Primary Indexes

Paradox creates a primary index based on key fields which you define. Key fields are indicated by an asterisk after the field type. Paradox can create a primary index based on multiple key fields. A requirement is that the combined key value must be unique for each record. Another is that key fields must start with the first field and must be consecutive. For example, to use three key fields, you must use fields 1, 2, and 3. This should not cause a problem because the physical structure of the table does not affect the order in which fields are displayed on a form or in a report.

There are other repercussions of "keying" a table (setting up a primary index) which you need to consider. One is that keyed tables are sorted in ascending order based on the key field(s) values. This sort order cannot be changed. To sort a keyed table on a field other than the key field, or fields, you must sort it to a new table. However, automatic sorting can be a real benefit in managing a table which you want to keep alphabetized or in numeric order. The order on which Paradox sorts records depends on the country code which you chose when you installed Paradox. For the U.S., the standard ASCII sort order is used. This means that blanks are sorted in before letters or numbers, and that all uppercase letters come before lowercase letters. Choosing a different country code will cause different rules for sorting to take effect.

The requirement that the key value for each record must be unique can cause problems if it is not considered ahead of time. For example, it would not do to key a customer table on First and Last Names if it were possible for two customers to have the same name. (Paradox does not allow two records with the same key value in the same table.) If you did not have a unique identification number for each customer, you could key the table on another combination of fields, such as Last Name, First Name, and Address. A longer key will slow performance, however. If you don't already have one, it may be worthwhile to consider setting up a unique identifier for each customer.

Note, too, that the maximum record length for a keyed table is 1,350 characters, rather than 4,000 characters. If you have several wide text fields, you may bump against this limitation. If so, rethink your database design and consider placing notes, or other long text fields, into separate tables. Paradox's performance is adversely affected by wide tables anyway, so it is a good idea to keep tables as narrow as possible, even when not using a primary index. Keeping information in several narrow tables is usually preferable to working with wide tables. Use wide tables only if you absolutely must. If you will always need to use all of your information at the same time, you may as well put it all into one table. But remember, you will not get optimal performance in that situation.

Benefits of Keyed Tables

As mentioned, keying a table to create a primary index will result in better performance during many operations. A primary index also will keep a table automatically sorted. This can save time doing sorts after a table is changed.

Another benefit of keying a table is that it is quite easy to update a subset of records using the **Tools/More/Add/Update** command. You can use the **Tools/More/Add/NewEntries** command to check for duplicate key values when adding new records to a keyed table. These commands will be covered in Chapter 4.

Restructuring Your Paradox Tables

Don't worry if you find that you need to make changes to table structures after they have been created. Changing the structure of a table is easy. You can add and delete fields, move them around, or change Field Types, by using the **Modify/Restructure** menu choices. After prompting for a table name, Paradox will display a table called STRUCT just as it does in Create mode.

If you are using field names that are similar, you can use Ctrl-D, "Ditto," to copy a name from the previous record and then change it.

The STRUCT table can be edited just like any other Paradox table. To delete a field, press the Del key with the cursor on the record for the field to be deleted; to add a field, press the Ins key on the record below where you want to insert the new field. To move a field, use the Ins key to insert a blank record into the new position for the field. Type the name of the field to be moved and press Enter. Paradox will recognize the name of an existing field and move it to the new location. (The Field Type for the moved field will be filled in automatically by Paradox.)

Changing the CUSTOMER Table

As noted earlier, we need to add a Customer # field to the CUSTOMER table. That field will be used to link CUSTOMER to ORDERS. Use the Restructure mode to do this.

1. Choose **M**odify/**R**estructure from the Main Menu. You will be prompted for a table name.

2. Type **CUSTOMER** and press Enter. This places Paradox into Restructure mode.

3. A STRUCT table will be displayed, as shown in Figure 2.8. This table contains the current structure of CUSTOMER. To add a field at the beginning of the table, leave the cursor positioned at the first record and press the Ins key. STRUCT now looks like Figure 2.9.

4. Type **Customer #** into the Field Name field and type **S** as the Field Type. Pressing F2 to save the table at this point gives the error message "Non-consecutive key found for Last Name" as shown in Figure 2.10.

5. Change the key fields so that Customer # is the only key field. The STRUCT table should appear as shown in Figure 2.11 with an asterisk only after the Field Type for Customer #.

6. Now you can press F2 to save the changes to the CUSTOMER table.

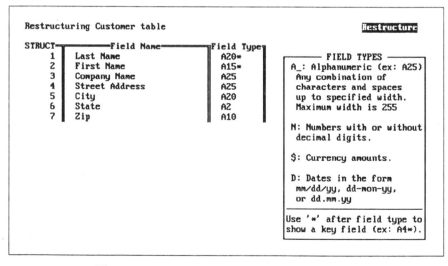

Figure 2.8 Restructuring the CUSTOMER table

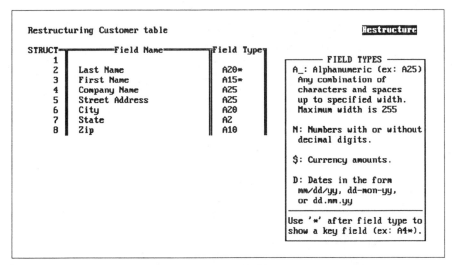

Figure 2.9 Inserting a new field into CUSTOMER

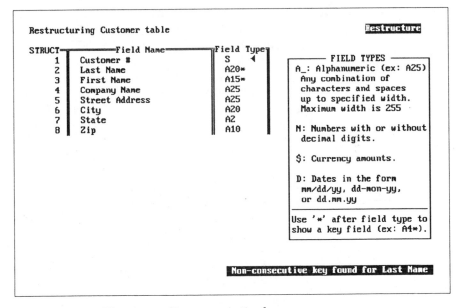

Figure 2.10 Non-consecutive key error message

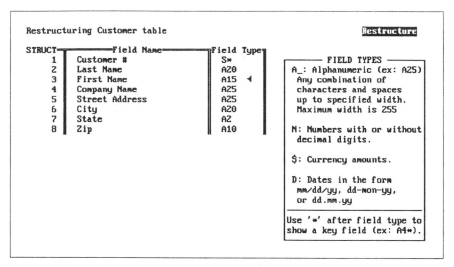

Figure 2.11 Keying CUSTOMER correctly

KEYVIOL Tables and What to Do with Them

 But what's this? A table called KEYVIOL is displayed on the screen as shown in Figure 2.12. KEYVIOL is a temporary table created during certain operations. KEYVIOL contains records whose key values duplicate key values for records in the original table, CUSTOMER in this case. Adding the new key field, Customer #, which has no entries for any records, will, of course, cause key violations. Every record in CUSTOMER would have a blank value in the key field. Paradox will not let you have more than one record with a blank key field in a keyed table.

Figure 2.12 KEYVIOL table after restructuring CUSTOMER

To fix the problem, go through the following steps.

1. Press F10 to display the Main Menu. Choose **View** and then type

CUSTOMER, and press Enter. This places the CUSTOMER table onto the workspace.

2. Press F9 to go into Edit mode. All tables now on the workspace can be edited. (Changing modes affects all tables on the workspace.)

3. Type **1** in the Customer # field for the record shown in CUSTOMER.

4. Press F4, "Up Image," to move the cursor to the KEYVIOL table. Add numbers to the Customer # field in KEYVIOL. Press F2 to complete editing and to return to Main mode. The tables will look like those shown in Figure 2.13.

5. All records now have a unique key value. The KEYVIOL table can be added to CUSTOMER without subsequent key violations. To do this, press F10 to display the Main Menu and choose **T**ools/**M**ore/**A**dd/NewEntries. The NewEntries Update menu is displayed when the target table, like CUSTOMER, is keyed. (See Figure 2.14.)

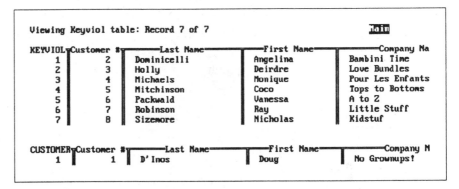

```
Viewing Keyviol table: Record 7 of 7                              Main

KEYVIOL Customer #        Last Name         First Name        Company Na
   1         2      Dominicelli       Angelina          Bambini Time
   2         3      Holly             Deirdre           Love Bundles
   3         4      Michaels          Monique           Pour Les Enfants
   4         5      Mitchinson        Coco              Tops to Bottoms
   5         6      Packwald          Vanessa           A to Z
   6         7      Robinson          Ray               Little Stuff
   7         8      Sizemore          Nicholas          Kidstuf


CUSTOMER Customer #       Last Name         First Name        Company N
   1         1      D'Inos            Doug              No Grownups!
```

Figure 2.13 KEYVIOL and CUSTOMER after adding unique key values

```
NewEntries Update                                                Main
Insert records from the source table into the target table.
KEYVIOL Customer #        Last Name         First Name        Company Na
   1         2      Dominicelli       Angelina          Bambini Time
   2         3      Holly             Deirdre           Love Bundles
   3         4      Michaels          Monique           Pour Les Enfants
   4         5      Mitchinson        Coco              Tops to Bottoms
   5         6      Packwald          Vanessa           A to Z
   6         7      Robinson          Ray               Little Stuff
   7         8      Sizemore          Nicholas          Kidstuf


CUSTOMER Customer #       Last Name         First Name        Company N
   1         1      D'Inos            Doug              No Grownups!
```

Figure 2.14 NewEntries Update Menu during
Tools/**M**ore/**A**dd to keyed table

See Chapter 5 for information on using changeto queries to update a subset of the fields in a table.

Choosing `NewEntries` will instruct Paradox to create a KEYVIOL table if records from the source table, KEYVIOL, duplicate key values in the target table, CUSTOMER. In this case, we have already created unique key values. The `Update` menu choice is used to update records in the target table with records in the source table which have matching key values. Updating a record means replacing it with the corresponding record from the source table. Don't try to update individual fields using this method. Chapter 9 has more information about using the `Tools` commands to update tables.

General Rules for Handling KEYVIOL Tables

1. View the KEYVIOL table. See if your key should consist of more fields, or if the records have inaccurate information resulting in duplicate keys.

2. If necessary, add additional key fields to your original table using **M**odify/**R**estructure.

3. Edit the records in KEYVIOL, if necessary, to eliminate duplicate key information.

4. Use **T**ools/**M**ore/**A**dd to add the records in the KEYVIOL table back into the table.

When You Can Get PROBLEMS Tables

Besides adding fields, you can use **M**odify/**R**estructure to delete fields, change field lengths and names, move fields around, and change field types. If you delete or shorten fields, Paradox will prompt you to verify whether you meant to delete fields, or to trim data from fields which have been shortened.

Check to see that your information is in the proper format before changing field types to avoid creating a PROBLEMS table.

Changing the Field Type may cause more serious problems. In fact, any records which are incompatible with the new structure will be placed into a temporary table called PROBLEMS. An example of what might cause this is changing an Alphanumeric field to a Date field. If any records in the table being restructured contain values inconsistent with Paradox's date format, those records will end up in a PROBLEMS table. PROBLEMS is treated like all other temporary tables. It will be deleted when you exit from Paradox or when you perform another operation which creates a new PROBLEMS table. If you want to save the PROBLEMS table, be sure to rename it using **T**ools/**R**ename/**T**able.

What to do with PROBLEMS Tables

Here are some steps to follow to add records from the PROBLEMS table into a restructured table:

1. Edit the PROBLEMS table to make the records compatible with the new table structure.

2. Use **Tools/Rename/Table** to rename the PROBLEMS table. This is necessary because Paradox will not allow you to restructure the PROBLEMS table.

3. Restructure the renamed PROBLEMS table. Make all changes to its structure which you made to the original table.

4. Use **Tools/More/Add** to add the records in the renamed PROBLEMS table to the original table. If the original table is keyed, you will be prompted for `NewEntries` or `Update`. Choose `NewEntries` to make sure you do not accidentally overwrite any records.

Importing Information into Paradox

You don't need to create tables from scratch if the information already exists in a format which Paradox can import. Using the **Tools/ExportImport/Import** commands, you can create tables from information in one of the following formats:

- ASCII Text (up to 132 characters wide)
- Delimited ASCII
- dBASE II, dBASE III, dBASE III PLUS, and dBASE IV
- Quattro
- Lotus 1-2-3 (Releases 1A, 2.0, 2.01, and 3.0)
- Symphony (Releases 1.0 and 1.1)
- Reflex (Releases 1.0 and 1.1)
- PFS:File
- VisiCalc (.DIF)

FLimport is included on the PProg disk 6 in the \ Util directory if you have Version 3.01.

You can also import fixed-length ASCII files using a free utility program FLimport which is available from Borland International. Those files must have each record on a separate line followed by a CR/LF (Carriage Return/Line Feed). Each field must start at the same character position on each line.

Chapter 9, "Managing Your Paradox Objects," contains detailed information about using the **Tools/ExportImport/Import** command. If your files are in one of the above formats, you will save a considerable amount of time by using the `Import` command.

If you import information from a different file format, you may have to work with the resulting Paradox table to get the final table structure which you want. For example, Paradox sometimes imports values, stored as dates in the original file, into Alphanumeric fields. You can use a short PAL script to convert the date values into an acceptable Paradox date format. The table can then be restructured to convert the Alphanumeric field to a Date field. A script to do this is included in Chapter 11.

Some Important Things to Know About Paradox Tables

Table Width and Performance

Paradox is quite sensitive to table width. If you work with wide tables (tables containing many fields and/or very long text fields), you won't get optimum performance. It is best to keep your tables as narrow as possible.

Working with long tables does not cause this problem. Of course, it will take longer to process a table with many records. You can optimize performance when working with long tables, though, by minimizing the table width.

Table Size and Disk Space

During queries, sorting, and other operations, Paradox creates temporary files which are deleted when the operation has been completed. The disk space needed for these files depends on the size of the table(s) being used and the complexity of the task being done. A good rule-of-thumb is that you should have two to three times the size of the table(s) in use available in free disk space. On rare occasions, you may need even more.

Usually, the free disk space requirement does not cause a problem. However, you may encounter a problem when working with large tables or limited disk space. Paradox may abort whatever it is doing and display the message "Resource Limit Exceeded–not enough disk space to complete operation." If this happens, see if you can free enough disk space *on the drive in which your private directory is located* to accommodate Paradox's needs. This is a very important point. Paradox creates its temporary files in your private directory. If you are not sure on which drive your private directory is located, use **T**ools/**N**et/**S**etPrivate to check the location.

This free disk space requirement holds when you are restructuring or importing tables. If you plan to import a huge file, make sure you have enough disk space for Paradox to create the new table.

Damaged Paradox Tables

Paradox tables can become damaged as can any other computer files. If you are using a table and something happens which affects your computer's memory, it is possible to damage that table. Some causes are:

- Power surges
- Power failures
- Bad memory chips in your computer
- Rebooting your computer before properly exiting from Paradox

Sometimes Paradox will indicate that a table is damaged when you attempt to use the table. Many times you will not get such a message. You will simply start to notice problems with the table. Symptoms of table damage include:

- Computer "hangs" when a table is being used
- Blank records appear when paging through a table
- Random "garbage" characters show up in the table
- Records "disappear" from the table
- Duplicate key values show up in a keyed table
- Reports print "garbage"

Using Tutility to Recover Damaged Tables

A utility program, called Tutility, is included with your Paradox program files. This program can often be used to recover damaged tables. Tutility is run from the DOS prompt and has a Paradox-like menu which allows you to Verify or Rebuild tables, change directories, or to exit from the program. If you suspect that there may be a problem with a table, don't use the Verify option. Verify does not always catch all problems. You should use the Rebuild option to fix any possible problems. Rebuilding a table will delete the primary index if one exists. If necessary, be sure to use **M**odify/**R**estructure to rekey a table after using Rebuild.

Tutility cannot always be used to recover a damaged table. Sometimes the "header" of a table is so badly damaged that Tutility cannot read it. At other times, Tutility can recover some, but not all, of the records in a table. If you are working with information which is important, **BACKUP FREQUENTLY**. Backing up your tables regularly is the best way to avoid, or minimize, losing information. More information on backing up Paradox tables and their families is included in Chapter 9, "Managing Your Paradox Objects."

Entering Information into Your New Tables

There are several ways that you can enter information into Paradox tables. Chapter 4, "Modifying Your Paradox Tables," will go into detail about the various methods and when it is appropriate to use each. For now, you can use the Modify/Edit command to enter the sample records from Figure 1.9 into your tables. Another way to get into Edit mode easily is to View a table and then press F9. To enter information into a table, type the desired value in a field and press Enter, Tab, or the right-arrow key, to move to the next field. The other arrow keys are used to move in other directions within your table. A few quick tips:

- If you make a mistake, use Backspace to erase a single character or Ctrl-Backspace to erase the entire field value.
- To cancel what you have done, press F10 and choose Cancel and Yes from the menus.
- To change a value in a field, press Alt-F5 or Ctrl-F to enter "field view." In field view, the arrow keys moves the cursor within a field, rather than moving the cursor between fields. The Ins key toggles between insert and overwrite modes. To exit from field view, press Enter.
- You can delete a record by pressing the Del key.
- You can insert a new record by pressing the Ins key. When you are in the last record in a table, you can also bring up a new record by pressing the down-arrow key. Pressing the right-arrow key while you are in the last field of the last record in a table gives the same result.
- You can "Undo" all of your changes, one record at a time, by pressing Ctrl-U.
- When you have finished adding records, press F2 or F10/DO-IT! to save your changes. You will be returned to Main mode.

In Edit mode, Paradox has many features available to speed up and streamline the data-entry process. We will not cover all of these now. For now, simply add the records in Figure 1.9 to the CUSTOMER table to illustrate the concepts to be covered in Chapter 3, "Looking at Your Paradox Tables." Table view and form view were mentioned briefly in the preceding chapter. Chapter 3 contains information about using all features available in table view and form view. Being familiar with these before you start entering information into your tables will be helpful.

Summary

This chapter explained how to design and create Paradox tables. It also highlighted some things you should know about tables before you start creating them:

- Information should be divided among separate tables when it makes sense to do so.
- Related tables need common fields so that Paradox can link them.
- Key fields in tables are important to improve performance; they are also needed to link tables with forms and reports.
- Tables are created using `Create` on the Main Menu.
- Tables can have up to 2 billion records, 255 fields and can be 4,000 characters wide (1,350 for a keyed table). Maximum field length is 255 characters.
- Tables should be kept as narrow as possible to maximize performance; 15 to 20 fields is a good rule-of-thumb.
- **Tools/ExportImport/Import** can be used to create tables from file formats such as Lotus 1-2-3 and dBASE.
- The Flimport program can be used to import fixed-length ASCII files.
- Damaged tables can sometimes be recovered using Tutility, a utility program which is included on your Paradox diskettes.

Looking at Your Tables

Once your tables have been created, you can explore different ways to view the information in them. Paradox can display tables using a *table view*, a *form view*, or graph the data. This chapter will cover the differences between table view and form view, show you how to create forms, and describe using the Image command to tailor the presentation of your information. All Image command options except Graph will be explained in this chapter. Graphs will be covered in Chapter 8.

How to View Your Tables

To view a table, you use the View command on the Main Menu. Using the View command allows you to look at a table, but you will not be able to change it unless you leave Main mode. The one exception to this is when you use a query to change a table. Queries execute in Main mode and can be used to alter the contents of a table.

Putting a table onto the Paradox workspace, using the View command, is simple:

1. Make sure that you are in Main mode. If you currently are editing a table, press F2 to save your changes and to return to Main mode.
2. Press F10 to display the Main Menu.
3. Choose View by pressing V or by pressing Enter with the cursor on View.

4. Paradox will prompt for the name of a table. Type the name of the table which you want to view and press Enter. You also can press Enter to get a list of tables in the current directory if you have more than one table in the directory. The list will look similar to the second line of Figure 3.1.

To view a table from a directory other than the current, or working, directory, type the complete pathname of the table which you want to view. Figure 3.2 shows how to do this. Typing the path, without specifying a table name, will cause Paradox to display a list of tables in the specified directory.

5. If you press Enter, or type a path, you can choose a table from the list which is displayed. There are two ways to do this. You can use the right- or left-arrow keys to move the cursor to the desired table and press Enter to select it.

You can also select a table by pressing the first letter of the table name. If there is more than one table which starts with the letter pressed, Paradox will display a shortened list of these tables. This feature can save you time if there are many tables in a directory and you don't remember how to spell the table's name, but know the first letter.

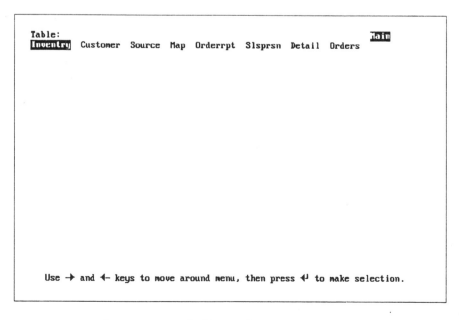

Figure 3.1 List of tables in the current directory

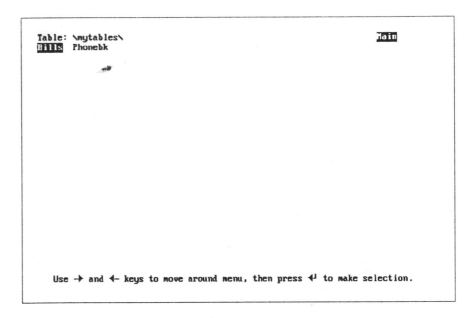

Figure 3.2 Viewing a table outside of the current directory

Table View

When you place a table on the workspace using `View` or some of the `Modify` commands, it will appear in table view, the default. The CUSTOMER table for The Raspberry Patch is displayed in table view in Figure 3.3.

Moving Through a Table in Table View

When a table is displayed in table view, records are displayed as rows. Each field appears as a column. If there are more fields than can be displayed at one time, you can use the left- or right-arrow key to move horizontally across the table. As you move across the table, you will see different fields for the group of records currently displayed.

You can use Ctrl-Z "Zoom," and Alt-Z, "Zoom Next," to quickly move to a record with a specific value.

Similarly, Paradox will display as many records from the current table as it can fit onto the screen. (The *current table* or *current image* is the table the cursor is in. This becomes important if you are working with more than one table at once, or if you have query images, as well as tables, on the workspace. More about this later.) You can use the up- or down-arrow key to move vertically through the records.

There are other keys and key combinations which can be used to move quickly through a table. Becoming familiar with these keystrokes can save you much time. Using Ctrl with the right- or left-arrow keys will move the cursor horizontally one screenful at a time. PgUp and PgDn will move the cursor up or down as many records as are currently displayed in a table's image. (The number of records displayed in an image can be adjusted. See the references later in this chapter to the Image command.) A complete listing of keystrokes for moving through tables is included on the Quick Reference Card.

You can place several Paradox tables on the workspace at the same time by using the View command successively. In fact, it is even possible to place more than one image of the same table on the workspace at the same time. This is very useful if you want to compare two records from a large table. To move between tables on the workspace, use F3 to move up one image and F4 to move down an image.

```
Viewing Customer table: Record 1 of 8                        Main

CUSTOMER Customer #        Last Name        First Name        Company N
    1        1        D'Inos          Doug             No Grownups!
    2        2        Dominicelli     Angelina         Bambini Time
    3        3        Holly           Deirdre          Love Bundles
    4        4        Michaels        Monique          Pour Les Enfant
    5        5        Mitchinson      Coco             Tops to Bottoms
    6        6        Packwald        Vanessa          A to Z
    7        7        Robinson        Ray              Little Stuff
    8        8        Sizemore        Nicholas         Kidstuf
```

Figure 3.3 CUSTOMER table in table view

Using the Image Command in Table View

Paradox normally displays a table in table view with the fields ordered according to the table structure. The number of records displayed depends on how many records will fit on the screen. The Image command can be used to change these parameters as well as others. Choosing Image on the Main Menu, with a table on the workspace in table view, brings up the menu shown in Figure 3.4. Choosing Image while a table is in form view will display a slightly different menu which will be described later in this chapter. You can also use Image while you are in Edit, Coedit and DataEntry modes. The Image command in these modes is the same as it is in Main mode, except that Graph is not available. If there are multiple tables on the workspace, the Image command will affect only the current image.

```
┌─────────────────────────────────────────────────────────────────────┐
│ TableSize  ColumnSize  Format  Zoom  Move  PickForm  KeepSet  Graph  Join │
│ Change the number of records to show in the current image.           │
│ CUSTOMER┬Customer #┬────────Last Name────────┬─────First Name─────┬───────Company N │
│    1    ││    1    ││ D'Inos          ││ Doug           ││ No Grownups!    │
│    2    ││    2    ││ Dominicelli     ││ Angelina       ││ Bambini Time    │
│    3    ││    3    ││ Holly           ││ Deirdre        ││ Love Bundles    │
│    4    ││    4    ││ Michaels        ││ Monique        ││ Pour Les Enfant │
│    5    ││    5    ││ Mitchinson      ││ Coco           ││ Tops to Bottoms │
│    6    ││    6    ││ Packwald        ││ Vanessa        ││ A to Z          │
│    7    ││    7    ││ Robinson        ││ Ray            ││ Little Stuff    │
│    8    ││    8    ││ Sizemore        ││ Nicholas       ││ Kidstuf         │
└─────────────────────────────────────────────────────────────────────┘
```

Figure 3.4 Image Menu while in table view in Main mode

The Image Menu choices allow you to change the way your table information is presented.

- TableSize lets you change the number of records displayed.
- ColumnSize is used to change the width of fields in table view.
- Format controls the way numeric values and dates are shown.
- Zoom moves the cursor based on criteria you enter.
- Move shifts the order in which fields are displayed.
- PickForm chooses a form with which to view the table.
- KeepSet saves the Image changes, except TableSize, for a table.
- Graph creates graphs or crosstab views of tables.

TableSize

TableSize allows you to adjust the number of records which are displayed for a particular table. This is useful when you are working with more than one table and want to view records from more than one image at the same time. When you bring a new table onto the workspace, Paradox displays all records up to 22 (the most that can fit onto the screen). If there are other tables on the workspace, they will scroll off the top of the screen if room is needed for the new image. By reducing the number of records displayed in the images, you can view more than one image at once.

After choosing TableSize on the Image Menu, a blinking cursor will appear at the bottom of the current image. You can use the up- or down-arrow key to adjust the number of records displayed. A minimum of two records must be displayed, and a maximum of 22 can be displayed. Pressing Home or End will move the number of records to the displayed minimum and maximum values, respectively. Pressing Enter will save the changes you make for the current session. As with most Paradox menus, you can press Esc to cancel the process.

ColumnSize

The `ColumnSize` command is used to adjust the width of each field in table view. There are some limits, however, to the changes which you can make:

- The minimum field width which can be displayed is one character.
- N, S, and $ fields may be increased only to the length of their field name, if it is longer than the default field size.
- Date fields may be increased only to 14 characters unless the field name is longer.
- Alphanumeric fields may not be increased to more than the defined field width or the field name, whichever is longer. The displayed field width cannot exceed the width of the screen.

If you shorten a field so that all of its value cannot be displayed:

- Alphanumeric fields will be truncated.
- Values in N, S, and $ fields will be displayed as asterisks if whole numbers and formatted decimal places cannot be displayed.
- Values in N, S, and $ fields will be displayed if only unformatted decimal values will be truncated.

 Changing the displayed field width does not change, in any way, the values stored in the table. You can still view values which are not completely displayed by using the field view command. You can enter field view by pressing Alt-F5 or Ctrl-F. When you are in field view, you can move the cursor through a field value using the left- or right-arrow, Ctrl-left-arrow, Ctrl-right-arrow, Home, or End keys. In addition, you can use the up- and down-arrow keys to move through *wordwrapped* field values. To exit from field view, press Enter.

Format

The `Format` command allows you to change the displayed format of N, $, and Date fields. Again, changing the display format does not affect the way values are stored on disk. The options you will have after choosing `Format` on the Image Menu depend on the type of field you indicate at the field prompt shown in Figure 3.5.

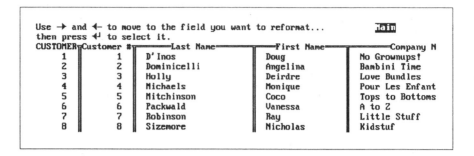

Figure 3.5 Field prompt for the Image/Format command

If you are formatting an N or a $ field, Paradox will display the menu shown in Figure 3.6.

```
General  Fixed  Comma  Scientific                                Main
Standard format; all numbers justified in the column.
DETAIL┬─Order #─┬─Item #─┬───────Description──────┬──Quantity──┬──Price─
   1  │    1   │  707  │  Black Jeans           │    10      │   7.50
   2  │    1   │  708  │  Black Jeans           │    10      │   7.50
   3  │   13   │  501  │  Bikini                │    12      │  10.00
   4  │   13   │  502  │  Bikini                │    12      │  10.00
```

Figure 3.6 Image/Format Menu for N and $ fields

- General is used to display a number with as many decimal places as are needed.
- Fixed is used to specify how many decimal places to display.
- Comma allows you to display numbers with whole number separators and parentheses for negative values. The separator used depends on the country group that you selected during installation. Commas are used as the separators for the U.S., and periods are used for the International format.
- Scientific displays numbers in exponential notation. In this format, all numbers are displayed as a decimal number between 1 and 10, multiplied by a power of 10.

Use the Custom script to change from the U.S. or Int'l format for numbers.

When you use Format on a Date field, you will see the menu shown in Figure 3.7. Dates will be displayed in the format you choose from this menu.

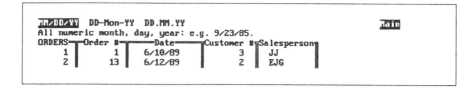

```
MM/DD/YY  DD-Mon-YY  DD.MM.YY                                    Main
All numeric month, day, year: e.g. 9/23/85.
ORDERS┬─Order #─┬─────Date──────┬─Customer #┬Salesperson┐
    1 │      1 │ 6/10/89        │        3 │ JJ        │
    2 │     13 │ 6/12/89        │        2 │ EJG       │
```

Figure 3.7 Image/Format Menu for Date fields

Zoom

Choosing Zoom displays the menu shown in Figure 3.8. You can move to a different field, record, or value, if it exists in the table.

- Field lists fields in the current table. The cursor will move to the field you select from the list.

- Record prompts you for a record number. The cursor will move to the current field of the record you specify.

- Value prompts for a field and for a value to search for in that field.

```
Field  Record  Value                                           Main
Move to a named field.
CUSTOMER┬Customer #┬────Last Name───┬────First Name───┬────Company N
      1 │       1 │ D'Inos         │ Doug            │ No Grownups!
      2 │       2 │ Dominicelli    │ Angelina        │ Bambini Time
      3 │       3 │ Holly          │ Deirdre         │ Love Bundles
      4 │       4 │ Michaels       │ Monique         │ Pour Les Enfant
      5 │       5 │ Mitchinson     │ Coco            │ Tops to Bottoms
      6 │       6 │ Packwald       │ Vanessa         │ A to Z
      7 │       7 │ Robinson       │ Ray             │ Little Stuff
      8 │       8 │ Sizemore       │ Nicholas        │ Kidstuf
```

Figure 3.8 Zoom Menu

Using the Zoom/Field and Zoom/Record commands is self-explanatory. The Zoom/Value command, however, deserves more of a description. It allows you to search for a specific value in a field or to use wildcard operators to search for values which match the pattern you type.

Wildcards are special characters which are used to represent any character, or even a group of characters. Paradox recognizes two wildcard operators in queries and in the Zoom/Value command:

.. represents any number of characters, including none and blank spaces.

@ stands for any single character.

Make sure you have the proper indexes set up to get good performance using "Zoom."

Here is an example of how wild-card operators work. If you want to look for the name *Pasquesi* but don't remember exactly how to spell it, you can type **Pa..** at the prompt after indicating a field for **Z**oom/**V**alue to search in. Paradox will look for any name which starts with *Pa*. If the search is successful, the cursor will be moved to that record. Similarly, if you want to find a product number which you know has only three digits, type @@@ at the value prompt. Paradox will look for a product number which has exactly three digits.

An important tip: All value searches in Paradox are case-sensitive unless wild-card operators are used. *Case-sensitive* means that Paradox when searching for matching values, considers whether letters have been typed in upper- or lowercase. (This is true for queries as well as when using **Z**oom/**V**alue.) If you are looking for a name which could have been typed with initials caps only, or entirely in uppercase letters, use the .. wildcard after the name at the value prompt. Paradox will then search for any occurrence of that name regardless of upper- or lowercase.

Searches done with the **Z**oom/**V**alue command always start from the first record in the table, regardless of the current cursor position. Paradox will search through the entire table. If no record contains the value being searched for, Paradox will display the message "Match not found" in the lower-right corner of the screen.

There is a shortcut for **Z**oom/**V**alue: Ctrl-Z, the "Zoom" key. Place the cursor in the field in which you want Paradox to search and press Ctrl-Z. The value prompt will be displayed at the top of the screen. If you have already used Zoom on the same field, the value typed previously will be displayed. You can type a new value or simply press Enter to have Paradox search again for the same value. Field view can be used in this context to change the current value after the "Zoom" prompt.

Alt-Z, the "Zoom Next" key, will search for additional occurrences of the value specified with Ctrl-Z. Alt-Z always starts searching from the record where the last match was found. If it does not find a match, the message "Match not found" will be displayed.

Move

The **Move** command rotates fields in table view. By default, table view displays fields according to the table structure. **Move** allows you to rotate fields so that you can view them in any order. This feature is quite useful for comparing fields which otherwise may not be displayed on the same screen. When you choose **Move** on the Image Menu, Paradox will display a list of the fields in the current table and prompt you to choose one. After you choose a field, Paradox will prompt you to move the cursor to indicate the new position for the field. Remember, this does not affect table structure; only the view of the table on the screen is changed.

The shortcut for `Move` is Ctrl-R. You can move a field to the right end of the table by placing the cursor in that field and pressing Ctrl-R. All other fields in the table will be moved one position to the left.

Unless the `KeepSet` command is used, changes which are made to a table using Ctrl-R or the `Move` command are in effect only while that image is on the workspace.

PickForm

`PickForm` is used to choose a form with which to view a table. If `PickForm` is chosen from the Image Menu, Paradox will display a menu of the forms for the current table. The current record is displayed using the form which you specify. If you specify a multi-table form, matching records from any linked tables also are displayed. For unlinked tables in a multi-table form, the first record(s) of that table are shown. After a form is picked using `PickForm`, F7 will bring up that form in table view as long as a table is on the workspace.

KeepSet

`KeepSet` will save selected `Image` settings in a special file so that the settings take effect whenever the table is placed on the workspace. The file is called TABLE.SET where *TABLE* is the name of the current table. These are the `Image` settings which can be saved with `KeepSet`:

- `ColumnSize`
- `Format`
- `Move`
- `PickForm`

Using `KeepSet` can save time if you frequently use a form other than the standard form, or if you prefer to view a table in a field order other than the default.

`TableSize` settings and `Graph` information are not stored in the `KeepSet` file. `Graph` information is stored differently. Chapter 8 contains more information on how to save and change Graphs.

Graph

Choosing `Graph` on the Image Menu will bring you into the Graph subsystem. This area has many features and will be covered fully in Chapter 8. The `Graph` command brings up the menu shown in Figure 3.9. Paradox creates Graphs using graph settings files which contain information on graph type, titles, axis labels, scales, and even the type of printer in use. The Graph Menu commands are used to control the graph settings files, as well as to generate graphs and crosstabs.

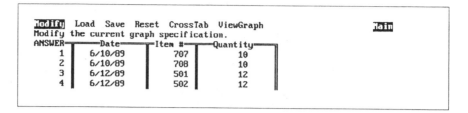

Figure 3.9 Graph Menu

- **Modify** lets you change the current graph settings.
- **Load** loads a graph setting which was saved earlier.
- **Save** saves the current graph settings in a file you name.
- **Reset** changes the current graph settings to their default values.
- **CrossTab** cross-tabulates the values in the current table.
- **ViewGraph** creates a graph using the current graph settings and the current table. You can view this graph on the screen, send it to a printer or plotter, or save it to a file.

Ctrl-F7 is a shortcut for the **I**mage/**G**raph/**V**iewGraph/**S**creen commands. The graph produced depends on the way that the current table is displayed and the current graph settings. Paradox will look to the first field in the current table for graph categories. (Use Ctrl-R to move the field containing the graph categories to the first field position if necessary.) The cursor must be in the first Numeric field because Paradox will graph the current field and the next five fields as series values. Each field being graphed represents a *series*. (A series is a group, or category, of information.) The default graph is a stacked bar graph. This can be changed using the **Modify** command on the Graph Menu.

Depending on the table being graphed, the information may need first to be summarized, using a query or the **CrossTab** command. Examples of how to do this are included in Chapter 8. **CrossTab** generates a separate table of cross-tabulated information which then can be graphed. The shortcut for the **CrossTab** command is Alt-X.

As mentioned, the **Image** command is available whether you are in table view or form view. The menu choices displayed, however, are different in form view. These differences will be covered after the following information on Paradox forms.

Form View

You can also view a table using a Paradox form. After placing a table on the workspace, you can change to form view by pressing F7, or by using the **I**mage/**P**ickForm command. F7 is a toggle key which moves between table view and form view. Form view is different from table view because it allows you to focus on one record or a group of records from a table (or tables!) using a screen layout which you design.

Paradox forms are created using the `Forms` command on the Main Menu. (You may want to refer to the card which illustrates the Paradox menu tree as you read through this section.) This chapter includes step-by-step examples of how to create simple forms which include information from only one table as well as forms which display information from multiple tables. You can create up to 15 forms for each table. For each form, Paradox creates a file called TABLE.Fn. *TABLE* is the name of the table to which the form belongs, and n is either nothing or a number from 1 through 14.

The Standard Form

The standard form is the form which Paradox uses when you press F7 to change from table view to form view (unless **I**mage/**P**ickForm had been used earlier on the same image.) TABLE.F is the name of the file which Paradox creates for a standard form. You can create your own standard form or let Paradox create its default. The default standard form can be used to view one record at a time from a table. This form lists the field labels with their corresponding field values, vertically. If there are more fields than will fit onto one page of the form, Paradox will create additional form pages as needed. Forms can be up to 15 pages long. If you press F7 while viewing a table in table view, Paradox will generate the standard form. The message "Creating standard F form...", will appear briefly in the lower-right corner of the screen. The standard form generated by Paradox for the CUSTOMER table is shown in Figure 3.10.

The standard form contains the table name and current record number in the upper-right corner of the form. The downward-pointing triangle on the first line of the screen indicates that there are more records below the current record in the table. If there are records above the current record as well, an upward-pointing triangle is displayed, too.

Moving Through a Form

Navigating through the fields on a form is different than moving through fields in table view. In table view, using the Enter, Tab, or right-arrow keys will move the cursor to the next field in the current record (or to the first field in the next record if the cursor is currently in the last field of a record). In form view, these keys move the cursor from field to field in

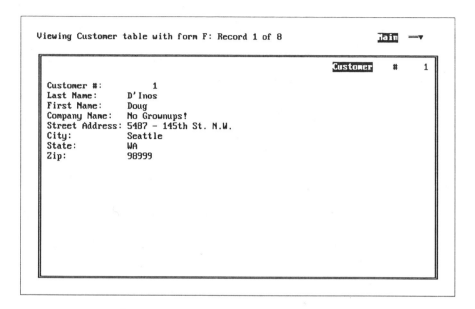

Viewing Customer table with form F: Record 1 of 8   **Main** ——▼

```
                                              Customer   #    1

        Customer #:        1
        Last Name:       D'Inos
        First Name:      Doug
        Company Name:    No Grownups!
        Street Address: 5487 – 145th St. N.W.
        City:            Seattle
        State:           WA
        Zip:             98999
```

Figure 3.10 CUSTOMER table viewed using standard form
generated by Paradox

left-to-right and top-to-bottom order. (For a form which has another form
embedded in it, this rule holds true within each form.) The only to way
change this is to write a PAL program to control cursor movement
through fields in a form or to create a multi-table form with a separate
form for each column.

In form view, you can move up or down one page using PgUp and
PgDn, respectively. Whether this will move the cursor to a new record
depends on whether you are using a multi-page form. If you are in a
multi-page form, using Ctrl-PgUp or Ctrl-PgDn will move the cursor to
the previous or to the next record in the table, respectively. Home and
End will move the cursor to the first record and the last record in a table,
respectively. The keystrokes used to move through a table in form view
are listed on the Quick Reference Card.

If you use F3 or F4 to move to another image on the workspace, the
image to which you move will be displayed in table view, even if the
previous current image was in form view. You must press F7, or use the
Image/PickForm command, to change back to form view.

Image Menu in Form View

The Image Menu in form view is slightly different than that menu in
table view. The commands for `TableSize`, `ColumnSize` and `Move` are not

applicable in form view. This leaves Format, Zoom, PickForm, KeepSet, and Graph. Those commands work the same as they do in table view. Figure 3.11 shows the Image Menu in form view.

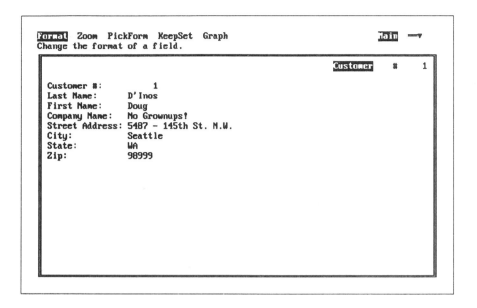

Figure 3.11 Image Menu with table in form view in Main mode

Using the Forms Command

This section briefly outlines the Form Menu commands and the functions each provides. After this section are examples of how to create simple and complex forms, illustrating the use of many of the Forms commands. Additional commands, along with several tips on using forms, are described at the end of the chapter.

Getting to the Forms Subsystem

Choosing Forms on the Paradox Main Menu displays a menu with two choices:

- Design allows you to create a new form.
- Change allows you to modify an existing form.

Use Tools/Copy/Form to save time if you are designing a form similar to one that already exists. Then, change the copy instead of designing a new form from scratch.

In both cases, you are prompted for a table name and for a form number (or **F** for the standard form). You are also given an opportunity to type a description for the form. After completing these steps, you are in the Forms subsystem. If you are designing a new form, you will see a blank screen with information about the current Paradox state on the top two lines. (See Figure 3.12 for an example.) The first line indicates the table, and the form which you are designing or changing. The right side of the screen shows which page of the form you are in. The left side of the second line indicates the current cursor position. If you are changing an existing form, you will see the current state of the form on the screen below the top two lines.

Press F10 to display the Form Menu. You will need to use the Form Menu commands for all work, except typing literals, while designing a form.

```
Designing new F form for Orders                    Form    1/1
< 1, 1>
```

Figure 3.12 Initial form design screen

The Form Menu

The Form Menu is shown in Figure 3.13.

```
Field  Area  Border  Page  Style  Multi  Help  DO-IT!  Cancel  Form    1/1
Place, erase, reformat, recalculate, or wrap a field.
```

Figure 3.13 Form Menu

- `Field` is used to place, erase, reformat, recalculate, and wordwrap fields.
- `Area` allows you to move or erase areas.
- `Border` places or erases borders.
- `Page` inserts or deletes pages.
- `Style` allows you to change the style and color of text: It has features which allow you to display field names and to highlight embedded form areas during form design.
- `Multi` is used to create and modify multi-record and multi-table forms.

- Help provides access to Paradox's context-sensitive help system.
- DO-IT! is used to save a form and return you to Main mode.
- Cancel cancels the work in progress and returns you to Main mode.

Each command has its own tree of menu commands. (The complete Form Menu tree is shown on the card which is included in this book.) Most commands are self-explanatory. Some of them are not obvious, though. The following examples illustrate the process of using the Form subsystem.

Creating a Single-Table, Single-Record Form

The simplest forms display one record from one table at a time. The following steps illustrate how to create a simple form for the ORDERS table created in Chapter 2 for The Raspberry Patch. The example is quite simple in order to point out the basic steps needed to create a form from scratch. (Instead of starting with the blank screen you get after choosing **F**orms/**D**esign, you can start with the standard form generated by Paradox by choosing **F**orms/**M**odify/**F**. This can save time if the form you want to create is similar to the standard form.)

This form will also serve as a building block for a multi-table form for ORDERS. This form will be used later as the master form into which forms for CUSTOMER and DETAIL will be embedded.

1. Choose **F**orms/**D**esign from the Main Menu.

2. Type **ORDERS**. If you do not remember the name of the table to use, press Enter and select Orders from the list. Then select F (or a number) from the list of available forms.

3. Paradox will prompt for a description of the form which you are creating. You can type a description or press Enter to accept the default Paradox description. Typing a description can be helpful if you intend to create more than one form for a table. The description can be used to indicate the purpose of each form.

4. When you are designing a new form, Paradox displays a screen like the one which was shown in Figure 3.12. Except for some information on the first two lines of the screen, the screen will be blank. The information on the left side of the first line reminds you what you are currently doing. Towards the right side of the screen, the word Form indicates that you are in Form mode. The 1/1 indicates that you are on the first page of a one-page form.

5. Literals, such as field labels, are typed onto the form design screen. To place fields on a form, though, you must use the Form Menu. This menu is accessed by pressing the universal menu key in Paradox, F10. The Form Menu was shown in Figure 3.13.

6. The first thing we will do is to place a border for the form. Choose **B**order/**S**ingle-Line from the menus. Paradox will prompt you to move the cursor to one corner for the desired border and to press Enter. Next, you will be prompted to move the cursor to the border's diagonal corner and press Enter again. Voila! After these keystrokes, you will see a border around the area you indicated. Paradox can create single- or double-line borders or a border using a character you specify.

Unfortunately, there is no quick way to move the cursor in Form mode. You must repeatedly press the arrow keys to move around the screen.

7. The next step is to type any literal information which you want displayed on the form. In the upper-left corner of the form, type the field labels, followed by colons. You can use the Ins key to toggle between insert and overwrite modes, if necessary.

8. After typing all of the literal information to be displayed on the form, use the menu commands to indicate where field values should be displayed. This is called "placing a field." To place a field, press F10 and choose **FI**eld/**P**lace/**R**egular from the menus. Type the name of the field to be placed or press Enter and choose the desired field from the list which is displayed. It is not necessary to place all fields from a table onto each form. You can place just a subset of the fields in a table.

9. After you indicate the field to be placed, Paradox will prompt you to use the cursor to show where you want the field value displayed on the form. Move the cursor to the desired location and press Enter.

10. Paradox will prompt you to use the arrow keys to indicate, the length of the *field mask*. The "field mask" is the area of the form used to display a field value. Press Enter when you have completed sizing the field mask. The effect of field mask size depends upon the field type. For an Alphanumeric field, Paradox will simply truncate the field value if it will not fit into the field mask. For a Numeric field, Paradox will display asterisks if the value cannot be displayed in the space available.

This is an important note: Paradox needs at least five extra spaces available in the field mask for a number field; six if the fields may have negative values. For example, to display the number *123*, make sure your field mask is at least eight spaces long. Paradox needs extra space to display Numeric values because of the way they are stored internally. If you leave enough space for number fields when you first set up a form, you can avoid trying to figure out later why numbers are displayed as asterisks.

11. Repeat Steps 8 through 10 for each field you want to place on the form. You can save time by placing the cursor on the desired location for a field before going through these steps. You can then press Enter twice as you go through the menu choices which prompt for the field location and length. If you will be placing many fields, the time-saving can be significant.

12. When you have placed the desired fields, the form should look like Figure 3.14. Press F2 to save the form. The form is now available for viewing table information.

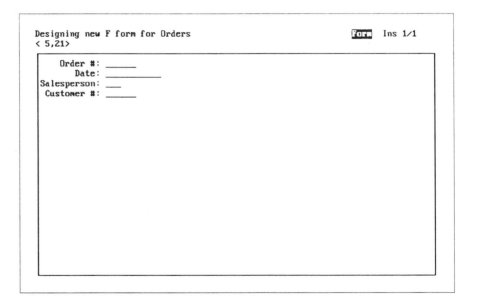

Figure 3.14 Form for ORDERS

Multi-record and Multi-table Forms

The standard form which Paradox creates will display one record from one table. In many cases, it is desirable to view several records from the same table on one form, or to view information from more than one table at the same time. You can create multi-record or multi-table forms to do this. It is even possible to combine the two types of forms, giving you many possibilities for creating custom views of your tables.

To enter orders for The Raspberry Patch, we will create a form which utilizes both multi-record and multi-table forms. The steps for doing this are included later in this chapter.

Creating a Multi-record Form

Creating multi-record forms is easy; simply follow the menu path which Paradox prompts you through after choosing **Multi/Records** from the Form Menu. An example is included in Step 8 of the section "Creating a Multi-table Form" later in this chapter. The multi-table form that will be created is used to enter and view records for The Raspberry Patch.

The multi-record form example in this chapter contains only fields from DETAIL. These fields are placed on one line which is duplicated in a "multi-record region" using the **Multi/Records** command. It is possible to embed another table's form on a multi-record form, but only if it is unlinked.

There are two other things to note about multi-record forms: if you are designing a form to be embedded in a master form, make sure you work in the upper-left corner of the form. Paradox determines the size of the form to be embedded by looking at everything from the upper-left corner to the bottom-most, right-most character in the form. The second thing to note is the positions of the fields which you place. This information will be useful when typing literal column headings for the multi-record area on the master form.

Creating multi-table forms is more complex, but still relatively easy, if you understand the basic concepts.

Multi-table Form Basics

Multi-table forms in Paradox are created by embedding a form from one table (the detail table) in the form of another table referred to as the master table. You can embed up to five forms in a master table's form. Another important note is that you cannot embed a form in a form which already is embedded in another table. The Form Menu commands **Multi/Tables/Place** are used to embed one table's form in another form. There are two types of embedded forms, linked and unlinked.

Unlinked Forms

It is possible to embed the form of one table into a master table's form even if there is no relationship between the tables. This can be useful for viewing and editing information in a table which is not related to the master table. That table may need to be accessed while the master table's form is being used. To embed an unlinked form, use the commands **M**ulti/**T**ables/**P**lace/**U**nlinked while designing or modifying a form for a master table. Paradox will prompt for the name of the table and for the number of the form to embed. You must be in Form mode on the master table.

This will be illustrated in the section "Creating a Multi-table Form" later in this chapter. It might be beneficial, for example, to be able to scroll through an unlinked INVENTRY table, to check available stock while entering orders in ORDERS for The Raspberry Patch. The person taking the order then could suggest alternative items if necessary.

Linked Forms

Linked forms are used when there is a relationship between the master table and the table whose form is being embedded. Paradox relates records from different tables by looking for matching values in linked fields. Records from the detail table are displayed with a record from the master table on a multi-table form based on matching values in the linking fields.

Rules for Linking Tables in a Multi-table Form

The following are the rules for linking tables with multi-table forms:

- The detail table must be keyed on one or more fields.
- Keying the master table is optional unless you want Paradox to enforce "referential integrity" (which is defined below).
- The linking field(s) must be a contiguous group of fields from the detail table's key fields, and must start with the first key field. The linking field(s) may or may not include all the key fields from the detail table.
- The linking fields must be placed on the master table form (which is the basis for the multi-table form), rather than in the embedded form for the detail table.

- The detail table form which is embedded in the master table form must contain any detail table key fields that are not used as linking fields.

Types of Links for Linked Multi-table Forms

There are four types of links possible between the master and detail tables in a multi-table form. The type of link is determined automatically by Paradox. How the master and detail tables are keyed determines the type of link between the tables.

- *One-to-one*: It is possible for only one record in the detail table to match a record in the master table. This occurs when the master table and the detail table are keyed on exactly the same field(s). Both tables must be keyed in order for Paradox to recognize this as a one-to-one link.

- *One-to-many*: More than one record in the detail table may correspond to a record in the master table. In this case, both the master and detail tables are keyed. The key of the master table is a subset of the key of the detail table.

- *Many-to-one*: It is possible for more than one record in the master table to match one record in the detail table while only one record in the detail table matches a record in the master table. If the master table is keyed, the linking fields are a subset of the master table's key fields.

- *Many-to-many*: Records in the detail table may correspond to more than one record in the master table and vice-versa. This can happen if the master table is not keyed, or if all of its key fields are not used as linking fields. Also, the linking fields must be a subset of the detail table's key fields.

Considering these rules while looking back at Figure 2.4, you will see that the relationship between ORDERS and CUSTOMER is many-to-one. The linking field, Customer #, is keyed only in CUSTOMER. ORDERS and DETAIL have a one-to-many relationship, because Order # is the entire key in ORDERS and a subset of the key in DETAIL.

Referential Integrity

When Paradox recognizes a one-to-one or a one-to-many link between tables, certain rules are enforced while editing tables with a multi-table form. Paradox uses these rules to maintain the relationships between matching records in linked tables. As an example, Paradox automatically changes the linking values in a detail table when the corresponding value is changed in the master table. This is referred to as "referential integrity." Referential integrity will be described fully in Chapter 4, "Modifying Your Paradox Tables." To take advantage of this capability, however, you must be sure to key your linked tables appropriately. There are some possible pitfalls in this area.

To illustrate this, let's look at the tables used to track orders for The Raspberry Patch. There will be only one record for each order in the ORDERS table. For each order, however, there may be several corresponding line items in the DETAIL table. You might think that a one-to-many link exists between the ORDERS and DETAIL tables and assume that Paradox will enforce referential integrity when you edit these tables using a multi-table form. This is not necessarily so, though. Unless the master table, ORDERS, is keyed, Paradox will not recognize the link between ORDERS and DETAIL as one-to-many and so will not enforce referential integrity. (This is because unless ORDERS is keyed on the Order #, there could be more than one record for each Order # in the table.)

If you change the Order # in ORDERS, using a multi-table form, without ORDERS being keyed, Paradox will not automatically change the corresponding Order #s in the DETAIL table. This can be disastrous unless you are aware of it. In this case, changing an Order # in ORDERS without changing the corresponding Order #s in the DETAIL table will result in "lost" detail records.

To insure that Paradox sees the link between ORDERS and DETAIL as one-to-many, thereby enforcing referential integrity, the ORDERS table *must* be keyed. Further, because the DETAIL table must be keyed and more than one record in DETAIL may correspond to a record in ORDERS, DETAIL must be keyed on more than one field to insure a unique key value for each record. Thus it makes sense to key the DETAIL table on the Order # *and* the Part # fields.

Creating a Multi-table Form in Paradox

Let's create a multi-table form for viewing and entering The Raspberry Patch's orders to illustrate this process.

1. Determine which table will be the master table. In this case, it is the ORDERS table, because ORDERS is the common link between CUSTOMER and DETAIL. A form for the ORDERS table could, in fact, be embedded in another table's form for some other task.

2. Make a list of other tables to be used with ORDERS. To enter orders, we will also use the CUSTOMER and DETAIL tables. (Information in the SLSPRSN and INVENTRY tables will be referenced but not added to, or changed, during order entry. These tables will be used as "lookup" tables. More about this will be covered in Chapter 4 in the section on table lookup validity checks.)

3. For all embedded forms, decide whether the forms need to be linked or unlinked. The CUSTOMER and DETAIL tables are related to the ORDERS table, as was shown in Figure 2.4 so the forms will be linked. (Although we are not going to show this, you could also embed the form for an unrelated table such as INVENTRY. Such a form would be unlinked.)

4. Check the key fields for the master table, ORDERS, and the detail tables, CUSTOMER and DETAIL, to be sure that they satisfy the requirements for linking tables in a multi-table form. ORDERS is keyed to make sure Paradox enforces referential integrity. It is keyed only on the first field, Order #, while DETAIL is keyed on both Order # and Part #. The tables will be linked only on the Order # field, ensuring a one-to-many link between ORDERS and DETAIL.

   CUSTOMER is keyed on the Customer # field. The corresponding field for Customer # in ORDERS is not keyed. This means that there will be a many-to-one relationship between ORDERS and CUSTOMER. Changing a Customer # on a record in ORDERS will not cause the matching record in CUSTOMER to be changed.

5. Design a form for ORDERS which will be used as the master form. The form designed in the single-table example earlier in this chapter is suitable.

6. Before embedding the forms for CUSTOMER and DETAIL in the form for ORDERS, these forms must, of course, be designed. For the CUSTOMER table, we will use a form which does not contain the Customer #. Customer # is placed in the master form for ORDERS and cannot be placed in the form for CUSTOMER. This is how Paradox knows to link the tables on the Customer # field. The form design screen for Form 1 for CUSTOMER is shown in Figure 3.15. Notice that Form 1 is designed in the upper-left corner of the screen. When Paradox embeds a form, it uses all parts of the embedded form from the upper-left corner to the right-most, bottom-most character on the form.

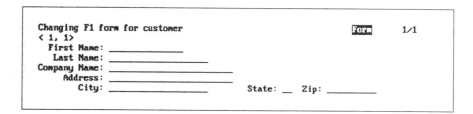

```
Changing F1 form for customer                          Form    1/1
< 1, 1>
   First Name: _____
    Last Name: _____
 Company Name: _____
      Address: _____
         City: _____   State: __  Zip: _____
```

Figure 3.15 Form for CUSTOMER to be embedded in ORDERS form

7. The form for DETAIL, which is embedded in the ORDERS form, must be able to display multiple line-items. This step illustrates how to create a multi-record form. Choose **Forms/Design** from the Main Menu. Type **DETAIL** when prompted for a table name and **1** for the form number. After typing a description and pressing Enter, an "empty" form screen will be displayed. Remember that the form for DETAIL must be designed in the upper-left corner of the screen so it can be embedded easily later in the form for ORDERS.

The column headings for the fields from DETAIL on the master form need to be shown only once. They should be typed on the master form for ORDERS after the DETAIL form is embedded. The DETAIL form need only include unique information for each line item in an order. This includes all of the fields from DETAIL, except Order # which is included on the master form for ORDERS. Use the F10/**F**ield/**P**lace/**R**egular commands to place each of the remaining fields from DETAIL on the first line in the form. We will also place a calculated field on the same line using the F10/**F**ield/**P**lace/**C**alculated commands. When prompted for an expression, type **[Quantity] * [Price]** as shown in Figure 3.16. This Calculated field will be used to display the extended price for each line item on the form. It will not create a true field in the DETAIL table.

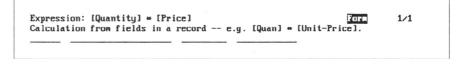

Figure 3.16 Calculated expression on DETAIL form

After placing all of the desired fields *once* on the form for DETAIL, we are ready to define a "multi-record region." Use F10/**M**ulti /**R**ecords/**D**efine to do this. Figure 3.17 shows how Paradox prompts you to indicate a corner of the area to be used for each section of the multi-record region. (You can use more than one line per record on a multi-record form.) Move the cursor to the desired corner and press Enter. Do the same when prompted to indicate the diagonal corner of the record area. This area will be highlighted. It represents the area which Paradox will duplicate for the multi-record region. Lastly, Paradox will prompt you to use the up- and down-arrow keys to indicate the size of the multi-record region (see Figure 3.18). Press the down-arrow key to adjust the number of records to be shown on the form and press Enter.

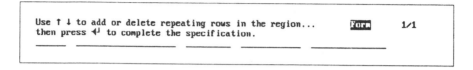

Figure 3.17 Prompt to indicate corner of multi-record region

```
Use ↑ ↓ to add or delete repeating rows in the region...     Form     1/1
then press ↵ to complete the specification.
```

Figure 3.18 Prompt to adjust multi-record region

The resulting form design screen is shown in Figure 3.19. Press F2 to save the form for DETAIL.

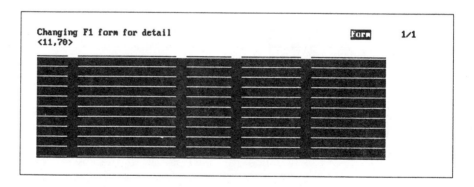

Figure 3.19 Multi-record form for DETAIL

8. To embed *Form 1* for CUSTOMER in *Form F* for ORDERS, use the following commands on the Main Menu: **Forms/Change** and specify ORDERS when prompted for a table name. Choose **F** for the form number and press Enter when prompted for a form description (unless you want to change the description. The description can be edited using field view, Backspace, or Ctrl-Backspace.)

   Once the form for ORDERS is displayed, press F10 to display the Form Menu. Choose **Multi/Tables/Place/Linked** and then type **CUSTOMER** when prompted for a table name. Press **1** to choose the form to embed. Paradox will then prompt you, as shown in Figure 3.20, to select a field from ORDERS to match the Customer #

field in CUSTOMER. Choose the Order # field from the list which is displayed.

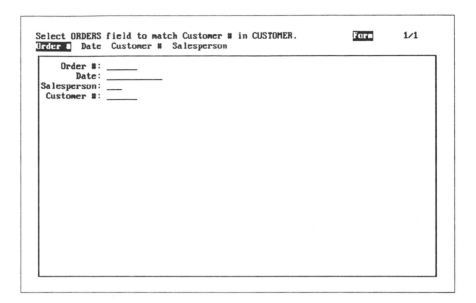

Figure 3.20 Prompt for linking fields during form design

Paradox knows that Customer # is to be used as a linking field because it is not placed on the form for CUSTOMER. We will not be prompted for any other linking fields because there are no other key fields in CUSTOMER. If there were multiple key fields in CUSTOMER, Paradox would request that a matching field be specified for each key field not placed on the form to be embedded.

After specifying a field in ORDERS to be matched to Customer # in CUSTOMER, Paradox will display a highlighted area in the lower-right corner corresponding to the size of the form to be embedded. Use the arrow keys to "drag" this area to the desired location for the embedded form. Press Enter to complete the "embedding" process.

9. Use F10/**M**ulti/**T**ables/**P**lace/**L**inked to embed the multi-record form for DETAIL in the form for ORDERS. Type **DETAIL** when prompted for a table name and press **1** for the form number. When prompted for a field from ORDERS to match to Order # in DETAIL, choose Order #. (If DETAIL was not keyed, the message, "Trying to embed non-keyed table" would be displayed.) Paradox knows that Order # is the linking field because it is not placed on the form for DETAIL.

The final step is to type the literal column headings for the fields displayed from the DETAIL table. As Figure 3.21 shows, the fields positions on the embedded form are not obvious when viewing the master form in Form mode. You will see only a highlighted area for each embedded form. Press F2 to save the form again and the multi-table form is complete!

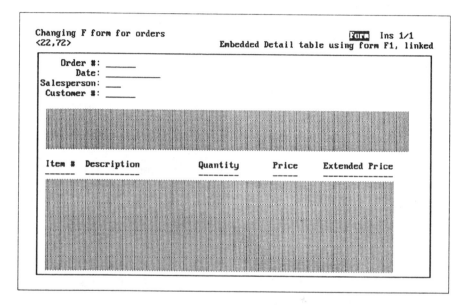

Figure 3.21 Multi-table form for ORDERS

Additional Form Commands

Many Form Menu commands were covered in the above examples. Additional commands are described below.

Field Commands

Changing a Field Length

Field/Reformat can be used to change the length of a field mask. It cannot be used to change the display format for a field value in the same way that the **Image/Format** command can. Use this command to lengthen Numeric field masks if you see asterisks instead of numbers.

Changing a Calculated Expression

You can use Alt-F3 to save the expression for a calculated field to a script. Then, play the Instant Script using Alt-F4 to "type" in the formula again.

Field/CalcEdit is used to change the expression of a Calculated field. When you use this command, the current expression for the selected Calculated field will be displayed. You can edit this expression using field view or use Ctrl-Backspace to erase the current expression and start over.

Word-Wrapping Fields on a Form

F10/Field/WordWrap is used to display a single field value on more than one form line. This is useful because you cannot scroll horizontally on the pages of a form. For fields which are wider than the screen width, WordWrap can be used to automatically present a field value in a paragraph-type format, allowing the entire value to be viewed on the screen.

You can use Home, End, and Ctrl with the arrow keys to move quickly through a word-wrapped field.

Using WordWrap is simple. First, decide how wide you want the "paragraph" to be. Then use F10/Field/Place/Regular to place a field mask on the form for the field to be wrapped. Calculate how many lines will be necessary to display the longest possible field value. (It depends on the length of the field mask as well as on the length of the field itself.) For example, if the field to be wordwrapped is 255 characters and the field mask is 65 characters, you will need four lines to display the longest possible field value. Next, make sure there are enough blank lines below the field mask for Paradox to display the wordwrapped value.

After completing these steps, use F10/Field/WordWrap to complete the process. You will be prompted for the field to be "wrapped" and the number of lines to use to display the value. That's it!

Paradox will split field values at spaces or hyphens at the end of a line. You can use field view on a wordwrapped field just as you can on any other field. You can also use the Area command to move a word-wrapped field. When doing this, you need indicate only the field mask as the area to be moved. Paradox will move the extra lines automatically. Make sure there is room in the new location for all possible lines.

DisplayOnly Fields

You can use a DisplayOnly field to protect a field's contents from undesired changes.

Field/Place/DisplayOnly is used to display field values on a form without providing user-access to the value. You cannot move the cursor to a field placed as a DisplayOnly field. This feature can be useful in displaying fields which have been placed as Regular fields on a multi-page form. (Regular fields can be placed only once on a form.)

Placing the Record Number on a Form

Use Field/Place/#Record to display the current record number automatically on a form. This field is included in the upper-right corner of the standard form.

Deleting Fields

The Backspace key will not erase field masks from a form. You must use the Field/Erase commands to remove a field mask.

Style Commands

Changing Form Colors

Style/Color can be used to set off the area where information is entered from the field labels.

Style/Color allows you to specify the colors to be used on a form. You can set the color for entire areas, borders, or lines on a form. This command will have effect only if you are using a color system. It overrides any monochrome attributes previously set for a form area. Pressing Alt-C while you are adjusting the colors will display a color palette.

Be careful if you use Style/Color on a form to be used on a monochrome screen. How the form will look depends on the relationship between colors and monochrome attributes which are currently set. This relationship can be changed using the Custom script. More details about this are included in Chapter 13, "Customizing Your Paradox System."

Changing Monochrome Display Style

Style/Monochrome gives you access to the commands used to set the text display style on a monochrome monitor. These commands can be used only on text or borders. You cannot alter the way field values will be displayed (too bad!).

It is possible to make text on a colored screen blink by using the Style/Monochrome commands *after* you use the Style/Color commands to set the desired color.

Multi Commands

Moving an Embedded Form

To move an embedded form on a master form, use the Multi/Table/Move commands. An embedded form *cannot* be moved using the Area command.

Removing a Multi-Record Region

When you make changes to the first line of a multi-record region, the changes take affect for all records.

The **M**ulti/**R**ecord/**R**emove commands allow you to remove a multi-record region. Using **F**ield/**E**rase will not erase the region; it will erase only the field masks from the multi-record region.

Additional Notes on Using Paradox Forms

Using Field Placement to Enforce Validity Checks

Edit mode has a feature which allows you to set up "validity checks" on values entered in a table. How to do this will be explained in Chapter 4, "Modifying Your Tables." Validity checks take effect only as you attempt to leave a field. If a field is never entered, Paradox will not use the validity check, even a "required field" valcheck, to check the field value. By placing each field on a line by itself, you guarantee that the field will be passed through on the way to other fields. This is why the master form for ORDERS was designed with each field on a line by itself.

Moving Through Multi-table Forms

Even though a multi-table form allows you to display information from more than one table on the same screen, it is still necessary to use the F3 and F4 keys to move between the tables used in the form. In the background, Paradox is working with separate table images on the workspace.

Reporting from Forms

Forms can be used only to display information. They cannot be used to print information from tables. The only way to print such information is by using the Paradox Report Generator or a PAL program. To print table records as they are displayed on a form, you must first create a report specification which looks like the desired form.

It is also impossible to print blank forms for a table. The Report Generator will report only on records in a table. You cannot use it to print blank forms, even if the table being reported on is empty. Paradox will give the message "Nothing to report" if you attempt to print a report for an empty table.

Calculated Fields in Forms

Paradox forms can have Calculated fields such as the one created in the form for the ORDERS table. These Calculated fields are for display purposes only. They do not exist in the table and cannot be referenced in expressions for other Calculated fields. It is not possible to format a Calculated field on a form unless at least one of the fields used in the calculation is a $ field. Then, only two decimal places will be displayed. If you are using a multi-table form, you cannot create a Calculated field from fields in more than one table.

Also, you cannot create calculated fields from other Calculated fields. Because of this, it is not possible to show a sum of the extended prices for each line item on the ORDERS form. Another limitation of Calculated fields is that you cannot use PAL functions, even the TODAY() function, in the expression for a Calculated field. If you need to print sums, this can be done through the Report Generator. To save sums in a table, you must use a query to do the calculations.

If you get blanks on a form when you expect to see a calculated value, check to see if any of the field values being used in the calculation are blank. Unless you have set Blanks=0 to Yes using the Custom script (see Chapter 13), Paradox will display a blank as the result of any calculation involving blanks.

Creating Fancy Borders

You can use special characters for borders by using the Border/Place/Other commands. Paradox will prompt for a character. Any character from the keyboard can be used. You can also use a character from the IBM Extended Character Set (ASCII codes 128–254). These characters are typed by holding down the Alt key while typing the ASCII code for the character you want on the numeric keypad. These ASCII codes are listed in Appendix C.

How Restructuring Tables Affects Forms

When you restructure a table, you will see a message in the lower-right corner of the screen that Paradox is updating each form and report for that table. Changing a field using the Modify/Restructure commands can sometimes result in the field mask being deleted from a form or report. An obvious example is when you delete a field or change a Field Type. If you are not sure what will happen after you restructure a table, be sure to check your forms and reports.

Damaged Forms

Sometimes the files which contain form information get damaged. You might get an error message when you try to use F7 or use `PickForm`. This is rare, but it can occur. Or, a restructure may fail as Paradox tries to make changes to a form. If this happens, delete the problem form and recreate it. There is no way to "fix" a damaged form file.

Backing Up and Restoring Forms

Remember, Paradox moves entire families as a unit. If you have to delete a form and restore its backup, or if you want to copy a form from one table to another, be sure you use the **Tools/Copy/Form** commands. If you use DOS to copy or restore a form without its .DB file, you will get a message that the form is corrupted or obsolete.

To restore a damaged form, first rename the table to which the form belongs. Then restore the backup copy of the table and its form. Once you have both tables available, you can perform a **Tools/Copy/Form/DifferentTable** from the restored table to the renamed table. Finally, give the renamed table its original name using **Tools/Rename/Table**.

Clearing Images from the Workspace

Although there is no logical limit to the number of images you can place on the workspace, you are realistically limited by how much RAM Paradox can use for the workspace and the width of the tables in use. As you work in Paradox, it is a good idea to clear tables which are not currently in use off the workspace.

The current image can be cleared by pressing F8, "Clear Image," while you are in Main mode. To clear the entire workspace, press Alt-F8, "Clear All." While you are using Paradox interactively, Alt-F8 has the additional benefit of writing the contents of RAM related to your tables to the disk and completely closing any tables in use. This is especially important if you are working with tables on floppy disks. To use a table on a floppy disk, other than the one currently in use, be sure to press Alt-F8 before taking the first floppy disk out of the disk drive. Paradox will then clear the RAM of all information related to the directory of the first diskette. If you neglect to do this, the files on the next floppy disk you attempt to use during the same Paradox session using the same drive will probably become damaged. You will also encounter error messages later in your Paradox session if you remove a floppy disk before pressing Alt-F8 or exiting from Paradox.

Summary

This chapter explained how to view tables, use the `Image` command, and create custom forms. These are the important points to remember:

- You can place a table on the workspace using the `View` command or one of the `Modify` commands

- Tables are displayed either in table view or in form view; you can toggle between these views using F7.

- Ctrl-R rotates fields in table view.

- The `Image` command is accessed from Main, Edit, Coedit, or DataEntry modes; it allows you to specify how information should be displayed without changing how it is stored, pick forms and locate specific records. In Main mode, Image also gives access to Graph mode.

- Ctrl-Z, "Zoom," and Alt-Z, "Zoom Next," can be used to search quickly for values in a table.

- Forms are designed and changed using the `Forms` command in Main mode; each table can have up to 15 forms.

- Multi-table and multi-record forms are created using the `Multi` command in Form mode.

- You can embed up to five linked or unlinked tables in a multi-table form.

- Linked tables on a multi-table form must be keyed; the linking fields cannot appear on the embedded form.

- There are four types of relationships possible between master and detail tables: one-to-one, one-to-many, many-to-one, and many-to-many. The relationship is determined by the key fields and the linking fields.

- Paradox enforces "referential integrity" for linked tables with one-to-one and one-to-many relationships.

Modifying Your Tables

Chapter 2 showed you how to enter information into your tables using the Modify/Edit command. There are actually several different ways to enter and change records in your tables using Paradox:

`Modify` gives you access to Edit, Coedit, DataEntry, Restructure, and Sort modes.

Using queries to make global changes to tables can be a real timesaver.

`Ask` lets you use queries to change, add, or delete records, using one table or linked tables.

`Tools` has commands to add, subtract, and empty entire tables.

The method you should use depends on the nature of the changes you are making. This chapter will explain the various methods that are available and give examples of using each.

The Modify Command

The `Modify` command provides several different ways to change tables:

- `Sort` allows you to sort records based on one or more fields.
- `Edit` is used to insert, delete, and change records in one or more tables at a time.
- `Coedit` can be used by more than one user at a time to edit the same tables.
- `DataEntry` gives you an ENTRY table which is used to add new records to one or more tables.

- `MultiEntry` is used to add new records from an ENTRY table into more than one target table.
- `Restructure` is used to change the structure of a table.

When you choose any of the above commands on the Modify Menu, you enter a new Paradox mode. `Edit`, `Coedit`, `Sort`, and `Restructure` take you into a mode of the same name. `DataEntry` and `MultiEntry` both take you into DataEntry mode. Each mode has its own set of menus. These menus are described in the sections for each command below.

Edit Mode

When you place a table on the workspace using the `View` command, you can move through the table freely but cannot make any changes to it. To change the table, you must be in Edit mode. Edit mode is used to add new records to a table (or tables using a multi-table form) as well as to change, insert, and delete records.

Entering Edit Mode

To edit a table which is not on the workspace, choose `View` on the Main Menu, specify a table when prompted, and then press F9. Or, choose Modify/Edit from the Main Menu and type the name of a table. If a table is already on the workspace, simply press F9 to go into Edit mode.

 Before you press F9, though, be sure to read the section later in this chapter on the differences between Edit and Coedit modes. You may want to press Alt-F9 for Coedit mode instead, *even if you are not using Paradox to share tables on a network!*

Editing Multiple Tables

If you want to edit more than one table at a time without using a multi-table form, first place all of the desired tables on the workspace using the `View` command. Then press F9. Once you go into Edit mode, all tables on the workspace can be edited. You can move between table images using F3 and F4.

This is because Paradox modes affect the entire workspace, not just one table. Also note that once you are in Edit mode, you cannot place another table on the workspace until you return to Main mode.

Moving Through Tables in Edit Mode

Moving through tables in Edit mode is basically the same as it is in Main mode. You can use the numeric keypad to move through a table quickly. The Quick Reference Card lists the keys which can be used and their effects in table view and form view.

Toggling Between Table View and Form View in Edit Mode

In Edit mode, you switch between table view and form view using the F7 key. F7 displays the current record using the standard form. You can specify that another form be used by using the Image/PickForm command from the Edit Menu.

There are some restrictions on switching between table view and form view while using a multi-table form. Those rules will be covered later in this chapter.

Changing Field Values in Edit Mode

There are different ways to change field values in Edit mode. You can use the Backspace key to erase the character to the left of the cursor. Pressing Ctrl-Backspace erases the entire value in the current field. To change a value without first erasing the entire value, use field view.

Field View

Field view allows you to move the cursor within a field instead of moving it only from field to field. To enter field view, press either Alt-F5 or Ctrl-F. In field view, you can change any character in the field value. The Ins key acts as a toggle between insert and overwrite modes. Pressing Ctrl and the left- or right-arrow keys will move the cursor one word at a time. Pressing Home or End will move the cursor to the beginning or end of the field value. To exit from field view and move to other fields in the table, press Enter. If you press F2 to "Do-It!" in field view, Paradox will display a message reminding you to press Enter before you attempt to "Do-It!"

Inserting and Deleting Records

 To insert a new record in Edit mode, press the Ins key. A new record will appear above the current one. To delete a record, press the Del key. Paradox will delete the record without further prompting. You can use the "Undo" command, which will be explained in the next section, to get deleted records back, but only if you know you deleted them in the first place. Be careful about leaning on the Del key accidentally or resting something against it. Your table will shrink quickly!

Using "Undo"

In Coedit mode, Undo reverses only the last change made to the table.

In Edit mode, you can use the "Undo" command to reverse the last change made to the table. You can use "Undo" incrementally to erase all changes made since the beginning of the current edit session. "Undo" is invoked by pressing Ctrl-U or by choosing Undo on the Edit Menu.

Copying Field Values

To copy an entire field value, you can use Ctrl-D, the "Ditto" command. "Ditto" copies the value from the same field in the preceding record to the current field. "Ditto" works only on a field basis. There is no interactive command which will allow you to copy an entire record. Neither is there a command to copy the value from one field to another in the same record. To transfer values from one field to another, you can use a *Changeto* query. Changetos will be described in Chapter 5, "Queries: The Exciting Part of Paradox."

The Edit Menu

Press F10 in Edit mode to display the Edit Menu. Figure 4.1 shows the Edit Menu displayed while editing the ORDERS table. The Edit Menu has some commands with which you are already familiar: Image, Help, DO-IT!, and Cancel. The Image command in Edit mode displays the same menu as when Image is chosen on the Main Menu, with one difference. In Main mode, Graph is included on the Image Menu. It is not possible to generate graphs while you are editing a table. You must first return to Main mode. There are two new choices on the Edit Menu:

- Undo allows you to "undo" the last change made to the table. It works the same as pressing Ctrl-U.
- ValCheck is used to place various validity checks on fields.

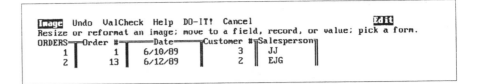

Figure 4.1 The Edit Menu

Validity Checks

Choosing `ValCheck` on the Edit Menu allows you to define or remove field validity checks. Validity checks are used to control the way information must be typed into fields or to fill in information automatically. There are six types of "valchecks":

- `LowValue` is used to specify a minimum value for a field.
- `HighValue` sets a maximum value for a field.
- `Default` lets you specify a value for Paradox to fill in when a field is left and no value has been entered.
- `TableLookup` can be used to check values against those in another table and, optionally, to fill in matching fields.
- `Picture` is used to control the format of values entered into a field and can be used to fill in constants.
- `Required` does not let the user leave a field blank.

Why Use Validity Checks?

Using validity checks is a powerful way to ensure that the information in your tables has a degree of uniformity. This is especially important when considering the way in which Paradox links tables. Paradox uses matching field values to link records in tables. Values must be *exactly* the same in order for Paradox to use them as links. This means that the case of letters in Alphanumeric strings must be the same. Paradox also includes leading, and sometimes trailing, blanks when determining whether values match. By using validity checks carefully, you can ensure that field values have consistent formats.

How Validity Checks are Enforced

Placing a valcheck on a field will not affect values already in the table.

An important note about valchecks: *Paradox enforces valchecks only when you attempt to leave a field*. For example, if you set a `Required` valcheck on a field, Paradox will not allow you to leave the field until you type a value. However, if you never move the cursor to that field, a valcheck for that field will have no effect. (For `Picture` valchecks, there is a slight difference. Paradox checks each character as it is typed, instead of waiting to check the entire string when you try to leave the field.) You can increase the probability that a valcheck will be enforced by placing a field on a line by itself in a form. Unless the user presses F2, cancels, or moves to another table on the workspace, the cursor will have to be moved through the field, guaranteeing that the valcheck will be used.

When you place validity checks on a table field, Paradox creates a file called TABLE.VAL where *TABLE* is the name of the table in use. Validity checks can be set up in either Edit or DataEntry mode. Although you cannot set up valchecks in Coedit mode, they will still take effect if the .VAL file is present when you go into Coedit mode. The valchecks you define will be used during Edit, Coedit, DataEntry, and MultiEntry modes until you clear them, using the **ValCheck/Clear** commands, or erase the .VAL file. You can erase the .VAL file with DOS or by using **Tools/Delete/ValCheck**.

Valchecks are *not* available when you use **Tools/More/Add** or a method other than Edit, Coedit, DataEntry, or MultiEntry mode to add or change records in a table. You may need to use PAL to format information in tables properly before adding them to other tables if the format of information is important. Examples of doing this will be found in Chapter 11, "Introduction to PAL."

Setting Up Validity Checks

To illustrate the use of valchecks, let's use this feature on the ORDERS table and the tables to which it is linked with the multi-table form created earlier. This form is shown in Figure 4.2. For each field, we will look to see what type of valcheck can be useful and use the **Val-Check/Define** command to put it in place.

Required ValCheck

The first field is Order #. Ideally, we would like to have Paradox assign the next Order # to this field when a new order is entered. Unfortunately, this is not possible using valchecks. This can be done just by using a little PAL program and is shown in Chapter 11. Even though we cannot yet control the number which is being typed, you can use a `Required` valcheck to make sure that some number is entered in the field. To set up the valcheck, you must have the ORDERS table on the workspace in Edit mode. Then, press F10 and choose **ValCheck/Define** from the Edit Menu. Select the Order # field when prompted and then choose **Required/Yes** from the ValCheck Menu which is displayed. This menu is shown in Figure 4.3. The `Required` valcheck for the Order # field is

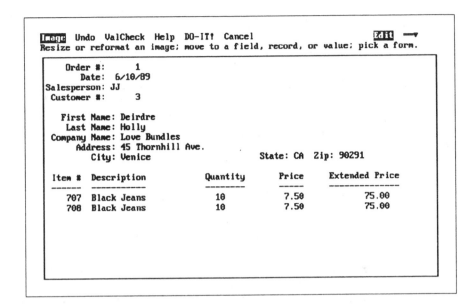

Figure 4.2 Multi-table form for ORDERS

now in place. Remember it will be enforced only when you attempt to leave the Order # field. Since Order # is the first field in the table and on the form, it would be impossible to circumvent the valcheck in this case.

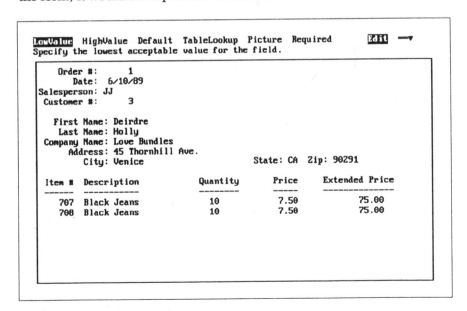

Figure 4.3 ValCheck Menu

Default ValCheck

The second field is Date. You can use the `Default` valcheck to have Paradox automatically fill in the system date when you move the cursor through the field and leave it blank. Choose `Default` from the ValCheck Menu and type **today** when prompted for a default value. (This is one of two places where you can use the expression *today* in Paradox. The other is in a query.) Paradox will fill in the system date when you leave the Date field. You can type another date if you want to.

TableLookups

The main advantage of `TableLookup` is that it allows you to ensure that a field value exists in another table referred to as a *lookup table*. The lookup table contains all possible valid entries, such as state codes or customer numbers, for a field. Once a `TableLookup` valcheck is in place on a field, you cannot type any value into the field unless that value exists in the lookup table. There are two rules for lookup tables:

1. The lookup field must be the first field in the lookup table.
2. The lookup field must be of the same field type as the field which the `TableLookup` valcheck is set for. The field names do not have to be the same, though.

   `TableLookup` has two additional features:

- Automatic fill in of corresponding fields
- Lookup help

These features are set through `TableLookup`'s own menu tree. Let's set up a table lookup for the Customer # field of ORDERS with both of the above features. After choosing **ValCheck/Define** and indicating the Customer # field, choose `TableLookup` from the next menu. Paradox will prompt for the name of a lookup table. Type **CUSTOMER**. Next you will see the menu shown in Figure 4.4. If you want Paradox to validate only the current field value against the lookup table, select `JustCurrentField`. In this case, that is sufficient. We do not need to have Paradox fill in information from the CUSTOMER table. It will be displayed automatically on the linked multi-table form when you use F4 to move to the CUSTOMER part of the form. The `AllCorrespondingFields` feature will be used in the DETAIL portion of the table.

A second menu is displayed as shown in Figure 4.5. If you choose `PrivateLookup`, Paradox will not allow the user to see the lookup table. Choosing `HelpAndFill` makes the lookup table available to the user if F1 were to be pressed. This is a nice feature if you don't know exactly how a

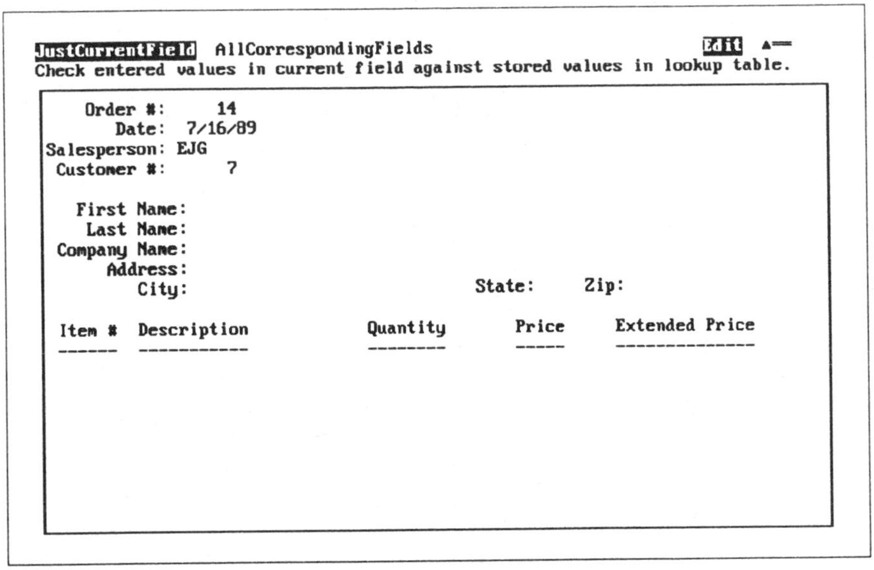

```
┌─────────────────────────────────────────────────────────────┐
│ ▓JustCurrentField▓ AllCorrespondingFields              ▓Edit▓ ▲─ │
│ Check entered values in current field against stored values in lookup table. │
│   ┌──────────────────────────────────────────────────────┐  │
│   │     Order #:     14                                   │  │
│   │      Date:   7/16/89                                  │  │
│   │ Salesperson: EJG                                      │  │
│   │  Customer #:      7                                   │  │
│   │                                                       │  │
│   │   First Name:                                         │  │
│   │    Last Name:                                         │  │
│   │ Company Name:                                         │  │
│   │      Address:                                         │  │
│   │         City:                  State:    Zip:         │  │
│   │                                                       │  │
│   │  Item #  Description       Quantity    Price   Extended Price │  │
│   │  ──────  ───────────       ────────    ─────   ────────────── │  │
│   │                                                       │  │
│   └──────────────────────────────────────────────────────┘  │
└─────────────────────────────────────────────────────────────┘
```

Figure 4.4 TableLookup first menu

value is to be typed. (Paradox's case-sensitivity can cause problems here.) When you press F1, and if HelpAndFill has been specified, Paradox will display the lookup table as the only table on the screen. You can move the cursor to the desired record and press F2 to tell Paradox which record you want to use. It is also possible to use "Zoom" on the lookup table. This is handy if you are working with a long lookup table.

Choose HelpAndFill for the lookup on CUSTOMER for Customer #. This way, Paradox will allow you to move the cursor through the CUSTOMER table if you need help with a Customer #. Once a record from CUSTOMER has been selected, Paradox will fill in the Customer # field in ORDERS. The other customer-related information on the form is automatically displayed on the linked multi-table form when you move to the CUSTOMER part of the form.

There is one more field in the ORDERS part of the form. That field is Salesperson. We can again place a simple TableLookup on this field using the SLSPRSN table, and choosing JustCurrentField.

The CUSTOMER portion of the multi-table form needs no validity checks. All information there is displayed automatically, based on the Customer # entered in the ORDERS part of the form.

The TableLookup valcheck can be used again in the DETAIL part of the form. Here we will utilize the AllCorrespondingFields feature. To put the valcheck in place, press F10 and choose ValCheck/Define from the Edit Menu. After indicating the Item # field, choose Table-Lookup and type **INVENTRY** as the lookup table. Choose AllCorrespon-

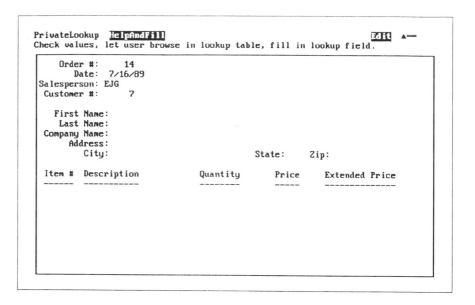

Figure 4.5 `TableLookup` second menu

dingFields/**HelpAndFill** from the menus. Now you will be able to press F1 while in the Part # field in DETAIL and have the INVENTRY table displayed. Paradox will automatically fill in the Description and Price fields in DETAIL after a record has been selected from the lookup table.

Working with Keyed Lookup Tables

While not necessary, it is useful to have a long lookup table keyed on the first field. This will speed the lookup process. Only the first field should be keyed. A lookup table keyed on more than one field causes problems. When you attempt to use a multiple-key lookup table with `HelpAndFill`, Paradox will tell you that you cannot do this with a lookup table keyed on more than one field.

A related problem involves using `HelpAndFill` on an unkeyed table which has non-unique values in the first field. No matter which entry in the lookup table you select, Paradox uses the first record for a particular value. This can cause problems if you are expecting the information from another record to be filled in. The only solution is to code your own "lookup-and-fill" routine using PAL.

These are all the valchecks necessary for entering orders for The Raspberry Patch. There are three additional valchecks: `LowValue`, `High-Value`, and `Picture`. `LowValue` and `HighValue` are self-explanatory. They simply set minimum and maximum values which can be entered into a field.

Using Pictures

Pictures are more complex. They allow you to set up formats to which field values must conform. Pictures are especially useful with Alphanumeric fields.

There are several ways you can use Pictures. Here are some things which they can do for you:

- Fill in the rest of an expression after one or more characters have been typed
- Check to see that a string matches a certain pattern of character types and/or literals
- Automatically capitalize or initial-capitalize words
- Check that a value is one of a group of alternatives

You use the same command to set up any of these types of Pictures. Choose Picture from the ValCheck Menu and type a Picture when prompted. Now, what does a Picture look like?

A Picture can consist of literals as well as characters which stand for any character of a certain type. There are a few special characters which indicate other things. The special characters you can use in Pictures are listed in Table 4.1.

Table 4.1 Characters Used In Pictures

Character	Used For
#	Numeric digit
?	Letter(A-Z or a-z)
&	Letter to be converted to uppercase
@	Any character
!	Any character to be converted to uppercase
;	Take the next character literally
*	Repetition indicator
[ ]	Optional character(s)
{}	Group operator
,	Separates alternative values

Looking at sample Pictures will help to clarify how these characters are used. One of the simplest Pictures is just a string of #s. If you type ### as a Picture, Paradox will allow you to enter only a string of three numbers. If you attempt to type a non-numeric character, Paradox will beep. If you try to leave the field before entering a value which conforms to the Picture, Paradox will display the message "Incomplete field."

To enter a variable number of numbers, you can use the Picture *#. This allows you to enter any number of numbers. A variation of the ### Picture is *3#. This Picture tells Paradox to accept only three numbers for a value. You can also mix literals with the # symbol. Using the Picture ###-##-#### will facilitate entering Social Security numbers. Paradox will fill in the hyphens automatically as numbers are typed.

Square brackets, [ ], indicate that part of a Picture which is optional. #####[-####] can be used as a picture for ZIP Codes which are either 5 or 9 digits long.

Another type of Picture involves alternative values. If you want a field value to be either **Y** or **N**, use the Picture **Y,N**. You can type either **y**, **Y**, **n**, or **N**. If you type a letter in lower case and it is capitalized in the Picture, Paradox will automatically convert the letter to uppercase. If you use longer strings as alternative values, Paradox will fill in the value as soon as you type enough characters for Paradox to make a choice from the Picture. If the picture is **Yes,No**, Paradox will fill in the word *Yes* if **Y** is typed.

Be sure to use the ; in front of any commas or other special characters that are part of the value the user can type in.

A listing of sample Pictures is included in Appendix I. The examples given here are quite simple and are used just to illustrate the different Picture possibilities. You can create nested Pictures which are much more complex, allowing the user to enter a number of possible values. This is useful for controlling fields for addresses or complicated part numbers.

Tips on Editing Keyed Tables

Use Coedit mode if you want to be notified about duplicate key values when records are entered or changed.

When you edit key values in a table, be careful. You may unexpectedly lose records if you do not understand how Paradox is working on the changes that you specify. If you duplicate a key when you add a new record, or change the key of an existing record, Paradox will assume that you want to replace the existing record with the new record for that key. Similarly, if you enter more than one record leaving the key field(s) blank, Paradox will keep only the last record entered. You will get no warning that a record is being deleted from the table.

Another potential problem involves reassigning key values in a table. Assume that you have a keyed table with 10 records as shown in Figure 4.6. The records have the values *1* through *10* in the key field. If you renumber the records as shown in Figure 4.7 and then press F2 to "Do-It!," you will be left with only one record in the table. Figure 4.8 shows the table which will result from such changes. Because of the way

Paradox handles its transaction log, all of the records, except the last one, are deleted.

```
┌──────────────────────────────────────────────────────────────────────────┐
│ Editing Projects table: Record 1 of 10                         Edit        │
│                                                                            │
│ PROJECTS┬─Number─┬─────────Project─────────┬─Target Date─┬─Complete┬Completion Da │
│    1    │     14 │ Mow lawn                │   9/15/89   │         │         │
│    2    │      2 │ Redo phonebook pages    │  12/01/89   │         │         │
│    3    │      3 │ Have car serviced       │   8/31/89   │         │         │
│    4    │      4 │ Update baby books       │  10/17/89   │         │         │
│    5    │      5 │ Feed camellias          │   9/15/89   │         │         │
│    6    │      6 │ Organize PC mags        │  12/31/95   │         │         │
│    7    │      7 │ File expense info       │   4/01/90   │         │         │
│    8    │      8 │ Repair skates           │   8/01/89   │         │         │
│    9    │      9 │ Proposal for KK Inc     │   9/01/89   │         │         │
│   10    │     10 │ Add setups to Pdox      │   8/15/89   │         │         │
└──────────────────────────────────────────────────────────────────────────┘
```

Figure 4.6 Keyed table before changing key values

```
┌──────────────────────────────────────────────────────────────────────────┐
│ Editing Projects table: Record 10 of 10                        Edit        │
│                                                                            │
│ PROJECTS┬─Number─┬─────────Project─────────┬─Target Date─┬─Complete┬Completion Da │
│    1    │      2 │ Mow lawn                │   9/15/89   │         │         │
│    2    │      3 │ Redo phonebook pages    │  12/01/89   │         │         │
│    3    │      4 │ Have car serviced       │   8/31/89   │         │         │
│    4    │      5 │ Update baby books       │  10/17/89   │         │         │
│    5    │      6 │ Feed camellias          │   9/15/89   │         │         │
│    6    │      7 │ Organize PC mags        │  12/31/95   │         │         │
│    7    │      8 │ File expense info       │   4/01/90   │         │         │
│    8    │      9 │ Repair skates           │   8/01/89   │         │         │
│    9    │     10 │ Proposal for KK Inc     │   9/01/89   │         │         │
│   10    │  11  ◄ │ Add setups to Pdox      │   8/15/89   │         │         │
└──────────────────────────────────────────────────────────────────────────┘
```

Figure 4.7 Same table as shown in Figure 4.6 with key values changed

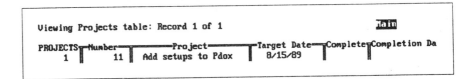

```
┌──────────────────────────────────────────────────────────────────────────┐
│ Viewing Projects table: Record 1 of 1                          Main        │
│                                                                            │
│ PROJECTS┬─Number─┬─────────Project─────────┬─Target Date─┬─Complete┬Completion Da │
│    1    │     11 │ Add setups to Pdox      │   8/15/89   │         │         │
└──────────────────────────────────────────────────────────────────────────┘
```

Figure 4.8 Table shown in Figure 4.7 after pressing F2

Editing and Using Multi-table Forms

When you view tables using a multi-table form, you can toggle between table view and form view. (Only the master table will be shown when you go to table view.) In form view, you use F3 and F4 to move between the tables on the form, the same way you do in table view. When you are in Edit mode, though, some restrictions apply when using multi-table forms.

Updating Linked Tables

When you enter, or change, information in the master table on a multi-table form, corresponding information in the linked tables is displayed when you press F3 or F4 to move to the linked table. Just entering the information into the master part of the form will not cause the detail records to be displayed.

To display the detail information without leaving the master table, you must press Ctrl-L, "Resynch." This causes Paradox to resynchronize the master and detail records, resulting in an update of the records displayed in any linked table on the multi-table form. "Resynch" works only while you are in the master table on the multi-table form.

Toggling Between Table View and a Multi-table Form

1. You cannot toggle from table view to a multi-table form once you have started editing the table in table view.

   If you attempt to do this, you will see the message shown in Figure 4.9. In this case, ORDERS had been placed on the workspace in Edit mode and then F7 was pressed in an attempt to display multi-table form F. Changes were already made to the table so Paradox would not display the multi-table form.

2. You cannot toggle to table view from a multi-table form in Edit mode and continue editing.

   Paradox will display the message shown in Figure 4.10 if you try to do this. When tables are being edited using a linked multi-table form, Paradox considers the tables to be "link locked." Once tables are link locked, they can be edited only by using the multi-table form which links them.

Referential Integrity

To check link type: with the cursor in the detail table, press Alt-F10. Choose Value and type linktype( ).

The rules above apply to all tables which are linked with a multi-table form. If there is a one-to-one or one-to-many relationship between the master table and the detail table, Paradox will also enforce additional rules to maintain "referential integrity." Referential integrity refers to

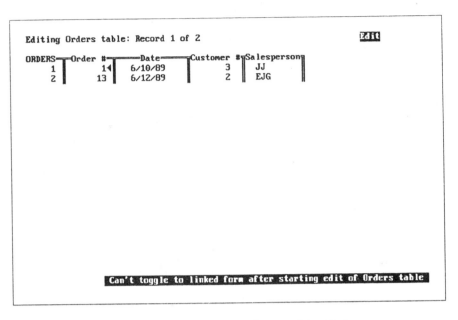

Figure 4.9 Attempting to toggle to multi-table form
while editing in table view

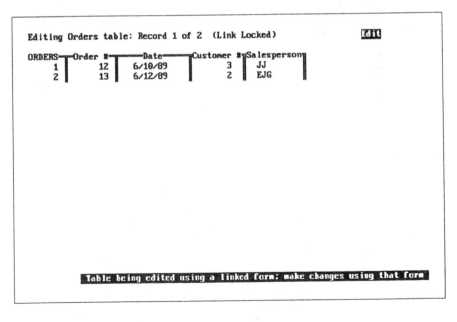

Figure 4.10 Trying to edit a link locked table in table view

the way Paradox maintains consistency of linking values. Two things are done to insure this:

1. Paradox will not allow you to delete a master record while detail records depend on it.

   This rule is enforced only while you are editing using a multi-table form. If you attempt to delete a master record which has corresponding records in a detail table, you see the message shown in Figure 4.11. You can see that the cursor is in the Order # field in the master table part of the form. Also note that linking records are displayed in the detail table parts of the form. Paradox will allow you to delete the master record only if there are no corresponding records in the linked tables.

   An important note here is that although Paradox will not let you use the Del key to delete a master record which has detail records, you can inadvertently do this by entering a record with a duplicate key. Paradox will delete the old record which has the same key, along with its detail records.

2. If you change a linking value in a master record, Paradox will automatically update the corresponding linking values in the detail table. Once again, this will happen only while you are editing the tables using a multi-table form.

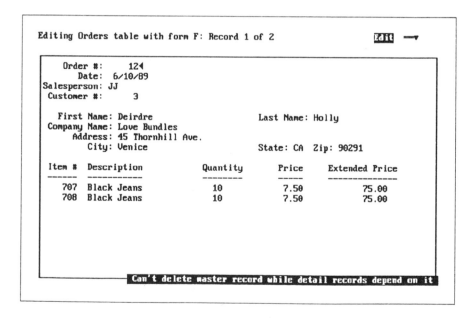

Figure 4.11 Attempting to delete a master record that has corresponding detail records

Remember that Paradox uses the key fields of the master and detail tables to determine the type of relationship between linked tables. Even though there may be a one-to-one or one-to-many relationship between records in two tables, unless the tables are keyed appropriately, Paradox may see the link as being many-to-one or many-to-many. Referential integrity is maintained only for tables with a one-to-one or one-to-many relationship.

A Few More Notes on Edit

Taking Advantage of Image/Format

When you use the Image/Format commands while editing to tell Paradox how to format Number or Date fields, you get a side benefit. Pressing the spacebar at the appropriate place will fill in slashes, periods, or commas if they are the only possible next character. Paradox will also fill in letters in month names, cents in Currency fields, and closing parenthesis for negative number values.

"Zooming" in Edit Mode

Paradox makes use of any indexes that are in place in Coedit mode, but not in Edit mode.

You can use the "Zoom," Ctrl-Z, and "Zoom Next," Alt-Z, commands in Edit mode. This is useful if you are editing a large table and need to search for scattered records. If you need to do this often, though, you may want to use Coedit, instead of Edit, mode. See the section in this chapter on "Differences Between Edit and Coedit Modes."

AutoSave

If your disk drive light flashes during an editing session and you are not making any changes, don't worry. Paradox occasionally writes any changes made to your tables to the disk if AutoSave is set to Yes. This will minimize the amount of information which will be lost in a power outage. You can change this option by playing the Custom script. See Chapter 13, "Customizing Your Paradox System," for details.

Coedit Mode

Coedit enables more than one network user to edit a table at the same time. It does this by using record locking, rather than by using table locking. When you go into Edit mode, Paradox places a "full lock" on any tables on the workspace. This prevents any other users from being able to access the tables. Coedit mode, instead, places a "prevent full lock" on any tables being used. (More information about the different types of locks which Paradox uses will be found in Chapter 15, "Networking With Paradox.") This allows multiple users to make changes to the same tables at the same time. When a user begins to edit a record in Coedit mode, a lock is placed on that record until the user is finished with it. Only one user can lock any given record at a time. This is to ensure that records are not updated simultaneously by more than one person.

Record Locking

In Coedit mode, Paradox does not lock a record until you begin to change it. As soon as you start changing a record, however, you will see the cursor become highlighted. This indicates that the current record is locked. A message will be displayed on the second line of the screen to indicate this. The record will remain locked until you move the cursor off the record, "Do-It!," or use Alt-L to unlock the record explicitly. No other user can change that record until it is unlocked.

You may want to unlock a record after entering the key value to see if the key already exists. The record may "fly away" though. See Section below.

In Coedit mode, you can use Alt-L to explicitly lock or unlock records. Alt-L works as a toggle key. The action it takes depends on whether the current record is locked or unlocked. Typically, you do not need to lock records explicitly while you are in Coedit mode. There are times, though, when being able to lock or unlock a record yourself is helpful.

When you are entering a new record in Coedit mode, you may notice the message "Entering new record–not yet posted to table" shown in Figure 4.12. When you create a new record in Coedit mode, there is no need to lock it as it is not yet part of the table. Until you leave the record, it will not be posted to the table. Once the record is posted, it

Figure 4.12 Entering a new record in Coedit mode

is available to other users as a part of the table. Until that point, it can be seen only on your screen.

If you press Alt-L on a new record which has not been posted to the table, it will have the effect of unlocking the record and posting it to the table.

Entering Coedit Mode

To enter Coedit mode, you can choose Modify/Coedit from the menus and specify a table when prompted or you can press Alt-F9 if the table is on the workspace. If there are multiple tables on the workspace, all tables will be in Coedit mode. As usual, you can move between images using F3 and F4.

The Coedit Menu

Any valchecks placed on the table in Edit mode are enforced during Coedit mode.

The Coedit Menu is shown in Figure 4.13. It differs from the Edit Menu in that it does not have the ValCheck or Cancel options. In Coedit mode, you cannot cancel the changes made during your coediting session because each change is permanently posted to the table when you leave, or otherwise unlock, a record. Valchecks cannot be added to a table because multiple users might attempt to place conflicting valchecks on the same field(s). There is one additional choice on the Coedit Menu which is not available in Edit mode: AutoRefresh.

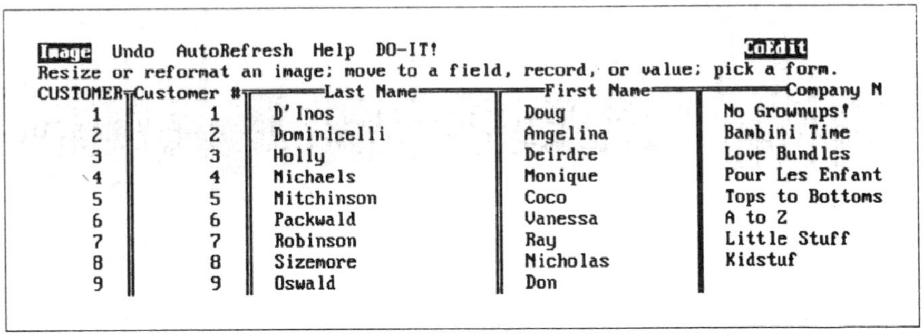

```
Image  Undo  AutoRefresh  Help  DO-IT!                         CoEdit
Resize or reformat an image; move to a field, record, or value; pick a form.
CUSTOMER Customer #      Last Name         First Name          Company N
    1         1    D'Inos             Doug              No Grownups!
    2         2    Dominicelli        Angelina          Bambini Time
    3         3    Holly              Deirdre           Love Bundles
    4         4    Michaels           Monique           Pour Les Enfant
    5         5    Mitchinson         Coco              Tops to Bottoms
    6         6    Packwald           Vanessa           A to Z
    7         7    Robinson           Ray               Little Stuff
    8         8    Sizemore           Nicholas          Kidstuf
    9         9    Oswald             Don
```

Figure 4.13 The Coedit Menu

AutoRefresh

You may want to increase the auto refresh internal to decrease network traffic.

AutoRefresh allows you to set the interval at which Paradox will refresh the screen with changes made by other users to the tables with which you are working. The default interval is three seconds. This can be set anywhere from 0 to 3600 seconds. The `AutoRefresh` interval also can be set using **T**ools/**N**et/**A**utoRefresh commands.

Paradox will refresh the screen at the specified intervals. It will also refresh the screen if you press Alt-R or if you begin to change an out-of-date record.

Using Coedit to Change Records

Making changes to tables in Coedit mode is basically the same as in Edit mode. You use the same keys to move around the table and to edit field values. "Zoom," "Ditto," and "Undo" can be used. The only difference is that you can "Undo" only the last change you make to a table in Coedit mode. Otherwise, you can use all of the same techniques you use in Edit mode. See the section on "Coediting Multi-table Forms" for notes on using "Undo" and "Zoom" with multi-table forms.

A note of caution: Since you cannot use "Undo" on more than one record while you are in Coedit mode, be careful about pressing the Del key. Once you delete a record, and then make another change to the table in Coedit mode, you cannot get the deleted record back. More than one person (including the author of this book!) has accidentally leaned on the Del key and deleted an unknown number of records from a table in use by several people on a network.

Coediting Keyed Tables

When you Coedit a keyed table, Paradox will notify you immediately if it attempts to post a record which has a duplicate key value. In Edit mode, Paradox assumes that any record with a duplicate key should replace the existing record with the same key. In Coedit mode, Paradox checks for a key conflict as soon as you leave a record or unlock it. If there is a key conflict, you will see the message shown in Figure 4.14. In this case, an attempt has been made to add another record with the key value 8 (the current record is indicated by the highlighted cursor). When this happens, you can use Alt-K to toggle between displaying the new record and the existing record with the same key value. This enables you to delete or change either record to resolve the key conflict.

"Fly Away" Records

Another thing to note about using Coedit mode on keyed tables: when you leave a record or unlock it, Paradox will move it to a new position in the table, if necessary, to maintain the proper sort order. This may be

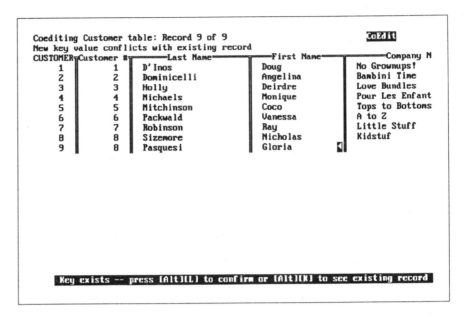

```
Coediting Customer table: Record 9 of 9                    CoEdit
New key value conflicts with existing record
CUSTOMER Customer #        Last Name        First Name        Company N
    1         1    D'Inos              Doug              No Grownups!
    2         2    Dominicelli         Angelina          Bambini Time
    3         3    Holly               Deirdre           Love Bundles
    4         4    Michaels            Monique           Pour Les Enfant
    5         5    Mitchinson          Coco              Tops to Bottoms
    6         6    Packwald            Vanessa           A to Z
    7         7    Robinson            Ray               Little Stuff
    8         8    Sizemore            Nicholas          Kidstuf
    9         8    Pasquesi            Gloria        ◄|




     Key exists -- press [Alt][L] to confirm or [Alt][N] to see existing record
```

Figure 4.14 Entering a record with a duplicate key in Coedit mode

disconcerting if you don't expect it. Your record is still in the table even if you can't see it. It is just in a new position. This is illustrated in Figures 4.15 and 4.16. In Figure 4.15, the record for *Don Oswald* is being entered but the record has not been locked. Note that the cursor is not highlighted and the message on the second line of the screen shows that the record has not yet been posted to the table.

Figure 4.16 shows what happened after Alt-L was pressed. The new record is posted to the table and it is moved to a new position based on its key value. Since it is blank, it goes to the first position in the table. Note that the cursor did not move with the record. The cursor is now on the last record in the table.

```
Coediting Customer table: Record 9 of 9                    CoEdit
Entering new record - not yet posted to table
CUSTOMER Customer #        Last Name        First Name        Company N
    1         1    D'Inos              Doug              No Grownups!
    2         2    Dominicelli         Angelina          Bambini Time
    3         3    Holly               Deirdre           Love Bundles
    4         4    Michaels            Monique           Pour Les Enfant
    5         5    Mitchinson          Coco              Tops to Bottoms
    6         6    Packwald            Vanessa           A to Z
    7         7    Robinson            Ray               Little Stuff
    8         8    Sizemore            Nicholas          Kidstuf
    9              Oswald              Don           ◄
```

Figure 4.15 Entering new record in Coedit mode

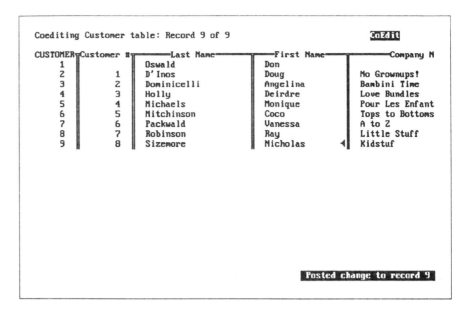

Figure 4.16 Table shown in Figure 4.15 after pressing Alt-L

You can easily see where your records go in a table this size. With large tables, though, it can be confusing to have your records disappear from the screen. Paradox moved them simply to maintain the proper key order.

Differences Between Edit and Coedit Modes

Although Coedit mode was originally added to allow users on a network to share a table, it can be used on a standalone system as well. The following information on the differences between Edit and Coedit modes should be useful in determining which mode is more appropriate for changing your tables. At first glance, it may seem that Edit mode is always the one to use if you do not share tables. However, there are some benefits to using Coedit mode, even on a standalone system, which may justify its use instead of Edit mode.

Table Locking vs. Record Locking

When you go into Edit mode, Paradox places a full lock on the tables in use. (How Paradox locks tables and records will be described in more detail in Chapter 15, "Networking With Paradox.") When a full lock is placed on a table, no other user can access that table. Coedit mode, in comparison, places a less restrictive lock on tables. Instead of limiting table access to one user, Coedit mode locks individual records in a table as needed. This allows more than one user at a time to use a table. To share tables on a network, you *must* use Coedit mode instead of Edit mode.

"Undo" in Edit vs. Coedit Modes

One advantage which Edit mode offers is the ability to incrementally "Undo" changes you make during an editing session. In Edit mode, Paradox maintains a transaction log of all changes. You can use the "Undo" command to reverse all changes you have made since the beginning of the current editing session. In Coedit mode, you can "undo" only the last change made to a table.

Using Indexes in Edit and Coedit Modes

In Edit mode, Paradox will not make use of any indexes for the table in use. Neither the primary nor the secondary index is updated until you exit from Edit mode. If you are merely adding records to a table, this does not make a big difference. But, if you are using the "Zoom" command to find records in a large table while you are in Edit mode, this can slow things down considerably.

Coedit mode offers an advantage here because indexes are updated incrementally in Coedit mode. This means that Paradox updates a table's index file(s) after each new or changed record is *posted* to the table. (Paradox "posts" a record to the table when it makes the change to the table permanent.) Since the index is always current, Paradox will use any indexes which are available for the field being searched using "Zoom" (or the LOCATE command if you are using PAL).

Key Violations in Edit and Coedit Modes

Remember, if you are editing using a linked multi-table form, detail records are deleted for any master record that is replaced.

When you change a keyed table in Edit mode, Paradox does not warn you if you enter a record with a key value that already exists in the table. Paradox assumes that you want to replace the existing record with the new record. This is true for new records that you add to the table and for changes which you make to key fields of existing records. When you press F2 to "Do-It!," Paradox keeps only the last record in the transaction log for each unique key value. See the section on "Editing Keyed Tables" for possible pitfalls in this area.

When you use Coedit mode on a keyed table, key violations are handled differently. In Coedit mode, each record is posted to the table as soon as you move off the record or explicitly unlock the record using Alt-L. At this point, Paradox checks to see if the key value already exists in the table. If it does, you will see the message shown in Figure 4.17. You can use Alt-K to display the record with the conflicting key, and decide what to do. This feature is quite useful. You can use it on a standalone system to avoid losing records.

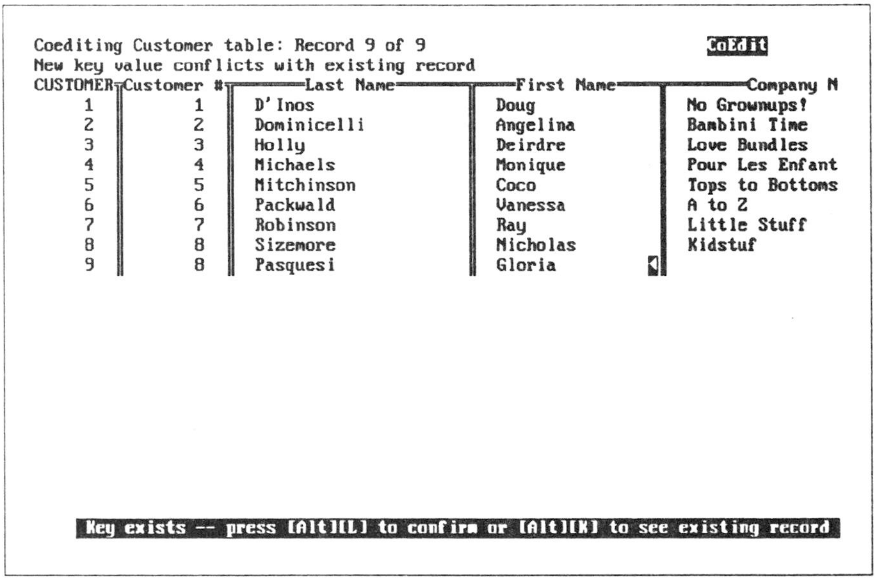

```
Coediting Customer table: Record 9 of 9                        CoEdit
New key value conflicts with existing record
CUSTOMER┬Customer #┬──────Last Name─────┬─First Name─────┬──────Company N
   1   ║    1    ║ D'Inos          ║ Doug          ║ No Grownups!
   2   ║    2    ║ Dominicelli     ║ Angelina      ║ Bambini Time
   3   ║    3    ║ Holly           ║ Deirdre       ║ Love Bundles
   4   ║    4    ║ Michaels        ║ Monique       ║ Pour Les Enfant
   5   ║    5    ║ Mitchinson      ║ Coco          ║ Tops to Bottoms
   6   ║    6    ║ Packwald        ║ Vanessa       ║ A to Z
   7   ║    7    ║ Robinson        ║ Ray           ║ Little Stuff
   8   ║    8    ║ Sizemore        ║ Nicholas      ║ Kidstuf
   9   ║    8    ║ Pasquesi        ║ Gloria      ◄ ║



                Key exists -- press [Alt][L] to confirm or [Alt][K] to see existing record
```

Figure 4.17 "Key exists" message in Coedit Mode

Coediting Multi-table Forms

Coediting multi-table forms is the same as editing using multi-table forms with a few exceptions:

- The current record must be posted before toggling from a multi-table form to table view; you can post the record without moving the cursor off it by pressing Alt-L.

- If one user is Coediting using a multi-table form, all other users must use the same multi-table form to make changes to any of the tables involved.

- You cannot post a record with a duplicate key; you must change the key or delete the record with the same key first.
- Master records are not posted when you move to a detail table on the multi-table form; they are posted only when you move to a new master record or unlock the master record.
- Detail records are posted as soon as you move the cursor off the record or leave the detail table.

An important note for Paradox 3.0 users (which does not apply to users of Version 3.01 or higher): If you post a record with a duplicate key, you will lose the old record with the same key *and* its associated detail records. Be careful or, better yet, get an updated version of Paradox!

While you are Coediting the master table in multi-table form view, you can use Ctrl-L, "Resynch," to resynchronize the master and detail records. This is useful if you change a linking value in the master table and want to see the new records which are associated with the master. Ctrl-L also displays detail records after entering a new master record, without having to move the cursor off the master record.

A note on using "Undo" while Coediting a multi-table form: once you leave a master table record, you cannot "Undo" a change to corresponding records in the detail table.

DataEntry Mode

DataEntry is used to prevent access to the table records are being added to.

`DataEntry` is used only to add new records to a table. You cannot use it to change existing records in a table (or tables using a multi-table form). When you choose `DataEntry` on the Modify Menu and select a table, Paradox displays an empty table with the same structure as the table you specified. This ENTRY table is a temporary table. An ENTRY table for the CUSTOMER table, which was created in Chapter 2, is displayed in Figure 4.18. You can enter records and change records in ENTRY as you do in any other table.

When you have finished entering new records into ENTRY, press F2 to "Do-It!" and Paradox will add the records in ENTRY to the original

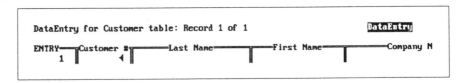

Figure 4.18 ENTRY table for data-entry into CUSTOMER

table. ENTRY will be available until you exit from Paradox or perform another operation which creates an ENTRY table. You will not see ENTRY on the workspace when you complete your DataEntry session, but you can view it as you can any other table.

Using DataEntry with Keyed Tables

If the original table is keyed and there are duplicate keys in ENTRY, Paradox will create a temporary table called KEYVIOL. It can be edited to eliminate duplicate keys and then those records can be added to the original table using **T**ools/**M**ore/**A**dd/**N**ewEntries. Be careful to rename KEYVIOL if you don't want to lose it when exiting from Paradox or by performing another operation which creates a KEYVIOL table.

The DataEntry Menu

The DataEntry Menu is the same as the Edit Menu with one addition: KeepEntry. See the DataEntry Menu in Figure 4.19.

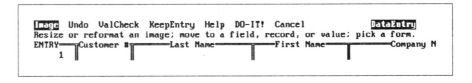

Figure 4.19 The DataEntry Menu

Using KeepEntry

The KeepEntry command causes the current ENTRY table to be saved and ends the current DataEntry session. The records are not added to the original table as they usually are when you exit from DataEntry mode. The ENTRY table must be renamed if you want to save it. The records in it can be added to the original table using **T**ools/**M**ore/**A**dd. You may want to use KeepEntry if you are doing DataEntry on a network table which is locked at the time you attempt to "Do-It!."

DataEntry with Multi-table Forms

It is possible to use DataEntry mode with a multi-table form. Once you are in DataEntry mode, use F10/**I**mage/**P**ickForm and specify the multi-table form you want to use. You can add records to this form in the usual manner. If you use KeepEntry, Paradox will create multiple ENTRY tables: ENTRY, ENTRY1, ENTRY2, and so forth, as needed. Paradox will also create a temporary LIST table which shows all of the ENTRY tables and the corresponding tables from the multi-table form. The LIST table for ORDERS after doing DataEntry using a multi-table form, is shown in Figure 4.20. Instead of using **Tools/More/A**dd to add the records in the ENTRY tables to the original table, use **Tools/More/F**ormAdd. FormAdd maintains referential integrity between the linked tables.

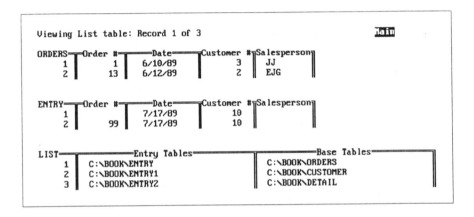

Figure 4.20 LIST of ENTRY tables used with multi-table form

If you create duplicate keys doing data-entry on a multi-table form, you will get multiple KEYVIOL tables: KEYVIOL, KEYVIOL1, and so on. These temporary tables can be saved by renaming them using **Tools/R**ename/**T**able. After editing them, you can use **Tools/M**ore /**F**ormAdd to merge the records into the original table.

MultiEntry

MultiEntry is useful when you need to update fields that exist in more than one table but are not linking fields.

MultiEntry is used to enter records into more than one target table from one source table. It enters one record into each target table for each record in the source table. The records in the target tables are created from subsets of the fields in the source table.

MultiEntry was a part of earlier versions of Paradox, before multi-table forms were available. With the availability of multi-table forms, it usually is not necessary to use MultiEntry. It works differently than using multi-table forms and you may see a way of using this to your advantage. In most cases, though, it is simpler to use multi-table forms. Follow the example below to see why.

How MultiEntry Works

There are two parts to `MultiEntry`: `Setup` and `Entry`. The first step in using `MultiEntry` involves setting up a source table and a map table. This is done by placing a query on the workspace which shows the relationship between the target tables and then choosing Multi-Entry/SetUp from the Modify Menu. You are prompted for the name of a *source table* and for the name of a *map table*. The source table is used for the actual entry of records. The structure of the source table is the same as that of the ANSWER table which would result from executing the query. The map table is a listing of all fields in the source table and the corresponding fields in the target tables.

When you use MultiEntry/Entry, you are in DataEntry mode. Paradox creates an ENTRY table with the same structure as the source table you specified. After you press "Do-It!," Paradox uses the map table to create records in the target tables. Once you have completed using `MultiEntry`, the ENTRY table is deleted when you exit from Paradox or perform another operation which creates an ENTRY table. The records do not exist in the source table.

Using MultiEntry/Setup

1. Create a query which links the tables into which you want to enter records using `MultiEntry`. (Queries are explained in Chapter 5.) Be sure to check any linking fields only once in the query. If you check a field more than once, it will appear more than once in the source table.

The query here is not processed; it is just used to show the relationship between the tables to be used with MultiEntry.

To enter records for The Raspberry Patch using MultiEntry instead of multi-table forms, you have to create a query linking ORDERS, CUSTOMER, and DETAIL. Figures 4.21A and 4.21B show a query which does this. (The query images for CUSTOMER and DETAIL cannot be displayed on one screen. Figure 4.21B shows the query after these images have been scrolled through using Ctrl-right-arrow.) Remember that you will be able to enter only one record into DETAIL for each order using this method.

2. Press F10. Choose Modify/MultiEntry/SetUp from the menus.

3. Paradox will prompt for the name of a source table. Type **SOURCE**. (This name can actually be anything.) Figure 4.22 shows the structure of the source table which Paradox creates after this step.

4. When prompted for the name of a map table, type **MAP**. (It does not need to be MAP. MAP is easy to remember.) This completes the `Setup` part of `MultiEntry`. This needs to be done only once. Figure

4.23 shows the map table that is displayed on the screen when the Setup has been completed.

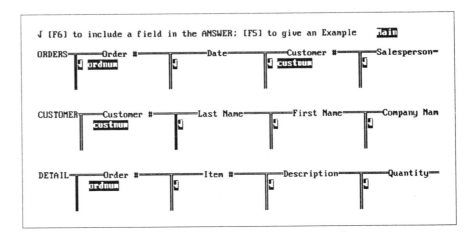

Figure 4.21A Query to use for MultiEntry/SetUp

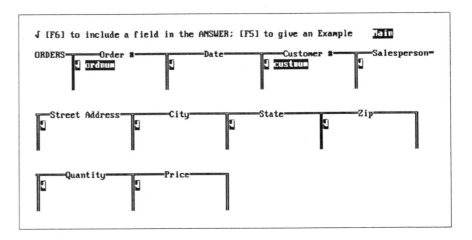

Figure 4.21B Query to use for MultiEntry/Setup (cont.)

Using MultiEntry/Entry

1. To enter records into the target tables using MultiEntry, choose Modify/MultiEntry/Entry from the menus.
2. When prompted for a source table, type **SOURCE**.
3. Type **MAP** for the name of the MAP table.

4. Paradox will display an ENTRY table. Enter your records. Then press F2 to "Do-It!" and conclude the MultiEntry session.

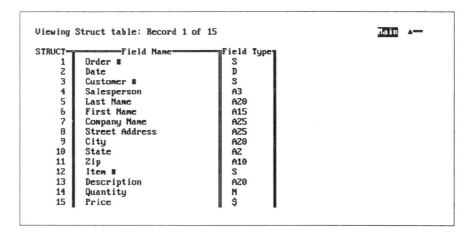

Figure 4.22 Structure of SOURCE table

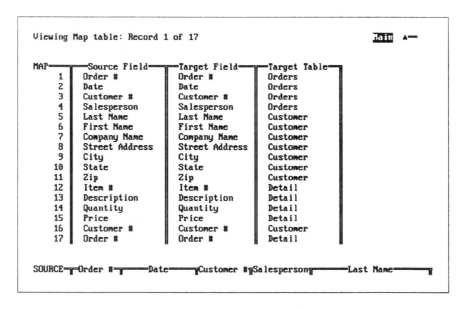

Figure 4.23 MAP table displayed after **MultiEntry/Setup**

Using MultiEntry on Keyed Tables

If a record in the source table has a conflicting key with a record in any one of the target tables, that entire record will be placed into a KEYVIOL table. KEYVIOL can be edited and added to the target tables using **Tools/More/MultiAdd**. Records with duplicate keys will not automatically be discarded unless the entire record is duplicated in each of the target tables.

The MultiEntry Menu

When you use **MultiEntry/Entry**, you go into DataEntry mode. The menu you see when you press F10 is the DataEntry Menu. KeepEntry and the other menu choices work as described elsewhere in this chapter.

Editing Records Entered with MultiEntry

MultiEntry provides a fairly easy way to enter records from one source table into multiple target tables. Once the records are entered, though, you cannot automatically view them using the source table. If you want to view and/or edit your records in one table, you must first do a query to link the records. If you use the same query that you used in the **MultiEntry/SetUp** step, you will get an ANSWER table with the same structure as your source table. You can edit the ANSWER table and then use **Tools/More/MultiAdd** to add the records back to the target tables. This will work, though, only if your target tables are keyed and if you do not change any of the key values. Otherwise, Paradox will create duplicate records in your target tables. You will have all the old records and the new records from ANSWER.

We have reviewed the commands which are available under Modify to allow you to edit or add records to a table. There are two additional Modify commands, Sort and Restructure.

The Sort Command

The Sort command is used to sort a table on one or more fields. The sort order used depends on the country code you chose when you installed Paradox. If you chose the U.S., Paradox will use the standard ASCII sort order. In an ascending sort, this means that blank values will come before values that begin with letters or numbers. All values beginning with uppercase letters will precede values that start with lowercase letters. Appendix J contains a listing of the various sort orders which can be used in Paradox.

When Paradox sorts Alphanumeric fields, it sorts according to the first character, then the second character, and then any additional characters in a field value. The sort is based on the country code, as noted above. This is important to note if you are entering numeric values into an Alphanumeric field and expect them to sort numerically. In an Alphanumeric field, 21 would come before 9 in an ascending sort because 2 is less than 9.

Sorting Keyed Tables vs. Non-Keyed Tables

When you choose the `Sort` command on the Modify Menu and specify a table, what you see next depends on whether the table you want to sort is keyed or not. If the table is not keyed, Paradox will display a menu with the choices `Same` and `New`. A non-keyed table can be either sorted into itself or sorted into a new table. If you choose `New` from the menu, Paradox will prompt for the name of a new table. The new table will contain the records sorted according to the fields you specify. The old table will remain as it was.

If the table you are sorting is keyed, Paradox will prompt you for the name of a new table. You cannot sort a keyed table into itself. Paradox *always* keeps a keyed table sorted in ascending order according to the key fields, the combination of which must be unique for each record. Because of this, you must specify a new table name when sorting a keyed table. You cannot view records in a keyed table in an order other than the one in which the records are stored.

How to Use Sort

When you choose `Sort` from the Modify Menu, Paradox will prompt for the name of the table to sort. If you specify an unkeyed table, Paradox will display a menu asking whether you want to sort to the same table or to a new table. If you choose `NewTable` or if you specified a keyed table to start with, you will be prompted to enter a new table name. Paradox will not allow you to sort a keyed table into itself.

You can also sort a table quickly using a query. See Chapter 5 for details.

Next, you will be presented with a form listing that table's fields. A Sort form for the CUSTOMER table is shown in Figure 4.24. Using this form, you can sort on as many fields as you like. Just press a number, starting with 1, next to each field you want to use for the sort. To sort CUSTOMER on State, and then on City, place 1 next to the State field and 2 next to the City as shown in Figure 4.25. The default sort order is ascending. It is also possible to sort in descending order. Simply type **D** after the number in front of the desired field. Press F2 and Paradox will complete the sort.

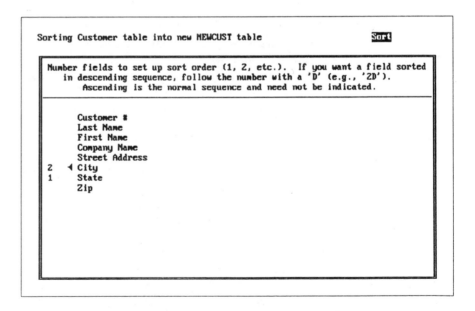

```
Sorting Customer table into new NEWCUST table                    Sort

┌──────────────────────────────────────────────────────────────────────┐
│  Number fields to set up sort order (1, 2, etc.).  If you want a field │
│   sorted in descending sequence, follow the number with a 'D' (e.g.,  │
│           '2D').  Ascending is the normal sequence and need not be     │
│                             indicated.                                 │
│ ────────────────────────────────────────────────────────────────────  │
│                                                                        │
│        ◄ Customer #                                                    │
│          Last Name                                                     │
│          First Name                                                    │
│          Company Name                                                  │
│          Street Address                                                │
│          City                                                          │
│          State                                                         │
│          Zip                                                           │
│                                                                        │
└──────────────────────────────────────────────────────────────────────┘
```

Figure 4.24 Sort form for CUSTOMER

```
Sorting Customer table into new NEWCUST table                    Sort

┌──────────────────────────────────────────────────────────────────────┐
│  Number fields to set up sort order (1, 2, etc.).  If you want a field │
│   sorted in descending sequence, follow the number with a 'D' (e.g.,  │
│           '2D').  Ascending is the normal sequence and need not be     │
│                             indicated.                                 │
│ ────────────────────────────────────────────────────────────────────  │
│                                                                        │
│            Customer #                                                  │
│            Last Name                                                   │
│            First Name                                                  │
│            Company Name                                                │
│            Street Address                                              │
│       2  ◄ City                                                        │
│       1    State                                                       │
│            Zip                                                         │
│                                                                        │
└──────────────────────────────────────────────────────────────────────┘
```

Figure 4.25 Completed Sort form for CUSTOMER

CUSTOMER must be sorted to a new table because it is keyed. The new table looks like NEWCUST, as shown in Figure 4.26.

```
  Viewing Newcust table: Record 2 of 8                              Main

  NEWCUST Customer #       Last Name          First Name            Company Na
     1        8     Sizemore            Nick            Kidstuf
     2        4     Michaels            Monique         Pour Les Enfants
     3        2     Dominicelli         Angelina        Bambini Time
     4        6     Packwald            Vanessa         A to Z
     5        5     Mitchinson          Coco            Tops to Bottoms
     6        3     Holly               Deirdre         Love Bundles
     7        7     Robinson            Ray             Little Stuff
     8        1     D'Inos              Doug            No Grownups!
```

Figure 4.26 NEWCUST table

The Sort Menu

The Sort Menu has only three choices, `Help`, `Do-It!`, and `Cancel`. Each choice does what the name suggests.

Notes on Sorting

You may be able to avoid doing separate sorts by using the `Group` command in the Report Generator. (The Report Generator will be covered in Chapter 6.) In fact, if you are going to set up any groups in the Report Generator, do not use **M**odify/**S**ort. As soon as you use `Group` in a report, the sorted table order is disregarded. If you sort the table by one field using **M**odify/**S**ort, and group it on a different field in a report, Paradox won't maintain the sorted order of the table within the groups in the report. If there are multiple entries in a group that is created by a report, Paradox will sort the table by the next field. It is pointless, then, to sort the table before generating a report in such a case. You must use the `Group` command in the Report Generator to specify which fields should be used for additional sorting.

In most cases, queries will also sort tables. Before doing sorts, double check to see if you really need to use **M**odify/**S**ort. You may already be getting your tables sorted in your queries and reports!

Restructuring Tables

To modify the structure of your table, not just its information, you must use **M**odify/**R**estructure. Examples of using `Restructure` were included in the latter part of Chapter 2. **M**odify/**R**estructure allows you to insert, delete, rename, and reorder fields. You can also use it to key a table or to change key fields, as long as key fields begin with the first field and are consecutive.

The Restructure Menu

The Restructure Menu has the following choices:

- Borrow lets you use the structure of an existing table.
- Help accesses the Help system.
- Do-It! tells Paradox to make the changes you requested.
- Cancel returns you to Main mode without changing the table.

Borrowing to Save Time

The Borrow command can save time if the changes you want to make already exist in another table. When you choose Borrow, Paradox will prompt for the name of a table from which to borrow the structure. The new structure will be displayed in the STRUCT table. You then can edit STRUCT as needed. Don't worry about making a mistake. You can always Cancel the restructuring. Paradox also will prompt for an OK to delete or shorten any fields.

KEYVIOL and PROBLEM Tables

When you restructure a table and add or change key fields, you may end up with a KEYVIOL table. KEYVIOL will contain any records which have keys which already exist in the table. An example of when a KEYVIOL table is created and how to handle it was included in Chapter 2 in the section on "Restructuring Tables."

If you change the structure of a table so that records in the table are no longer compatible with the new structure, those records will be placed into a PROBLEMS table. An explanation of PROBLEMS tables, and what to do with them, was also included in Chapter 2.

Problems with Restructure

See Chapter 16 for details about Tutility.

If you restructure a table and your computer "hangs" or seems to be in an endless loop, it is likely that the table is damaged. After waiting to be sure that Paradox is no longer doing productive work, you will have to reboot your computer. Don't worry about damaging the table. The most likely cause of such problems is a table that is already in bad shape. After rebooting the computer, run the Tutility program. Rebuild the problem table and attempt the restructure again if Rebuild was successful. (Remember to add any key fields to a table after rebuilding it. Rebuilding a table deletes the primary index.)

Another problem which you can encounter while restructuring a table is running out of disk space. Paradox needs at least 2-3 times the size of the table being restructured available in free disk space. If the restructure runs for a while before giving an "Out of disk space" message, it is possible that you just don't have enough room on your disk. See how much space is available and compare it to the table size. If you are certain that there is enough free disk space, use Tutility to rebuild the table. When a table is damaged, Paradox can get stuck in an endless loop trying to complete an operation.

If you get the "Out of disk space" message immediately after pressing F2 while restructuring a table, there is probably not enough disk space available on the disk drive where your private directory is located. You may have enough free disk space on the disk drive where the table itself is located. Paradox creates its temporary files, however, in your private directory. You can check the location of your private directory by using **T**ools/**N**et/**S**etPrivate.

Other Ways to Modify Tables

In addition to the Modify command, you can use queries and the Tools command to change tables.

Using Queries to Modify Tables

Basic queries involve checking fields in a query image, optionally entering selection criteria, and pressing F2 to "Do-It!." This action creates an ANSWER table and leaves the original table unchanged. There are other types of queries, though, which can be used to change tables.

Changeto queries allow you to perform global "find-and-replace" changes on tables. You can use selection criteria with Changetos, making it possible to use them on a subset of records in a table. Changetos can also be used to update one table against another table or tables, using selected fields for linking and updating.

There are two other types of queries which can be used to change tables, Insert and Delete queries. These queries can be used to insert or delete records from tables using selection criteria in one or more tables. Changetos, Insert, and Delete queries can be used to easily accomplish many tasks which otherwise would take hours to do manually. Chapter 5 will explain how to use these types of queries.

Changing Tables with Tools

Several times, we have referred to the use of the **Tools/More/Add**, **Tools/More/MultiAdd**, and the **Tools/More/FormAdd** commands to add records to tables. These commands offer another way to update tables. Used in conjunction with queries and `Edit` or `Coedit`, they provide a quick way to update a subset of information in a keyed table or tables.

Let's say you want to update a subset of records which are scattered throughout a large table. You can use "Zoom" or use Find queries to find one record at a time and edit it. Or, you can query out the desired records using appropriate selection criteria and edit the resulting ANSWER table. After the edit has been completed, use the **Tools/More/Add/Update**, **Tools/More/MultiAdd/Update**, or the **Tools/More/FormAdd/Update** commands to update the original table with the edited records. This technique will work only if the original table(s) are keyed. If you are not working with keyed tables, Paradox will add the edited records to the original table(s) as new records.

Summary

There are several ways to modify tables. You can use the `Modify` command, queries, or some of the `Tools` commands. The method to use depends on what you are trying to do. Here are some of the most important points about modifying tables:

- `Modify` gives you access to Edit, Coedit, DataEntry, Sort, and Restructure modes.
- In Edit mode, you can set up validity checks that enforce data integrity during editing.
- In Edit mode, Ctrl-U can be used to "Undo" changes incrementally. In Coedit mode, Ctrl-U can be used to "Undo" the last change only.
- Coedit mode must be used to allow sharing of a table on a network; there are reasons why it may be beneficial to use Coedit mode on a standalone system as well.
- Key violations are handled differently in Edit than in Coedit mode.

- Certain restrictions apply to modifying tables using multi-table forms; you cannot toggle between table view and form view once editing has begun.
- While you are using a multi-table form, Paradox will not allow you to delete a master record which has dependent detail records.
- DataEntry mode is used to add records to a table without giving access to the existing table.
- MultiEntry mode is used to add information from one source table into multiple target tables; there is always a one-to-one relationship between records in the source table and the target tables.
- Sort mode is used to sort tables according to the country code specified when you installed Paradox.
- Restructure mode is used to add, delete, or change fields in a table.
- Tools mode has commands to add, subtract, and empty tables. Changeto, Insert, and Delete queries can be used to make changes to tables. See the next chapter for more information.

Queries:
The Exciting Part
of Paradox

What Is a Query?

A query is usually thought of as a question. In Paradox, though, queries can be much more than just questions. You can use the Ask command to create queries which:

- Join tables to form new tables using the fields and records which you select
- Give you answers to questions about information in your tables
- Change information in tables
- Perform calculations using one or more tables
- Find records in a table
- Compare groups of information in one or more tables
- Update tables against other tables

When you use the Ask command, you create queries using a technique called Query-By-Example, or QBE.

Query-By-Example

QBE allows you to tell Paradox, without having to write special programs, what information to extract from your tables. With QBE, you give Paradox an example of the records you want, using a few special keystrokes and include any values for which you want Paradox to search. QBE is also used to tell Paradox how to link tables, change records, or do any of the other tasks listed above.

Types of Queries

There are many different types of queries. They can be divided into two main categories:

- Queries which generate ANSWER tables
- Queries which change tables

ANSWER Table Queries

You can use an ANSWER table just like any other Paradox table.

When you use the `Ask` command to select records from a table, using the fields and values which you specify, Paradox places any records which result into a temporary table called ANSWER. Queries which create ANSWER tables can be categorized further:

- Single-table queries
- Multi-table queries
- Calculation queries
- Outer joins
- Set queries

These queries are described in this chapter, along with examples of how to use each.

Changeto, Insert, and Delete Queries

There are also queries which don't generate ANSWER tables. These queries act on the original tables used in the `Ask` command and create their own special temporary tables.

- *Changeto* queries change values in fields.
- *Insert* queries add records to tables.
- *Delete* queries delete records from tables.

These queries are often overlooked when people consider ways to manipulate groups of records in tables. If you thought queries were only for getting ANSWER tables, be sure to check the examples for these queries shown in this chapter and in Chapter 7, "Putting Queries and Reports to Work." You may find some time-saving tips.

"Find" Queries

There is one more type of Paradox query. A *Find* query is used to locate a record which satisfies certain criteria. If such a record is found, that record becomes the current record on the workspace. When more than one record satisfies the query, an ANSWER table is also created.

Using the Ask Command

To create a query, you must be in Main mode. Let's perform a query on the CUSTOMER table to illustrate the process. First, press F10 to display the Main Menu. Then, type **CUSTOMER** when prompted, or press Enter to get a list of tables in the current directory. After you type or select a table name, Paradox will place a query image for that table onto the workspace.

Query Images

Commands for moving through a query image are the same as those for moving through a table image.

The query image for the CUSTOMER table is shown in Figure 5.1. It looks similar to a table view of the CUSTOMER table, but without any records in it. This is where you create your query.

When Paradox places a query image onto the workspace, it is displayed at the top of the screen, above any table images which may be present. Query images are displayed in the same way as are tables in table view. Fields which do not fit onto the screen can be brought into view by pressing the arrow keys or the Enter key to move from field to field. You can also move through an entire screenful of fields at a time by pressing Ctrl with the right- or left-arrow key. Query images are edited the same way you edit table images. You can move through a query image using the commands listed in the Quick Reference Card for moving through a table. There are also special commands which can be used only with query images. These commands are:

- F5, the "Example" key
- F6, for "Checkmark"
- Alt-F6, used for "Check Plus"

- Ctrl-F6, the "Check Descending" key
- Shift-F6, for "Groupby"

These commands can also be used with query images:

- Ctrl-R, to rotate fields
- Alt-F5 or Ctrl-F to enter field view
- Ctrl-D, to "Ditto" information from the field above
- F2, the "Do-It!" key

"Del" will delete an entire query line.

These commands work the same way in query images as they do in table images. The first list, though, are special commands which can be used only while creating queries.

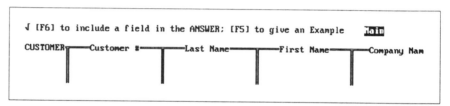

Figure 5.1 Query image for CUSTOMER

Checkmarks

When you use a query to create an ANSWER table, you indicate which fields from the original table should be included in the ANSWER table. You do this by using F6 to place a Checkmark into each field which you want to appear in the ANSWER table. F6 is a toggle key and can be used to check or "uncheck" fields if you change your mind about including them in the query.

If you press F6 while the cursor is in the left-most column of the query image, all fields will be Checkmarked as shown in Figure 5.2. This is useful to create an ANSWER table which has the same structure as the original table.

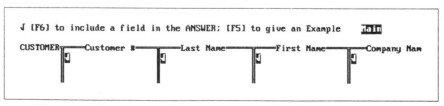

Figure 5.2 Query Image for CUSTOMER with all fields Checkmarked

For the example here, let's Checkmark only the Last Name, First Name, and Phone # fields, as shown in Figure 5.3. Note that you cannot see the Phone # field in the first screen of the query image shown in Figure 5.1. You must move the cursor to the Phone # field, or use Ctrl-R to bring it into view, before Checkmarking it.

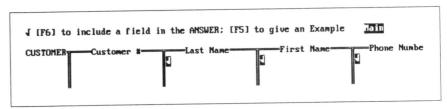

Figure 5.3 Query image for CUSTOMER with Last Name, First Name and Phone # Checked

Doing-It!

When you have completed filling out your query image, press F2 to tell Paradox to "Do-It!" Paradox will display the message "Processing query" in the lower-right corner of the screen. When the query has been completed, an ANSWER table is displayed and becomes the current image.

ANSWER Tables

Figure 5.4 shows the ANSWER table which was created from the query shown in Figure 5.3. Note that it contains information from all records in CUSTOMER, but includes only the fields which were Checkmarked in the query.

The ANSWER table is a temporary table and is deleted when you exit from Paradox or when you perform another query which creates an ANSWER table. To save your ANSWER table, rename it using **T**ools/**R**ename/**T**able.

ImageOrder vs. TableOrder

Changing the field order of ANSWER by using ImageOrder will also affect how the ANSWER is sorted.

Usually, Paradox creates an ANSWER table according to the structure of the table queried. It is possible to alter this by changing the `QueryOrder` setting to `ImageOrder` using the Custom script. Then, when you rotate the fields in your query image using Ctrl-R, the ANSWER table will have the same structure as the query image. Information on how to change the `QueryOrder` setting is included in Chapter 13, "Customizing Your Paradox System."

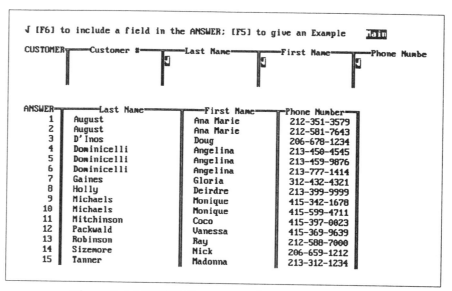

Figure 5.4 ANSWER from query shown in Figure 5.3

Figure 5.5 shows the query image shown in Figure 5.3 after the field order has been rotated using Ctrl-R. With `QueryOrder` set to `ImageOrder`, the ANSWER table from this new query looks like Figure 5.6.

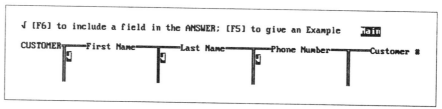

Figure 5.5 Rotated query image for CUSTOMER

Duplicate Records and ANSWER Tables

When Paradox creates the records to be included in an ANSWER table from a query with Checkmarks, it includes only unique records. Any duplicate records are not displayed. (A duplicate record refers to an entire record, not just to key fields.) If you are creating an ANSWER table which is a subset of only the original fields in a keyed table, you may end up with an ANSWER table which has fewer records than the original table. If you want to include duplicate records in an ANSWER table, use Alt-F6, "Check Plus," when you create your query.

To illustrate this, look at the query on CUSTOMER shown in Figure 5.7. Only the Company Name field is Checkmarked using F6. The resulting ANSWER table is shown in Figure 5.8. Note that there is only one record in the ANSWER table for each unique company name.

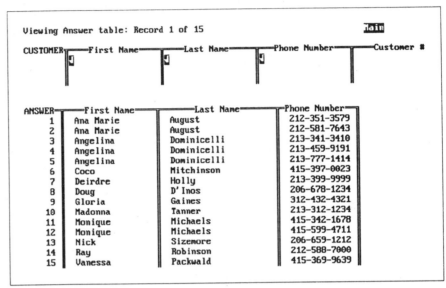

Figure 5.6 ANSWER from query in Figure 5.5

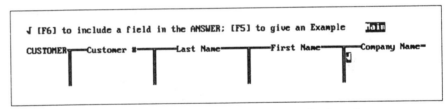

Figure 5.7 Query on CUSTOMER using Checkmark

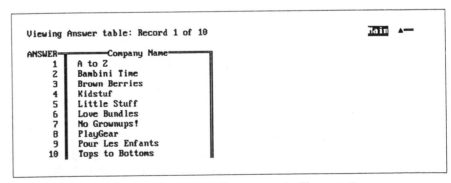

Figure 5.8 ANSWER from query in Figure 5.7

The same query, using "Check Plus" instead of "Check," is shown in Figure 5.9, along with the resulting ANSWER table. In this new ANSWER table, records are created from all of the original records, even if some are duplicates.

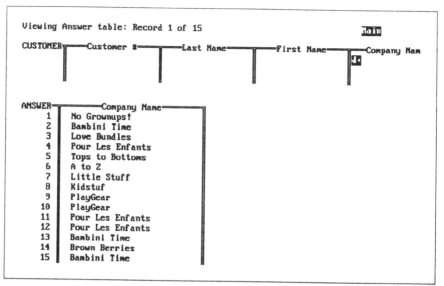

Figure 5.9 Query on CUSTOMER using "Check Plus" and resulting ANSWER table

There is one other reason you may want to use "Check Plus." It relates to how ANSWER tables are sorted. You may have noticed that the ANSWER table shown in Figure 5.9, unlike other ANSWER tables seen so far, is not sorted. When you use "Check Plus," Paradox does not sort the records in the ANSWER table.

How ANSWER Tables Are Sorted

When Paradox creates an ANSWER table, the new table is usually sorted beginning with the first field in the table. The only exception to this is when you use "Check Plus" to select fields in a query. In this case, the original record order of the table will be preserved.

Using "Check Descending"

There may be times when you want to sort a table in descending order on a particular field. You can do this by using Shift-F6, "Check Descending," to indicate that such a field should be included in the ANSWER table. Figure 5.10 shows a query on CUSTOMER which used "Check Descending" in the Company Name field. The ANSWER table from this query is shown as well. Company names are listed from Z to A instead of A to Z.

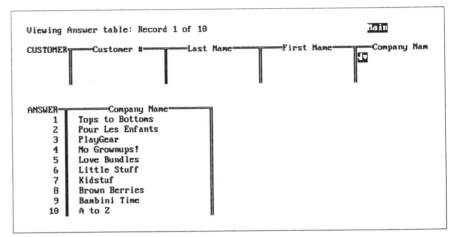

Figure 5.10 Query and ANSWER using "Check Descending"

Naming Fields with "As"

The field names in ANSWER tables are usually taken from the field names in the original table. It is possible to specify a different name using the special query command, *As*. To do this, type **As**, followed by the desired field name, in the query image.

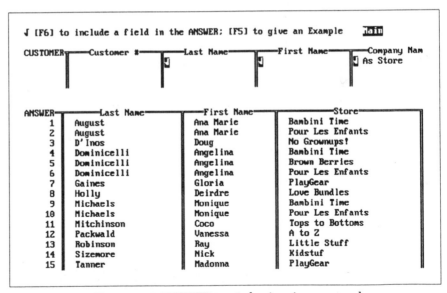

Figure 5.11 ANSWER created using As command

Let's say we want to create a new table from CUSTOMER where the Company Name for each record will appear in a field called *Store*. Create the query shown in Figure 5.11 and press F2. The ANSWER table in the same figure has all of the fields which were Checkmarked in the query, but the Company Name field is now called *Store*.

The As command can be extremely useful, especially when you are creating new Calculated fields in ANSWER tables and want to specify a name for the new field. An example of how to do this is included in the section on Calc queries later in this chapter.

Using Search Criteria

All queries shown so far use only Checkmarks to tell Paradox how to build ANSWER tables. Now that we have mastered the use of Checkmarks, and know about ANSWER tables, let's explore the use of search criteria to select records.

How Paradox Looks for Values

When you perform a query, you usually will want Paradox to look for records which match some set of criteria. It is easy to have Paradox look for records with certain values. Simply type the desired value into the appropriate field of your query image, Checkmark any fields which you want included in ANSWER, and press F2.

Let's say you want to find all Raspberry Patch customers who are in California. You can use the query image shown in Figure 5.12. (The fields in the query image have been rotated using Ctrl-R so that the pertinent fields are displayed.) The ANSWER table from this query is shown in the same figure.

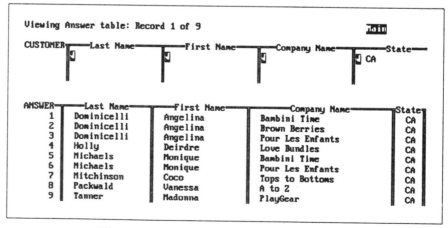

Figure 5.12 Query to find California customers

There are some important things to note about how Paradox looks for values while processing queries. First of all, Paradox will use only records which *exactly* match the search criteria you specify. This means that Paradox pays attention to whether letters are typed in upper- or lowercase. Paradox also is picky about blanks which are part of a value. You must be sure to type the value precisely as Paradox should look for it if you want those records to be found.

Don't despair, though. There are several commands which you can use with queries to help you find records when you don't know exactly how the information in the table looks. The next few sections explain how to use these tricks.

Wild Cards

There are two wild card operators . . and @ you can use with your query search criteria. The . . stands for any number of characters and @ can be used for any one character. You can combine these wild card operators with other characters to look for values which match certain patterns. A useful benefit of using wild card operators is that Paradox is not case-sensitive when looking for patterns.

To illustrate this, look at the record for *Gloria Gaines* in CUS-TOMER as shown in Figure 5.13. The name *Gloria* was typed with the first two letters capitalized. If you try to find this record using the query in the same illustration, you will get an empty ANSWER table. However, if you create the query using Gl. . in the First Name field as shown in Figure 5.14, the desired record is included in the ANSWER table.

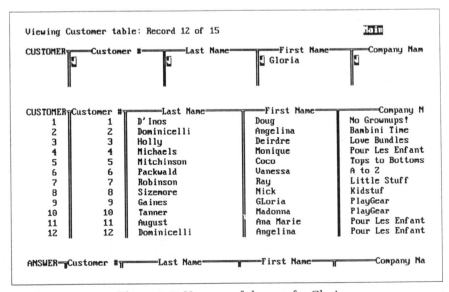

Figure 5.13 Unsuccessful query for Gloria

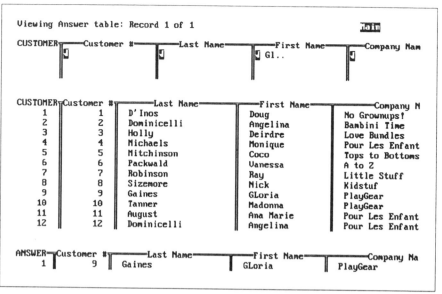

Figure 5.14 Successful query for Gloria using wild card operator

You can use multiple wildcard operators with literals in the same field in a query image, to create patterns for a Paradox search. Here are a few examples of patterns and the values which they select:

A..e.. selects *Angelina* and *Ana Marie*

@@@@ selects *Coco, Doug,* and *Nick*

..donna selects *Madonna*

If you need to use periods or other special characters in a search pattern, enclose them within quotation marks. That way, Paradox knows that the punctuation is part of the search value and not part of the query commands.

Range Operators

Another useful way to search for records is with range operators. Paradox recognizes these range operators in queries:

= is used for equal and is the default for all search criteria entered with no other range operator.

⟩ means greater than.

⟨ means less than.

> = means greater than or equal to.

< = means less than or equal to.

You can use range operators with all field types, including Alphanumeric fields. For Alphanumeric fields, Paradox uses the sort order specified at installation time to determine which characters are "greater" than others. (Remember that the sort order depends on the country code you chose when you installed Paradox. The different sort orders are shown in Appendix J.)

Figure 5.15 shows a query which uses two range operators in a date field to look for all orders placed during June, 1989. (You could also use the wild card operator **6..89** to find the same records.) Note that a comma is used to separate the two conditions.

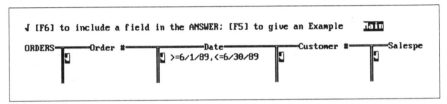

Figure 5.15 Query with range operators in Date field

Query Keywords

Paradox has several words which are used for special purposes in queries. These words are called "operators" or keywords. When you use them in a query, Paradox does not use them as literal search criteria. A few of these words are described here. Others are included in the sections on Calc queries, Summary operators, and Set queries.

"Like" Queries

You can use *Like* in a query to look for a value which resembles the value you type. This can be useful if you forget how to spell a name, or don't remember exactly how it was typed originally. Paradox uses a special algorithm which is sensitive to the length of the value you type with the Like keyword. It is also sensitive to punctuation, so it may not always work for long values or for values which contain many special characters. In most cases, it is preferable to use the .. wild-card operator because it is more flexible. Figure 5.16 shows a Like query and the resulting ANSWER table.

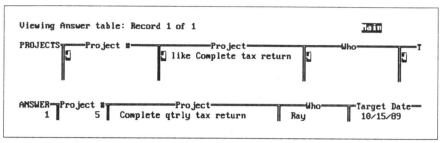

Figure 5.16 Like query and ANSWER

"Not" Queries

The word *Not* can be used in a query to have Paradox select all records which do *not* match a specified value. Perhaps you want to find all Raspberry Patch customers who are not in California. The query shown in Figure 5.17 will work for this type of search.

Be careful if you try to use *Not* with multi-table queries (which will be covered later in this chapter). It may not work as you expect it to. Look at the section on "Multi-table Not Queries" if you need more information.

Looking for Blanks

When you create a query, Paradox assumes that you don't want selection criteria in a field if you have left it blank. Then how do you search only for records which are blank in specific fields? The solution is to use the operator *Blank* in your query image. Typing **Blank** in a query image field will select only records which are blank in the specified field.

Searching for "Today"

Another time-saver is being able to use the keyword *Today* to select records with the system date in a date field. This is especially helpful in

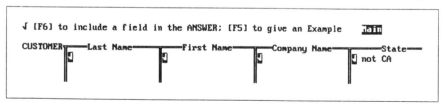

Figure 5.17 "Not" query

queries which you have saved and would like to execute on any day. (Information on saving queries is included at the end of this chapter. For now, you just might want to note that it is possible to create a generic query using *Today*.)

While Today by itself in a query is useful, the full power of using Today is realized when you combine it with arithmetic and range operators. For example, you can search for all orders entered within the last 30 days with the query shown in Figure 5.18.

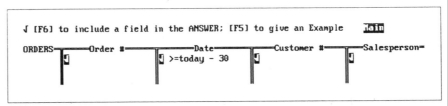

Figure 5.18 Query for orders entered within last 30 days

Keywords as Search Criteria

Whenever you need to include query keywords, such as *Like* or *Blank*, as conditions in a query, you must surround them with quotation marks. This also applies to characters which have special meaning in queries. The query keywords and special characters are listed by category here.

Reserved Words

Calc

Changeto

Check

Check Descending

Check Plus

Delete

Find

GroupBy

Insert

Set

Arithmetic Operators

+

−

*

/

( )

Range Operators

=

〉

〈

〉=

〈=

Pattern Operators

..

@

Special Operators

Like

!

As

Blank

,

Not

Or

Today

Summary Operators

All

Average

Count

Max

Min

Sum

Unique

Set Comparison Operators

Every

Exactly

No

Only

See Figure 5.19 for an example of searching for the company *No Grownups!* using the .. wildcard operator. The "No" portion of the pattern must be surrounded by quotation marks for the query to work. This is because the pattern contains the set comparison operator "No."

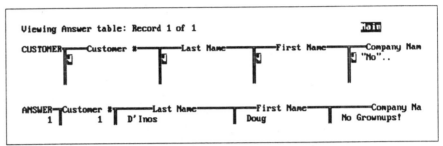

Figure 5.19 Special operator as query condition

Searching for Quotation Marks and Backslashes

One additional note about using quotation marks in queries: if you need to search for a value that already contains quotation marks, precede the quotation marks in the value with backslashes. For example, to search for *"Sugar" Ray Robinson*, type \ **"Sugar \ " Ray Robinson** in the query image. The backslash indicates that the next character is to be taken literally. Because of this, you also need to "double up" any backslashes used in search criteria.

So far we have used queries only on one table with one selection criterion. Queries can be used to ask much more complex questions about your tables. Let's see how to use some of the operators listed above.

"And" Queries

And queries look for records which satisfy multiple criteria. You can enter more than one condition in the same field of a query image, as shown in Figure 5.20, as long as they are separated by a comma and are not mutually exclusive. In this query, we are looking for orders entered after *5/31/89 and* before *7/1/89*. It is also possible to enter conditions into more than one field. You can enter search criteria in as many fields as you would like.

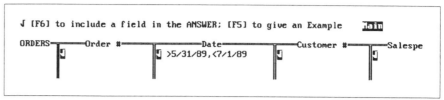

Figure 5.20 "And" query: Two conditions in Date field

"Or" Queries

Or queries look for records which satisfy at least one of a group of conditions. There are two ways to specify Or queries.

The "Or" Keyword

If you are looking for records which match at least one of a group of conditions in the same field, use the Or keyword. Enter the search conditions on the same line in the query and separate them with the keyword Or. This technique is used in the query shown in Figure 5.21. That query looks for customers in California or Washington.

Multi-line "Or" Queries

You can also create Or queries by using multiple lines in a query image. The query shown in Figure 5.22 searches for records for any *Bambini*

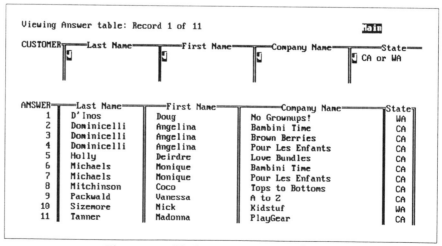

Figure 5.21 "Or" query using "Or" keyword

Time store or for *Angelina Dominicelli*. Note that the records in the ANSWER table can meet one or more conditions entered in the query image.

"And" and "Or" conditions can be combined in the same query. You simply need to be sure you check the same fields on each line, if you are using a multi-line query. Otherwise, Paradox will give you the message, "Query appears to ask two unrelated questions"! See the section on "Linking Records in the Same Table" for information on the only case where you don't need to Checkmark the same fields on each line in a query.

Multi-table Queries

Until now, all of the examples have involved only one table. This was to simplify the illustration of the use of query elements such as Checkmarks and special operators. Now that the basics have been covered, we can move on to some more exciting queries, those which make use of Paradox's relational capabilities.

The first step in creating a multi-table query is putting a query image on the workspace for each table involved. Use F10/**A**sk to do this. The next step is to show Paradox how to relate the tables being queried. Remember, Paradox attempts to use all query images on the workspace in a query. You must indicate how each table is related to other tables in the query.

How Paradox Links Tables

It was mentioned earlier that Paradox links tables by looking for matching values in common fields. In multi-table forms, the linking fields are determined by key fields in the master and detail tables. With multi-table queries, you have much more flexibility. You can link tables on any combination of fields, as long as the fields are of the same type. It is even possible to link multiple tables, without having one table be the master in all of the relationships. In other words, you can have more than one level of linking in queries.

Using Example Elements

An example element does not have to be the same as any selection criteria; it is totally separate.

You tell Paradox which fields to use for linking fields in queries by using *example elements*. Example elements are expressions which you place into a query image by using F5, the "Example" key. When you press F5 and then type an expression into a query image, that expression will be highlighted or displayed in a different color. This indicates that the expression will be used as an example element, *not* as literal search criteria. Except for a few basic rules, it doesn't matter what you use as an example element. It does not have to have any relationship to the type of field or to the field name. The only thing which matters is that you are consistent in referring to the same example element in a linking field or in another expression. The use of example elements will be illustrated in the next several sections.

You can use letters or numbers as example elements. No other characters, not even spaces, can be used. As soon as a character other than a letter or a number is typed, Paradox assumes that the example element is ended. This is why it is possible to use example elements, along with search conditions and Calc expressions, in the same field.

Example elements are used to indicate which fields should be used as linking fields in multi-table queries. They are also used to indicate values to use in calculations, Changetos, and other operations.

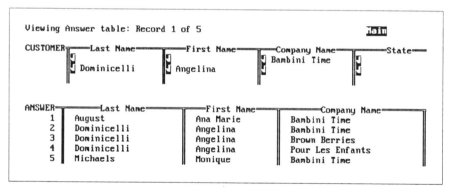

Figure 5.22 Multi-line "Or" query

Creating a Multi-table Query

Let's create a query linking ORDERS and CUSTOMER for The Raspberry Patch. First, place a query image for each table onto the workspace, using F10/**A**sk twice. The two query images will be displayed on the workspace as shown in Figure 5.23.

The next step is to place example elements into the linking fields to show how the tables should be related. The linking field in this case is Customer #. Use F3 to move to the query image for ORDERS. Move the cursor to the field for Customer #, press F5 and then type **custnum**. Note that the string *custnum* is highlighted or is shown in a different color. This is how you know that it is an example element and not a query condition. Next, press F4 to move to the CUSTOMER table and use F5 to place the same example element, **custnum**, into the Customer # field. The query should look like the one shown in Figure 5.24.

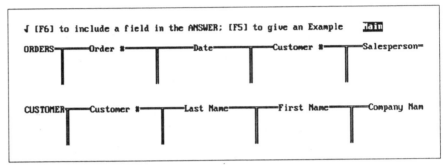

Figure 5.23 Query images for ORDERS and CUSTOMER

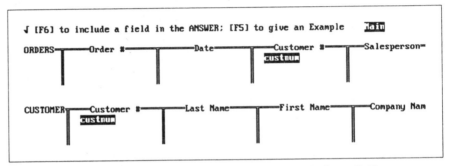

Figure 5.24 Query with example elements in linking fields

Now that the example elements have been placed, we can add any desired Checkmarks and conditions to the query. Figure 5.25 shows a completed multi-table query which will create an ANSWER table for all customers who have placed orders in June, 1989. Note that the linking field is Checkmarked only in one query image. If you Checkmark the linking field in both query images, Paradox will create a field called *Customer #-1* in addition to the Customer # field in ANSWER.

Paradox will include only those records from ORDERS and CUSTOMER which have a matching value in the linking field being used. In this query, customers who have not placed any orders will not appear in the ANSWER table. Similarly, any orders for customers who do not have a record in CUSTOMER will not be included in ANSWER.

As mentioned above, the order in which you place example elements, Checkmarks, search criteria, or other special operators, in your query images is not important. It is done step-by-step here only to illustrate the process clearly. You can place one query image on the workspace using Ask, fill it out completely and then do Asks on any other tables which are to be included in the query.

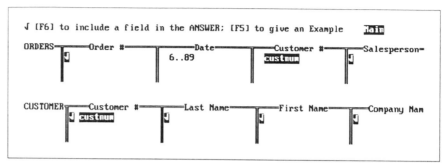

Figure 5.25 Query linking ORDERS and CUSTOMER

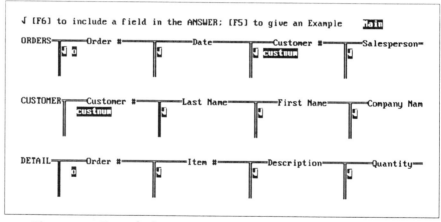

Figure 5.26 Query linking ORDERS, CUSTOMER, and DETAIL tables

Linking Three Tables

You can use commands in Report mode to suppress repeated values.

You can use example elements in more than one field in each query image. Figure 5.26 shows a query which links ORDERS, CUSTOMERS, and DETAIL. That query creates an ANSWER table which has complete order information for all orders placed in June, 1989. The first screenful of fields in ANSWER is shown in Figure 5.27. The second set of fields in ANSWER can be displayed using Ctrl-right-arrow. (The fields shown in Figure 5.27 have been reduced in width using F10/**I**mage /ColumnSize to fit more fields onto the screen.) You may notice that there is one record in ANSWER for each record in DETAIL. All customer and order header information is duplicated in each record in ANSWER. This may seem like a funny way to store information, but it works for creating Paradox reports.

Using ANSWER Table From Linked Tables

The ANSWER table shown in Figure 5.27 can then be used to print order-confirmation letters. The Report Generator has a feature which allows you to create groups of related records in a report. You can place any common information into a "group header," rather than printing it for each record in ANSWER. This is a common process while using Paradox. You link tables in a query and report from the ANSWER table. Since ANSWER is a temporary table, there are a few steps necessary to avoid constantly re-creating reports for ANSWER. Chapter 7, "Putting Queries and Reports to Work," has examples of how to set this up.

```
Viewing Answer table: Record 1 of 32                              Join ▲━

ANSWER━━Order #━━━━━Date━━━━━Customer #━Salesperson━━━━━━Last Name━
       1        1     6/10/89          3   JJ        Holly
       2        1     6/10/89          3   JJ        Holly
       3        1     6/10/89          3   JJ        Holly
       4        1     6/10/89          3   JJ        Holly
       5        1     6/10/89          3   JJ        Holly
       6        1     6/10/89          3   JJ        Holly
       7        1     6/10/89          3   JJ        Holly
       8        1     6/10/89          3   JJ        Holly
       9        2     6/10/89          6   UT        Packwald
      10        2     6/10/89          6   UT        Packwald
      11        2     6/10/89          6   UT        Packwald
      12        3     6/10/89          6   UT        Packwald
      13        3     6/10/89          6   UT        Packwald
      14        3     6/10/89          6   UT        Packwald
      15        3     6/10/89          6   UT        Packwald
      16        3     6/10/89          6   UT        Packwald
      17        3     6/10/89          6   UT        Packwald
      18        4     6/12/89          2   EJG       Dominicelli
      19        4     6/12/89          2   EJG       Dominicelli
      20        4     6/12/89          2   EJG       Dominicelli
      21        5     6/13/89          4   EJG       Michaels
      22        5     6/13/89          4   EJG       Michaels
```

Figure 5.27 ANSWER table from query shown in Figure 5.26

Number of Tables which Can Be Linked

Instead of creating an ANSWER table, you may want to use the Report Lookup feature instead.

There is no logical limit to the number of tables which can be linked in queries. You are realistically limited, though, by the amount of computer memory which is available for the workspace, the width of the tables you are querying, and the characteristics of the query itself. In general, complex queries require more memory than do simple queries. If you get a "Not enough memory to complete operation" message after pressing F2 to process a query, you should first make sure that your workspace contains nothing but your query. Clear all tables off the workspace using Alt-F8. If the workspace is already clear, you may need to break your query up into smaller tasks. You can always create new queries on ANSWER tables, or rename ANSWER tables to save them if necessary.

Multi-table "And" Queries

It is easy to set up multi-table queries where more than one condition must be met by records to be included in ANSWER. Simply link your tables using example elements and type any desired conditions into the query images. As long as all of the conditions are on the same line of the query images, Paradox will create an *And* query like the one shown in Figure 5.28.

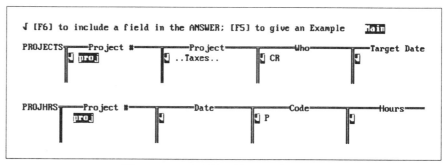

Figure 5.28 Multi-table "And" query

Multi-table "Or" Queries

You can combine "And" and "Or" freely in the same query.

Or queries on linked tables can be a little more tricky, depending on the approach you use. If you are using the "Or" operator to specify multiple conditions in the same field, as shown in Figure 5.29, the query is still simple. But, if you need to use multiple lines in your query to specify "Or" conditions in different fields, be sure to use different example elements on each line of the query. See Figure 5.29 for an example of how to set up a multi-table, multi-line, "Or" query correctly.

If you do not use different example elements for each line of the query, Paradox will instead create an "And" query. Remember that example elements are placemarkers. Let's say that you use an example element, with search conditions included, on a line. Paradox will find all records which meet the conditions on that line *and* which have a corresponding value in other fields containing the same example element. When you use the same example element in the same field on a separate line with different conditions, Paradox then looks for records which satisfy the conditions on both lines.

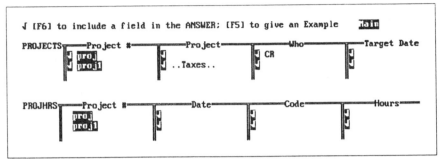

Figure 5.29 Multi-table, multi-line, "Or" query

Multi-table "Not" Queries

Using a multi-table query with the "Not" operator seems like a logical way to find all records in one table which are *not* contained in another table. For example, take the situation where we want to find all the customers in CUSTOMER who have not placed any orders. You might think we could use a query such as the one shown in Figure 5.30. Here, we link the tables on Customer # and use the "Not" operator before the example element in ORDERS. The problem is that Paradox compares *each* record in CUSTOMER to *each* record in ORDERS, rather than to the records in ORDERS as a group. Because of this, every customer appears in the ANSWER table, even if that customer has placed an order.

To get a table of the customers who have not placed orders, you can use either a "Set" query or a "Delete" query on a copy of CUSTOMER. Both approaches will be discussed later in this chapter.

Outer Joins

In all multi-table query examples so far, you may have noticed that the ANSWER tables contain only records where Paradox found a matching value in linking fields. When you use an example element to tell Paradox which fields to use to link tables, Paradox looks for matching values in those fields to decide which records to include in ANSWER. If a record in one table has a value in the linking field which is not matched in any record in the linked table, Paradox will not include that record in the ANSWER table.

Sometimes you may want to create an ANSWER table which has all records from one table and includes linking information from another table *if it exists*. This type of query is called an "Outer Join." You can create this type of query using !, the "Inclusion" operator. When you use the Inclusion operator with an example element in a query image, Paradox will include records from the table for that query image in ANSWER, whether or not they have matching values in the linked table.

Figure 5.31 shows how to create an Outer Join between INVENTRY and DETSUM, a summary table of The Raspberry Patch's order detail information. (Later in this chapter, examples of how to create summary tables using Calc queries will be shown.) In this query, the Inclusion operator is entered into the query image for INVENTRY, following the example element which links it to the DETSUM table. The resulting ANSWER table contains a record for each item in INVENTRY and corresponding summary information from DETSUM, if it is available.

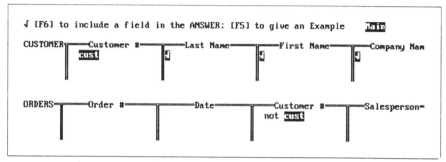

Figure 5.30 Multi-table "Not" query incorrectly set up

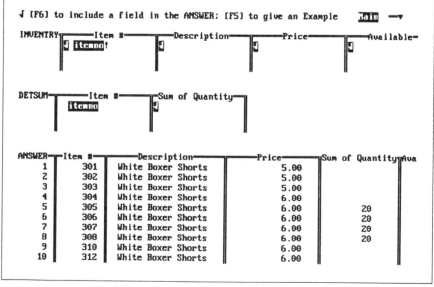

Figure 5.31 Outer Join of INVENTRY and DETSUM tables

Outer Joins and Selection Criteria

When you create an Outer Join query, you also can include selection criteria in any of the query images. Paradox will apply the selection criteria to any records from all tables before it creates the final ANSWER table.

Asymmetrical vs. Symmetrical Outer Joins

The query shown in Figure 5.31 is an example of an "Asymmetrical Outer Join." Here the Inclusion operator is used only with one of the two tables being queried. It is possible to use the Inclusion operator with all tables being linked in a query. This guarantees that all records from all tables will be included in ANSWER, whether or not they have matching values in the linking fields. This is a useful way to view information from tables which may or may not be related.

Figure 5.32 shows an example of a "Symmetrical Outer Join" query which creates an ANSWER table from the records in PROJECTS, PROJHRS, and CODES. PROJECTS contains information on who is working on certain tasks, PROJHRS has time information related to PROJECTS, and CODES has descriptions of the codes used in PROJHRS.

Both PROJECTS and CODES have records which do not have corresponding records in the other table. By combining the three tables with an Outer Join query, we can create an ANSWER table to see which projects are being worked on. You can also see which projects are not currently being worked on. These areas are indicated by any record which has a code and no other information.

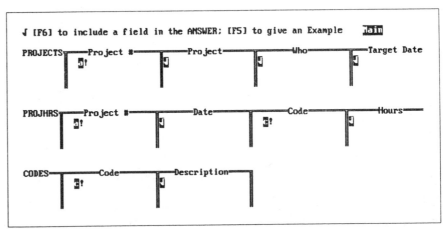

Figure 5.32 Symmetrical Outer Join of PROJECTS, PROJHRS, and CODES tables

Using Example Elements in Conditions

Example elements can be used in queries more than just as indicators of linking fields. They can be used to relate conditions in a query, giving you more flexibility in what you can search for. It is also possible to use example elements in expressions which include range operators, arithmetic, and other special operators. Sometimes it can be difficult to imagine all of the ways you can use example elements. Let's look at what is possible in a few queries.

Linking Records in the Same Table

The query shown in Figure 5.33 shows how you use example elements to link records in the same table to each other. This is an "And" query, but differs from other "And" queries we have looked at in one important way. In the other "And" queries in this chapter, Paradox looked for records which satisfied conditions in more than one field or that fell into a specified range. Each record was considered on its own as to whether it met the conditions for inclusion in the ANSWER table. In this new query, Paradox compares records in the table to each other. Here, we are looking for customers who own both a *Bambini Time and a Brown Berries* store. Using the same example elements in the name fields on both query lines tells Paradox to look for records which satisfy the conditions on *both* query lines.

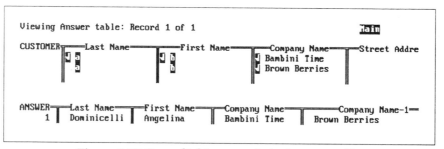

Figure 5.33 Query linking records in the same table

In this query, note that the name fields are not checked on both lines. This is the only type of query in which each line does not need to have exactly the same Checkmarks. If you Checkmark the name fields in both query lines, Paradox will create two sets of name fields in ANSWER.

Example Elements as Conditions

The conditions used so far have all been literal values, ranges, or special operators such as "Blank" or "Today." You can also use example elements as unknown conditions which are related to known conditions. Let's say we want to find the customer who owns the same type of store as Angelina Dominicelli does, but we don't remember the name of Angelina's store. We could perform a query to find the name of Angelina's store, and then perform a second query looking for other customers with the same store name. Using example elements, we can perform just one query to get the same answer. Figure 5.34 illustrates how to set this up. (The "Not Angelina" is included so we don't see the records for Angelina in ANSWER.) The resulting ANSWER table has records for people who own *Bambini Times* or *Pour Les Enfants* stores since Angelina owns one of each of these types of stores.

Example Elements in Expressions

You can also use example elements with ranges and arithmetic expressions. The query shown in Figure 5.35 looks for *bathing suits* in INVENTRY where the amount on hand is at least twice that of the *Cobalt Stripe Bikinis* for size 4. This query may look like a little convoluted, but it is an example of how to use multiple example elements, along with other expressions, to get quick answers to questions.

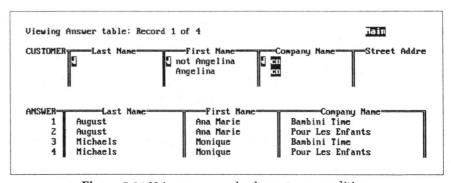

Figure 5.34 Using an example element as a condition

Doing Calculations with Queries

If you don't need to save calculated results, use Calculated fields in a report to save time doing unnecessary queries.

Performing calculations using information in tables is an important task in many applications. There are a few ways to do this in Paradox. You can create Calculated fields in forms, but they are for display purposes only. Using the Report Generator, you can include Calculated fields in your report, but they do not exist anywhere else. Or, you can use queries to save your calculated results in tables.

There are two different types of queries, which you can use to do calculations, Calc queries and Changeto queries. Calc queries allow you to create *new* Calculated fields which are included in ANSWER tables. Changeto queries are used to assign calculated results to an *existing* field in a query table, rather than in an ANSWER table. This section shows how to use Calc queries. Examples of using Changeto queries for calculations are included later in this chapter.

Calculations on Number Fields

Calc queries use the "Calc" keyword to tell Paradox to evaluate an expression which you place into a query image. The expressions used with the Calc keyword can contain literals, example elements (used to refer to field values), and the following arithmetic operators:

+

−

*

/

( )

As shown in Figure 5.36, you can use values from fields in more than one table in a Calc query. Here we link the ORDERS, SALES, and SLSPRSN tables and use a Calc expression to calculate commissions. Commission is calculated by multiplying the order amount (in SALES) and the commission rate (in SLSPRSN). The Calc expression can be typed into any field of the query image.

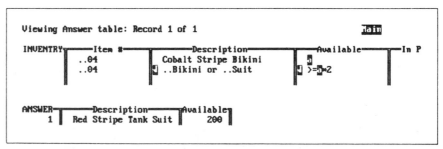

Figure 5.35 Example element used as part of an expression

Renaming Calculated Fields Using As

The query, shown in Figure 5.36 also illustrates the use of the As operator to specify a name for the Calculated field in ANSWER. If you don't use As to specify your own field name, Paradox creates a field name, using up to 25 characters, from the expression used to generate the field. In this case, the name of the Calculated field would be "Commission Rate * Detail." While this name correctly describes the field's contents, it gives no clue as to what the field will be used for. Naming the field *Commission*, by using As, can simplify later creating checks with the Report Generator.

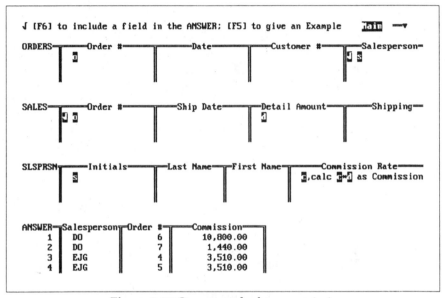

Figure 5.36 Query to calculate commissions

Where Calculated Fields Appear

You can always use Ctrl-R to rotate the fields of ANSWER later if needed. Also, in a report, you can place fields in any order.

Any Calculated fields created in a Calc query are placed into the ANSWER table after any other fields Checkmarked in the same query image as the Calc expression. The only exception is if you have `QueryOrder` set to `ImageOrder` in your Paradox configuration file. In that case, all Calculated fields appear at the end of ANSWER. (For more information on `QueryOrder`, see Chapter 13, "Customizing Your Paradox System.")

Order of Operations

When you use arithmetic operators in an expression, Paradox first evaluates any operations within parentheses ( ). Then, from left to right, multiplication or division is done before addition and subtraction. Here are a few sample expressions and the way they are evaluated by Paradox:

$$2 * 3 - 2 = 4$$
$$2 * (3 - 2) = 2$$
$$2 * (4 - 1)/3 = 2$$
$$2 * 4 - 1/3 = 7.666666666666$$

Alphanumeric Fields and Calc

You can also use Calc queries on Alphanumeric fields. When you use Calc with an Alphanumeric value (a string) rather than with a number, Paradox strings the specified values together. Literals can be used with example elements, giving you the power to create fields with new formats. Suppose you want to create a table which has customer names in the same field. You can do this easily using the query shown in Figure 5.37. Notice that you need to tell Paradox to place a blank between the names found in the First Name and Last Name fields. You do this by enclosing a blank space within quotation marks and including it in the calculated expression.

Including Literals in Calculated Expressions

Literals are values which are taken just as they have been typed and are not interpreted in any way. Most literals can be typed as part of the calculated expression for an Alphanumeric field. An exception occurs when you use spaces or any character which Paradox uses as a special operator in queries. In those cases, enclose the character within quotation marks so that Paradox uses it as a literal.

Date Calculations

Calculations also can be done on Date fields. When you add a number to a date, Paradox adds that number of days to the original date and creates a new date. You can subtract dates to find the number of days between dates. Dates can be literals or dates taken from fields indicated with example elements. The query shown in Figure 5.38 selects projects which are not yet complete and calculates the number of days until the due date. You can calculate the number of weeks until each due date by dividing the number of days by seven as shown in Figure 5.39. (The *Weeks Left* field in ANSWER has been formatted, using **Image/Format**, to display one decimal place.)

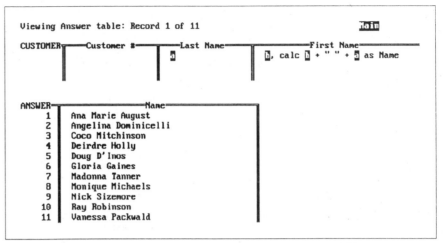

Figure 5.37 Calc query using Alphanumeric fields

Using Groups of Records in Queries

All queries shown so far have worked with individual records from tables. Records have been considered individually to see if they match selection criteria, and calculations have been done on one record at a time. You can also ask questions about groups of records in your tables using *Summary* operators. The Summary operators which Paradox recognizes are:

- Average
- Count
- Min
- Max
- Sum

Count, Min, and Max can be used with all field types. Average can be used with all field types *except* Alphanumeric. Sum is limited to Number, Short number and Currency fields.

How Summary Operators Work

You can use Summary operators both as search criteria and in calculated expressions. A Summary operator means nothing by itself, though. Simply typing a Summary operator into a field in a query image does not accomplish anything. A Summary operator *stands for* a value from a group of records; it does not display a summary value in an ANSWER table. (To display the actual value of a Summary operator for a group of records, you must use a Calc query. See the section, "Calculating Summary Information," for information on how to do this.)

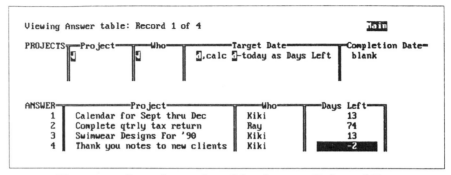

Figure 5.38 Query for number of days between Today and Date

Defining Groups

A Summary operator takes its value from a group of records, rather than from just one record, in a table. You tell Paradox which group of records to use with a Summary operator with Checkmarks. When you use Checkmarks in a query using Summary operators, the Checkmarks indicate which fields should be included in ANSWER *and* they determine how the records should be grouped.

Look at the query shown in Figure 5.40 to see how Summary operators can be used. In that query, the fields for customer name and company are Checked. Also, the Summary operator "Average" is used in the Detail Amount field with the range operator > 500. This tells

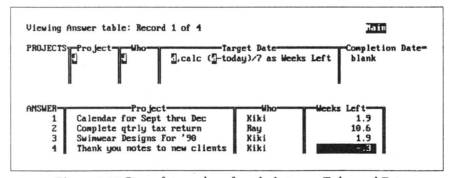

Figure 5.39 Query for number of weeks between Today and Date

Paradox to use the average amount *for each customer* when deciding which records to include in ANSWER.

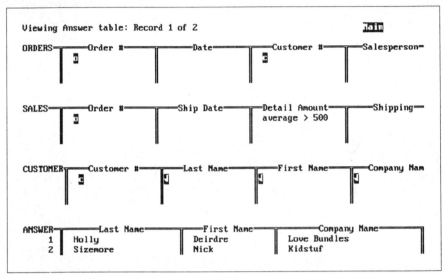

Figure 5.40 Query to find customers whose average orders exceed $500

Calculating Summary Information

To show the actual value of a Summary operator, you must use the Summary operator in a Calc query. For example, to find the average amount of all sales, use the query shown in Figure 5.41. Here, because no fields are Checkmarked, we are calculating the average amount of all records in the table.

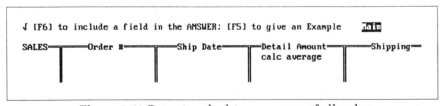

Figure 5.41 Query to calculate an average of all orders

To calculate the average amount by customer, simply link the ORDERS table to SALES, and Checkmark the name fields as shown in Figure 5.42. In that query, we have also linked CUSTOMER to ORDERS to display the name of each customer. Because the Customer #/Name combination is unique, Checkmarking name fields in CUSTOMER is the same as Checking Customer #. The resulting ANSWER has one record for each customer, showing the average order amount for each customer.

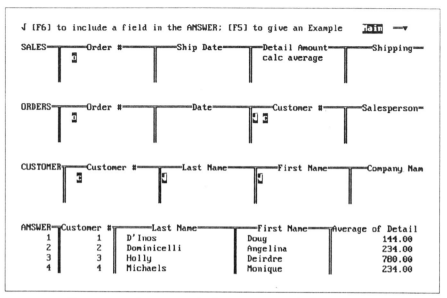

Figure 5.42 Query to calculate average order by customer

Using "Count," "Max," and "Min"

Forgetting to use "All" with "Calc Count" is a common mistake.

Using the Count Summary operator can be tricky. The reason is that the default grouping for "Count" is "Unique." This means that when you use "Count," Paradox will count only the unique values in the field, rather than count all values. This holds true for the "Max" and "Min" Summary operators, as well. If you want to use "Count," "Min," or

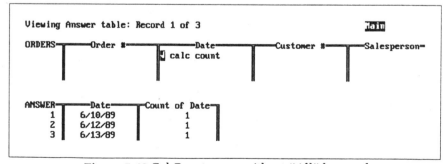

Figure 5.43 Cal Count query without "All" keyword

"Max" on all values in a group, you must include the keyword "All" after the Summary operator.

Figure 5.43 shows a query to calculate a Count where the keyword "All" has been omitted. Figure 5.44 shows the same query, but with "All" included after the Calc Count expression. Notice that the ANSWER tables are different. In Figure 5.43, we see a count of 1 for each date. In Figure 5.44, there is a different number for each date. This number represents the actual number of records for each date.

You can also do counts in reports.

In most cases, what you want is a count of *all* the records in a group. So be careful to use "Calc Count All" when counting.

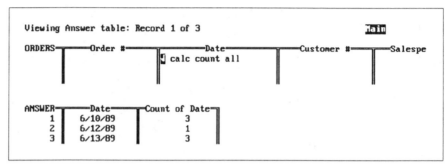

Figure 5.44 Calc Count query using "All" keyword

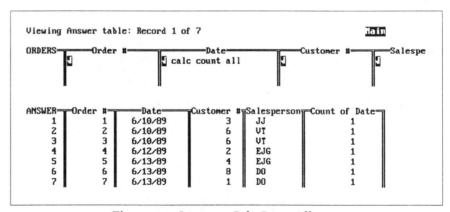

Figure 5.45 Incorrect Calc Count All query

Another thing to watch out for when doing Counts is the use of Checkmarks. Remember, Paradox uses all Checkmarks which you enter to determine the groups for counting. If you place Checkmarks into every field in a table and type **Calc Count All** in the Customer # field, as shown in Figure 5.45, Paradox will count the number of customers for each unique record on the table. In this case, the answer is meaningless.

To get a count of all of the different customers in ORDERS, use no Checkmarks.

"Only" Queries

"Only" is also used in set queries.

Another type of query which works with groups of records is an *Only* query. "Only" is a special operator which looks for records which satisfy *only* the specified condition and no other. "Only" is not considered a Summary operator because it is not used in calculations. However, it causes Paradox to consider each record which satisfies the "Only" condition relative to other records in the same table. Figure 5.46 shows the use of "Only" in a query which looks for any people who are working only on the Party project.

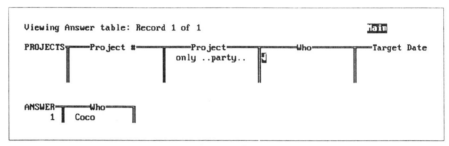

Figure 5.46 "Only" query

Queries Which Change Your Tables

We have now looked at several different ways to use queries to search through your information. One thing these queries have in common is that they produce ANSWER tables. Even when you do Calc queries, or use Summary operators, Paradox creates an ANSWER table and places information selected there.

There is another group of queries which can be used to make changes to the tables themselves. The special query commands used to create those queries are:

- Changeto
- Insert
- Delete

The following sections show how to use these special queries. Examples are included which illustrate how to use queries to manipulate entire groups of records easily. As you create your own Paradox database, be sure to consider how you might use these types of queries to your advantage. The query is often overlooked as a tool for updating and maintaining tables.

"Changeto" Queries

Changeto queries can save lots of time doing search-and-replace type editing.

Changeto queries are a powerful way to use queries to make changes to your tables. The simplest Changeto queries allow you to change the value of a field to a new value, optionally using conditions to select the records to change. The query shown in Figure 5.47 does a simple Changeto on the CUSTOMER table. This query looks for any records with *Kidstuf* in the Company Name field and changes the name to *Kidstuff*.

You can use a Changeto query similar to the one shown in Figure 5.47 to erase field values. Simply type **Changeto Blank** in the field you want to erase. This technique can be used with selection criteria to erase fields only in selected records.

CHANGED Tables

When you perform a Changeto query, Paradox creates a table, called CHANGED, which contains original copies of any records which have been changed. That is, CHANGED contains the records as they appeared before any changes were made to them. CHANGED is a temporary table. It will be deleted the next time you perform a Changeto query, change directories, or you exit from Paradox.

If Your Changeto Query Doesn't Work

When a Changeto query has been completed, CHANGED becomes the current image on the workspace. If it appears that your records aren't changed, double check to see if you are looking at your original table. You may be looking at your old (unchanged) records in the CHANGED table, instead.

One cause of unsuccessful Changeto queries is using "And" conditions when you really want to specify "Or" conditions. Look at the query shown in Figure 5.48. Here we have told Paradox to change the description for *Black Jeans* to *Black Pants*. On the same line, we have told Paradox to change any price of $5 to $5.50. The change will occur only if Paradox finds records in INVENTORY where the description is *Black*

Jeans and the price is $5. Since there are no records like this, we get an empty CHANGED table.

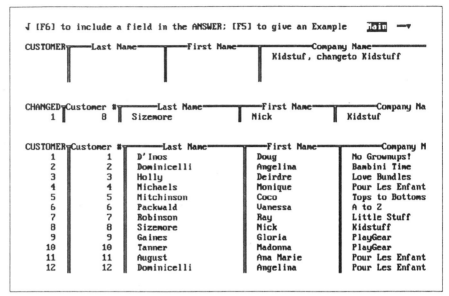

Figure 5.47 Changeto query on one field

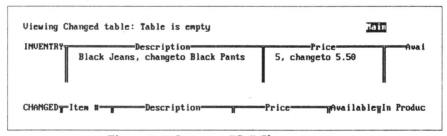

Figure 5.48 Incorrect "Or" Changeto query

The query shown in Figure 5.49 results in the desired changes to INVENTRY. It is set up correctly as an "Or" query where the separate conditions are entered on separate lines of the query image. You can see in INVENTRY that the prices for items *301*, *302*, and *303* have been changed. (Other records have been changed as well, but they are not visible on this screen. The images for CHANGED and INVENTRY have been reduced, using **I**mage/**T**ableSize, to accommodate viewing both tables on the screen at once.)

If you have mutually-exclusive Changeto conditions, be sure to create a separate query line for each condition and its Changeto.

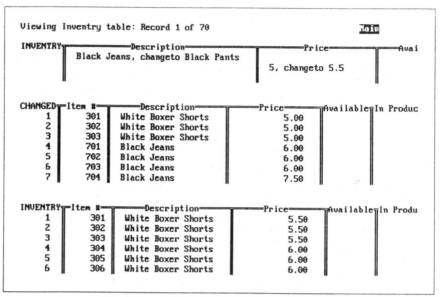

Figure 5.49 Correct "Or" Changeto query

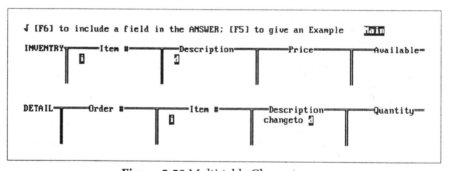

Figure 5.50 Multi-table Changeto query

Multi-table Changetos

You can use a changeto query to update one table against another.

Using a multi-table Changeto query is the easiest way to update one table from another when the tables have different structures. (If you are using keyed tables which have the same structure, you can use **T**ools/**M**ore/**A**dd/U**date.) We can use the INVENTRY and DETAIL tables to show how to do this. Suppose that the descriptions for some items in INVENTRY have been changed, and that the DETAIL table needs to be updated accordingly. Figure 5.50 shows a Changeto query which can be used to perform this update. The tables are linked on the Item # field using an example element. Another example element is used in the Description fields.

In this query, Paradox looks for the record in INVENTRY which corresponds to each record in DETAIL. When it finds the matching INVENTRY record, it notes the Description field value and writes that value to the Description field in DETAIL. Only one field is being changed in each record. Provided you have enough memory available, you can change as many fields as you like in this fashion, using "And" or "Or" queries.

Arithmetic and Changetos

Use changeto queries to calculate new values and assign them to the original field.

Earlier in the chapter, Changeto queries were mentioned as a way to assign new calculated values to tables. When you need to create new values in your table, not just in an ANSWER table, Changetos are perfect. To update pricing information for The Raspberry Patch, we can use the query shown in Figure 5.51. Here, we show not only how to use a calculated expression with a Changeto, but how to apply selection criteria as well. Prices for items in sizes 1–3 *only* are increased by 10%.

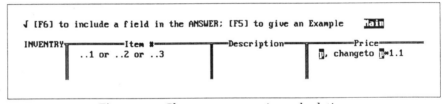

Figure 5.51 Changeto query using calculations

Be sure to review Chapter 7, "Putting Queries and Reports to Work," for other examples of how to make Changetos work for you.

"Insert" Queries

Insert queries are ideal for adding records from one table to another when the tables do not have the same structure. Take the case where we want to add all records from CUSTOMER into PHONEBK. If these tables had the same structure, we could use **T**ools/**M**ore/**A**dd to accomplish this. The tables are structured differently, though, so we have to use a different approach. Figure 5.52 shows how to use an Insert query to create new records, from records in CUSTOMER, for PHONEBK.

An Insert query creates new records in a table. Insert cannot be used to add information to existing records in a table. To add information from one table to corresponding records in another table, check to see if a Changeto query will work instead.

When you create an Insert query, you do not have to insert information into every field of the target table. You can use selected fields from the tables involved. Any fields which you leave blank in the query image will be blank in the new records which are added to the table.

When you perform an Insert query, you get a table called INSERTED. INSERTED has the same structure as the table to which the records have been added. INSERTED is a temporary table. You can use INSERTED to reverse the effects of your Insert query, if you need to. If you find that you have mistakenly added records to a table, you can use a Delete query, described in the next section, to delete INSERTED from the original table.

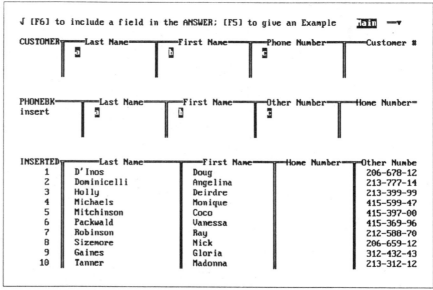

Figure 5.52 Insert query to add records from CUSTOMER to PHONEBK

"Delete" Queries

Use Delete queries for quick "clean ups" of tables uisng literal or linked selection criteria.

Delete queries are used to delete records from tables. You can use literal values as query criteria or you can link your DELETED table to other tables as shown in Figure 5.53. In that query, we are deleting all records from PHONEBK which have corresponding names in CUSTOMER. This will work only if the names appear exactly the same way in both tables.

When a Delete query has been completed, Paradox places all deleted records into a temporary table called DELETED. Be sure to rename this table if you want to keep these records. You can add them back into the original table if you find you made a mistake!

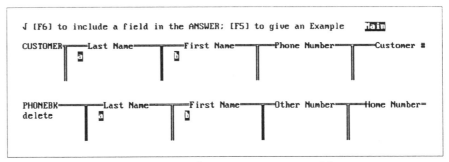

Figure 5.53 Delete query using two tables

"Find" Queries

For multi-field "zooms," use Find queries.

Find queries are different from the other queries described so far. They don't change a table; they act on the original table. You use a Find query to place the cursor in a specific record in a table, rather than placing that record into an ANSWER table. This can be useful if you need to get to a record using conditions in more than one field. "Zoom," in comparison allows you to search only on one field at a time. Find queries are easy to set up. Type the keyword **Find** in the left-most column of the query image as shown in Figure 5.54. Then type any search criteria you want to use and press F2 to "Do-It!" No Checkmarks need be used with Find queries.

If the Find query was successful, Paradox places the cursor in the first record which matches the query conditions. If additional records match the conditions, they are placed into an ANSWER table which has the same structure as the queried table.

You can link tables for use with a Find query. The table which is searched is the table which has "Find" in its query image.

"Set" Queries

Set queries produce ANSWER tables just like the ones produced by the queries described in the first sections of this chapter. They are included in a separate section here, though, because there are significant differences in the way they search for records. Set queries are similar to queries which use Summary operators in that they look at groups of records, but they are far more powerful.

Summary operators can be used to compare values in records to a value such as an average or a maximum value, that comes from a group of records. Set queries compare entire groups of records to each other, instead of just looking at summary values. Please be sure that you are familiar with all elements of queries discussed so far, especially example elements, before you attempt to perform Set queries.

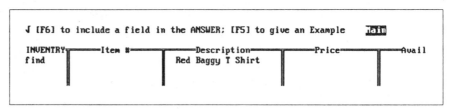

Figure 5.54 Find query

What Is a "Set" Query?

A set is a group. You can define a set to be anything you like. You might think of the people you know in terms of sets:

- All friends whom you have known since you were 10 years old
- All people whom you have met since you were graduated from high school
- Your entire "social set"
- Your family
- Your children
- The people whom you see at the gas station

In Paradox, a set is a group of records. It can consist of records from one table, or of related records from linked tables. A Set query allows you to define a set of records and then compare them to other records in the set. Paradox compares records using values in fields which you indicate. It does not compare entire records to each other.

Set Comparison Operators

There is a group of special comparison operators which you use to tell Paradox the kind of comparison to make. The results of the comparison determine which records go into ANSWER. Here is a list of these operators and what they do:

- *Only* tells Paradox that you want to see only records which have values in the set you define.

- No tells Paradox you want to see records which do not have values in the defined set.

- *Every* gives you records which have every value in the set.

- *Exactly* looks for records which have every value in the set and no other values.

"Value" refers to the field value(s) being used for comparison in the Set query. These definitions should become clearer after looking at examples of what each comparison operator does.

When to Use a Set Query

Set queries can be used to accomplish tasks which might otherwise require more than one query. If you need to find a group of records where the characteristics of the records as a group (as opposed to the content of the individual records) are important, then a Set query may be what you need. Let's look at an example of when a Set query can be used, and create it during the process.

Here is a question which appears relatively simple: Which customers have not ordered any Bikinis? Trying to answer this question is impossible with one conventional query. If you use the query shown in Figure 5.55, you get the names of customers who have placed orders for items which are not Bikinis. But the query looks only at individual order items. Customers who have placed these orders may also have ordered Bikinis, in the same order or in another.

One way to get the answer, using conventional queries, would be first to perform a query to get the names of all the customers who have ordered Bikinis. Then, copy the CUSTOMER table. Finally, use a Delete query to delete all customers in the first ANSWER table from those in the copy of ORDERS. This will leave records in the copy of CUSTOMER only for customers who have not ordered Bikinis.

This approach can be tedious. Just figuring out the steps to get the answer you want can be a problem. A Set query can be of great benefit here. It will give the answer you need in just one step.

How to Create a Set Query

To create a Set query, follow these steps:

1. Define your set. To do this, place the keyword "Set" into the left-most column of the query image(s) for the table(s) in which the set resides. Then, place example elements, along with any selection

criteria you want to use, into any fields which are part of the set. Figure 5.56 shows how to define a set of all orders for Bikinis.

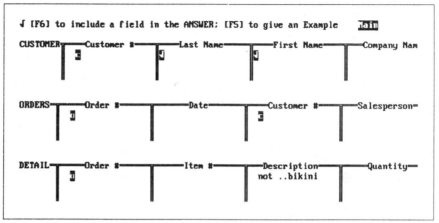

Figure 5.55 Incorrect query for customers who have not ordered Bikinis

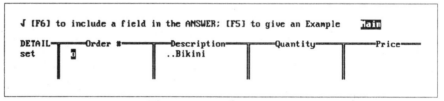

Figure 5.56 Defining a set

2. Create a query line which will select records for ANSWER based on some comparison to the set. Use the same example elements used in Step 1 to link the comparison group to the defined set. Checkmark any fields to be included in ANSWER. The Check-marked fields also serve to define the group on which the compari-son will be done.

In Figure 5.57, the lines which tell Paradox to find customers who have not ordered Bikinis are added to the above query. Customer # is Checkmarked because this is the group we want to see in ANSWER. The example element in the Order # field tells Paradox to compare orders for all customers to orders in the defined set. The "No" comparison operator is used to select only customers who do not have any orders in the defined set.

You need to include a Checkmark on this line, even if you don't want to display the Customer # in ANSWER. If you don't include the Checkmark, Paradox will tell you "No grouping is defined for set operation." (See the section on "Groupby" for a way around this.)

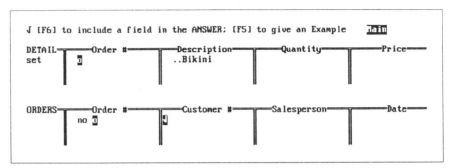

Figure 5.57 Using comparison operator in Set query

3. Optionally, link other tables to the line in Step 2 to select other related information. In Figure 5.58, CUSTOMER is linked to ORDERS on the Customer # field so that Customer Names, as well as numbers, will be displayed in ANSWER.

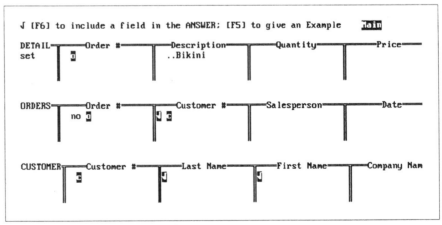

Figure 5.58 Complete Set query to find customers who have not ordered Bikinis

Using "Only"

Figure 5.59 illustrates the use of the "Only" operator to find customers who have ordered only Bikinis. The approach for setting up the query is the same as that shown in the "No" example. (This query can be performed using just the "Only" operator. If you have conditions on more than one table, though, you will need to use a Set query. See the section on "Multi-table Set Queries" below.)

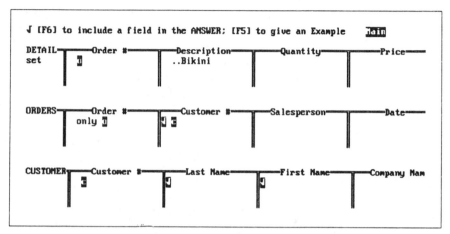

Figure 5.59 "Only" Set query

Using "Every"

Every is used to select records which have all the values in a set, but whose values are not necessarily limited to the set. An example of an "Every" question is: Which customers own the same type of stores as does Monique Michaels? The Set query shown in Figure 5.60 can be used to answer this question. The set is comprised of the stores owned by Monique Michaels and the group being compared to the set is all Raspberry Patch customers. "Every" is used to select only the customers who own *at least* the same type of stores, but may own other stores as well.

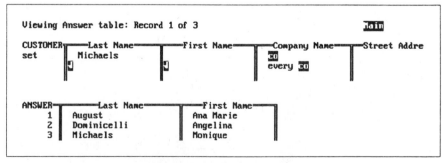

Figure 5.60 "Every" query

Using "Exactly"

Exactly looks for records which have exactly the same values as those in the defined set. If we want to find out which Raspberry Patch customers own exactly the same types of stores as Monique Michaels does *and own no other stores*, we can use an "Exactly" query. Figure 5.61 shows how to construct this query. The query is the same as the one shown in Figure 5.60, with the comparison operator "Exactly" used in place of "Every." Notice that the resulting ANSWER table is a subset of the ANSWER from the "Every" query. "Exactly" is a more restrictive condition than is "Every."

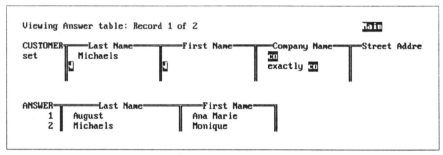

Figure 5.61 "Exactly" query

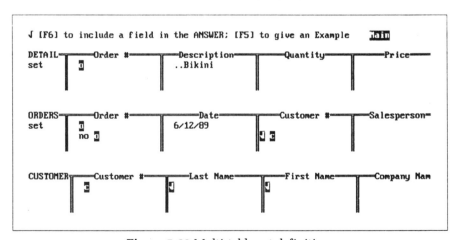

Figure 5.62 Multi-table set definition

Defining a Set with More Than One Table

The sets used in the above queries have been taken only from one table. It is possible to use more than one table to define a set as long as the tables can be related.

Let's say we need to contact all customers who *did not* order Bikinis on June 12, the special Bikini promotion day. The set here is all Bikini orders for June 12. The conditions used to define the set are part of two different tables. While the Bikini criteria needs to go into the query image for DETAIL, the date criteria must be entered into the query image for ORDERS. Figure 5.62 has an example of how to define this set using both query images.

Simply use the "Set" keyword in both query images and link them using an example element in the Order # field. The rest of the query is similar to the "No" query shown in Figure 5.58.

The "Groupby" Operator

You may have noticed that you must use a Checkmark in the set comparison line, even if you don't want to include that field in ANSWER. In the order examples above, we don't really need to know the Customer #, only the Customer Name. However, if you leave the Checkmark out of the Customer # field in the query image for ORDERS, Paradox gives the message, "No group is defined for the set operation" as shown in Figure 5.63. You can get around this by using the Groupby command, Shift-F6.

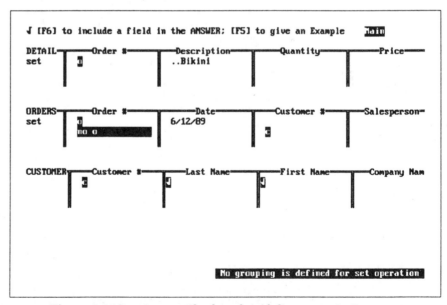

Figure 5.63 Leaving out Checkmark to define group in Set query

If you want to group records by a field, but do not want to include that field in ANSWER, press Shift-F6, instead of F6, in that field of the query image. Paradox will display a G in the field as shown in Figure 5.64. The ANSWER table from this query is shown in the same Figure. Note that it includes only Customer Names, not Customer #.

Saving Queries

Save queries you use more than once to scripts so you don't have to recreate them.

Most of the queries shown have been purposely simple in order to illustrate how different query features can be used. However, you can use the Ask command to create much more complex queries, or a series of queries. When you do, you may want to save the queries for future use. There are two ways to do this. Both use the Paradox Scripts command.

We have not talked about scripts, yet. Scripts are files of commands which tell Paradox what to do. You can create scripts by "recording" your keystrokes using Scripts/BeginRecord or Alt-F3, the Instant Script Record command. You can also create scripts by typing them directly into a script file using PAL, the Paradox Application Language. Chapters 10-12 of this book will describe how to create scripts using these methods.

Using Scripts/QuerySave

There is a special way you save queries as scripts using the Scripts/QuerySave command. You don't need to record your keystrokes

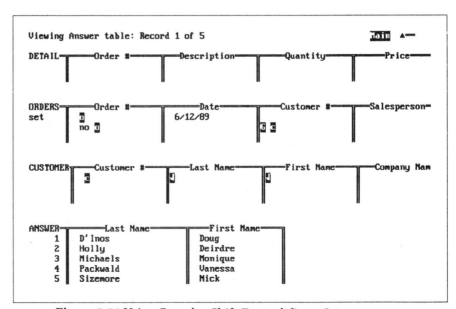

Figure 5.64 Using Groupby, Shift-F6, to define a Set query group

or to write any special commands into a script file. You simply create your query in the normal fashion. Then, when the query is properly set up, press F10 to access the Main Menu. Choose **S**cripts/**Q**uerySave from the menus. Paradox will prompt for a filename and save the query to the file you specified.

Using a Saved Query

You can place a query on the workspace by playing a script and then modify it if desired before pressing F2.

To recall a query which you have saved as a script, choose **S**cripts/**P**lay from the Main Menu. When prompted, select or type the name of the script containing your query and press Enter. Paradox will place the query onto the workspace. It will look exactly as it did when you saved the query originally.

To process the query, press F2 to "Do-It!" as you do with any other query. When you create a script using **S**cripts/**Q**uerySave, you are placing only the commands to create the query into the script file. No command is included to tell Paradox to "Do-It!" when you play the script.

Looking at a Saved Query

You can look at how a query is stored in a script file by choosing **S**cripts/**E**ditor/**E**dit from the Main Menu. When prompted, select or type the name of the script file at which you want to look and press Enter. Paradox will take you into the Paradox Script Editor.

You will see your query on the screen in the special format which Paradox uses to save queries to script files. Figure 5.65 shows the file containing the query from Figure 5.64 as it is displayed in the Paradox Script Editor.

You can see that the format Paradox uses for a query in a script is different from the way queries are displayed on the workspace. Here, you see only the fields which are used in a query, along with special commands like "Check" to indicate which fields have been marked with Checkmarks. Example elements are indicated by the underscore character "__".

Changing Saved Queries

While you can use the Script Editor to make changes to your saved queries, doing so is not recommended. It is easy to damage the special format which Paradox has created. If you need to make changes to a saved query, it is better to play the query script to place the query onto the workspace, make any changes and then save the new query. You can save the new query to the same file or to a new file. If you specify the old file's name, Paradox will give you a chance to cancel the operation before it replaces the existing file.

```
 ┌─────────────────────────────────────────────────────────────────────┐
 │                                                                       │
 │  Changing script C:\nobikini                              Script      │
 │                                                                       │
 │  ....+...10....+...20....+...30....+...40....+...50....+...60....+...70....+...80
 │  Query                                                                │
 │                                                                       │
 │    Detail │ Order # │ Description │                                   │
 │    set    │ _o      │ ..Bikini    │                                   │
 │           │         │             │                                   │
 │           │         │             │                                   │
 │                                                                       │
 │    Orders │ Order # │ Date    │    Customer #    │                    │
 │    set    │ _o      │ 6/12/89 │                  │                    │
 │           │ no _o   │         │ CheckGroupby _c  │                    │
 │           │         │         │                  │                    │
 │                                                                       │
 │    Customer │ Customer # │ Last Name │ First Name │                   │
 │             │ _c         │ Check     │ Check      │                   │
 │             │            │           │            │                   │
 │             │            │           │            │                   │
 │                                                                       │
 │    Endquery                                                           │
 │  ───────────────────────────────────────────────────────────────    │
 └─────────────────────────────────────────────────────────────────────┘
```

Figure 5.65 Using the Paradox Script Editor to look at a saved query

Combining Query Scripts

It is easy to combine query scripts into one script which you can play to process a series of queries. Here are the steps to do this.

Use the PAL "RENAME" command to save the ANSWER if necessary, in your script.

1. Save each query to a separate file using **Scripts/QuerySave**.

2. Use **Scripts/Editor/Edit** and specify the name of the first query you want processed. Once you are in the Script Editor, press End to move to the last line of the script. It will say **Endquery**. Press Ctrl-right-arrow and then press Enter to create a new line at the end of the script. On that line, type **DO__IT!**. This PAL command is equivalent to pressing F2. Make sure you use the underscore character, and not a hyphen, when typing **DO__IT!**.

3. You are now ready to insert another script after "DO__IT!" Press F10 to access the Script Editor Menu. Choose **Read** and specify the name of the script containing the next query you want to process. Paradox will insert the new script file below the current cursor position. As long as you didn't move the cursor after Step 2, the cursor should be after "DO__IT!"

4. Repeat Step 2 to add a "DO__IT!" after the second query in the script. You can repeat these steps to string several queries together.
5. When you have finished press F2 to save the script.

The next section of this book will show you how to automate your queries even further. You can include commands to rename ANSWER tables, generate reports or graphs from ANSWER tables, and even prompt the user for what conditions to use in a query. None of this is hard to do.

Query Notes

What You Really Use Queries For

At first glance, you may have thought that queries were only for finding records in tables. From the examples in this chapter, you saw that queries are a powerful tool which you can use for many varied tasks. Here are just a few of the ways you can use queries:

- Combine tables to get ANSWER tables on which to report
- Do global search-and-replace-type changes
- Update one table against another table when the tables have different structures
- Create summary tables to use with graphs and crosstabulations
- Analyze information to see patterns and trends

Chapter 7 contains additional examples of queries which show how they can be used to accomplish these tasks.

Query Performance

Because queries can be used to do much of your work in Paradox, you will probably want to be sure they run as quickly as possible. Chapter 14, "Performance Tips," has information on how to streamline your queries and keep them speedy.

Common Query Problems

Chapter 16, "Troubleshooting," has a section on solving query problems.

If you still have problems after studying the examples in this chapter, review Chapter 16 for additional tips.

Queries on a Network

Chapter 15, "Networking With Paradox," will describe how queries work on a network. Different types of queries place different types of locks on the tables in use. This affects the type of queries different users can perform at the same time. Chapter 15 will also cover topics such as private directories as they relate to query performance and disk space requirements. If you are using Paradox on a network, and will be using queries on shared tables, be sure to review Chapter 15.

A Note on Paradox Queries and SQL

The queries which you set up using Paradox, as mentioned at the beginning of this chapter, utilize a technique called QBE. Many mainframe computers and network servers store database information in a format which is accessible through Structured Query Language, or SQL. Borland is working on a version of Paradox which will allow you to formulate queries, using Paradox's QBE, to access information on these other types of systems. You will create a query the way you always do using Ask and Paradox will translate it to an SQL request for information "behind the scenes." The SQL request will be sent to the other computer. After the information is retrieved, Paradox will put it into a Paradox table for your use.

If you are a programmer, you will also be able to include SQL commands in your PAL programs. This will help integrate information from different types of systems. For users of both Paradox and SQL databases, this will be a real benefit.

Summary

The Ask command is used to create queries. You can generate ANSWER tables of selected records from one or more tables using the simple QBE (Query-By-Example) available through the Ask command. Queries also can be used to update tables as well as to search for information. Here are some important points about queries:

- When you use the Ask command, a query image for the table you specify is placed onto the workspace. Query images for multiple tables can be used together as long as the tables can be linked.

- F6 is used to indicate which fields are to be included in an ANSWER table.

- F5 is used to place example elements for linking tables or referring to field values in expressions.

- Summary operators can be used in queries as selection criteria or with calculations.

- You tell Paradox to do an Outer Join query by using the ! operator.

- Insert, Changeto, and Delete queries are used to change the query table instead of to create an ANSWER table. You can use these queries to update one table against others.

- Find queries let you find a record in a table using selection criteria.

- Set queries are used to compare groups of records in one or more tables using special group operators.

- You can save a query to a script file quickly using **Scripts** /**QuerySave** from the Main Menu.

Using the
Report Generator

The Instant Report

The easiest way to print a report within Paradox is to use Alt-F7, the "Instant Report" key. When you press Alt-F7 while viewing a table, Paradox sends a tabular listing of the current table to the printer. The report that is generated is similar to what you see when a table is displayed in table view. This report is known as the *Standard Report*. In Figure 6.1, you see the Standard Report for CUSTOMER. Paradox creates as many pagewidths as necessary to print all fields in the table horizontally.

Paradox reports are not limited to the Standard Report, though. You can change the Standard Report and create up to 15 different report specifications for each table. The `Report` command gives you access to these capabilities.

Overview of the Report Command

The `Report` command is used to create, change, and generate reports. When you choose `Report` on the Main Menu, you will see the menu displayed in Figure 6.2.

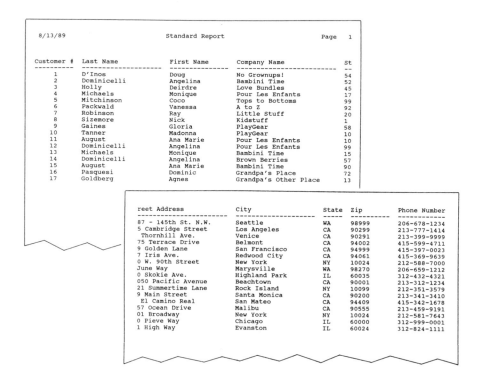

Figure 6.1 Standard Report for CUSTOMER

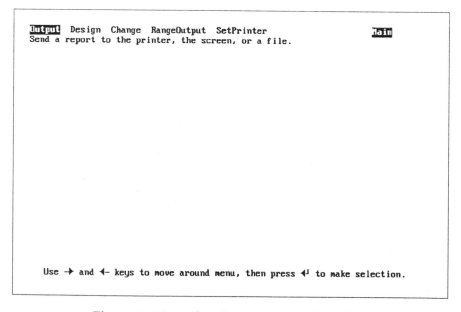

Figure 6.2 Menu after choosing Report from the Main Menu

The default SetPrinter options can be set using the custom script. See Chapter 13 for details.

- `Output` generates a report using the table and report specification you choose.
- `Design` is used to design your own report specification.
- `Change` allows you to change an existing report specification.
- `RangeOutput` sends a specified portion of a report to the printer.
- `SetPrinter` lets you determine which printer port and setup string to use; it also lets you set the `FormFeed` option.

`Output`, `RangeOutput`, and `SetPrinter` are used to generate a report from a table, using one of that table's report specifications. `Design` and `Change` are commands which give you entry to Report mode, where custom report specifications are created and changed. Report mode has its own set of menus for creating custom reports. Most of this chapter is devoted to information on using Report mode.

Before we get into Report mode, let's look at what is possible with the `Output`, `RangeOutput`, and `SetPrinter` commands.

Output

`Output` is the command which actually creates a report from a table and a report specification. When you choose **R**eport/**O**utput, Paradox will prompt for a table name. After specifying a table, Paradox will present a list of report specifications which exist for that table. Report specifications correspond to R (for the "Instant Report") or to a number from 1 through 14. When you create a report specification, you give a number to a report, as you do when you create a form. On the line below the report numbers, Paradox will display the description, if any, for the highlighted report specification. After choosing a report specification, Paradox will display a menu which allows you to send your report to a printer, the screen; or a file.

Sending Reports to a Printer

What happens after you choose `Printer` from the **R**eport/**O**utput menus depends on what is defined in your report specification or in your PARADOX3.CFG file. The default printer port is LPT1. You can change this default for any *new report specifications* which you create using the Custom script. How to use the Custom script for changing the default printer port, as well as several other report settings, will be described in Chapter 13, "Customizing Your Paradox System."

Within a report specification, it is also possible to specify a different printer port. Any printer port settings in a report specification will override the default settings in the PARADOX3.CFG file. How to define a printer port in a report specification will be covered later in this chapter in the section on "Settings."

Viewing Reports on the Screen

You can look at a report on the screen by choosing `Screen` from the **Report/O**utput menus. When you send a report to the screen, Paradox will display it one screen at a time, prompting you to press a key to display each new screenful of information. You can page only forward through a report.

If your report pagewidth is greater than 80 characters, you will be able to view only the first 80 characters. The additional information will not be shown. For a report with more than one pagewidth, Paradox will display all first pagewidths first, then all second pagewidths, until all pagewidths have been displayed. You can stop the display by pressing Ctrl-Break.

To scroll freely through a report file, you should send the report to a file and then use a text editor to view the file.

Sending a Report to a File

Be sure to follow the DOS conventions for naming a file.

It is easy to send a report to a file using the **Report/O**utput command. Simply choose `File` when Paradox prompts for the report destination. Paradox will then prompt for a file name. An ASCII file will be created on disk with the file name given. If you don't specify a file extension, Paradox will supply the .RPT extension.

RangeOutput

`RangeOutput` lets you output a subset of a report. When you choose `RangeOutput`, Paradox prompts for a table name, a report specification, and a report destination, as it did with `Output`. You will also be prompted for the beginning and ending page numbers to be generated. If you press Enter, Paradox will use the default starting page of one and the last page for the ending page.

Paradox determines report page numbers by creating the report file and then looking at the results. Unless you have created a report specification with one record per page, the page number will not correspond to the record number. Be careful to specify the *report* pages, not the record numbers you want.

If you have set the pagelength in your report to `C` for *Continuous*, Paradox will use the beginning and ending page numbers you specify to print those lines of your report.

SetPrinter

`SetPrinter` can be used to temporarily change the printer port, setup string, and form feed option used for reports. When you choose `Set-Printer`, you will see a menu with the following choices:

- Regular uses the settings stored in report specifications, instead of using the Override values. If there are no settings stored in a report specification, Paradox will send the report to LPT1 with no setup string.
- Override gives Paradox a new printer port and setup string to use. Anything specified with this option will override any settings stored in a report specification or in the PARADOX3.CFG file. You can also change the FormFeed option with Override.

When you choose Override, Paradox will display a menu with the choices PrinterPort, SetupString, and FormFeed.

PrinterPort

If you choose PrinterPort from the Override menu, Paradox will display a menu of printer ports: LPT1, LPT2, LPT3, COM1, COM2, and AUX. Paradox will use the port you choose for any reports to be sent to a printer.

SetupString

Using SetupString, you can specify a setup string which is different from the one stored in a report specification. This is a nice feature to use if you are testing setup strings. You can send new, temporary, setup strings to the printer without modifying the report specification until you have it right.

FormFeed

FormFeed lets you tell Paradox whether it should send a form feed to the printer at the end of each page. You can specify the default for this option using the Custom script, but setting it with **S**etPrinter/**O**verride lets you make temporary changes.

How Reports Work

Report specifications are built around one table. When Paradox creates a report, it includes each record in the table. You cannot set up conditions for printing individual records in the report specification. To do that, you must first query out the desired records and then report on the ANSWER table. There is information later in this chapter on how to do that.

Multi-table Reports

To report on information from more than one table at the same time, you may be able to use Paradox's multi-table report feature. This feature allows you to use another table as a lookup table for the main report table. You can link a lookup table to the main report table using Report mode's Field/Lookup command. Corresponding information from lookup tables can then be included in a report.

Multi-table Report Restrictions

Multi-table reports are not as flexible as queries, or multi-table forms, for linking tables. Before assuming that you can use a multi-table report on your related tables, consider the following:

- The lookup table must be keyed.
- Each key field in the lookup table must correspond to a field in the main report table.
- You can't link a lookup table to another lookup table.

This means that the main report table must contain all key fields of any lookup tables. This is different from multi-table forms where a "master" table may or may not contain all key fields of any linking tables. Let's look at the multi-table form we designed in Chapter 3 to illustrate this.

For The Raspberry Patch order entry, we designed a form in which the ORDERS table is the master table. Forms for CUSTOMER and DETAIL were embedded in the master form for ORDERS. DETAIL was keyed on both Order # and Item #, and was linked to ORDERS on Order #. Only part of the key for DETAIL was included in ORDERS. Because of this, ORDERS cannot be the basis for a multi-table report using the lookup table feature.

Let's consider using DETAIL, instead of ORDERS, as the main report table. ORDERS could then be used as a linked lookup table for DETAIL. However, there is no field in DETAIL which can be linked to CUSTOMER.

There are a few possible solutions. One is to link all three tables in a query, and report on the resulting ANSWER table. Another possibility is to link ORDERS and DETAIL with a query, and then report on ANSWER, linking CUSTOMER to the report table. An example of the latter approach is included later in this chapter to illustrate the use of report lookup tables.

Reporting on ANSWER Tables

Sometimes, using the multi-table report feature just won't work. This can be the case if your tables, as with ORDERS, DETAIL, and CUS-

TOMER, don't fit within the restrictions outlined above. Or, depending on the fields which you are linking, it may be quicker to perform a query and then report on ANSWER. For example:

1. Create a query to link tables.
2. Process the query to get an ANSWER table on which to report.
3. Report on ANSWER using **R**eport/**O**utput/ANSWER.

Using Custom Reports with ANSWER Tables

After you go through the above steps, you could design a custom report to use with your ANSWER table. However, the next time you perform a query, change directories, or exit from Paradox, ANSWER, along with all of its family members, will be deleted. Any custom reports which you have created will be lost. This is a problem if you want to be able to use the same query and report again.

The solution is to rename ANSWER, the first time you do the query, to make it permanent. Use **T**ools/**R**ename/**T**able/ANSWER /DUMMY where *DUMMY* (or any other name you choose) is the new name for the table. Then, design your custom report using DUMMY. This report will not be lost unless you, yourself, delete DUMMY or the report.

Once the report has been created, you can use it with any ANSWER tables which have the same structure as DUMMY. Use **T**ools/**C**opy/**R**eport/**D**ifferentTable/DUMMY/ANSWER to copy the custom report from DUMMY to ANSWER. Alternatively, you can empty DUMMY, use **T**ools/**M**ore/**A**dd/ANSWER/DUMMY, and then report on DUMMY using your custom report.

This may seem like many steps to go through just to generate a report. You can automate the process easily, though, using the Scripts command. Chapters 10 and 11 will show a few practical examples of how to do this.

Reporting on a Subset of Records

When you use **R**eport/**O**utput or Alt-F7, "Instant Report," Paradox prints out all records from a table. If you want to report on a subset of records in a table, you will first have to use a query to get the records you want into an ANSWER table. If you want to report on ANSWER using one of the custom reports you have for the original table, be sure to check all fields when you create your query. Then, you can use **T**ools/**C**opy /**R**eport/**D**ifferentTable to copy the desired report from the permanent table to ANSWER. This will work only if ANSWER has exactly the same structure as the original table. After the report is copied, you can use **R**eport/**O**utput on ANSWER to print the desired records.

Processing Order

When Paradox generates a report, it makes just one pass through the table. This means that any Summary or Calculated fields which you place will take into account only the records processed up to any given time. For example, say you placed a Calculated field which expresses the value of *Field A* as a percent of the sum of *Field A* into each report record. The sum used to calculate the percent will reflect only the records up to, and including, the current record. Because of this, it is not possible to use a Calculated Summary field to express "percent of total"-type values in a report. To do this, you need to place the necessary sum in a field in the table. You can then place a Calculated field which uses the sum field. See the last section of this chapter for details.

Report Characteristics

A report specification can be created for any table which is up to 2,000 characters wide. Paradox will not let you go into Report mode using a table that is wider than 2,000 characters. If you try, Paradox will display a message saying that the table exceeds the maximum allowable width. If you need to report on a wider table, you will have to perform a query first to get an ANSWER table which is less than 2,000 characters wide. Then, you can report on ANSWER.

A few other facts about reports:

- A page can be 2 to 2,000 characters wide.
- You can have any number of pagewidths, provided that the overall report width does not exceed 2,000 characters.
- A page can be from 2 to 2,000 lines long.
- You can use up to 255 fields, including fields from linked tables, in a report.
- Fields can be placed any number of times in each report.

Creating Your Own Reports

The rest of this chapter will be devoted to using Report mode to design reports. Each report design is called a report specification.

Getting to Report Mode

As mentioned, choosing Design or Change from the Report Menu is the way to access Report mode. When you choose Design to create a new report specification, Paradox will prompt for a table name, a report specification number (R or 1-14), and a description. The description will be displayed when you move the cursor through the menu of available reports. It will also display as the default report title in the page header. You can type up to 40 characters for the report description or leave it blank. Then press Enter to continue.

Tabular vs. Free-form Reports

At this point, Paradox will display the menu shown in Figure 6.3. You must choose whether to design a Tabular or a Free-form report.

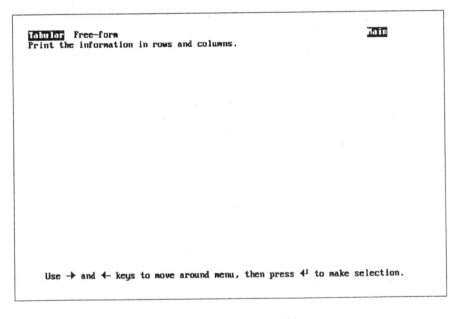

Figure 6.3 Tabular or Free-form Menu

- Tabular is used to create a report in which records are presented the way you see them in table view.
- Free-form lets you create a report in which each record can be displayed in its own form.

Tabular reports are good for simple listings. For other reports, it is usually easier to start with a Free-form report.

The way you use Report mode is basically the same for both Tabular and for Free-form reports. The main difference is that the default report specifications are different. Figure 6.4 shows the default Tabular report specification for CUSTOMER. The default Free-form report specification for the same table is shown in Figure 6.5.

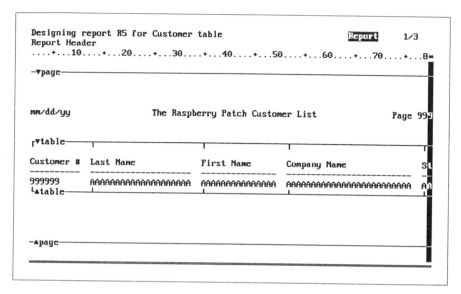

Figure 6.4 Default Tabular report specification for CUSTOMER

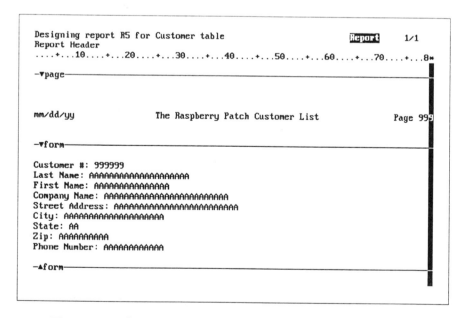

Figure 6.5 Default Free-form report specification for CUSTOMER

The Tabular Report

In the Tabular report specification, the fields are laid out horizontally on one row. Paradox uses a default pagewidth of 80 characters and creates as many 80-character pagewidths as are necessary to hold all of the fields. The area which holds the fields is called the *Table Band*. It is organized into columns, one for each field. Each column is labeled with the name of the field. The order of the columns in the default report specification is the same as it is in the table structure.

The Free-form Report

For Free-form reports, Paradox creates the default report specification by listing the fields vertically on the left side of the screen in an area called the *Form Band*. The form is as long as needed to list each field in the report table.

If you need one of the features that is unique to Tabular or Free-form reports, make sure you choose the right type when you create the report. You can't change the report type later.

There are a few other differences between the Report mode menus for each type of report. Basically, Tabular reports have menu options which allow you to work with entire report columns easily, suppress repeated values, and change the format of headings that are displayed. In Free-form reports, there are features which allow you to "squeeze" out blank space created by blank fields and to set up reports in a labels format.

Other than these differences, the rules for working with Tabular and Free-form reports are the same. The information which follows is the same for both types of reports unless otherwise noted.

Using Report Mode

After you choose `Tabular` or `Free-form`, Paradox displays a default report specification for the table with which you are working. You are now in Report mode. Let's look at the report specification shown in Figure 6.4 and see what it is made up of before we go through the Report mode menus.

What's on the Screen?

The report specification screen can look a little overwhelming at first. It doesn't resemble anything else seen in Paradox so far. It is not as complicated as it may appear, though. Looking at each line to see what it is used for should clarify things.

The Status Lines

The first two lines of the screen have some of the usual status indicators you see in Paradox. The left side of the top line tells you whether you are designing or changing a report and the name of the table with which you are working. On the right side of the same line, `Report` is an indicator of the current Paradox mode and the **1/3** shows that the current page is the first of three pagewidths.

The first part of the second line tells you where the cursor is in the report. There are separate areas of each report specification which are referred to as *headers*, *bands*, and *footers*. These will be described below. On the right side of the second line, Paradox will display the name of any field which the cursor is in. For a Calculated field, Paradox will display as much of the formula for the field as it can.

The Horizontal Ruler

On the third line, Paradox displays a horizontal ruler. This ruler indicates the character positions of the portion of the current report specification. This ruler is extremely helpful when you are working with pagewidths which are wider than the screen. The ruler will scroll as you move the cursor sideways through the report specification.

The Report Header

The area immediately below the ruler is used for the *Report Header*. This is where you type any literal information you want to use only at the beginning of the report. You can also place fields here. Paradox has special menu choices which let you place values such as Date and Time. You can place any other fields from your table here, but Paradox will take the values from the first record when it creates the Report Header. You can take advantage of this to place variable information into a Report Header by storing it in a "dummy" field in the first record.

Any lines which are included in the Report Header area, even blank lines, will show up only on the first page of the report. You can add lines here or delete all of them, eliminating the Report Header altogether.

The Page Header

For any field information in the Page Header, Paradox uses the next record to be printed.

The top of the Page Header is marked by the line with a downward-pointing triangle and the word `page`. The area from here to the next line in the report specification is where you can create a Page Header. Just as in the Report Header, you can type literal information and place fields which Paradox will use on the top of each page. Paradox uses all lines *between* the top page line and the next line when it determines what to place in the Page Header. Note that Paradox does not include any of the horizontal solid lines which are used to set off areas on the report specification when it decides what to print.

The title in the Page Header is taken from the description which you entered after you told Paradox which table and report specification you want to design or change. On the left side in the Page Header, you can see mm/dd/yy. This represents a *field mask* for the current date. (A "field mask" is the area Paradox reserves to print a field's value.) You can place a special field (one not in your table) which will contain the system date. How to do this is described in the section on the Field command below. On the right side of the same line, the word Page followed by 999 is displayed. "Page" is a literal and the "9"'s are a field mask for another special field which contains the current page number.

The default Page Header can be changed as you wish. You can delete all lines to eliminate the Page Header completely, or add lines as needed.

The Page Header will appear at the top of every page, unless you have the pagelength set to C for *continuous*. In that case, Paradox will ignore the Page Headers and Page Footers for all but the first and last pages. On the first page, the Page Header will appear directly after the Report Header.

The Table Band

In a Tabular report specification, you will see a line with a downward-pointing triangle and the word table marking the end of the Page Header. A few lines below that is another line labeled table with an upward-pointing triangle. The area between these lines is called the *Table Band*.

The Table Band contains a column for each field in the table. The column boundaries are indicated by "tickmarks" on the table lines. There is a break in the table lines after the last column. You cannot place anything in the Table Band past this point.

The first non-blank line within the Table Band contains the field labels. Field labels are printed at the top of each table. You can control whether they are printed only once, or at the top of each group or page, using special Report commands.

The line with the As contains a field mask for each field. Alphanumeric fields are indicated by a string of *As* as long as the field length. Number, Short number, and Currency fields are shown with 9s and other appropriate characters such as periods, commas, and parentheses (if specified). Date fields are shown with a date-type format, such as in the mm/dd/yy in the Page Header.

Place a blank line under the field masks to print out records double-spaced.

The line with the field masks, and any lines below it within the Table Band, are repeated for each record in a Tabular report. In the default Tabular report, records are printed single space. (There is no blank line under the field masks.) You can add or delete lines to this area to control spacing.

You can eliminate all lines in the Table Band to create a report which shows only summary information. It is possible to place Summary fields without using detail lines in the report. See the section on

"Summary Fields" in this chapter for more information on creating such a report.

The Form Band

If you look at Figure 6.5, you will notice that there are form lines instead of table lines. The area between the form lines is the *Form Band*. This area contains field labels (which can be deleted) and field masks for each field in the table. In a Free-form report, the lines in the Form Band are printed for each record in the table. You can change this area, rearranging fields in any order to get the report which you want.

The Page Footer

There is another line labeled `page` below the Table Band or the Form Band. This line has an upward-pointing triangle. This line delimits the area to be used for the Page Footer. All the lines below the bottom page line and the solid line above represent what Paradox will create for the Page Footer. This area can contain blank lines, literals, and Regular, Summary, Calculated, Date, Time, and Page fields.

The Page Footer will be printed at the bottom of every report page, including the last page. In fact, it is printed after the Report Footer on the last page as well.

The Report Footer

The last portion of the report specification, between the bottom page line and the double line below it, represents the *Report Footer*. Anything in this area gets printed after the last record (and the Group Footer, if there is one) in the report. Any Page Footer will follow the Report Footer on the last page.

Editing in the Report Generator

Whether you are using a Tabular or a Free-form report, the basic rules for moving through the report specification, editing, and using special commands are the same.

Moving Through a Report Specification

You move the cursor using the arrow keys and can use Ctrl with the left- and right-arrow keys to move horizontally one screen at a time. The Quick Reference Card lists the keyboard commands for moving through a report specification. What happens when you press Enter depends on where the cursor is on a line and whether you are in insert or overtype mode.

Placing Literals

In a Tabular report, Paradox will not let you "push" characters out of a column in the Table Band when you are in Insert mode. Use overwrite mode instead.

Literals can be typed anywhere they will fit on the report specification. You may notice Paradox beeping at times when you try to type literals. This happens in Insert mode when there is no room on the line on which you are typing. Paradox will move characters to the right in Insert mode until it reaches the last character of the pagewidth. At that point, it will not allow you to type additional characters. You can delete characters or spaces to make more room by using the Del or Backspace keys.

Adding Lines

If you are in Insert mode and press Enter with the cursor at the beginning of a line, Paradox will insert a new line in the report specification. Do this to add lines anywhere in the report specification. These new lines can be used as blank lines. Fields and other information can be entered on them, as well.

Deleting Lines

Deleting a line in Report mode is easy. Simply press Ctrl-Y with the cursor at the beginning of the line. Paradox will delete the current line, even if that line has field masks on it. The only lines which you cannot delete are the solid horizontal lines which indicate the page, group (not covered yet), table, or form areas.

Erasing Part of a Line

You can erase characters from the current cursor position to the end of the current line by pressing Ctrl-Y. All information, including field masks and any literals, will be erased.

Rotating Fields

If you are working with a Tabular report, you can rotate the field columns using Ctrl-R, the same as you did while viewing a table in table view. This is a quick way to reorder fields in order to create a different report.

The Vertical Ruler

While you are designing a report specification, it is often helpful to be able to count the lines in various areas of the report. Pressing Ctrl-V will display a vertical ruler on the left side of the screen as shown in Figure 6.6. All lines displayed as part of the report specification will be numbered. (These numbers will not print on a report, however.)

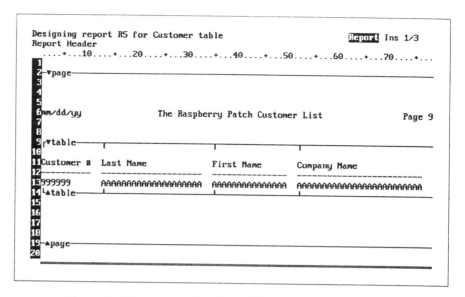

Figure 6.6 Report specification with vertical ruler displayed

See Chapter 16 for more information on how Paradox creates pages.

When you are calculating how many lines there are in each report area, remember not to count the solid lines used for page, group, table, and form because Paradox does not count these lines when it creates each page.

The Report Menu

Once you are in Report mode, you can access the Report Menu by pressing F10. The menu you see depends on whether you are working with a Tabular report or with a Free-form report. The Report Menu for a Tabular report is shown in Figure 6.7. Figure 6.8 shows the Report Menu for a Free-form report.

Here is a list of the Report Menu commands and what they are used for:

- `Field` is used to place, erase, reformat, justify, and wordwrap fields; it is also used to edit expressions for Calculated fields and to link report lookup tables.

- `TableBand` lets you insert, erase, resize, move, and copy columns *in a Tabular report only.*

- `Group` is used to set up groups for sorting and for organizing table information; it also lets you delete groups, as well as specify heading placement, sort direction, and type of grouping.

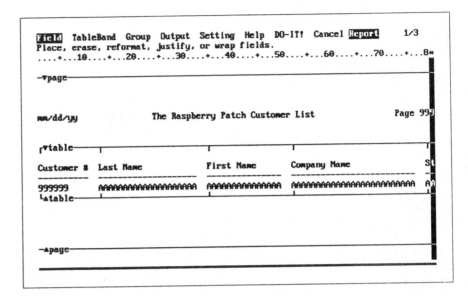

Figure 6.7 Report Menu for Tabular report

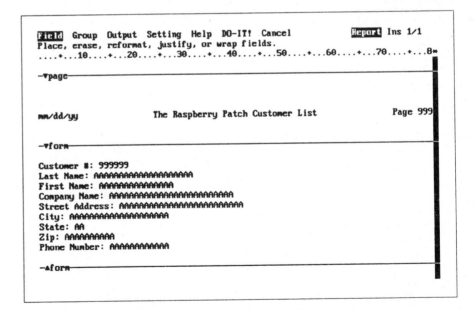

Figure 6.8 Report Menu for Free-form report

- Output lets you send the report being worked on to the printer, the screen, or to a file.

- Setting is used to control page layout, margin, setup string, printer port, and wait options; for Tabular reports, you can specify table format and group repeats; for Free-form reports, there are options to remove blank space and to generate a labels format.

- `Help` gives you access to Paradox's context-sensitive help system.
- `DO-IT!` saves the report specification on which you are working and returns you to Main mode.
- `Cancel` exits from Report mode, does *not* save the report specification being worked on, and returns you to Main mode.

The Tabular Report Menu has one choice, `TableBand`, which is not on the Free-form Report Menu. `TableBand` allows you to work with entire columns of a report specification. The only other differences between the menus for Tabular and Free-form reports are within the `Setting` command. There are a few `Setting` options which are unique to each type of report.

A diagram of the Report Menu tree is included in Appendix A. The `TableBand` and two `Setting` commands which are available only with Tabular reports are so labeled. The same is true for the two `Setting` commands which are seen only in Free-form reports. All other commands apply to both types of reports.

In this part of the chapter, we will list the report commands and what they are used for. The last part of the chapter contains step-by-step examples of how to create different types of reports using these commands.

The Field Command

`Field` has its own fairly extensive submenu as listed below. You can use:

- `Place` to place Regular, Summary, Calculated, Date, Time, Page, or Record # fields
- `Erase` to remove a field mask
- `Reformat` to change the display format of each field type
- `Justify` to specify how a field value should be aligned within the field mask
- `CalcEdit` to edit the expression for a Calculated field
- `WordWrap` to display a Regular or Calculated field in a paragraph-type format
- `Lookup` to link, unlink, or relink a lookup table whose fields can be placed in the report specification

Placing Fields

There are several types of fields which you can include in your report using Field/**P**lace:

- Regular fields are fields from the report table, or from a lookup table which has been linked using Field/Lookup.
- Summary fields can be used to show the sum, average, count, high, and low values for Regular and Calculated fields.
- Calculated fields are created from Regular fields and/or literals using arithmetic operators.
- Date places the system date in a report.
- Time is used to "timestamp" a report.
- Page contains the number of the current report page.
- #Record contains the report record number in a field.

Regular Fields: Use Field/**P**lace/**R**egular to place a field from your table in your report. Paradox will give you a list of field names from which to choose. If you have linked a lookup table to the report table using Field/Lookup, the list will include a pointer to each lookup table. Figure 6.9 shows the field list displayed for DETAIL after ORDERS and CUSTOMER have been linked using Field/Lookup. If you choose a pointer to a lookup table, Paradox will display a list of fields in the lookup table which can be placed.

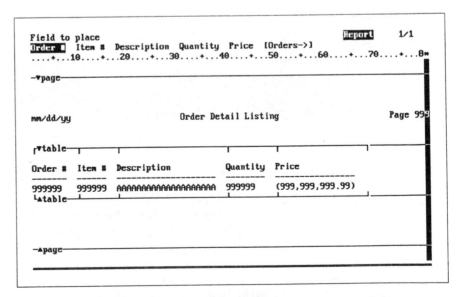

Figure 6.9 Field list displayed after Field/**P**lace/**R**egular

After you select a field from the list, Paradox will prompt for a position in which to place the field. You can place a field anywhere in a report specification, including Headers, Footers, Table Band, or Form Band. When you indicate where the field is to go, Paradox will display a string of As for Alphanumeric fields, 9s for Number and Currency fields, and a mask such as mm/dd/yy for Date fields. (The exact mask you see for Number and Date fields depends on the field format in use.) Paradox will also ask you (except for date fields) to use the arrow keys to show how long the field mask should be. You can change the field size or just press Enter. That's it!

Summary Fields: Field/Place/Summary is used to place a Summary value for a Regular or Calculated field in a report. A Summary value is taken from just one field. The value can be determined using all, or groups of records in a report table. (To calculate values from more than one field in a record, you can use Calculated fields, as explained in the next section.)

There are several types of Summary values which Paradox can produce. When you choose Field/Place/Summary, Paradox will ask whether you want to summarize a Regular field or a Calculated field. If you choose Regular, Paradox will present you with a field list. If you specify Calculated, Paradox will prompt you to enter a calculated expression.

After you choose a field, or enter a calculated expression (which cannot include Summary operators), Paradox will display a menu showing the types of Summary fields which you can place.

- Sum sums the values in a Number, Short number, or Currency field.
- Average calculates the average value in any field except an Alphanumeric type field.
- Count counts the number of values in a field .
- High shows the highest value in a field.
- Low shows the lowest value in a field.

The menu that you see will have a subset of these options if you are summarizing an Alphanumeric or a Date-type field. After you choose a summary type from the menu, Paradox will ask whether the summary should be PerGroup or Overall. If you choose PerGroup, Paradox will calculate the summary value using records only from the current group. If you choose Overall, Paradox will take the summary value from all records processed so far in the report. When the above steps have been completed, Paradox will prompt you to place and format the field just as with a Regular field.

You can also create Summary fields using Calculated fields. This can be a time-saver when you want to summarize a Calculated field. Instead of going through the steps necessary to place a Summary field, you can use summary operators in the expression for a Calculated field. The next section on Calculated fields has more information about how to do this.

Calculated Fields: Paradox lets you create new Calculated fields in a report using arithmetic operators. To place a Calculated field, choose **Field/Place/Calculated** from the Report Menu. Paradox will prompt for an expression as shown in Figure 6.10. The expression in that Figure will create a new field which contains the extended price for items in DETAIL.

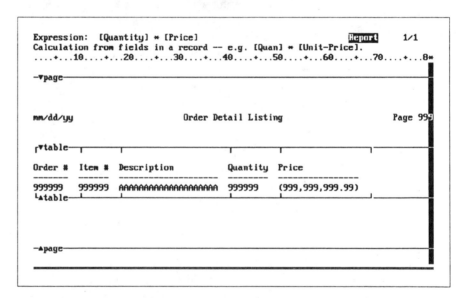

Figure 6.10 Expression prompt for Calculated field

You can use the following elements in the expression for a Calculated field:

- Field names from the report table enclosed within square brackets as in *[Target Date]*
- Field names from a lookup table where the lookup table name and field names are enclosed within square brackets as in *[Orders->Salesperson]*
- Arithmetic operators: + − * / ( )
- Literals, such as the number 5, a date, or a string within quotation marks as in *"These are the projects for:"*

- Summary operators: Sum, Average, Count, High, and Low

You can use Balance information in a lookup table in a Calculated Summary field to calculate a new balance. See Chapter 7 for an example.

Note that if you use a lookup table in another directory, you don't need to include its full pathname in a calculated expression. In fact, if you do, Paradox will not be able to interpret the expression. Just omit the path from the table name. Paradox knows where to find a lookup table, even if it is in another directory, from the Field/Lookup/Link which was done.

Calculated Summary Fields: If you use Summary operators in a calculated expression, you must enclose the field to be summarized in parentheses. You can optionally include `,group` after the field name to tell Paradox to calculate the summary value for the current group of records. Examples of using Summary operators in this way are included in the next paragraph. After you enter a valid expression, Paradox will prompt you to place and format the field.

There are many types of fields which can be created with Calculated fields. Here are some examples:

- *[Price] * [Quantity]* creates an extended price using Number and Currency fields from the current record.
- *[Quantity] * [Parts -> Price]* calculates an extended price using a quantity from the main report table and a price from a linked lookup table called *PARTS*.
- *Sum([Price] * [Quantity],group)* calculates the sum of extended prices for the current group of records.
- *Sum([Price] * [Quantity],group) * .07* calculates the sales tax for a group of records.
- *Sum([Price] * [Quantity])* calculates the sum of prices for all records printed so far.
- *[Completion Date] – [Target Date]* calculates the number of days between the completion and target dates.
- *[First Name] + " " + [Last Name]* creates a string consisting of a First Name and a Last Name separated by one space.
- *[City] + " " + [State Code] + " " + [Zip]* creates an address line.
- *"\012"* places an ASCII 12, a form feed character.
- *"\027E"* places a control code to begin bold print for some printers.
- *"\027F"* places a control code to end bold print for some printers.

Calculated fields are an easy way to send control codes to the printer in the middle of a report.

Note that when you use a Calculated field to place literals in the report, the field will still show up as a string of **A**s. You can see the actual expression displayed in the upper-right corner of the screen when the cursor is in the Calculated field.

Calculating with Blank Values: When you do calculations using fields which have blank values, be sure to set `Blanks=0` to `Yes` using the Custom script if you don't want to get blanks for results. Details on using the Custom script are included in Chapter 13, "Customizing Your Paradox System."

Changing a Calculated Expression: To change the expression for a Calculated field, use Field/CalcEdit on the Report Menu. Paradox will ask you to indicate the Calculated field whose expression is to be edited. When the expression is displayed, you can use Ctrl-Backspace to erase the entire current expression and type a new one. Or, you can use Backspace to erase the character(s) to the left of the cursor. You can also use Ctrl-F or Alt-F5 to go into field view. In field view, you can cursor through the expression, using the Del key to delete individual characters. You can also toggle between Insert and Overwrite modes using the Ins key. Home and End take you to the beginning or end of the expression, respectively.

Date, Time, Page, and #Record Fields: The remaining options on the Field/Place menu let you place fields for the system Date, Time, Page and Record number in a report. These fields are placed similarly to other fields.

When you place a `Time` field, Paradox will prompt you to choose hh:mm pm (or am) or hh:mm:ss (military). If you place a Date field, Paradox will also prompt you to choose one of these date formats:

```
mm/dd/yy
M o n t h dd, yyyy
mm/dd
mm/yy
dd-Mon-yy
Mon yy
dd-Mon-yyyy
mm/dd/yyyy
dd.mm.yy
dd/mm/yy
yy-mm-dd
```

You can change the date format later using Field/Reformat on the Date field.

For `#Record` fields, Paradox takes the record number from the *report* record number, not the table record number. If you specify `Per-Group`, Paradox will number each group of records starting with the number 1. Choosing `Overall` causes Paradox to number all records consecutively, starting with the first record in the report.

Removing a Field Mask

Removing a field mask from a report specification is easy. Choose Field/Erase from the Report Menu. Paradox will ask you to indicate the field mask to be deleted. After doing this, press Enter and the field mask will "disappear."

Field Format and Length

You can reformat any field mask by using the **Field/Reformat commands**. What you can do depends upon the type of field being reformatted:

- Alphanumeric fields can be shortened or lengthened up to the actual field length.

- Number fields can have the number of whole digits and decimal places specified, as well as having the format for displaying negative numbers and separators specified.

- `Date` and `Time` fields can be changed to one of the formats listed earlier.

- `Page` and `#Record` fields can have the number of digits to be displayed changed.

Regardless of how many digits show in the report, Paradox uses all significant digits in calculations.

When you choose **Field/Reformat**, Paradox will ask you to indicate the field to be reformatted. If you choose a Number, Short number, or Currency field, Paradox will display the menu shown in Figure 6.11.

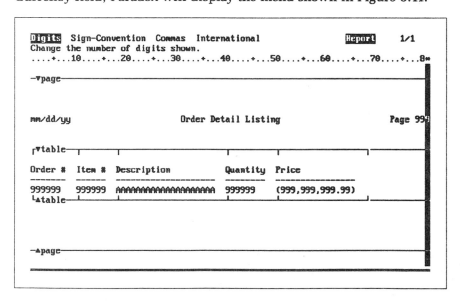

Figure 6.11 Field/Reformat Menu for Number, Short number, or Currency fields

- **Digits** is used to change the number of whole number digits and decimal places to be used in the field.
- **Sign-Convention** lets you specify how negative numbers are to be shown.
- **Commas** is used to choose whether to show numbers with separators between each group of three whole number digits.
- **International** lets you tell Paradox how to use periods and commas for whole number separators and decimal separators.

You can also change the defaults for formatting values using the Custom script. Details on doing so are included in Chapter 13.

Justifying Field Values

Field/Justify are the menu choices you use to change the way Paradox displays a value within a field mask. After you indicate a field to change, Paradox displays a menu with these choices:

- **Left** aligns values at the left side of the field mask; this is the default for Alphanumeric and Date fields.
- **Center** places a value in the center of a field mask.
- **Right** aligns values at the right side of the field mask; this is the default for Number, Short number, and Currency fields.
- **Default** is used to return a field to its default justification, based on the field type.

Wordwrapping Fields

Sometimes you may want to display an Alphanumeric field value on more than one line. Field/WordWrap is used to do this. There are a few steps involved. First, you must use Field/**R**eformat to adjust the length of the field mask to be used with **WordWrap**. Look at the field mask for Description as shown in Figure 6.12. It is set to the length of the field itself. Using Field/WordWrap on the field at this point will not display the field value on more than one line because it will fit within the current field mask.

Figure 6.13 shows the field mask for Description after it has been shortened using Field/**R**eformat. Now, if you use Field/WordWrap on the Description field, Paradox will "wrap" the field value onto more than one line if necessary.

When you choose Field/WordWrap from the Report Menu, Paradox will first ask you to indicate the field to be "wrapped." Then, Paradox will prompt for the number of lines onto which the value should be "wrapped." Figure 6.14 shows the report from the report specification

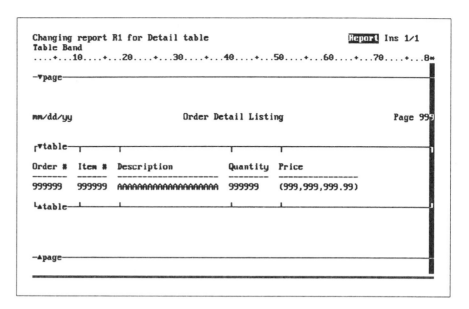

Figure 6.12 Description field mask at original length

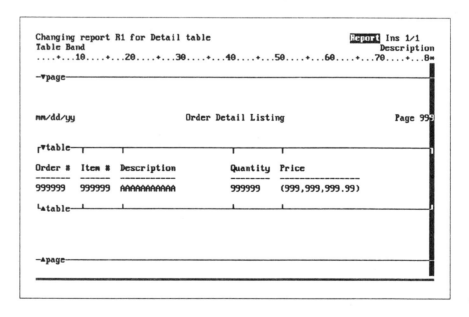

Figure 6.13 Description field mask after being reformatted

illustrated in Figure 6.13 after the Description field has been "WordWrapped."

```
 1/01/80                        Order Detail Listing                    Page    1


 Order #   Item #   Description      Quantity   Price
 -------   ------   -----------      --------   ----------------
    1       305     White               20           6.00
                    Boxer Short

    1       306     White               20           6.00
                    Boxer Short

    1       307     White               20           6.00
                    Boxer Short

    1       308     White               20           6.00
                    Boxer Short

    1       705     Black Pants         10           7.50

    1       706     Black Pants         10           7.50

    1       707     Black Pants         10           7.50

    1       708     Black Pants         10           7.50

    2       601     Red/White            5           8.00
                    Overalls

    2       602     Red/White            5           8.00
                    overalls

    2       603     Red/White            5           8.00
                    Overalls

    3       801     Red Stripe           5           6.00
                    Tank Suit

    3       802     Red Stripe           5           6.00
                    Tank Suit

    3       803     Red Stripe           5           6.00
                    Tank Suit

    3       901     Cobalt               5           6.00
                    Stripe

    3       902     Cobalt               5           6.00
                    Stripe

    3       903     Cobalt               5           7.50
                    Stripe

    4       901     Cobalt              12           6.00
                    Stripe
```

Figure 6.14 Report with "WordWrapped" Description field

If there is blank space below any field which you have Word-Wrapped, Paradox will use this space to show the value before it creates any new blank lines in the report. To preserve any blank lines, type **BLANKLINE** at the beginning of a blank line following the wordwrapped field mask. BLANKLINE is a report keyword which tells Paradox to leave a line blank. If necessary, Paradox will create a new blank line to "wrap" a value onto rather than use a BLANKLINE line.

Specifying a Lookup Table

Field/Lookup allows you to link a lookup table to the report table. You can also use it to unlink or relink a lookup table using different fields in the report table. The rules for using lookup tables in reports were explained in the Tabular report section at the beginning of this chapter. Check that section for an example of how to use this feature.

A Note on Moving Fields

Use Alt-F3, Instant Script Record, to save calculations you type in if you want to use them again in the same report.

If you want to move a placed field, you first must use Field/Erase to remove the field mask. Then, use Field/Place to put the field mask into a new position. There is no command to move a field mask. You can insert or delete spaces, however, to move a field mask.

TableBand

The `TableBand` command is present on the Report menu only while you are designing a Tabular report. `TableBand` has its own menu. It allows you to:

- `Insert` new columns into a report specification
- `Erase` columns of information
- `Resize` a column within certain limits
- `Move` a column to another position in the Table Band; Ctrl-R can be used as a shortcut for `Move`
- `Copy` a column to a new location in the Table Band

Working with Table Bands

Before you start experimenting with the `TableBand` command, it is helpful to know how Table Bands work. The Table Band in a Tabular report is the area between the two lines labeled *table*. It is separated into columns, one for each field in the report. If you look at the table lines shown in Figure 6.15, you can see little "tickmarks" which show the boundaries of each column. Each column is a separate work area. The following rules apply when working in a column:

- You cannot place a field across columns.
- You must adhere to the column boundaries when typing literals; using insert mode will not allow you to type across boundaries.
- A column cannot be shrunk to less than the width of the field mask or field label, whichever is larger.

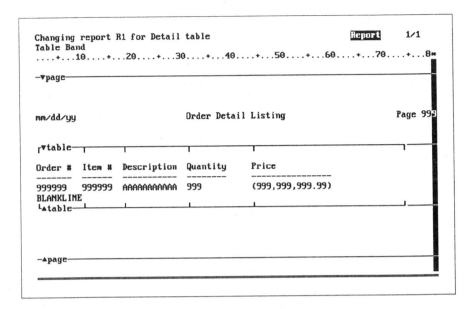

Figure 6.15 Report with Table Band

You may notice there is a slight break in the table line after the last column. This indicates the right boundary of the Table Band. There are restrictions on what you can do in the area beyond the last column in the Table Band. You can increase the size of columns, thereby extending the entire Table Band, but you cannot place fields, or type anything, beyond the last column in the Table Band. You can work only within one of the columns in the Table Band.

Use Tableband/Erase to delete a column.

Because of these restrictions, it is sometimes easiest to delete all columns except one in the Table Band. Then, use **TableBand/Resize** to expand the one remaining column to the entire pagewidth. You can then work freely within this area. This approach may sound drastic, but if you want to "shrink" several field masks to make room for more fields on the same page, this approach may take less time than deleting and resizing several columns. Figure 6.16 shows a Tabular report where this has been done to facilitate extensive redesign of the field layout.

Group

Why Use Groups?

Group can be used to organize your report records into groups. Your records are automatically sorted according to the groups you specify, and you can place Summary fields which are based on groups of records, rather than on the entire table.

Another important aspect of using groups in reports is that it allows you much flexibility in designing reports for ANSWERs created

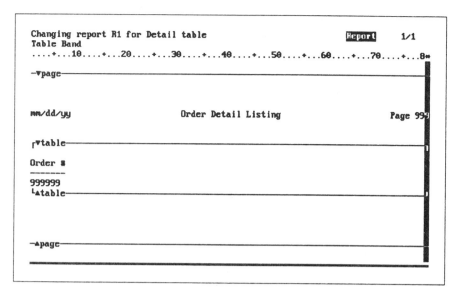

```
Changing report R1 for Detail table              Report    1/1
Table Band
....+...10....+...20....+...30....+...40....+...50....+...60....+...70....+...8*

─▾page─────────────────────────────────────────────────────────────────────

mm/dd/yy                    Order Detail Listing              Page 99

┌▾table─────────────────────────────────────────────────────────────────

Order #
───────
999999
└▴table─────────────────────────────────────────────────────────────────


─▴page─────────────────────────────────────────────────────────────────────
```

Figure 6.16 Tabular report with one "big" column

from linked tables. When you create a group, Paradox automatically creates a Group Header and a Group Footer. The Group Header can be used to display common information for a group of records, while a Group Footer can be utilized to show summary information.

Let's look at an example to illustrate this. Figure 6.17 shows the ANSWER which is created when you link the ORDERS, CUSTOMER, and DETAIL tables used for The Raspberry Patch orders. You can see that information such as Order # and Customer # is duplicated in each detail record for a particular order.

A report can be created which uses groups to organize the information for each order into a format quite different from that seen in ANSWER. Look at the report shown in Figure 6.18. That report was created using the report specification shown in Figure 6.19. The common information for each order is printed in the Header for each group. Next, the unique part of each record is listed, and, finally, the Group Footer contains summary information for each order.

Step-by-step examples of how to use groups to organize information in reports are included later in this chapter and also in Chapter 7, "Putting Queries and Reports to Work."

Groups and Sorting

You can create as many as 16 levels of grouping in each report. Paradox sorts records in a report with groups first by the outermost, or top, group and then by any successive groups. When you have a group in a report, record order in the table is ignored. If there is more than one

```
┌─────────────────────────────────────────────────────────────────────┐
│ Viewing Answer table: Record 1 of 79                         Main ▲━ │
│                                                                       │
│ ANSWER┬─Order #─┬───Date───┬Customer #┬Salesp─┬Last Name──┬First Name─┬──── │
│     1 │    1    │ 6/10/89  │    3     │  JJ   │ Holly     │ Deirdre   │ Lou │
│     2 │    1    │ 6/10/89  │    3     │  JJ   │ Holly     │ Deirdre   │ Lou │
│     3 │    1    │ 6/10/89  │    3     │  JJ   │ Holly     │ Deirdre   │ Lou │
│     4 │    1    │ 6/10/89  │    3     │  JJ   │ Holly     │ Deirdre   │ Lou │
│     5 │    1    │ 6/10/89  │    3     │  JJ   │ Holly     │ Deirdre   │ Lou │
│     6 │    1    │ 6/10/89  │    3     │  JJ   │ Holly     │ Deirdre   │ Lou │
│     7 │    1    │ 6/10/89  │    3     │  JJ   │ Holly     │ Deirdre   │ Lou │
│     8 │    1    │ 6/10/89  │    3     │  JJ   │ Holly     │ Deirdre   │ Lou │
│     9 │    2    │ 6/10/89  │    6     │  VT   │ Packwald  │ Vanessa   │ A t │
│    10 │    2    │ 6/10/89  │    6     │  VT   │ Packwald  │ Vanessa   │ A t │
│    11 │    2    │ 6/10/89  │    6     │  VT   │ Packwald  │ Vanessa   │ A t │
│    12 │    3    │ 6/10/89  │    6     │  VT   │ Packwald  │ Vanessa   │ A t │
│    13 │    3    │ 6/10/89  │    6     │  VT   │ Packwald  │ Vanessa   │ A t │
│    14 │    3    │ 6/10/89  │    6     │  VT   │ Packwald  │ Vanessa   │ A t │
│    15 │    3    │ 6/10/89  │    6     │  VT   │ Packwald  │ Vanessa   │ A t │
│    16 │    3    │ 6/10/89  │    6     │  VT   │ Packwald  │ Vanessa   │ A t │
│    17 │    3    │ 6/10/89  │    6     │  VT   │ Packwald  │ Vanessa   │ A t │
│    18 │    4    │ 6/12/89  │    2     │  EJG  │ Dominicelli│ Angelina │ Bam │
│    19 │    4    │ 6/12/89  │    2     │  EJG  │ Dominicelli│ Angelina │ Bam │
│    20 │    4    │ 6/12/89  │    2     │  EJG  │ Dominicelli│ Angelina │ Bam │
│    21 │    5    │ 6/13/89  │    4     │  EJG  │ Michaels  │ Monique   │ Pou │
│    22 │    5    │ 6/13/89  │    4     │  EJG  │ Michaels  │ Monique   │ Pou │
└─────────────────────────────────────────────────────────────────────┘
```

Figure 6.17 ANSWER table from query linking
ORDERS, CUSTOMER, and DETAIL

record with the same value in a field which is being used to group on, Paradox will sort the records by the leftmost field in the table, then the next field, and so on. Being aware of this can save you needless sorts. In fact, you should not sort any table that is to be used with a report specification which contains groups. The sorted order always will be overridden by any groups in a report. If you want Paradox to sort a table within a group, set up another group on the desired sort field within the first group.

The Group Menu

When you choose Group from the Report Menu, Paradox displays the Group Menu. With these commands you can:

- Insert a group and specify a basis for grouping on a field
- Delete a group from your report
- Headings tells Paradox whether to print only at the beginning of each group or at the top of every page as well
- SortDirection specifies that a sort for a particular group be ascending or descending
- ReGroup records using a different type of organization

```
    1/01/80                        Order List                        Page    1

    Order #:         1
    Date:        6/10/89
    Customer:    Deirdre Holly
    Company:     Love Bundles


    Item #   Description             Quantity  Price                Extended Price
    ------   --------------------    --------  ----------------     --------------
       305   White Boxer Shorts         20              6.00            120.00
       306   White Boxer Shorts         20              6.00            120.00
       307   White Boxer Shorts         20              6.00            120.00
       308   White Boxer Shorts         20              6.00            120.00
       705   Black Pants                10              7.50             75.00
       706   Black Pants                10              7.50             75.00
       707   Black Pants                10              7.50             75.00
       708   Black Pants                10              7.50             75.00


    Order #:         2
    Date:        6/10/89
    Customer:    Vanessa Packwald
    Company:     A to Z


    Item #   Description             Quantity  Price                Extended Price
    ------   --------------------    --------  ----------------     --------------
       601   Red/White Overalls          5              8.00             40.00
       602   Red/White Overalls          5              8.00             40.00
       603   Red/White Overalls          5              8.00             40.00


    Order #:         3
    Date:        6/10/89
    Customer:    Vanessa Packwald
    Company:     A to Z


    Item #   Description             Quantity  Price                Extended Price
    ------   --------------------    --------  ----------------     --------------
       801   Red Stripe Tank Suit        5              6.00             30.00
       802   Red Stripe Tank Suit        5              6.00             30.00
       803   Red Stripe Tank Suit        5              6.00             30.00
       901   Cobalt Stripe Bikini        5              6.00             30.00
       902   Cobalt Stripe Bikini        5              6.00             30.00
       903   Cobalt Stripe Bikini        5              7.50             37.50


    Order #:         4
    Date:        6/12/89
    Customer:    Angelina Dominicelli
    Company:     Bambini Time


    Item #   Description             Quantity  Price                Extended Price
    ------   --------------------    --------  ----------------     --------------
       901   Cobalt Stripe Bikini       12              6.00             72.00
       902   Cobalt Stripe Bikini       12              6.00             72.00
```

Figure 6.18 Report on ANSWER shown in Figure 6.17

Inserting a Group

To insert a group, use **Group/Insert**. Paradox will display a menu with the choices:

- Field
- Range
- NumberRecords

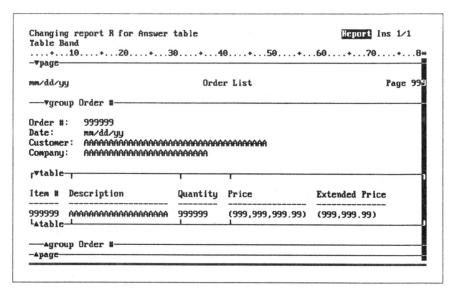

Figure 6.19 Report specification used to create report
shown in Figure 6.18

Use this menu to tell Paradox whether you want to group records accord-ing to field values, ranges of values, or a number of records. If you choose `Field` or `Range` as the type of grouping, Paradox will ask you to pick a field on which to group. For `NumberRecords`, Paradox will prompt you for the number of records to place within each group.

You can force each group to start at the top of a new page by using the PAGEBREAK command in the Group Header.

Grouping on a Field: When you group on a field, Paradox places records into groups based on field value. If there is only one record for a particular value in the grouping field, there will only be one record for that value in the group. The records will be sorted on the field values in ascending order, unless you use **Group/S**ortDirection to change this.

Using Range to Group Records: When you choose `Range` as the group-ing method, Paradox will ask you for more information to set up the ranges. If the field being grouped is a Number, Short number, or Cur-rency field, Paradox will prompt you to specify the size of the range as shown in Figure 6.20. Ranges always start with 0 and include as many numbers as you specify at the prompt. For example, if you specify 3 for the range size, records 0, 1, and 2 will be placed together. Records 3, 4, and 5 will be together, and so on.

To group by "quarter," use a query to assign a quarter number to a dummy field. Then, group on the dummy field in the report.

Date fields can be grouped on `Day`, `Week`, `Month`, or `Year`. Weeks run from Sunday through Saturday for Paradox. There is no way to specify another week order.

For Alphanumeric fields grouped using a `Range`, Paradox will ask you how many characters to build the Range on. If you specify 1,

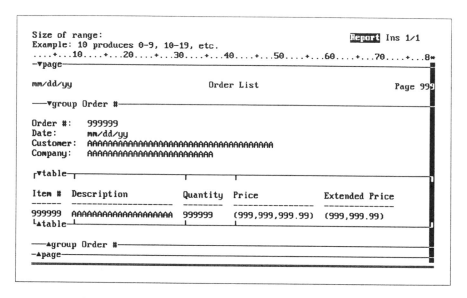

```
Size of range:                                                    Report Ins 1/1
Example: 10 produces 0-9, 10-19, etc.
....+...10....+...20....+...30....+...40....+...50....+...60....+...70....+...8*
─▼page──
                                                                              
mm/dd/yy                          Order List                         Page 999

──────▼group Order #──────────────────────────────────────────────────────

Order #:    999999
Date:       mm/dd/yy
Customer:   AAAAAAAAAAAAAAAAAAAAAAAAAAAAAAAAAAAAAAA
Company:    AAAAAAAAAAAAAAAAAAAAAAAAA

┌─▼table─┬───────────────────┬──────────┬──────────────────┬──────────────────

Item #  Description          Quantity  Price              Extended Price
──────  ──────────────────   ────────  ──────────────────  ──────────────────
999999  AAAAAAAAAAAAAAAAAAAA  999999    (999,999,999.99)   (999,999.99)
└─▲table─┴───────────────────┴──────────┴──────────────────

──────▲group Order #──────────────────────────────────────────────────────
─▲page──
```

Figure 6.20 Range prompt for Number and Currency fields

Paradox will group all records which start with the same character together. This is the only way to group on just part of an Alphanumeric field. You can only group an Alphanumeric field on a substring which begins with the first character of the value.

Sending Out Reports

The `Output` command on the Report Menu works similarly to the **R**eport/**O**utput command on the Main Menu. You will not be prompted for a table and a report specification, though. Paradox will use the report specification on which you are working to create the report. The `Printer Screen File` menu will be displayed so you can tell Paradox where to send the report.

When you send a report to the screen using the **R**eport/**O**utput command from the Main Menu, you can sometimes use Ctrl-Break to interrupt the flow of information to the screen. ("Sometimes" is used because pressing Ctrl-Break does not always cancel the report.) When you send a report to the screen while you are working on a report specification, don't press Ctrl-Break. If it works, it will take you to the Main Menu and you will lose any work you have done on the report.

Adjusting Settings

The `Setting` command allows you to change many different elements of a report specification. With `Setting` you can:

- **Format** a Tabular report into groups of tables or tables of groups
- **RemoveBlanks** left by blank field values in Free-form reports
- **GroupRepeats** specifies whether should be retained or suppressed in a Tabular report
- **Margin** adjusts the left margin in a report specification
- **Setup** adds a predefined or a custom string to a report specification
- **Wait** sets **Yes** or **No** for hand-fed forms
- **Labels** creates a format in a Free-form report

The Setting/Format Command

Use the **Format** *command in Report mode to control how headings are printed.*

Until now, **Format** commands have applied only to fields. The **Setting /Format** command is different. It controls how tables are laid out in a Tabular report which uses groups. A table is considered to be the records below a set of field headings. You can have your report be one large table of groups, as shown in Figure 6.21, or you can have each new group be a separate table, as shown in Figure 6.22. There is no impact on how records are grouped or summarized. The only thing **Setting/Format** affects is where table headings are seen in a report.

```
 8/15/89                      Projects By Person                      Page    1


 Who          Project                    Target Date  Completion Date  Comple
 ----------   ------------------------   -----------  ---------------  ------

 Coco         Staff Costumes For Party    10/25/89

 Jade         Cost Model For Raspberry Patch   6/30/89      7/08/89
              To Do List System            7/15/89      7/23/89
              Manage Party Tasks Completion  10/31/89

 Kiki         Calendar for Sept thru Dec   8/15/89
              Thank you notes to new clients  7/31/89
              Swimwear Designs For '90     8/15/89
              Clean Showroom Windows       6/30/89      7/04/89
              Create Plan:  Halloween Party  9/15/89

 Ray          Review Commission rates      7/15/89      7/15/89
              Complete qtrly tax return   10/15/89
              Complete qtrly tax return    7/15/89      7/15/89
              Assist at Bambini Time Opening  7/05/89      7/05/89
              Develop Budget For 10/31 Party  9/30/89
```

Figure 6.21 Report with **TableOfGroups** format

```
    8/15/89                      Projects By Person                    Page   1


    Who          Project                      Target Date  Completion Date  Comple
    ----------   -----------------------      -----------  ---------------  ------
    Coco         Staff Costumes For Party      10/25/89


    Who          Project                      Target Date  Completion Date  Comple
    ----------   -----------------------      -----------  ---------------  ------
    Jade         Cost Model For Raspberry Patch  6/30/89      7/08/89
                 To Do List System              7/15/89      7/23/89
                 Manage Party Tasks Completion 10/31/89


    Who          Project                      Target Date  Completion Date  Comple
    ----------   -----------------------      -----------  ---------------  ------
    Kiki         Calendar for Sept thru Dec     8/15/89
                 Thank you notes to new clients 7/31/89
                 Swimwear Designs For '90       8/15/89
                 Clean Showroom Windows         6/30/89      7/04/89
                 Create Plan:  Halloween Party  9/15/89


    Who          Project                      Target Date  Completion Date  Comple
    ----------   -----------------------      -----------  ---------------  ------
    Ray          Review Commission rates        7/15/89      7/15/89
                 Complete qtrly tax return     10/15/89
                 Complete qtrly tax return      7/15/89      7/15/89
                 Assist at Bambini Time Opening 7/05/89      7/05/89
                 Develop Budget For 10/31 Party 9/30/89
```

Figure 6.22 Report with `GroupsOfTables` format

Removing Blanks

When you design a Free-form report, Paradox gives you the option of "squeezing" out blank spaces created by blank field values. `RemoveBlanks` can be used with `LineSqueeze` or `FieldSqueeze`.

FieldSqueeze

`FieldSqueeze` will take out any blank space created in a blank line by a field value or one which is shorter than the defined field length. This feature works on only one line at a time. Remember that, while you can create letters and other documents with the Report Generator, it is not a word processor. `FieldSqueeze` will tidy up an individual line in a report, but it will not reformat groups of lines. Figure 6.23 shows a report where `FieldSqueeze` has not been set to `Yes`. You can see that there are unnecessary spaces between First and Last Names, and between the City, State, and Zip code. The report in Figure 6.24 shows the same report after `FieldSqueeze` has been set to `Yes`. You can see that Paradox has formatted the line differently. The values are "squeezed" together so that the appearance is more natural.

```
1/01/80                The Raspberry Patch Customer List              Page   1


Customer #: 1
Doug          D'Inos
No Grownups!
5487 - 145th St. N.W.
Seattle              WA 98999
206-678-1234


Customer #: 2
Angelina        Dominicelli
Bambini Time
525 Cambridge Street
Los Angeles          CA 90299
213-777-1414


Customer #: 3
Deirdre       Holly
Love Bundles
45 Thornhill Ave.
Venice               CA 90291
213-399-9999


Customer #: 4
Monique       Michaels
Pour Les Enfants
1775 Terrace Drive
Belmont              CA 94002
415-599-4711


Customer #: 5
Coco          Mitchinson
Tops to Bottoms
999 Golden Lane
San Francisco        CA 94999
415-397-0023


Customer #: 6
Vanessa       Packwald
A to Z
927 Iris Ave.
Redwood City         CA 94061
415-369-9639


Customer #: 7
Ray           Robinson
Little Stuff
200 W. 90th Street
New York             NY 10024
212-588-7000
```

Figure 6.23 Report without FieldSqueeze

FieldSqueeze always works on an entire line. If you want to squeeze just part of a line, you can use a Calculated field. Look at Figure 6.25. This is the same report as shown in Figure 6.24, with some notes added after the City, State, Address information. With FieldSqueeze on, the note is "squeezed" next to the address information and does not line up in a column. FieldSqueeze does not give the desired result here.

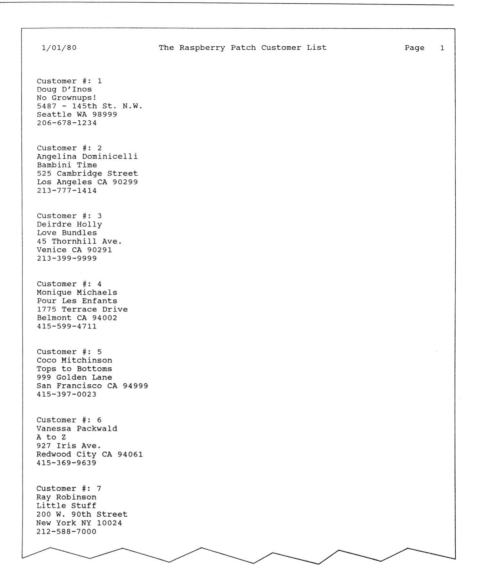

```
1/01/80              The Raspberry Patch Customer List        Page   1


Customer #: 1
Doug D'Inos
No Grownups!
5487 - 145th St. N.W.
Seattle WA 98999
206-678-1234


Customer #: 2
Angelina Dominicelli
Bambini Time
525 Cambridge Street
Los Angeles CA 90299
213-777-1414


Customer #: 3
Deirdre Holly
Love Bundles
45 Thornhill Ave.
Venice CA 90291.
213-399-9999


Customer #: 4
Monique Michaels
Pour Les Enfants
1775 Terrace Drive
Belmont CA 94002
415-599-4711


Customer #: 5
Coco Mitchinson
Tops to Bottoms
999 Golden Lane
San Francisco CA 94999
415-397-0023


Customer #: 6
Vanessa Packwald
A to Z
927 Iris Ave.
Redwood City CA 94061
415-369-9639


Customer #: 7
Ray Robinson
Little Stuff
200 W. 90th Street
New York NY 10024
212-588-7000
```

Figure 6.24 Report with FieldSqueeze

To work around the problem, you can place the City, State, and Zip code information using a Calculated field. Erase the fields for City, State, and Zip and replace them with a Calculated field which has the expression: **[City] + " " + [State] + " " + [Zip]**. Paradox will squeeze the City, State, and Zip code together as shown in Figure 6.26, without also pulling the note over.

218

```
   1/01/80                The Raspberry Patch Customer List              Page   1


   Customer #: 1
   Doug D'Inos
   No Grownups!
   5487 - 145th St. N.W.
   Seattle WA 98999          Notes: Will be opening new store
   206-678-1234                                     October '89


   Customer #: 2
   Angelina Dominicelli
   Bambini Time
   525 Cambridge Street
   Los Angeles CA 90299      Notes: Liked Color Combos
   213-777-1414


   Customer #: 3
   Deirdre Holly
   Love Bundles
   45 Thornhill Ave.
   Venice CA 90291          Notes:
   213-399-9999


   Customer #: 4
   Monique Michaels
   Pour Les Enfants
   1775 Terrace Drive
   Belmont CA 94002          Notes: Daughter named Hilary -
   415-599-4711                                     10/12/87


   Customer #: 5
   Coco Mitchinson
   Tops to Bottoms
   999 Golden Lane
   San Francisco CA 94999      Notes:
   415-397-0023


   Customer #: 6
   Vanessa Packwald
   A to Z
   927 Iris Ave.
   Redwood City CA 94061      Notes:
   415-369-9639


   Customer #: 7
   Ray Robinson
   Little Stuff
   200 W. 90th Street
   New York NY 10024          Notes:
   212-588-7000
```

Figure 6.25 Report with FieldSqueeze

LineSqueeze

LineSqueeze will remove any lines which are totally blank due to blank field values from a report. Blank lines which are part of the report specification will *not* be squeezed out. This feature is nice when you don't want to have blank lines in your report because of unused fields. For example, you can use LineSqueeze to show address lines together, even if one of the address lines is blank. Or, look at the example shown in Figure 6.27. This is a report for the PHONEBK table. LineSqueeze is set to No in this report.

```
   1/01/80                  The Raspberry Patch Customer List            Page    1


   Customer #: 1
   Doug D'Inos
   No Grownups!
   5487 - 145th St. N.W.
   Seattle WA 98999                        Notes: Will be opening new store
   206-678-1234                                   October '89


   Customer #: 2
   Angelina Dominicelli
   Bambini Time
   525 Cambridge Street
   Los Angeles CA 90299                    Notes: Liked Color Combos
   213-777-1414


   Customer #: 3
   Deirdre Holly
   Love Bundles
   45 Thornhill Ave.
   Venice CA 90291                         Notes:
   213-399-9999


   Customer #: 4
   Monique Michaels
   Pour Les Enfants
   1775 Terrace Drive
   Belmont CA 94002                        Notes: Daughter named Hilary - 10/12/87
   415-599-4711


   Customer #: 5
   Coco Mitchinson
   Tops to Bottoms
   999 Golden Lane
   San Francisco CA 94999                  Notes:
   415-397-0023


   Customer #: 6
   Vanessa Packwald
   A to Z
   927 Iris Ave.
   Redwood City CA 94061                   Notes:
   415-369-9639


   Customer #: 7
   Ray Robinson
   Little Stuff
   200 W. 90th Street
   New York NY 10024                       Notes:
   212-588-7000
```

Figure 6.26 "Squeezing" part of a line using a Calculated field

The same report is shown in Figure 6.28 with `LineSqueeze` set to `Yes`. If there is no second phone number and/or comments, Paradox omits those lines from the report.

When you set `LineSqueeze` to `Yes`, Paradox will ask you to choose `Fixed` or `Variable`. If you choose `Fixed`, Paradox will place any blank lines which it squeezes out of a form at the end of the form. This preserves the spacing between records in a Free-form report. Figure 6.28 has `LineSqueeze` set to **Yes/Fixed**.

Make sure `LineSqueeze` *is* `Fixed` *when printing labels or other fixed-length forms.*

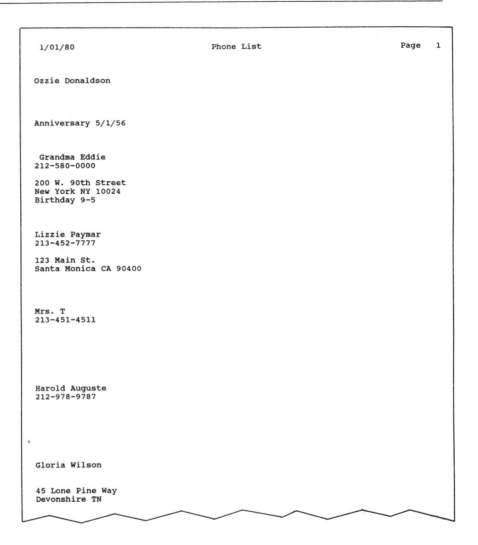

```
1/01/80                    Phone List                    Page    1


Ozzie Donaldson



Anniversary 5/1/56


 Grandma Eddie
 212-580-0000

200 W. 90th Street
New York NY 10024
Birthday 9-5


Lizzie Paymar
213-452-7777

123 Main St.
Santa Monica CA 90400



Mrs. T
213-451-4511




Harold Auguste
212-978-9787




Gloria Wilson


45 Lone Pine Way
Devonshire TN
```

Figure 6.27 Report with LineSqueeze/No

When you specify LineSqueeze/Yes/Variable, Paradox removes any blank lines but does not insert them at the end of the form. Records are printed with exactly as many lines as are necessary to print the record. The report shown in Figure 6.29 has LineSqueeze set to Yes/Variable. Note that the spacing between records is no longer uniform.

When you use LineSqueeze or FieldSqueeze, they work only with information in the Form Band. To squeeze blanks out of a Group Header, you have to use another approach. FieldSqueeze can be simulated by using a Calculated field as described above. For LineSqueeze,

```
  1/01/80                      Phone List              Page    1


  Ozzie Donaldson
  Anniversary 5/1/56




   Grandma Eddie
   212-580-0000
   200 W. 90th Street
   New York NY 10024
   Birthday 9-5




  Lizzie Paymar
  213-452-7777
  123 Main St.
  Santa Monica CA 90400




  Mrs. T
  213-451-4511




  Harold Auguste
  212-978-9787




  Gloria Wilson
  45 Lone Pine Way
  Devonshire TN
```

Figure 6.28 Report with LineSqueeze/**Yes**/**F**ixed

there is no simple solution. If you really need `LineSqueeze` in a Group Header or other than in the Form Band, you could query out any records which have blanks in fields which would otherwise create blank lines, leaving these fields uncheckmarked. Then, report on ANSWER using a different report specification. This solution is time-consuming but it will give the desired result.

Suppressing Repeated Values

This feature does not work with wordwrapped fields.

`GroupRepeats` is an option which is available only for Tabular reports. It can be used to tell Paradox to suppress the printing of repeated values in

```
1/01/80                        Phone List                        Page   1


    Ozzie Donaldson
    Anniversary 5/1/56


     Grandma Eddie
    212-580-0000
    200 W. 90th Street
    New York NY 10024
    Birthday 9-5


    Lizzie Paymar
    213-452-7777
    123 Main St.
    Santa Monica CA 90400


    Mrs. T
    213-451-4511


    Harold Auguste
    212-978-9787


    Gloria Wilson
    45 Lone Pine Way
    Devonshire TN


    Alexander Graet
    415-599-5990
    2005 Terrace Dr.
    Belmont CA 94002


    Jade Lee
    415-347-0000
    PAL programmer
```

Figure 6.29 Report from Figure 6.28 with LineSqueeze/**Yes**/**V**ariable

a grouping field. Look at the report for The Raspberry Patch which is used to print out a summary of who's working on what projects. The report specification shown in Figure 6.30 shows a simple Tabular report for PROJECTS grouped on the field, Who. In this report, Who is placed in the Table Band instead of in the Group Header. With `GroupRepeats` set to `Suppress` (instead of to `Retain`), the report prints as shown in Figure 6.31. Note that each name is printed only in the first record for each person.

Setting a Margin

You can use **Settings/Margin** to create a left margin in your report specification. Paradox will prompt for the margin size. You need to make sure that there is enough room on the right side of the page for Paradox to move everything over or else you will get an error message that there is "Not enough room for new margin."

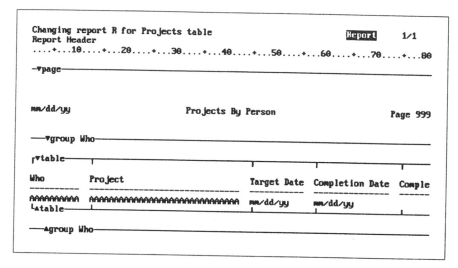

Figure 6.30 Tabular report specification for PROJECTS

```
1/01/80                          Projects By Person                    Page   1


Who             Project                       Target Date  Completion Date  Comple
----------      ------------------------------  -----------  ----------------  ------
Coco            Staff Costumes For Party        10/25/89

Jade            Cost Model For Raspberry Patch   6/30/89      7/08/89
                To Do List System               7/15/89      7/23/89
                Manage Party Tasks Completion   10/31/89

Kiki            Calendar for Sept thru Dec       8/15/89
                Thank you notes to new clients   7/31/89
                Swimwear Designs For '90         8/15/89
                Clean Showroom Windows           6/30/89      7/04/89
                Create Plan:  Halloween Party    9/15/89

Ray             Review Commission rates          7/15/89      7/15/89
                Complete qtrly tax return       10/15/89
                Complete qtrly tax return        7/15/89      7/15/89
                Assist at Bambini Time Opening   7/05/89      7/05/89
                Develop Budget For 10/31 Party   9/30/89
```

Figure 6.31 Report from Figure 6.30 with GroupRepeats/Suppress

Using Printer Setup Strings

Setting/Setup lets you send setup strings to your printer with the report specification. (You can also set up a default printer setup string using the Custom script; see Chapter 13 for details.) Paradox uses this approach rather than including printer drivers. With setup strings at the beginning of a report, you can send just about any commands which your printer can understand.

When you choose **Setting/Setup** from the Report menu, Paradox will display another menu with the choices `Predefined` and `Custom`. If you choose `Predefined`, Paradox will display a list of setup strings from which you can choose. Paradox includes a list of setup strings. You can also add strings to the list which is displayed using the Custom script.

If you choose `Custom` from the `Setup` menu, you will be prompted to choose a printer port and to enter a setup string. Examples of how to do this are included later in this chapter.

Pausing Between Printed Pages

The `Wait` command lets you tell Paradox to pause after each page that is printed. If you choose **Setting/Wait/Yes** from the Report Menu, Paradox will wait for a keystroke before printing each new page of a report. This give you a chance to manually feed paper, envelopes, or special forms to the printer.

Multi-column Labels

Use a setup string to change your printer pagewidth if necessary.

Paradox has a feature that makes it easy to print labels in more than one column. You turn this feature on by choosing **Setting/Labels/Yes** from the Report Menu while you are designing a Free-form report. There are a few other steps you need to go through to get `Labels` to work. You must:

- Set your pagewidth to the width of your labels (in characters, of course).
- Make sure that the number of report specification pages is equal to the number of columns of labels which you want to print.
- Design an appropriate form.
- Make sure `LineSqueeze`, if you are using it, is set to `Fixed`.
- Set the Paradox pagelength appropriately.

A step-by-step example is included later in this chapter.

Creating a Tabular Report

Let's create a Tabular report for The Raspberry Patch to illustrate the use of many of the features described above. We can design a report to print order-confirmations using the information in ORDERS, DETAIL, and CUSTOMER. The table which is the basis for the sample report is called ORDERLET. It is the renamed ANSWER table from a query linking ORDERS and DETAIL. ORDERLET contains all fields from ORDERS and information from each record in DETAIL. Figure 6.32 shows a STRUCT table which lists the structure of ORDERLET.

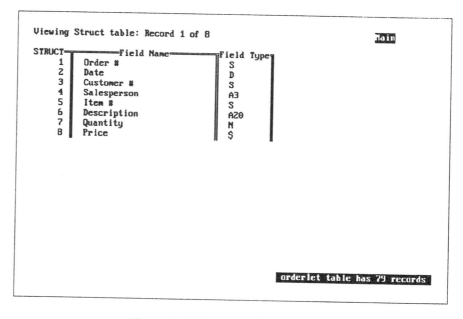

Figure 6.32 Structure of ORDERLET

The report will also include:

- A group on Order # to organize the information by order
- Calculated fields which display the extended price for each item in an order, as well as for all items in an order
- A Summary field which reflects the total number of items in an order
- A lookup on CUSTOMER to display customer information for each order
- Use of the PAGEBREAK command

The final report is shown in Figure 6.33. Looking at the finished report will give you an idea of what we are creating with the following steps. Each step is numbered and there are headings which describe the purpose of each group of steps.

```
   8/14/89                        ORDER CONFIRMATION                    Page    1


   Order #:      1
   Date:         6/10/89
   Salesperson: JJ
   Customer:     3

   Deirdre Holly
   Love Bundles
   45 Thornhill Ave.
   Venice CA 90291

   THANKS FOR YOUR ORDER!!!!



   Item #   Description            Quantity  Price       Extended Price
   ------   --------------------   --------  --------    --------------
      305   White Boxer Shorts        20      6.00          120.00
      306   White Boxer Shorts        20      6.00          120.00
      307   White Boxer Shorts        20      6.00          120.00
      308   White Boxer Shorts        20      6.00          120.00
      705   Black Pants               10      7.50           75.00
      706   Black Pants               10      7.50           75.00
      707   Black Pants               10      7.50           75.00
      708   Black Pants               10      7.50           75.00

            Total                    120                    780.00
```

Figure 6.33 Report for order-confirmations

Starting Out

The first step, of course, is to tell Paradox what we want to do.

1. Choose **R**eport/**D**esign from the Main Menu. Type **ORDERLET** for the table name, choose R for the report number and type **Order-Confirmation Letters** when prompted for a description. This description will appear in the report specification as the default title. It will be edited later. Then, choose Tabular from the menu.

Using the TableBand Command

Figure 6.34 shows the default Tabular report specification for ORDER-LET. Compare the information in the Table Band (the area between the table lines) to the information shown in the detail area of the report shown in Figure 6.33. There are some differences. The first thing we want to do is delete the columns for Order #, Date, Customer #, and Salesperson. This information will be placed in the Group Header later.

2. Press F10 to access the Report Menu. Choose TableBand/Erase from the menus, when prompted, and place the cursor in the Order # column using the arrow keys. When the cursor is in the column, press Enter. The column will be erased. Repeat the Table-Band/Erase command for the Date, Customer #, and Salesperson fields.

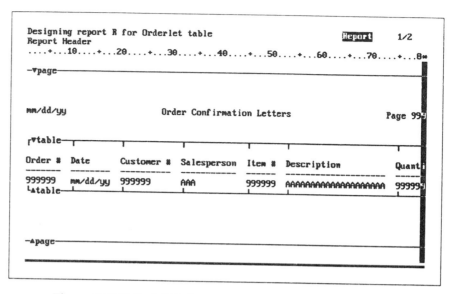

Figure 6.34 Default Tabular report specification for ORDERLET

3. We can also delete the Report Header and change the Page Header at this point. To delete the Report Header, place the cursor in the first position of the blank line above the top page line and press Ctrl-Y. Then, edit the title in the Page Header so it says *ORDER CONFIRMATION*.

Setting Up Groups

The next thing to do is set up a group on Order #. This tells Paradox to sort the records in ORDERLET by Order # and to place them into separate groups.

4. Press F10 and choose Group/Insert/Field from the menus. Press **O** to choose Order # from the list of fields displayed. Paradox will ask you to indicate where the group should be placed. Use the arrow keys to place the cursor below the title line and above the first table line. Press Enter. Paradox will insert two group lines, one above the top table line and one below the bottom table line.

Creating a Group Header

We now want to place the information for Order #, Date, Salesperson, and Customer # in the Group Header. That way, the header information will be printed only once for each order, even though it appears in each record in ORDERLET.

5. Add blank lines to the Group Header by pressing Enter in insert mode with the cursor at the beginning of a blank line just below the top group line.

6. Type the literals **Order #:**, **Date:**, **Salesperson:**, and **Customer:** in the Group Header so they appear as shown in Figure 6.32.

7. Place the appropriate fields after each literal using F10/**F**ield /**P**lace/**R**egular for the Order #, Date, Salesperson, and Customer # fields.

Adding a Lookup Table

Before we can include the name and address information from CUS-TOMER in the Group Header, we need to link CUSTOMER to ORDERLET.

You can use upper- or lowercase for table and field names. Paradox does not care.

8. Link CUSTOMER to ORDERLET by using F10/**F**ield/**L**ookup/**L**ink. Type **CUSTOMER** when prompted for the name of the table to link and choose Customer # from the list of fields displayed. Paradox will then use the Customer # to link a record from CUSTOMER to each record in ORDERLET.

Placing Fields from a Lookup Table

9. Use F10/**F**ield/**P**lace/**C**alculated. Type **[Customer-〉First Name] + " " + [Customer-〉Last Name]** at the expression prompt and press Enter. Place the field on the second blank line under the Customer # field in the Group Header. This will format the First and Last Names together as one string, separated by a space. Otherwise, the names would appear in two separate columns.

10. To place the address field, press F10. Choose **F**ield/**P**lace/**R**egular from the menus. When Paradox displays the field list, it will also display a pointer to the lookup table: [Customer-<]. Move the cursor to this pointer and press Enter.

Paradox will then display a list of fields from CUSTOMER. Choose Street Address from the list and then place it as any other Regular field under the Calculated field for name placed in Step 9.

11. For the remaining address information, place a Calculated field under Street Address where the expression to be typed is **[Customer->City]** + " " + **[Customer->State]** + " " + **[Customer->Zip]**.

After all fields have been placed in the Group Header, the report specification will appear as shown in Figure 6.35.

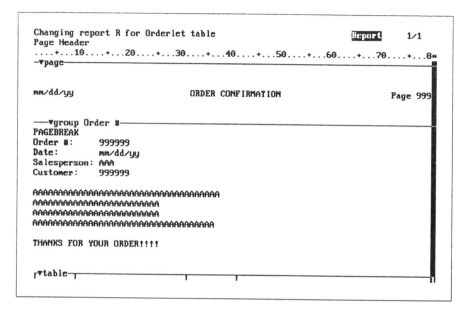

Figure 6.35 Report specification for order-confirmations

Placing Calculated and Summary Fields

We need to add a Calculated field which contains the extended price for each record to the Table Band. Before the field can be added, however, the Table Band needs to be enlarged.

12. Press F10. Choose **TableBand/Resize** and place the cursor in the last column for Price. Press Enter. Then, use the right-arrow key to widen the column. Move the cursor to the end of the first page-width and press Enter to complete the resizing process.

13. Use F10/Field/**Reformat** to reformat the field mask for Price. Decrease the number of whole numbers which will be displayed so that the field mask appears as shown in Figure 6.36.

14. Type **Extended Price** and a row of hyphens under it to the right of Price in the table band.

15. Use F10/**F**ield/**P**lace/**C**alculated, type **[Quantity] * [Price]** for the expression, and place the field under the literals typed in Step 14. This field will display the extended price for each line item in an order.

16. Add blank lines to the Group Footer to make room for the total information. Also type **Total** in the Group Footer under the Description field mask.

17. Place a field to show the total number of items ordered. Press F10, choose **F**ield/**P**lace/**S**ummary/**R**egular from the menus and pick Quantity from the field list. Then, specify Sum and PerGroup from the next menus. Place the field in the Group Footer under the field mask for Quantity.

18. Use a Calculated Summary field to show the total order amount. (This will be the cost for items ordered only. Chapter 7 has information about creating an invoice and including costs for shipping, and so on.) Choose **F**ield/**P**lace/**C**alculated from the Report Menu and type **S**um([Quantity] * [Price],group) at the expression prompt. Place this field in the Group Footer under the field mask for Extended Price. The report specification now looks like the one seen in Figure 6.36.

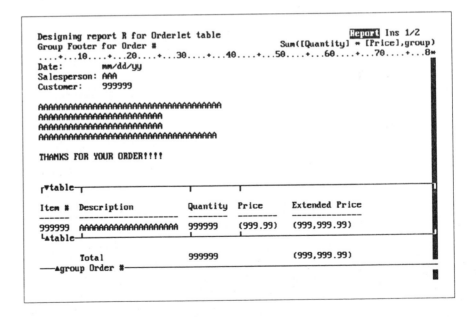

Figure 6.36 Report specification for order-confirmations

Refining the Page Layout

The following steps are as important as placing the fields in the report. If report pages are not formatted properly, you can have many things go wrong when the report is generated.

19. Insert a blank line under the group line. Type **PAGEBREAK** at the beginning of the line, being careful to use all uppercase letters and no spaces. This tells Paradox to go to a new page for each new order. PAGEBREAK must be at the very beginning of the line for Paradox to recognize it as a command.

20. Delete the extra pagewidth, using F10/**Setting**/**PageLayout** /**Delete**/**OK**, if you haven't done so already.

21. Optionally, you can use F10/**Field**/**Justify** to tell Paradox to left-justify the fields from ORDERS in the group header.

22. Finally, choose **Setting**/**Format**/**GroupsOfTables** from the Report Menu. This causes Paradox to place the table heading after the Group Header information. Otherwise, it will print at the top of the Order Confirmation before the header information.

Testing the Report Specification

Before saving the report specification, you can test it by choosing Output from the Report Menu. You can send the report to the printer, screen, or a file. If you do not want it sent to the default printer, use **Setting**/**Setup**/**Custom** to change the printer port.

Saving Your Work

When you have finished working on the report specification, press F2 or choose DO-IT! from the Report Menu. (You do not have to be finished with your work. You can use **Report**/**Change** from the Main Menu later to continue working on the same report specification.)

Be sure not to rename ANSWER to ORDERLET again. This would cause Paradox to delete ORDERLET *and its family*. All of the effort which went into creating a custom report would be lost. See the next section for information on using this custom report with future ANSWER tables.

Printing the Report

To print order-confirmations using ORDERLET, choose **Report**/**Output** on the Main Menu. Specify ORDERLET for the table and R for the report.

Paradox will then prompt for the report destination. Make your choice and the report will be generated.

Using the Custom Report with an ANSWER Table

Save all these commands, including the query, to a script to save time.

The next time that you want to use this report with an ANSWER from ORDERS and DETAIL, you can use **T**ools/**C**opy/**R**eport/**D**ifferentTable /ORDERLET/R/ANSWER/R. This will copy the order-confirmation report from ORDERLET to the ANSWER table. Then, report on ANSWER using **R**eport/**O**utput/ANSWER/R.

Creating a Free-form Report

The next example will show how to use a Free-form report to create 5″ × 7″ pages for a personal phone book. It serves to illustrate the following:

- How to create your own field layout
- Keeping records "neat" with the RemoveBlanks command
- Using an Alphanumeric Calculated field to avoid blank spaces
- Wordwrapping a field
- Using a non-standard-size form

After the report specification has been designed, the report will look like the page shown in Figure 6.37. Although you can't see it in the picture, each new group starts on a new page and all headings are shown at the top of each page.

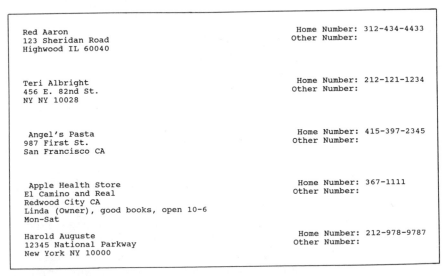

```
Red Aaron                                    Home Number: 312-434-4433
123 Sheridan Road                            Other Number:
Highwood IL 60040


Teri Albright                                Home Number: 212-121-1234
456 E. 82nd St.                              Other Number:
NY NY 10028


 Angel's Pasta                               Home Number: 415-397-2345
987 First St.                                Other Number:
San Francisco CA


 Apple Health Store                          Home Number: 367-1111
El Camino and Real                           Other Number:
Redwood City CA
Linda (Owner), good books, open 10-6
Mon-Sat

Harold Auguste                               Home Number: 212-978-9787
12345 National Parkway                       Other Number:
New York NY 10000
```

Figure 6.37 Phone book page created with Free-form report

Starting Out

The first task is to bring up the default Free-form report specification for PHONEBK and rearrange the fields into the desired format.

1. From the Main Menu, choose **Report/Design**, type **PHONEBK** for the report table, and press **R** for the report number. For the description, type **Phone Book Pages** or leave it blank. In either case, press Enter.

Designing the Form

The default report which Paradox brings up is shown in Figure 6.38. Notice that all field names, along with their field masks, are listed vertically in the form band. There are two approaches you can take to get the form layout you want. One option is to erase, or move, individual field masks and erase any unneeded field labels.

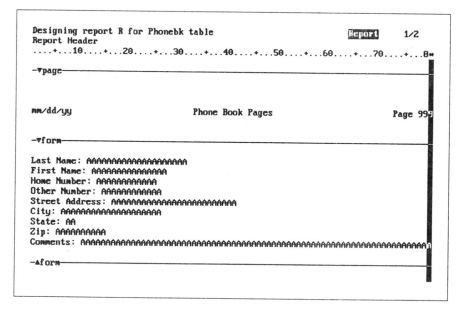

Figure 6.38 Default Free-form report for PHONEBK

The other option is to delete all lines in the Form Band, using Ctrl-Y, add new blank lines to the form, and then place all desired fields and literals. Fields are placed using F10/**Field**/**Place**, as explained earlier in the Tabular report example. Literals are simply typed into the report specification.

Refer to Figure 6.39 for the phone book field layout. You can follow these steps to place the necessary fields in an empty Form Band.

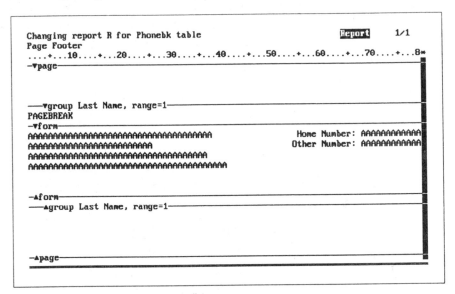

```
Changing report R for Phonebk table                          Report    1/1
Page Footer
....+...10....+...20....+...30....+...40....+...50....+...60....+...70....+...8*
-▼page────────────────────────────────────────────────────────────────────


───▼group Last Name, range=1──────────────────────────────────────────────
PAGEBREAK
-▼form─
AAAAAAAAAAAAAAAAAAAAAAAAAAAAAAAAAAAAAAAAAA          Home Number: AAAAAAAAAAAA
AAAAAAAAAAAAAAAAAAAAAAAA                           Other Number: AAAAAAAAAAAA
AAAAAAAAAAAAAAAAAAAAAAAAAAAAAAAAAAAA
AAAAAAAAAAAAAAAAAAAAAAAAAAAAAAAAAAAAAAAA


-▲form─
───▲group Last Name, range=1──────────────────────────────────────────────



-▲page────────────────────────────────────────────────────────────────────
```

Figure 6.39 Report specification for phone book pages

2. Use a Calculated field for the name with F10/Field/**P**lace /Calculated. At the expression prompt, type **[First Name] + " " + [Last Name]**. Place the field on the first line of the form.

3. Use **Field/Place/R**egular to place the Street Address field directly beneath the field mask for Name.

4. For the City, State, and Zip, place a Calculated field with the expression **[City]+ " " + [State] + " " + [Zip]** under the Street Address field mask.

5. Place Comments as a `Regular` field on the fourth line of the form.

6. Type the literal headings for the phone numbers. Place the numbers as `Regular` fields after their respective headings.

Wordwrapping a Field

Avoid using GroupsRepeats/Suppress on wordwrapped fields. It will not work.

Just for looks, we will wordwrap the Comments field onto a second line, rather than having the possibility of it spreading all the way under the phone numbers. To wordwrap a field, use the following steps:

7. Shorten the field mask for Comments using F10/Field/**R**eformat. Indicate the Comments field when prompted and use the left-arrow key to shorten the field mask so it is contained on the Name and

Address portion of the form. Press Enter to tell Paradox when the field mask is the desired size.

8. Use F10/**F**ield/**W**ordWrap to have Paradox display Comments on more than one line. Choose Comments from the field list which Paradox displays and type **2** for the number of lines on which to display the value. If we wanted Paradox to preserve a blank line below the field mask for Comments, we could type the report keyword BLANKLINE just below the wordwrapped field mask. However, we want the form to be fixed length, so we will omit BLANKLINE. The Comments field will now be "wrapped" onto an additional line if it will not fit within the field mask. There is nothing in the form to indicate that it is wordwrapped. If the cursor is in the Comments field mask, though, Paradox will display `wrap:` and the number of lines in the field indicator area.

Using RemoveBlanks

There is a place where we can use `RemoveBlanks` in this report, even if `FieldSqueeze` is not needed. Some records may not have company names or address information. We can use `LineSqueeze` to have Paradox format all the information for a person into one block, even if some fields are missing.

9. Press F10 and choose **S**etting/**R**emoveBlanks/LineSqueeze/**Y**es /**F**ixed from the menus. That way, any blank lines which are "squeezed" out will be added to the end of the record, preserving uniform spacing between records on the phone book pages.

Using PAGEBREAK

We also want to set up the report so that Paradox will alphabetize the entries and go to the top of a new page whenever a last name starts with a new letter. There are two steps to doing this:

10. Set up a group on the first character of the last name using F10/**G**roup/**I**nsert/**R**ange. Choose `Last Name` from the list of fields displayed and then press **1** for the number of characters on which to group. Place the group just outside the Form Band.

11. Type the Report keyword **PAGEBREAK** in the Group Header as shown in Figure 6.39. This command tells Paradox to go to the top of a new page for each new initial letter in Last Name.

Page Layout

The last tasks are related to page layout. The pagewidth, pagelength, and number of pagewidths must be set.

12. Change the pagelength to **C** if the pages are on continuous forms using F10/**S**etting/**P**ageLayout/**L**ength. If you are using separate sheets, set the pagelength to **42**. This works if you are printing six lines per inch on a 7-inch page length. Adjust the pagelength appropriately if you are using different vertical spacing, or a different size print, or a different length page.

13. Send a setup string to tell the printer to print in condensed print. That way you can fit 80 characters (the width of the report specification) onto a page that is 5″ wide. For many printers, the control code for condensed print is ∖ *015*. Use F10/**S**etting/**S**etup/**C**ustom, choose a port, and then type the necessary setup string at the string prompt.

14. Use F10/**S**etting/**P**ageLayout/**D**elete/**O**K to delete any pagewidth after the first. The current page and total number of pagewidths are displayed in the upper-right corner of the screen.

15. If you are using hand-fed forms, tell Paradox to pause after printing each page by choosing **S**etting/**W**ait/**Y**es from the Report Menus.

16. Remove the Report Headers and Footers by using Ctrl-Y at the beginning of all of these lines. Also, remove all blank lines from the Group Header and Footer. Adjust the Page Header and Page Footer so that the number of blank lines equals any margins on the phone book page.

17. Lastly, make sure that the number of lines between the Form Bands is equal to the space for each entry on the page. You can use Ctrl-V to display a vertical ruler on the report specification screen. Remember that Paradox does not count the lines for page, group, or form when it creates a report.

Printing Labels

Printing labels in one or more columns is easy using Paradox. We can convert the report specification used for phone book pages to one which can be used to print labels from PHONEBK in just a few steps.

1. Copy the report specification created for phone book pages using **T**ools/**C**opy/**R**eport/**S**ameTable. Type **PHONEBK** as the name of the table. Choose R for the report to copy and any other number for new report. For the example, we'll use *1*.

2. From the Main Menu, choose **R**eport/**C**hange and type **PHONEBK** when prompted for a table name. Choose **1** as the report specification to change.

3. Erase the phone number portion of the report specification by placing the cursor before the phone information on the line. Then, press Ctrl-Y. Paradox will erase all information to the right of the cursor. You can also erase the line with the Comments field mask in this way.

Using the Labels Feature

You need to use the labels feature only if you will be printing more than one column of labels. In addition to setting Labels to Yes, you must make sure that your pagewidth is equal to your label width. The number of pagewidths must equal the number of columns to be printed.

4. Turn on the labels feature by using F10/**S**etting/**L**abels/**Y**es.

5. Change the pagewidth to **44**, using F10/**S**etting/**P**ageLayout /**W**idth, if you will be using condensed print with 3-up labels on standard size forms. If you are using a different size label, make sure that the pagewidth is equal to the width (in characters) of one label.

6. Add pagewidths to the report specification as needed by using F10/**S**etting/**P**ageLayout/**I**nsert. To print three columns of labels, use this sequence of commands twice to add two pagewidths to the report.

See Chapter 16 if you are having problems with pagelength.

7. Make sure the pagelength is set appropriately. Use **C** for continuous forms or type the number of lines which your printer will print on a page if you are using separate label sheets. For example, if you are using a Hewlett-Packard LaserJet with special labels for that printer, you can set the pagelength to 60. If you are using other labels, you need to calculate the number of lines to be printed and the margins for each page. Then, send an appropriate setup string to the printer using F10/**S**etting/**S**etup/**C**ustom. The report specification for 3-up labels can be seen in Figure 6.40, and the resulting labels in Figure 6.41.

Report Tips

Creating a "Summary Only" Report

It is easy to create a report which includes only summary information. Simply delete all lines from your table band using Ctrl-Y. The resulting

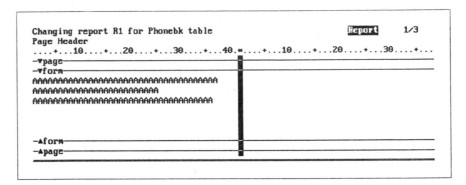

Figure 6.40 Report specification to print labels from PHONEBK

```
Ozzie Donaldson        Grandma Eddie          Lizzie Paymar
1775 Terrace Drive     200 W. 90th Street     123 Main St.
Belmont CA 94002       New York NY 10024      Santa Monica CA 90400


Harold Auguste         Gloria Wilson          Alexander Graet
12345 National Parkway 45 Lone Pine Way       2005 Terrace Dr.
New York NY 10000      Devonshire TN          Belmont CA 94002


Jade Lee               Apple Health Store     Marissa Bird
571 Lone Star Parkway  El Camino and Real     Two Pacific Blvd.
West Hills CA 95555    Redwood City CA 94600  Venice CA 90290


Red Aaron              Angel's Pasta          Teri Albright
123 Sheridan Road      987 First St.          456 E. 82nd St.
Highwood IL 60040      San Francisco CA 94000 NY NY 10028
```

Figure 6.41 3-Up labels from report specification in Figure 6.40

report specification will look like the one shown in Figure 6.42. With no detail information included for any of the records, the report shows only summary information for each order in ORDERLET.

Page Totals

It may seem logical to place a Summary field in a Page Footer if you want page totals. This will not work, however. Once a record has been printed, the current record is the next one to be printed. Because of this, Paradox will include the first record from the next page in any Summary fields in the Page Footer. One way around this is to group records using the number of records which will fit onto each page. Then you can place a Summary field in the Group Footer to get accurate page totals. (This works only if you can have a fixed number of records on each page.)

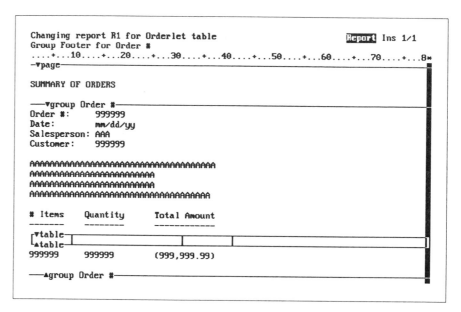

Figure 6.42 Report specification with empty Table Band

Placing Group Footers at the Bottom of a Page

As a last resort, place dummy records with blank detail values in your table so each group has the same number of records.

Whenever you have a Group Footer, Paradox prints the footer information after the last record in the group. Sometimes, it may be desirable to place the Group Footer in a fixed position on the page, rather than having it "float" after the last group record. For example, you may be printing invoices on pre-printed forms and want the total to print in a box at the bottom of the page. Unless every invoice has the same number of detail items, the Group Footer may not actually land in the right spot.

If your printer recognizes a vertical tab control code, you can use it to work around the problem. Place a Calculated field in the first line of the Group Footer. Use the printer control code for a vertical tab as the expression for the Calculated field. Be sure to enclose the control code within quotation marks because it is a literal value.

When Paradox reaches the Group Footer, it will send the vertical tab control code to the printer. The printer should then advance to the desired location on the page before the Group Footer is printed.

Sending Form Feeds

When you use the PAGEBREAK command, Paradox sends line-feeds to the printer. The number sent is based on the current line position and the pagelength specified. If you want to send a form-feed, ASCII 12, to the printer, place a Calculated field using the expression "\012" (being sure to type the opening and closing quotation marks, too).

This can be useful if you are having problems setting the pagelength. Try setting the pagelength to "C" for continuous and placing the form-feed Calculated field if you don't need any Page Headers or Footers. You may be able to incorporate any desired headers or footers into other report specification areas if they are needed.

Printing More than One Report on the Same Page

Print more than one short report on the same page by setting the pagelength to "C" for continuous.

Paradox usually advances the paper to the top of the next page at the end of a report. This can be a problem if you want to print more than one short report on the same page. You can get around this by setting the pagelength to "C." Then, Paradox will stop at the end of the report instead of advancing to the next page.

"Percent of Total" Fields

You cannot use Calculated Summary fields in a report to place "percent of total" fields for individual records or groups. That is because Paradox does not know the overall sum of a field until it has finished processing the entire report. To get around this, restructure your table and add a field to hold the sum needed for such a calculation. Then, use a Calc query to get the sum. You can assign the sum to the new field using a Changeto query. This new field can then be used in a calculated expression such as *[Field A] / [Sum of A] * 100* to show the "percent of total" value.

Summary

You can change the "R" report or copy another report specification to that slot for use with Alt-F7.

You can use the Report Generator to create different documents using information in your tables. Chapter 6 showed you how to use the commands available in Report mode to design and print reports. Here are the key things to remember about reports:

- Paradox will create a Standard Report for a table if you press Alt-F7 while viewing the table. The Standard Report is simply a tabular listing of all the records in the table.
- You can create up to 15 custom report specifications for each table using **Report/Design**.

- There are two types of reports, Tabular and Free-form. Each has slightly different menus in Report mode to offer features unique to each report type.

- To print a report other than the "R" report, use **R**eport/**O**utput from the Main Menu.

- There are other commands available on the Report Menu which let you send override setup strings to a printer, print a subset of a report, change a report specification, or send a report to the screen or to a file.

- You can link a lookup table to a report table using **F**ield/**L**ookup on the Report Menu. Lookup tables must be keyed and all the key fields must be in the master report.

- Reports are built around one table and report on all records in that table.

- To use a custom report with an ANSWER table, use **T**ools/**C**opy /**R**eport/**D**ifferentTable to copy the desired report from a table with the same structure as ANSWER; don't rename ANSWER with the name of the table the report is designed for—if you do, the table *and* its report will be deleted.

Putting Queries and Reports to Work

We have already looked at how to design tables, set up multi-table forms, create queries, and generate reports using the order-entry example for The Raspberry Patch. This chapter will show you how to build on these Paradox objects and set up procedures to:

- Print order-confirmation letters
- Generate invoices at shipment time
- Post payments
- Generate statements
- Update customer balances

The steps necessary to do these tasks interactively are outlined in this chapter. Chapters 10 through 12 will show you how to automate these tasks further using recorded scripts and PAL.

Note: For the reports and queries in this chapter to work, you must have Blanks=0 set to Yes. This option is set using the Custom script. See Chapter 13 for details on using the Custom script.

Order-Confirmation Letters

In Chapter 6, we designed a report for a table called ORDERLET to print order-confirmation letters. ORDERLET was the renamed ANSWER table from a query linking ORDERS and DETAIL. It contained the header and detail information for each Raspberry Patch order.

We can use the same report to create letters for new orders without re-creating the report specification. Here is the way to do it.

The Query

First, use Ask to create a query on ORDERS and DETAIL for any new orders which have been entered. Assuming that letters are sent out once a week, the query shown in Figure 7.1 will select all orders entered during the past week.

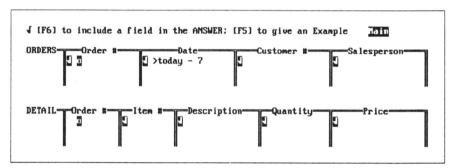

Figure 7.1 Query on ORDERS and DETAIL

The Report

In Chapter 6, we executed the same query on ORDERS and DETAIL but without selection criteria in the Date field. The ANSWER table was renamed ORDERLET. Then, a report was designed for ORDERLET to print order-confirmation letters. The report specification is shown in Figures 7.2 and 7.3.

The trick now is to be able to use the report from ORDERLET with ANSWER. We cannot simply rename ANSWER to ORDERLET again. This would cause Paradox to delete ORDERLET along with all of its family members. (Remember that Paradox will not save family members when the corresponding table has been deleted.)

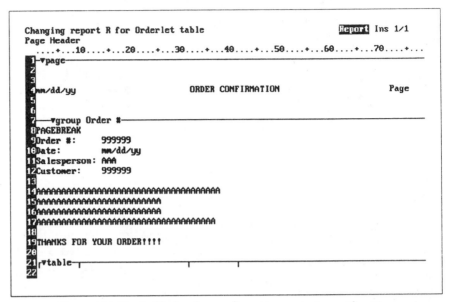

Figure 7.2 Top half of order-confirmation report specification

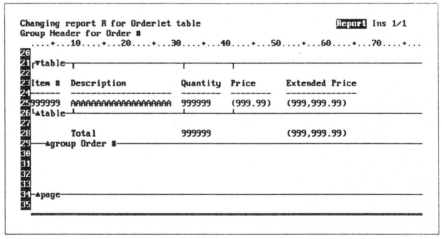

Figure 7.3 Bottom half of order-confirmation report specification

Using Tools/Copy/Report

Since the ANSWER from the query shown in Figure 7.1 has the same structure as ORDERLET, we can copy the custom report from ORDER-LET to ANSWER. Use **T**ools/**C**opy/**R**eport/**D**ifferentTable/ORDERLET /R/ANSWER/R from the Main Menu. You can then use **R**eport/**O**utput /ANSWER/R to get order-confirmation letters for the new orders in

ANSWER. Or, if you are viewing ANSWER, just press Alt-F7 to get the new letters.

This is one of the keys to using Paradox effectively. Perform a query, rename the ANSWER table, and design a report for the renamed table. Then, use **Tools/Copy/R**eport to use the custom report with other ANSWER tables which have the same structure.

Recording the Action

Although it is not necessary, you may want to add a field to ORDERS to note the date that a letter was sent. Figure 7.4 shows the structure of ORDERS after adding this field using **Modify/R**estructure.

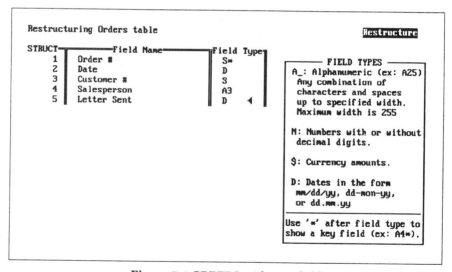

Figure 7.4 ORDERS with new field

Save these steps to a script to automate the process.

To update the Letter Sent field, you can use a query such as the one shown in Figure 7.5. Here, we look for any orders selected in the query shown in Figure 7.1 and change the Letter Sent value to today's date.

The approach outlined here will work to generate letters in a batch mode. The batch of orders processed depends on the selection criteria used in the query in the first step.

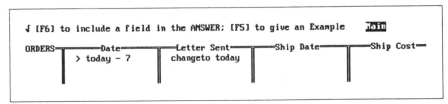

Figure 7.5 Query to update Letter Sent field in ORDERS

Invoices

Once orders are taken, we will want to fill them and send out invoices for the total sales amounts. Most of the information needed to print invoices is already in ORDERS, CUSTOMER, and DETAIL. There are a few more pieces of information to track, though. We need to be able to note the Ship Date for each order and also to add the shipping charges to each order's cost. The example will show one way you can do this.

We will also need to consider whether an order will be shipped exactly as it was entered. In the simplest case, you are always able to fill complete orders. The first part of this example shows how to generate invoices and assumes that complete orders are always shipped.

The last part of the example illustrates how to generate an invoice for a partially filled order. The approach is simple and can be utilized without programming. A means of tracking the unfulfilled portion of these orders is not included here, but could be implemented fairly easily using appropriate queries.

Selecting Shipped Orders

Let's assume that we always want to generate invoices the same day that orders are filled. We need a way to select those orders for printing. We can add a field, called Ship Date, to ORDERS for this purpose. ORDERS can then be queried using **today** in the Ship Date field to select orders for invoicing.

The field for shipping charges will be used later in a report calculated field to get the total order cost.

At the same time, we can add a field for shipping charges to ORDERS. Figure 7.6 shows the new structure of ORDERS after the two new fields have been added using **Modify/Restructure**. (For this example, assume that all orders are going to resellers and do not need to include sales tax. Another field, for sales tax, could be added if necessary, though.)

We can create a new form which includes these new fields to record the shipment of orders. Use **Tools/Copy/Form/SameTable /ORDERS/F/1** to copy the form used for entering orders. Then, use

Forms/Change/ORDERS/1 and add the new fields to the new form. This form will be used to record when an order is shipped and the shipping charges.

To record when an order has been shipped, you can Edit or Coedit ORDERS and use Image/PickForm/1. Paradox will display ORDERS with the new form as shown in Figure 7.7. Type the Ship Date, and the charges for each order which is being shipped. Press F2 to save these changes.

```
Restructuring Orders table                                    Restructure

STRUCT        Field Name          Field Type        — FIELD TYPES —
   1    Order #                        S*       A_: Alphanumeric (ex: A25)
   2    Date                           D            Any combination of
   3    Customer #                     S            characters and spaces
   4    Salesperson                    A3           up to specified width.
   5    Letter Sent                    D            Maximum width is 255
   6    Ship Date                      D
   7    Ship Cost                      $        N: Numbers with or without
                                                   decimal digits.

                                                $: Currency amounts.

                                                D: Dates in the form
                                                   mm/dd/yy, dd-mon-yy,
                                                   or dd.mm.yy

                                                Use '*' after field type to
                                                show a key field (ex: A4*).
```

Figure 7.6 New ORDERS structure

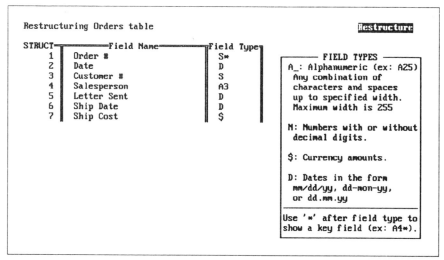

Figure 7.7 New form for ORDERS

To select orders for invoicing, you can use the query shown in Figure 7.8. This query links ORDERS and DETAILS and selects only orders which have today's date in the Ship Date field. All fields necessary for the invoices are Checkmarked.

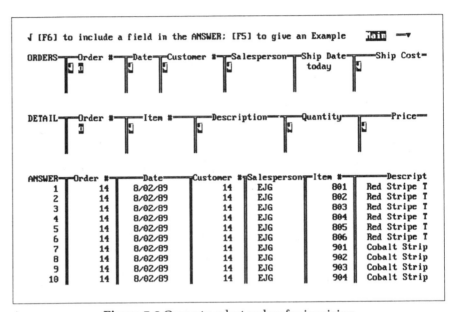

Figure 7.8 Query to select orders for invoicing

Creating an Invoice Report

After processing the query shown in Figure 7.8, *the first time only,* rename ANSWER using **T**ools/**R**ename/**T**able/ANSWER/INVRPT. This step needs to be done only once. For subsequent queries, go to the next section, "Using the Invoice Report."

After ANSWER has been renamed, design a report which can be used to generate invoices. The report specifications shown in Figures 7.9 and 7.10 utilize the following features to print invoices:

- A group on Order # organizes the detail records for printing.
- CUSTOMER is linked as a lookup table.
- All customer information is in the Group Header; Calculated fields are used for the Customer Name, and the City, State, and Zip lines.
- All unnecessary columns have been deleted from the Table Band using TableBand/**E**rase.

- PAGEBREAK is used in the Group Header to print each invoice on a separate page.
- A Calculated field, with the expression *Sum([Quantity] ∗ [Price], group) + [Ship Cost]*, is used to display the total invoice amount in the Group Footer.

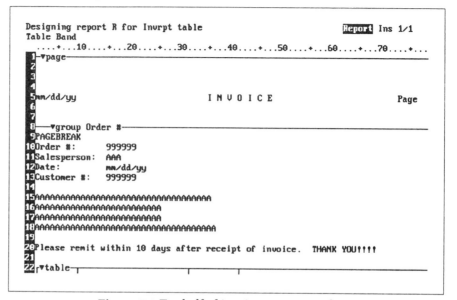

Figure 7.9 Top half of invoice report specification

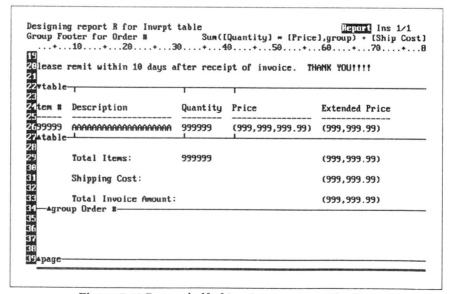

Figure 7.10 Bottom half of invoice report specification

Using the Invoice Report

The first time that you generate invoices, you can use **R**eport/**O**utput /INVRPT/R to print, using the records in INVRPT, the renamed ANSWER table. INVRPT can then be emptied using **T**ools/**E**mpty /INVRPT. The records in INVRPT are no longer needed once they have been invoiced. All underlying information is still in ORDERS and DETAIL.

You can also press Alt-F7 while viewing ANSWER to send the R report to the printer.

To print invoices from ANSWER tables generated on later dates, first use **T**ools/**C**opy/**R**eport/**D**ifferentTable/INVRPT/R/ANSWER/R to copy the invoice report created in the last section. Then use **R**eport/**O**utput/ANSWER/R to print the new invoices from the records in ANSWER.

Invoicing Partial Shipments

We will use a simple approach here to keep track of partial shipments and invoice them accurately. The example is based on the invoice query and report created in the last section. A few changes are necessary to handle additional information for possible ship amount differences.

New Field for DETAIL

First, add a Short number field, called Ship Qty, to DETAIL using **M**odify/**R**estructure. The new structure of DETAIL is shown in Figure 7.11. (The STRUCT table was created using **T**ools/**I**nfo/**S**tructure /DETAIL.)

Instead of creating a new table for shipments, minimize the duplication of information by adding a field to an existing table.

This new field will be used to record the actual number of items shipped for each item in DETAIL before an invoice is generated. For the example here, we will fill out this field for each record in DETAIL, even if the shipped amount matches the order amount. (You could fill in Ship Qty only for items where the number shipped is not equal to the number ordered. Then, use a Changeto query to update blank Ship Qty fields from the Quantity field before executing the invoice query and printing the report.)

New Forms for ORDERS and DETAIL

To record the shipment amounts in the new Ship Qty field, we need to create a new form for ORDERS. We can copy the ORDERS form used to enter new orders and then modify it. Use **T**ools/**C**opy/**F**orm/**S**ameTable /ORDERS/F/1 to get a new form.

Since the Ship Qty field is in DETAIL, we also need to create a new multi-record form to embed in the master ORDERS form. Use

Tools/Copy/Form/SameTable/DETAIL/1/2 to copy the multi-record form embedded in the order-entry form. Use F10/Forms/Change/DETAIL/2 to make the following changes to the new form:

- Use F10/Field/Erase to remove the Extended Price Calculated field from the first line of the multi-record area.
- Place the new Ship Qty field in the area created in the last step by using F10/**Field**/**P**lace/**R**egular.
- Optionally, remove the other fields on the form and re-place them as DisplayOnly fields to protect the order information.

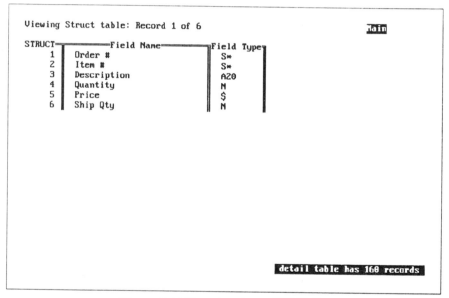

Figure 7.11 New structure of DETAIL

Save the changes to the new DETAIL form by pressing F2. Now we are ready to embed the new form in the master ORDERS form.

Choose Forms/Change/ORDERS/1 to bring up the new ORDERS form. We need to delete the old multi-record form before we can embed the new DETAIL form. Follow these steps to create a new shipping information form:

- Use F10/Multi/Tables/**R**emove. When prompted, move the cursor to the multi-record portion of the form, and press Enter to delete the old multi-record form.
- Use F10/Multi/Tables/Place/Linked, type **DETAIL** when prompted for a table name, and choose Order # as the linking field. Specify **2**

as the DETAIL form to embed, and place it into the area vacated by the old multi-record form.

- Backspace over the literal for Extended Price and type a new field label, **Ship Quantity**.

Save the changes using F2, and the new ORDERS form is ready for use. You can see it in Figure 7.12. When it is time to ship orders, Edit or Coedit ORDERS using this form and type the shipping information for date, shipping charges and amounts. You can use Ctrl-Z in the Order # field to locate individual orders quickly for updating.

```
Editing Orders table with form F1: Record 15 of 16            Edit  ▲-▼

    Order #:    14              Ship Date:   8/20/89   ◄
      Date:  8/02/89
 Salesperson: EJG               Ship Cost:    12.00
  Customer #:    14

   First Name: Angelina
    Last Name: Dominicelli
 Company Name: Brown Berries
      Address: 5757 Ocean Drive
         City: Malibu           State: CA  Zip: 90555

 Item #  Description           Quantity       Price     Ship Quantity
 ------  ------------          --------       -----     -------------
    801  Red Stripe Tank Suit      4           6.00           3
    802  Red Stripe Tank Suit      4           6.00           3
    803  Red Stripe Tank Suit      4           6.00           3
    804  Red Stripe Tank Suit      4           7.00           3
    805  Red Stripe Tank Suit      4           7.00           3
    806  Red Stripe Tank Suit      4           7.00           3
    901  Cobalt Stripe Bikini      4           6.00           4
    902  Cobalt Stripe Bikini      4           6.00           4
```

Figure 7.12 Shipping Form for ORDERS

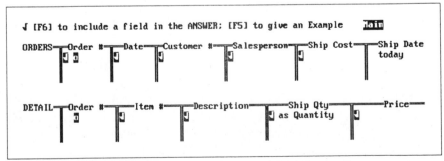

Figure 7.13 Query on ORDERS and DETAIL for invoices

The Query

To copy a report from one table to another, the tables must have the same structure.

The same query used in the simple invoice example can be used with one minor change. We need to tell Paradox to use the Ship Amount field, rather than the Quantity field, in the ANSWER table. You can see this in Figure 7.13. Note the use of the As keyword to rename the *Ship Qty* field to *Quantity* in ANSWER. This makes the structure of ANSWER identical to that of INVRPT, the table which has the invoice report created in the last example.

You can use PAL to prompt the user for a date to use in the query. See Chapter 11 for an example.

Again, we are still using *today* in the Ship Date field to select only those records which were shipped today. For this query to work, it must be run the same day orders are shipped and updated with shipping information.

The Report

Since ANSWER has the same structure as INVRPT, we can use F10/**T**ools/**C**opy/**R**eport/**D**ifferentTable/INVRPT/R/ANSWER/R to copy the custom invoice report to ANSWER. Then, with the cursor in ANSWER, press Alt-F7 to print invoices for the newly-shipped orders.

Recording Transactions

The ORDERS and DETAIL tables have all information on every order shipped. However, the final total for each shipped order is not shown in one place. To make it easier to post payments, let's create a table to hold that information. That same table can be used to post payments, credits and returns, and sales information.

The Table

"Flag" fields are a useful technique that make it easy to categorize information. Lookup tables can be used to fill in more descriptive information in reports.

First, create a table called *TRANS*. The structure of that table is shown in Figure 7.14. It has a one-character code field which can be used for a transaction code such as *S* for sale, *P* for payment, *C* for credit, *R* for return. It also has an Order # field to keep track of payments and charges.

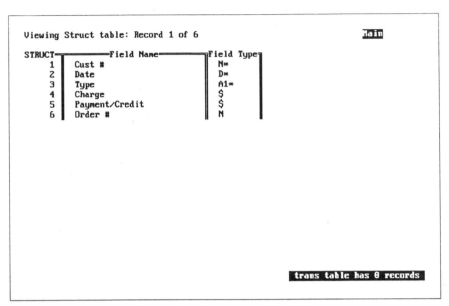

Figure 7.14 Structure of TRANS

The Queries

Before we can post sales to TRANS, we must consolidate the information in ORDERS and DETAIL. It will take three queries to get one sales total for each shipped order and place it in TRANS. Figure 7.15 shows the first query. That query calculates the extended price for each item in DETAIL which is part of an order shipped today. The second query, shown in Figure 7.16, calculates the sum of the extended prices for each order in ANSWER. You can see the ANSWER table from this query in Figure 7.17.

Finally, the query shown in Figure 7.18 inserts the sums and corresponding shipping charges from the ANSWER table seen in Figure 7.17, into TRANS as one record. That query illustrates how you can use an Insert query to place a calculated result into the target table.

Posting Payments

We could simply Edit or Coedit TRANS to record payment information. It would be useful, though, to be able to see a customer's past transactions while posting. To facilitate this, let's design a multi-table form using CUSTOMER and TRANS.

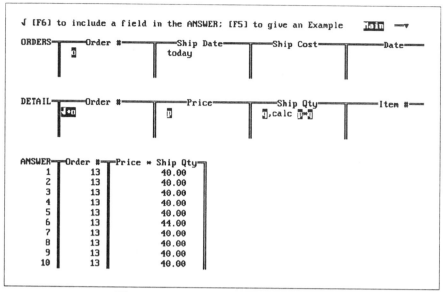

Figure 7.15 First query for posting sales

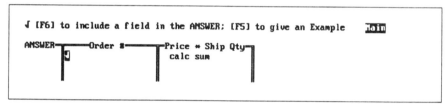

Figure 7.16 Second query for posting sales

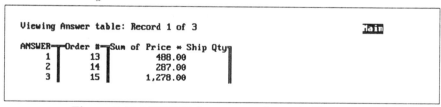

Figure 7.17 ANSWER from query shown in Figure 7.16

There is a one-to-many relationship between CUSTOMER and TRANS.

CUSTOMER will be the master table. That way, you can display a transaction history by customer. CUSTOMER is keyed on Customer #, while TRANS is keyed on Customer #, Date, and transaction Type. We can link the two tables on Customer # using a multi-table form.

First, we need to design a multi-record form for TRANS which can be embedded in the CUSTOMER form. This multi-record form should have all fields from TRANS, *except* the linking field, Customer #. To design the form, use **Forms/Design/TRANS** from the Main Menu.

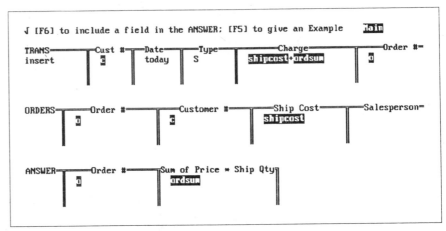

Figure 7.18 Final query to post sales

Take time to design forms so they are easy to read and use.

Once you are in Form mode, use F10/**Field**/**P**lace to place each field on the first line of the form. Be sure to leave a margin on either side of the line. If you don't, the form will not fit neatly within the border of the master form. All fields, except Charges, can be placed as `Regular` fields. The Charges field should be placed as a `DisplayOnly` field to protect it from being changed while payments are posted. It also makes posting payments easier because the cursor will move directly from the Type field to Payments/Credits.

To create the multi-record area, choose **Multi**/**R**ecords/**D**efine from the Form Menu. When prompted, use the cursor to point to either side of the first line, being careful to maintain the margin on either side of the line. Then, using the down-arrow key, extend the multi-record area 12 additional lines, and press Enter to complete the process.

Save the multi-record form for TRANS using F2. The next step is to embed this form into a form for CUSTOMER. First, design a form for CUSTOMER which looks like the top half of the form shown in Figure 7.19. Before saving the new CUSTOMER form, use **Multi**/**T**ables /**P**lace/Linked from the Form Menu and specify TRANS as the table to link. Choose Customer # as the linking field and the form designed above for TRANS as the form which to embed. Place the TRANS multi-record form on the bottom half of the CUSTOMER form, aligning it within the border. As the last step, you can protect the information in CUSTOMER from inadvertent changes by making it `DisplayOnly`. Use **Multi**/**T**ables/DisplayOnly/**M**aster to do this.

To post payments using the new form, Edit or Coedit CUSTOMER and use F10/**I**mage/**P**ickForm to bring up the multi-table form designed above. You can use Ctrl-Z on the Customer # or Customer Name field to locate a specific customer quickly. (If you use this method to find customers, you will get better performance using Coedit mode. Information on why this is so will be included in Chapter 14, "Performance Tips.") Then, press F4 to move to the TRANS portion of the form and post payments.

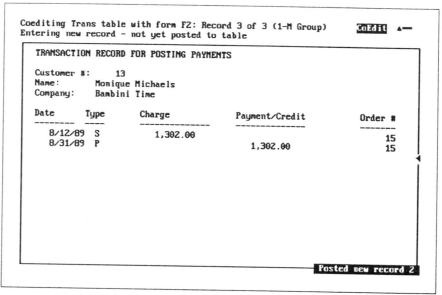

Figure 7.19 Multi-table form to post payments

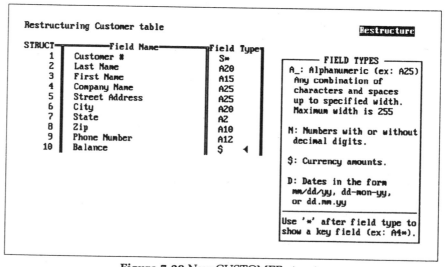

Figure 7.20 New CUSTOMER structure

Statements

Information about each customer's transactions is included in TRANS. The current balance for each customer's account can be calculated from the records in TRANS by subtracting the sum of the Payments/Credits field from the sum of the Charges field. You can use a Calculated Summary field in a report to do this easily.

To create a statement which includes the balance from the prior month takes a little more work. This example shows one way to do it. The approach is to add a field for Balance to CUSTOMER as shown in Figure 7.20. This field will be updated each month *after* statements have been generated. Queries are used to do the updating. First, let's look at how to create statements. After that has been covered, how to update the Balance field will be illustrated.

The Statements Query

Assuming that we want to include only the previous month's transactions on each statement, we need to perform a query to select these records. Figure 7.21 shows a query which will select only August's records for TRANS. (How to create a query using a variable for the month will be described in Chapter 11, "Introduction to PAL.")

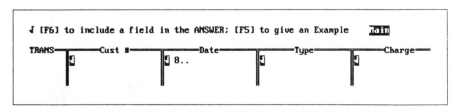

Figure 7.21 Query to select transactions for statements

As in other examples where we reported on an ANSWER table, the ANSWER table should be renamed, using **T**ools/**R**ename/**T**able /ANSWER/STMNTS, the first time the query is run. Then, a report can be designed to generate statements using the permanent table, STMNTS. Statements for future months can be printed by using **T**ools/**C**opy/**R**eport/**D**ifferentTable/STMNTS/R/ANSWER/R and then reporting on ANSWER.

The Report

STMNTS, the renamed ANSWER table, is used as the basis for the statement report. CUSTOMER is linked to STMNTS as a lookup table to provide information on the starting balance. The final report is shown in Figures 7.22 and 7.23. It includes the following:

- A group on Customer #
- A lookup on the CUSTOMER table so that the Balance field from CUSTOMER, along with other customer information, can be placed in the Group Header
- PAGEBREAK in the Group Header to start each statement on a separate page
- A list of all transactions for the previous month in the Table Band
- A Calculated field in the Group Footer with the expression *[Customer->Balance] + Sum([Charges] − [Payments/Credits], group)* to show the new balance
- **S**etting/**F**ormat/**G**roupsOfTables is used to place the Table Band header below each Group Header

An example of the statement produced by this report specification is shown in figure 7.24.

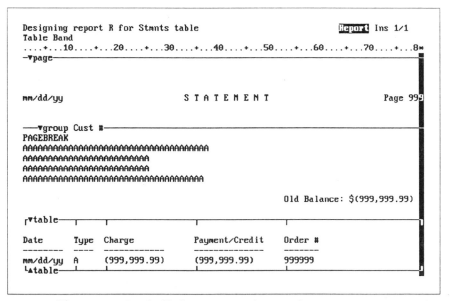

Figure 7.22 Top half of report specification for statements

Updating Balances

After statements are generated, the Balance field in CUSTOMER must be updated. We can do this with two queries. The first query is shown in Figure 7.25. Here, we total transactions, by customer, for the month of

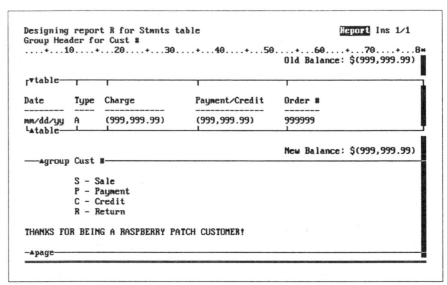

```
Designing report R for Stmnts table                    Report Ins 1/1
Group Header for Cust #
....+...10....+...20....+...30....+...40....+...50....+...60....+...70....+...8*
                                                  Old Balance: $(999,999.99)

  ┌▼table─┬──────┬──────────────┬─────────────────┬──────────────
  Date      Type   Charge          Payment/Credit    Order #
  ────────  ────   ──────────────  ─────────────────  ───────
  mm/dd/yy  A      (999,999.99)    (999,999.99)       999999
  └▲table─┴──────┴──────────────┴─────────────────┴──────────────

                                                  New Balance: $(999,999.99)

 ──▲group Cust #────────────────────────────────────────────────

          S - Sale
          P - Payment
          C - Credit
          R - Return

 THANKS FOR BEING A RASPBERRY PATCH CUSTOMER!

 ──▲page──────────────────────────────────────────────────────
```

Figure 7.23 Bottom half of report specification for statements

August. (Again, Chapter 11 will show you how to use a variable month in the query.) The resulting ANSWER table is shown in the same Figure.

The second query performs a Changeto on CUSTOMER, using summary information from the first query, to update the Balance field. Figure 7.26 illustrates that query. This is another example of how to perform arithmetic with a Changeto query to update one table against another.

Keeping Balances Current

You must execute the above two queries, using the appropriate month, of course, to update the balances after generating statements. If you don't update the balances, they will not be accurate for the next month's statements. In Chapter 11, we'll look at how to use scripts and a bit of PAL code to automate this process.

If You Forget

Since a record of all transactions is kept in TRANS, it is always possible to recalculate Balance information if necessary.

Using the TRANS table, and the Balance field in CUSTOMER, it is easy to recalculate balances if you suspect that they are not correct. First, use a Changeto query on CUSTOMER, such as the one shown in Figure 7.27, to change all balances to 0. Next, execute the two queries shown in Figures 7.25 and 7.26, *without* placing any criteria in the Date field of

```
      8/23/89                    S T A T E M E N T                    Page    1


      Angelina Dominicelli
      Pour Les Enfants
      999 Main Street
      Santa Monica CA 90200


                                                   Old Balance: $     500.00


      Date     Type  Charge        Payment/Credit    Order #
      --------  ----  ------------  --------------    -------
      8/02/89  S        506.00                          13
      8/12/89  P                       500.00           13


                                                   New Balance: $     506.00
```

```
      S - Sale
      P - Payment
      C - Credit
      R - Return

THANKS FOR BEING A RASPBERRY PATCH CUSTOMER!
```

Figure 7.24 Statement

TRANS, to select records. That way, Paradox will summarize all records in TRANS and use the overall totals to update the Balance field.

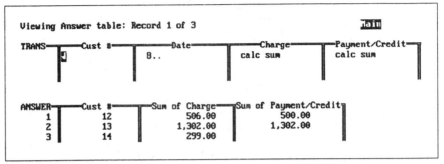

Figure 7.25 Query to summarize TRANS

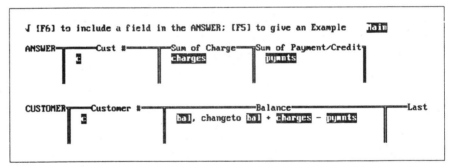

Figure 7.26 Query to update Balance

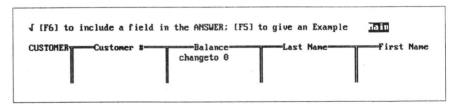

Figure 7.27 Changeto on CUSTOMER

Summary

This chapter showed you how you can use queries and reports together to create order-confirmation letters, invoices, and statements. It also showed you how to maintain a transaction record and update balances. These are the keys to the process:

- Using appropriate selection criteria, query out the records with which you want to work.

- The first time you perform a query for a particular operation, rename the ANSWER table and design any custom reports which are needed for the new table.

- The next time you use the same query, *don't* rename ANSWER with the name of the report table. Doing so will erase any custom reports which you have designed.

- Use **T**ools/**C**opy/**R**eport/**D**ifferentTable to copy the custom report from the permanent table to ANSWER.

- Then, report on ANSWER using **R**eport/**O**utput/ANSWER and the report copied in the last step.

- If you do calculations in queries and reports involving blank values, make sure you have `Blanks=0` set to `Yes` in your PARA-DOX3.CFG file; this option is set using the Custom script.

You will learn how you can automate regular processes such as those in this chapter using Scripts. Chapters 10 through 12 will show you how to create scripts and customize them using PAL.

Graphs

Chapters 6 and 7 showed you how to use Paradox reports to create
different kinds of documents with information from tables. Using
reports, you can summarize information and display it in many different formats. However, the information is always presented as text. You
may have to read reports carefully in order to glean important facts and
patterns.

It is usually easier to distinguish patterns or key characteristics of
information by looking at a "picture." You can use Paradox's Graph
mode to create pictures or graphs from your tables. This chapter covers:

- The types of graphs which you can create with Paradox
- How to use Graph mode to create graphs
- Examples of summarizing and crosstabulating tables for graphing

What Is a Graph?

A graph is a picture which can be used to illustrate the relationship(s)
between groups of information. At least one group of such information
must consist of number values. The comparison group may be made up
of other types of values, such as names or dates. Here are some examples
of information which you can graph using Paradox:

- Sales by item
- Sales amounts per salesperson

- Sales by item by salesperson
- Income over time
- Separate income components over time

Figure 8.1 shows the DETAIL table of The Raspberry Patch's orders. While all information on each item ordered is included, it is difficult to look at that table and immediately see the contribution each item made to overall sales. Looking at a graph like the one shown in Figure 8.2, however, you can see the picture instantly. This graph is a pie chart. There are several ways to look at the same information by using different types of graphs.

```
Viewing Detail table: Record 1 of 160                              Main

DETAIL──Order #──┬──Item #──────────Description───────Quantity─────────Price─
      1       1       305   White Boxer Shorts           20              6.00
      2       1       306   White Boxer Shorts           20              6.00
      3       1       307   White Boxer Shorts           20              6.00
      4       1       308   White Boxer Shorts           20              6.00
      5       1       705   Black Pants                  10              7.50
      6       1       706   Black Pants                  10              7.50
      7       1       707   Black Pants                  10              7.50
      8       1       708   Black Pants                  10              7.50
      9       2       601   Red/White Overalls            5              8.00
     10       2       602   Red/White Overalls            5              8.00
     11       2       603   Red/White Overalls            5              8.00
     12       3       801   Red Stripe Tank Suit          5              6.00
     13       3       802   Red Stripe Tank Suit          5              6.00
     14       3       803   Red Stripe Tank Suit          5              6.00
     15       3       901   Cobalt Stripe Bikini          5              6.00
     16       3       902   Cobalt Stripe Bikini          5              6.00
     17       3       903   Cobalt Stripe Bikini          5              8.00
     18       4       901   Cobalt Stripe Bikini         12              6.00
     19       4       902   Cobalt Stripe Bikini         12              6.00
     20       4       903   Cobalt Stripe Bikini         12              8.00
     21       5       901   Cobalt Stripe Bikini         12              6.00
     22       5       902   Cobalt Stripe Bikini         12              6.00
```

Figure 8.1 DETAIL table of The Raspberry Patch's orders

Types of Graphs

With Graph mode, you can create the following types of graphs:

- Regular bar graphs
- 3-D bar graphs
- Rotated bar graphs
- Stacked bar graphs

- Pie charts
- Line graphs
- Markers graphs
- Lines and Markers graphs
- Area graphs
- X-Y (or scatter) graphs
- Other combined graphs

Pie Charts

Some graphs illustrate relationships better than others. For example, pie charts are wonderful for showing the contribution of individual elements to a whole. The pie chart shown in Figure 8.2 illustrates the relative amounts of The Raspberry Patch items which have been sold.

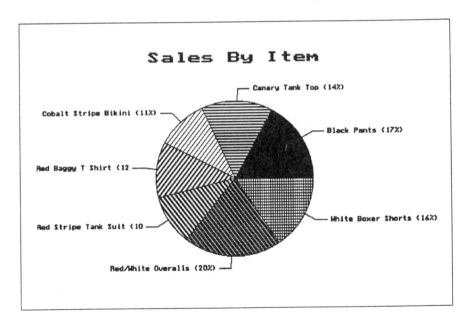

Figure 8.2 Pie chart of sales by item

Bar Graphs

Bar graphs, too, are useful for showing the relationship between groups of items. Figure 8.3 shows the information graphed in Figure 8.2, but using a regular bar graph. In this bar graph, there is one bar on the X (horizontal) axis for each item. The amounts for each item are graphed using the scale on the Y (vertical) axis.

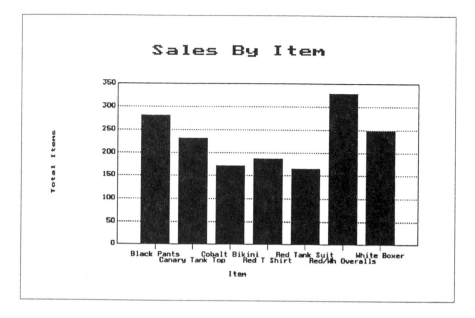

Figure 8.3 Regular bar graph

There are several variations of the bar graph that Paradox can create. Figure 8.4 shows the bar graph from Figure 8.3 but with 3-D shading. The same graph is also shown in Figure 8.5 with the axes switched. The result is a Rotated bar graph where the bars are displayed horizontally, instead of vertically.

Stacked Bar Graphs and Series

If you have more than 6 categories of information, you will need to consolidate some of them.

The graphs shown so far have included only one category of information, the total amount of each item. This amount could be broken down further. For example, the amount for each item could be shown as a separate number for each size. Each size would then represent a separate *series*. Using a Stacked bar graph, you can graph up to six series of information on the same chart.

The Stacked bar graph shown in Figure 8.6 shows sales amounts for each Raspberry Patch salesperson. The bar for each salesperson is made up of separate layers, one for each group of items which that person has sold. Each group of items in this graph represents a different series. The *legend* on the right side of the graph shows how each series is depicted in the bars.

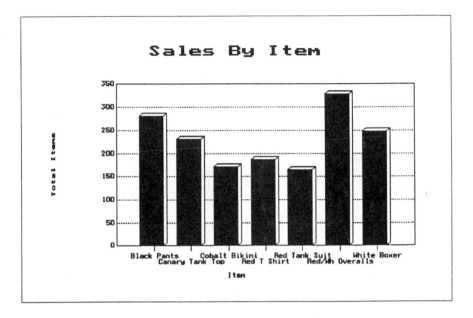

Figure 8.4 3-D bar graph

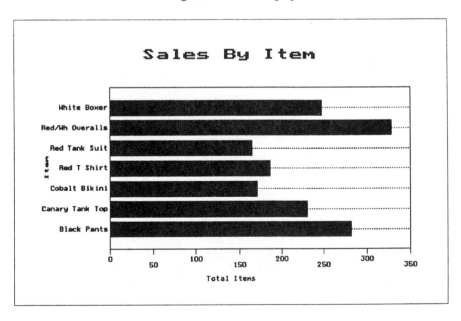

Figure 8.5 Rotated bar graph

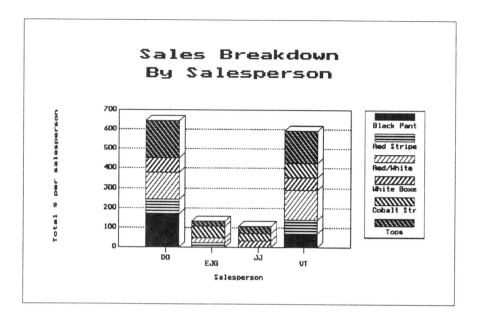

Figure 8.6 3-D Stacked bar graph

Lines and Markers Graphs

There is another category of graphs which are good to represent changes in values over time. These graphs use Lines, Markers, or a combination of these elements, to show trends. In Figure 8.7, you can see a Markers graph which illustrates the total monthly sales for four salespeople. The months run along the X (horizontal) axis and total amounts are plotted on the Y (vertical) axis. This graph illustrates graphing multiple series on the same chart. Here, each salesperson represents a different series.

This same graph is shown in Figure 8.8 with Lines and Markers. With the Lines added, it is easier to follow the sales trend for each person. You can also create a graph using Lines without Markers, for one or more series.

Area Graphs

Area graphs show the relative contribution of separate parts to a whole. They are similar to bar graphs in this way, but Area graphs also show change over time. One area is graphed for each series instead of separate bars for each element on the X-axis. The Area graph shown in Figure 8.9 shows the same information illustrated in the preceding two graphs. Note that the scale along the Y-axis is different here. The points on the graph are not important; it is the relative area of each series which illustrates how much each person has sold.

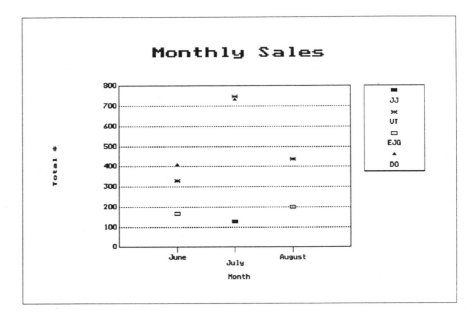

Figure 8.7 Markers graph

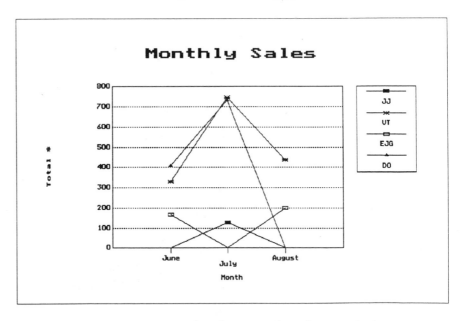

Figure 8.8 Combined Lines and Markers graph

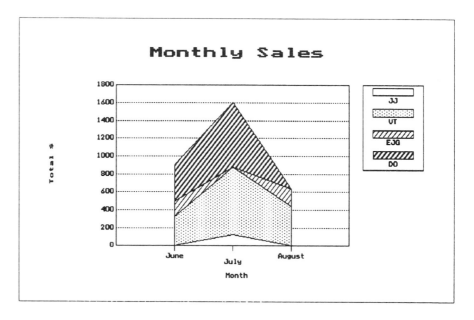

Figure 8.9 Area graph of Raspberry Patch sales

XY Graphs

You can also create XY graphs such as the ones we studied in school. An XY graph can be used to plot how one variable, shown on the X-axis, changes in relation to a second variable, plotted on the Y-axis. You can plot one series of variables as shown in the growth chart illustrated in Figure 8.10. It is possible to plot up to six series of variables on the same XY graph.

Elements of Graphs

If you know the definitions of the elements of a graph, it is easier to use the Image/Graph/Modify menus.

Before we go through examples of how to create some of the graphs shown above, let's look at the elements which make up a graph. It is important to be familiar with this terminology so that you can easily customize your own graphs using the **Image/Graph/Modify** command.

- *Axes* are the lines which define the boundaries of a graph; they also act as a scale for the range of values plotted.
- *Tickmarks* are the small marks along each axis which divide it into separate groups, or ranges, of values.
- The *scale* is the range of values which runs along an axis and determines the placement of tickmarks.

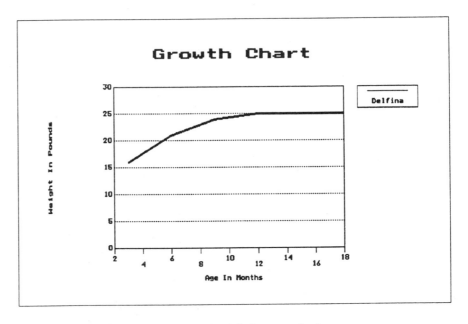

Figure 8.10 XY graph for growth chart

- *Labels* are placed near each tickmark, showing the value which the tickmark represents.
- *Titles* are used to label the graph and each axis.
- *Series* are the different groups of information which may be plotted on the same graph.
- *Legends* indicate how each series is depicted on a graph.

When you use Graph mode to create your graphs, you can specify options for each of these elements, in addition to choosing a graph type. There are forms which you fill out, using **Image/Graph/Modify**, for each element. How to do this will be shown in the examples which follow later in this chapter.

Creating Graphs

The "Instant Graph"

The graph setting contains information on graph type, titles and other graph elements.

There are two ways to generate a graph. You can press Ctrl-F7, the "Instant Graph" key, to send a graph to the screen, or, you can use the **Image/Graph/ViewGraph** commands. Either way, Paradox creates a graph using the current graph settings and the current table on the workspace. This is similar to pressing Alt-F7 to get an "Instant Report" from the current table.

If you have not modified the graph settings, Paradox will generate a Stacked bar graph, the default graph. Except for a change in the title, the graph shown in Figure 8.6 was created using the default graph settings. Paradox will graph up to six series using the default graph settings.

How Paradox Graphs Tables

Before you press Ctrl-F7, though, there is something else to consider. You need to tell Paradox how to use the information in the current table to produce the graph. As you can see in the graph examples shown above, Paradox plots one group of information against another, optionally dividing a group into series.

The fields Paradox uses to create a graph depend on the type of graph you are creating and whether the table to be graphed is keyed. The rules which follow apply for all graphs except pie charts and XY graphs:

The X-Axis

When you graph a keyed table, Paradox automatically uses the last key field for the values along the X-axis. For an unkeyed table, the first non-numeric field is used for the X-axis values. The range of values along the X-axis is determined by the values in the field used for the X-axis.

The Y-Axis

You can use Ctrl-R to put fields in the proper order for graphing.

The values used for the Y-axis are taken from the field that the cursor is in. This field must be Numeric. Paradox will use up to five subsequent Numeric fields for graph values. Each Numeric field is used as a separate series in the graph. The names of the series fields are used as the default titles for the legend.

Pie Charts

Pie charts can include only one series of values. The labels, or categories, for the values are taken from the first non-numeric field in the table. In the example shown in Figure 8.2, the Description field was used for the labels. The values themselves are always taken from the field the cursor is in. This field must be Numeric.

XY Graphs

XY graphs use information in Numeric fields only. The values for the X-axis are taken from the first Numeric field in the table. Values for the first series on Y-axis are taken from the field the cursor is in. This field must be a Numeric field. Values are taken from up to five subsequent Numeric fields for the remaining series.

Use Image/Graph/ViewGraph to send a graph to the printer or a file.

Once you have determined which fields to use for the X- and Y-axes, and for any additional series in your graph, position the cursor appropriately and rotate any fields as needed. Then, press Ctrl-F7. The "Instant Graph" will be sent to the screen automatically.

Summarizing Your Tables for Graphing

Sometimes, your table may not be in a form which can be graphed according to the above rules. There are several ways to change your information. They include:

- Rotating fields
- Queries
- CrossTabs

Rotating Fields

In Chapter 3, we have already seen how to rotate tables using Ctrl-R. To rotate a field to the right-end of the table, place the cursor in the field to be moved and press Ctrl-R. All fields to the right of the cursor will be moved one place to the left.

Rotating fields is an easy way to change the series to be used for a graph. You can create different graphs using the same table, and the same graph setting, by rotating fields to get different series.

Queries

You can use queries to summarize information for graphing. For example, you may want to graph the number of customers for each salesperson. Using a Calc Count query on CUSTOMER, you can get an ANSWER table with the required structure for graphing. The examples later in the chapter will make extensive use of queries to create tables for graphing.

Queries can also be used as a quick way to sort tables. You may at times want to sort a table to force a certain order for values on one or both axes before graphing it.

CrossTabs

You can *crosstabulate* a table using the **Image/Graph** command. Cross-Tabs are necessary to create a graph with different series from a table which has the information for all series in one field. Look at the graph shown in Figure 8.8. All information in this graph was derived from the DETAIL and ORDERS tables. However, the values for different items were all in one field in DETAIL. The `CrossTab` command was used to create a table with one field for each separate item. That way, Paradox could use each item field to create a separate series. An example later in the chapter will illustrate this process.

Customizing Graphs

As mentioned above, the default graph is a Stacked bar graph. Paradox uses the name of the graphed table for the graph title and uses other default titles for the axes and labels. You can change these elements, and others as well, and the graph type, using the **Image/Graph** command.

The Graph Menu

When you choose **Image/Graph** from the Main Menu, you will see a menu with these choices:

- `Modify` lets you change the current graph settings.
- `Load` is used to load a new graph settings file.
- `Save` prompts you for the name of a file in which to save the current graph settings.
- `Reset` sets the graph settings back to their default.
- `CrossTab` provides a way to quickly crosstabulate a table.
- `ViewGraph` generates a graph from the current table and graph settings; the graph can be sent to the screen, a printer or a file.

The Graph Settings File

When you choose a graph type, or change the elements of a graph, Paradox keeps this information in a graph settings file. You can save the changes you make to a graph settings file using the **Image/Graph/Save** command. Paradox will prompt for a file name. All graph settings files have a .G extension.

Any changes which you make using **Image/Graph/Modify** stay in effect for all graphs created in the current session or until you reset or change the graph settings file. You can use **Image/Graph/Reset** to load the default settings or **Image/Graph/Load** to load another graph settings file by name. When you load a graph settings file, the settings determines the format for all graphs which are generated until you exit from Paradox or change the settings again by using the **Image/Graph/Load** or **Image/Graph/Reset** commands. You can set the default graph settings file using the Custom script.

Changing Graph Settings

Graph settings are changed with the **Image/Graph/Modify** commands. When you choose these commands from the Main Menu, you will see the screen shown in Figure 8.11. This screen is the first of many which are available to customize graphs.

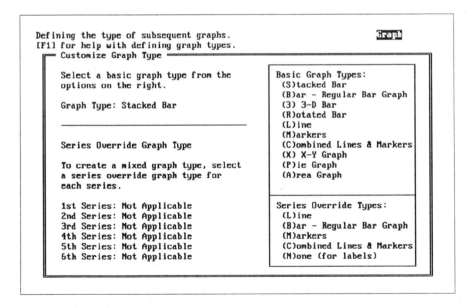

Figure 8.11 Image/Graph/Modify "Graph Type" form

Graph Type

Using this screen, you can quickly change the graph type without going through any other menu choices. The graph types are listed on the right side of the screen. To change the graph type, press the key corresponding to the letter of the desired graph type when the cursor is in the field labeled `Graph Type`. Paradox will automatically fill in the name of the graph type you want.

This screen also is used to tell Paradox which type of graph to use for each series if you want to combine graph types. To do this, move the cursor to the field on the bottom half of the screen for the series you want to change. Again, press the letter of the graph type you want to use.

Getting to the Graph Mode Menu

At this point, if you want to return to Paradox, press F2 or F10/Do-It! Paradox will exit from Graph mode and return you to Main mode. Or, you can go on and change other elements of your graph settings. To move on in the process, press F10 to access the Graph mode Menu.

After pressing F10, you will see the menu shown in Figure 8.12. You can see that it is displayed at the top of the screen for changing the graph type. From this menu, you can access screens for changing all the other graph elements. The screens look similar to the one shown in Figure 8.11 for changing the graph type. You edit them as you do any other Paradox form, using the instructions on the screen. To exit from a screen, you must press F10 to access the Graph mode Menu. There are choices there which allow you to `DO-IT!` or `Cancel` your changes. You cannot use Esc to move up a level as you can in other areas of Paradox.

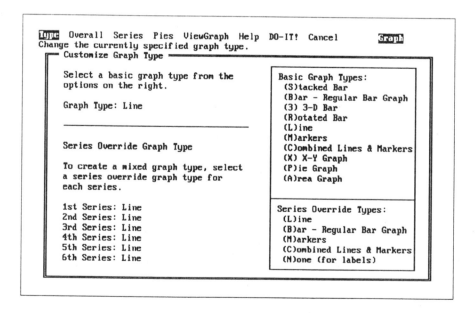

Figure 8.12 Graph mode Menu

Overall Options

When you choose Overall, you will see another menu listing the elements you can change with this command. A different screen will be displayed for each menu choice. The options which you can change are:

- Titles for the graph and the axes, as well as font and sizes
- Colors for the screen and for the printer
- Axes for setting scales and tickmarks
- Grids to choose grid lines and colors and also a graph frame
- PrinterLayout for margins, graph size, orientation, page breaks, and plotter speed
- Device to set the printer (from one of the four defined using the Custom script) or the file type (current printer, .EPS or .PIC)
- Wait to tell Paradox whether to display a graph on the screen until a keystroke is entered or for a duration of time

Series Options

If you choose Series from the Graph Menu, you will see a menu with these choices:

- LegendsAndLabels is used to tell Paradox whether to use a legend, and to change the legend labels if desired.
- MarkersAndFills lets you choose patterns for fills and symbols for markers.

Pies

Using Pies, you can change the label format, colors, and patterns for each "slice" of a pie. You can also tell Paradox whether or not to explode individual pie slices on the graph.

Viewing Your Graph

You can view your graph as you make changes by choosing ViewGraph from the Graph mode Menu or from the **Image/Graph** menu. That way, you can view a graph to see the effect of changes you have made before saving the changes to a settings file. When you choose ViewGraph, you are presented with a menu which lets you send a graph to the screen, a printer, or to a file.

Viewing a Graph on the Screen

When you send a graph to the screen, Paradox gets information about the type of display and graphics being used from the PARADOX3.CFG. If you have problems seeing your graph on the screen, play the Custom script and use **Graphs/Screen** to check the current graph settings. The default is Auto. Paradox should be able to detect the kind of screen you have, but at times you may have to set this yourself.

Sending a Graph to the Printer

Paradox will send a graph to the current printer after you use **Image /Graph/ViewGraph/Printer** or **Image/Graph/Modify/F10/ViewGraph /Printer**. The default current printer is the one in the PARADOX3.CFG file. You can change this to one of four different printers using **Image /Graph/Modify/F10/Overall/Device/Printer** where you are prompted to choose from among the 1st, 2nd, 3rd, or 4th printer. These four printers are defined using the Custom script.

Sending a Graph to a File

If you choose File from the ViewGraph Menu, Paradox sends the graph to a file. The default file format is simply a file which can be sent to the current printer. (See the section above on sending a graph to a printer for information about changing the current printer.)

You can also send a graph to a .PIC or .EPS file. To change the file format, use the commands **Image/Graph/Modify/F10/Overall /Device/File**. Paradox will display a menu with the choices: Current-Printer, EPS and PIC. Choosing EPS creates an Encapsulated PostScript file. PIC saves the file in Lotus .PIC format.

Examples

As mentioned before, it is often necessary to summarize a table before it can be graphed. The following examples show how to create the graphs shown in the first part of this chapter.

Creating a Pie Chart

The pie chart shown in Figure 8.2 is derived from information in the DETAIL table. It shows the total quantity ordered of each Raspberry Patch item. Here are the steps necessary to produce this chart:

1. The first task is to create a table which has the fields necessary for the chart. These fields are Description and another field which has the total amount of each item ordered. The query shown in Figure 8.13, along with its resulting ANSWER table, will do this.

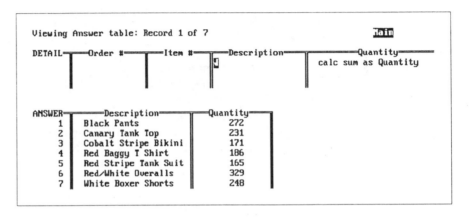

Figure 8.13 Query on DETAIL and resulting ANSWER

At this point, you can generate the default Stacked bar graph by placing the cursor in the Description field and pressing Ctrl-F7. Because there is only one series of values to graph—the quantities—a pie chart is more appropriate. To produce a pie chart, we need to go through a few more steps.

2. Press F10 and choose **I**mage/**G**raph/**M**odify from the menus. The graph type screen will be displayed. Press **P** to change the current graph type to Pie.

3. Press F10 to access the Graph mode Menu. Press **P** to choose `Pies` and press **P** again to change the label format to `Percent`.

The title may appear differently on the screen than on the printed report.

4. Press F10. Choose **O**verall/**T**itles. Type **Sales By Item** in the first field, the field for the Main title. Optionally, you can add a second title line or change the font to be used for the title.

5. The graph can now be viewed on the screen by using F10/**V**iew-Graph/**S**creen or sent to the printer using F10/**I**mage

/ViewGraph/**P**rinter. To save the changes made, press F2 or choose DO-IT! from the Graph Menu.

6. The pie chart graph settings can be saved to a file by using F10/Image/Graph/**S**ave. Paradox will prompt for a file name and save the settings to the file you specify.

Creating Bar Graphs

The ANSWER table used to create the pie chart shown in Figure 8.2 was also used to generate the graphs shown in Figures 8.3 through 8.5. Figure 8.3 shows a Regular bar graph; Figure 8.4 shows a 3-D bar graph; and Figure 8.5 shows a Rotated bar graph. In each case, Image/Graph/**M**odify was used to change the graph type.

A few other changes were also made. First, the ANSWER table was edited to shorten the descriptions for some items. Figure 8.14 shows the edited ANSWER table. The descriptions were shortened so they could be displayed legibly as labels for the X-axis.

It makes sense to change the title for the Y-axis here so that it is more descriptive. Use F10/Image/Graph/**M**odify/F10/**O**verall/**T**itles to change the title. Move the cursor to the field for the Y-axis title and type **Total Items**.

Because there is only one series of values to be graphed, there is no need for a legend on any of these graphs. You can use Image/**G**raph/**M**odify/F10/**S**eries/**L**egendsAndLabels and press **N** in the first field of the form to tell Paradox not to include a legend in a graph.

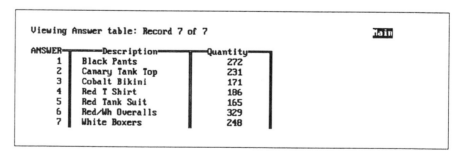

Figure 8.14 Edited descriptions in ANSWER

Creating a Stacked Bar Graph Using CrossTab

When you have more than one series of values to graph, you can use the default Stacked bar graph. The Stacked bar graph in Figure 8.6 shows the total sales amounts for each Raspberry Patch salesperson, divided among six categories of items. Each category, or series, is represented as a separate portion of the bar for each salesperson.

All information in the graph is contained in DETAIL and ORDERS. The trick here is to get the information into a table with a separate field for each series to be graphed. In this case, each item represents a different series. Paradox's `CrossTab` command makes it easy to do this. To generate the graph, take these steps:

1. First, link the ORDERS and DETAIL tables to get an ANSWER table with a separate record for the quantity of each item sold by a particular salesperson. This query and ANSWER are shown in Figure 8.15. The entire ANSWER table is not visible, just the portion which can be displayed on the screen with the query.

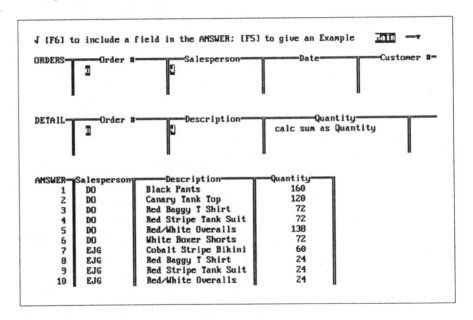

Figure 8.15 Query and ANSWER for Stacked bar graph

2. The next task is to generate a table from ANSWER which has a separate field for each item. That way, the quantities for each salesperson can be in one record. *Salesperson* can be the value for the X-axis, and the quantity fields for each item can be used as a series in the graph.

The `CrossTab` command will generate a table such as this automatically. There are two ways to invoke `CrossTab`: using Alt-X or use Image/Graph/CrossTab. If you use the menu commands, you will be prompted for the type of crosstabulation of values Paradox is to perform. Paradox can calculate the sum, count, minimum, or maximum of the values used to generate the new records in CROSSTAB. Paradox will then prompt for the row label, column label, and values fields.

In this example, we can use Alt-X to generate the default CROSS-TAB table. Place the cursor in the Salesperson field of ANSWER. Press Alt-X to generate the CROSSTAB table shown in Figure 8.16.

```
Viewing Crosstab table: Record 1 of 4                    Main  ▲═

CROSSTAB╤Salesperson╤═Black Pants══╤Canary Tank Top╤Red Baggy T Shirt╤Red Strip
    1 ║   DO        ║     160      ║     120      ║       72        ║    72
    2 ║   EJG       ║       0      ║       0      ║       24        ║    24
    3 ║   JJ        ║      40      ║      36      ║        0        ║     0
    4 ║   UT        ║      72      ║      75      ║       90        ║    69
```

Figure 8.16 CROSSTAB from ANSWER shown in Figure 8.15

This new table has one field for each of the seven items contained in DETAIL, and one record for each salesperson. The number in each field represents the quantity of that item sold by each salesperson.

3. Because Paradox will include only a maximum of six series on a graph, we need to consolidate some of the information in CROSS-TAB further. Figure 8.17 shows a query which sums the amounts for Canary Tank Tops and Red Baggy T Shirts and places the total in a new field called *Tops*. All other fields in CROSSTAB are Checkmarked so that they will be included in ANSWER.

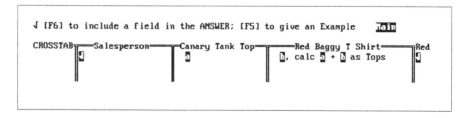

Figure 8.17 Query to consolidate CROSSTAB fields

4. The graph shown in Figure 8.6 can be generated from the resulting ANSWER table. If necessary, use F10/**I**mage/**G**raph/**R**eset to reset the graph settings to the default. Change the graph title, and the

Y-axis title, using F10/**I**mage/**G**raph/**M**odify/F10/**O**verall/**T**itles and press F2 to save the changes. Then, place the cursor in the Black Pants field, the first series, and press Ctrl-F7 to generate the Stacked bar graph on the screen.

Creating a Lines and Markers Graph

Lines and Markers graphs are usually easier to read than Markers graphs.

The graph shown in Figure 8.8 shows the sales figures for The Raspberry Patch salespeople over a period of three months. All information needed to produce the graph is contained in DETAIL and ORDERS, but it needs to be summarized first.

1. Use **Ask** to create an ANSWER table from ORDERS and DETAIL which contains the total amount sold by each salesperson by date. Figure 8.18 shows this query and ANSWER.

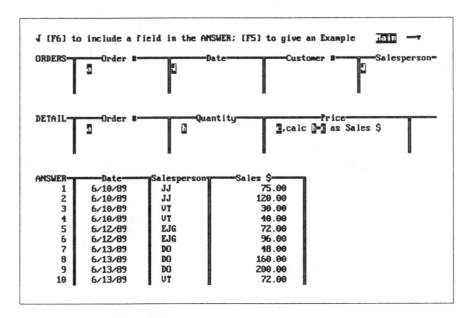

Figure 8.18 Query on ORDERS and DETAIL

2. We need to change the date value in each record in ANSWER to a month name. That way, the records can be summarized, using CROSSTAB, to get totals by month. Before the dates can be changed to the month names, which are Alphanumeric, we need to change the Date field type. Use F10/**M**odify/**R**estructure to change the Date field type from D to **A8**.

3. Execute a Changeto query on ANSWER, such as the one shown in Figure 8.19, to change each date to its corresponding month.

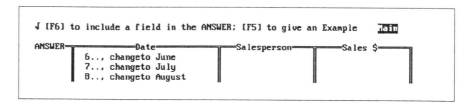

Figure 8.19 Changeto query on ANSWER

4. Place the cursor in the Date field of ANSWER and press Alt-X. Paradox will generate a CROSSTAB table with one record for each month and a field for each salesperson. This table is shown in Figure 8.20.

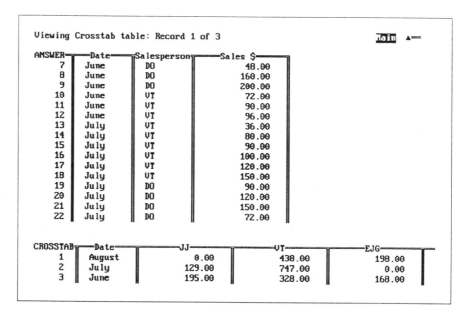

Figure 8.20 CROSSTAB from ANSWER

This example works because of the spelling of the months involved. For other months you might need to create a number month field to sort on.

5. One last thing needs to be done. In the process of creating CROSS-TAB, Paradox sorted the records alphabetically on the month name. If a graph were created now, it would list the months from *August* to *June* along the X-axis. The table needs to be sorted in descending order on the Date field. You can use F10/**Modify**/**Sort**

to do this, or use the query shown in Figure 8.21. Here, the "Check Descending" key, Ctrl-F6, is used to sort the table in descending order. The resulting ANSWER is shown in the same Figure.

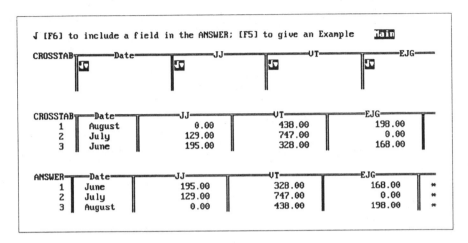

Figure 8.21 Query to sort CROSSTAB

6. The graph can now be produced from the ANSWER table created in the last step. Before pressing Ctrl-F7, let's make a few changes which will make the graph easier to understand. First, use F10/**I**mage/**G**raph/**M**odify to change the graph type to Combined Lines & Markers. Use F10/**O**verall/**T**itles to access the screen and change the title to **Monthly Sales**. Also, change the Y-axis title to **Total $**. Then, press F10 to access the Graph Menu and choose `Series/MarkersAndFills`. Use the screen options to specify the markers you want used for each series. After making these changes, press F2 to exit from Graph mode. To save these settings, use F10/**I**mage/**G**raph/**S**ave and, when prompted, type a name for the graph settings file.

7. Place the cursor in the JJ field of ANSWER and press Ctrl-F7 to send the graph to the screen.

You can create a Line graph, Markers graph or Area graph from the same ANSWER table. To do this, use F10/**I**mage/**G**raph/**M**odify and, in the first field of the form, press the letter corresponding to the desired graph type.

A note on Line graphs: if you are using a monochrome monitor or a black-and-white printer, you will not be able to distinguish between the lines on the graph. You will need to use a Combined Lines & Markers graph if you are graphing more than one series. Otherwise, you will not be able to tell which line corresponds to each series.

Creating a Mixed Type Graph

It is possible to combine Line, Bar and Marker-type graphs on the same graph. You use the same screen which you used to change the graph type. The bottom half of that screen has a line for each of the series which can be included on a graph. By pressing Enter to move to the line for a particular series, you can change the graph type for that series. The letters for each of the possible series override types are listed on the right side of the screen as shown in Figure 8.11.

Presentation Tips

There are several things you can do to maximize the impact of the graphs which you create. Here are a few tips:

Limit Your Categories

Remember that each record is used for a point on X-axis or a slice of a pie chart.

As you saw from the above examples, the most important part of creating a graph is setting up the underlying table correctly. There are two parts to this: making sure that the table has the necessary structure to generate the desired graph, and limiting the number of records in the graphed table. In the above examples, there are very few records in the final tables. This limits the number of points along the X-axis (or the number of slices in a pie chart) and makes the graph easier to comprehend.

Depending upon the graph, you may also want to limit the number of series to less than the six which Paradox allows. You can always consolidate series using a query, as shown in the Stacked bar example above. Looking at "less" information is usually more impactful than trying to figure out an overly-busy graph.

Using Titles and Labels

An accurate title can make all the difference in the usefulness of a graph. If the viewer does not know what the graph values represent, the graph is meaningless. Make sure, too, to include information along the axes which clarifies the graph content.

Scales

There are commands which you can use to change the scales of the axes used in graphs. You may want to "narrow" or to "widen" the ranges used on the axes to maximize the impact of a graph. F10/**I**mage /**G**raph/**M**odify/F10/**O**verall/**A**xes leads you to the screen where the scales can be changed.

Colors and Fills

You may want to emphasize certain areas of a graph. If you are using a color screen or printer, you can use F10/**I**mage/**G**raph/**M**odify/F10 /**O**verall/**C**olors to specify which colors are to be used. For a monochrome screen, or for black-and-white printers, you can use F10 /**I**mage/**G**raph/**M**odify/F10/**S**eries/**M**arkersAndFills to customize the way areas for different series are filled in.

Summary

Sometimes looking at a picture is the easiest way to understand important information. You can create graphs from your Paradox tables using the **I**mage/**G**raph command. Here is a summary of the points which were covered in this chapter:

- You can create a graph from the current table on the workspace by pressing Ctrl-F7.
- Before you press the "Graph Key," Ctrl-F7, make sure the underlying table has the right structure and that the cursor is in the proper field. Paradox uses the current cursor position, and the position of other fields, to determine a graph's structure.
- You can create several different types of graphs: pie charts, Stacked bar graphs, 3-D bar graphs, Regular bar graphs, Line graphs, Markers graphs, XY graphs, and Area graphs. The default graph is a Stacked bar graph.
- Paradox always uses the current graph settings to generate a graph. You can change the settings using **I**mage/**G**raph/**M**odify. You can save graph settings to a file and later load them by name using the **I**mage/**G**raph command.
- **I**mage/**G**raph/**M**odify lets you change the graph type, titles, axes labels, scales and tickmarks, legends and labels, device type and

numerous other graph characteristics. You can change the defaults for these using the Custom script. (See Chapter 13 for details.)

- You can send graphs to the screen, a printer, or to a file.

- Details make the difference—making sure the table you want to graph is summarized ahead of time is necessary. Pay close attention to details such as titles and scales to make sure that your graphs have the greatest possible impact!

Managing Your
Paradox Objects

A table's family can consist of many files. You should keep track of what each file is used for.

One of the most important parts of database management is keeping your files organized and up-to-date. It is also critical, especially while you are developing your system, to know what each file is used for. As you create your queries and other Paradox objects, you may go through an iterative process which will result in many files.

This chapter discusses some of the ways you can manage your database and its related files. Information on the following topics is included:

- Using subdirectories to stay organized
- Taking care of tables and their families
- Using the Tools command, including Exporting and Importing files
- Setting up passwords

The information on the Tools command in this chapter is especially important. At first glance, it may look like Tools is simply a group of file and table utilities. There are several features tucked away in the Tools menus, though, which are quite useful. You have already seen **Tools/Copy/Report** used in the examples in this book. That command was an essential part of most of the processes which were outlined in Chapter 7, "Putting Queries and Reports to Work." Tools commands can be key parts of the Paradox procedures you develop for your database work. As you read this chapter, keep your eyes open for ways you can use Tools for your own purposes.

Staying Organized

See Appendix G for information on Paralex, an add-on product which can help you keep track of lookup tables and other Paradox objects.

As you develop your Paradox system, it is essential to keep track of the files which you create. You may end up with dozens of files for each project. There are a few basics of managing files of which you are probably aware, but we'll review them anyway. The first step in organizing files is making proper use of subdirectories.

Using Subdirectories

When you installed Paradox, the Paradox system files probably were placed into a subdirectory called \ *PARADOX3*. It is best not to clutter that subdirectory with other files. The tables and associated files for each project should reside in their own directory.

Changing Directories or Drives

Use the DOS MD command to create new directories.

You must create any subdirectories outside of Paradox before they can be used. Once a directory exists, you can access it easily from within Paradox by using the **Tools/More/Directory** commands from the Main Menu. Paradox will prompt you for a new directory name. Type the name of the desired directory, with or without a drive specifier if needed, and press Enter. Choose OK from the next menu and Paradox will make the specified change.

When you change directories from within Paradox, the workspace is cleared and all temporary tables are deleted. Be sure to rename any temporary tables you want to save *before* you use **Tools/More/Directory**. If you are changing from a directory on a floppy disk drive to a directory which is on a different drive, make sure you leave the floppy diskette in its drive until the directory change has been completed. Otherwise, Paradox may try to delete or close files later and be unable to complete the operation.

Default Directories and Paths

Place \ *PARADOX3 at the beginning of your DOS path for optimum performance.*

Usually the default or working directory is the directory from which you start Paradox. The working directory is where Paradox looks for tables or other files that you specify without using a full pathname. (A file pathname includes the name of the directory, and possibly the name of the drive, where the file resides.) By placing the directory for your Paradox system files on your DOS path, you will be able to start Paradox from any directory.

You can use a DOS batch file to control the directory you start Paradox from.

You can change the directory which Paradox uses when it is loaded in two ways, using the Custom script or an *Init* script. Both of these options will be described in Chapter 13, "Customizing Your Paradox System." Of course, you can always load Paradox from \PARADOX3 and use **Tools/More/Directory** to change directories.

Using Pathnames

Lookup tables can reside in a separate directory.

At times, you may want to access a Paradox object which resides outside of the current or working directory. You can do this by specifying the pathname of any object at the appropriate prompt. Figure 9.1 shows how to access a table called *BILLS* in the directory \MYDIR while working in a different directory. You can use this method to keep tables with the same name in different directories at the same time. Paradox does not place restrictions on using tables from different subdirectories together. The only thing to note in this regard is that all family members for a table must reside in the same directory.

```
Table: \mydir\bills                                              Main
Enter name of table to view, or press ↵ to see a list of tables.




                                              

Use → and ← keys to move around menu, then press ↵ to make selection.
```

Figure 9.1 Using a pathname to access a table

Keeping Directories Compact

For optimum performance, you should limit the number of files in each subdirectory. A rule-of-thumb is that you should not have more than 100 files in any subdirectory. (Some people prefer to have no more than 64.) More than this and you may start to notice degradation in performance.

Be sure to delete unnecessary files from your subdirectories to conserve disk space. Paradox usually needs two to three times the size of any tables being used together in free disk space for its temporary work files. You can delete Paradox files easily using the **Tools/More/Delete** commands. If you are using any "dummy" tables to hold report specifications or forms, keeping them empty will help to save disk space, too. **Tools/More/Empty** empties a table of all of its records.

Keeping Track of Files

Many people find it useful to devise a system to keep track of what their different files are used for. Using paper-and-pencil or relying on memory are popular methods. You can get more creative, though, and come up with ways of documenting the components of your database using Paradox tables and `Tools`.

You may have noticed how Paradox makes use of its own tables during many operations: table structures are displayed in a STRUCTure table; file lists are shown in a LIST table; and records selected by queries are placed into ANSWER tables. You can create special tables, to manage information about your database, with the `Tools` commands.

For example, you can list all tables in a particular directory using **Tools/Info/Inventory/Tables**. (See Figure 9.2 for a sample inventory list of Raspberry Patch tables.) Note that Paradox places the inventory list into a temporary table called *LIST*. Then, rename LIST using **Tools /Rename/Table**. In this example, we'll call it *RPTABLES*. Restructure the newly named table to add a description field and you will have a handy reference for your tables, a "table of tables," such as the one shown in Figure 9.3. (In that example, the Name field was changed to A8 from A53, the field length created by Paradox in LIST, to save space.)

```
 Viewing List table: Record 1 of 13                          Main

 LIST            Name                                         Date
      1 │  Customer                                       │ 8/23/89
      2 │  Detail                                         │ 8/23/89
      3 │  Inventry                                       │ 8/16/89
      4 │  Invrpt                                         │ 8/20/89
      5 │  List                                           │ 8/27/89
      6 │  Orderlet                                       │ 8/14/89
      7 │  Orders                                         │ 8/23/89
      8 │  Phonebk                                        │ 8/14/89
      9 │  Projects                                       │ 8/14/89
     10 │  Projhrs                                        │ 8/02/89
     11 │  Slsprsn                                        │ 7/29/89
     12 │  Stmnts                                         │ 8/20/89
     13 │  Trans                                          │ 8/20/89
```

Figure 9.2 LIST resulting from **Tools/Info/Inventory/Tables**

Similarly, you can use **Tools/Info/Structure** to display the structure of a table in STRUCT. Figure 9.4 shows the STRUCTure table which was generated after using **Tools/Info/Structure/CUSTOMER**. With the cursor in STRUCT, press Alt-F7, and you will have an "Instant Report" of a table structure. You should label the report so that you know the table to which it corresponds.

```
┌─────────────────────────────────────────────────────────────────────────┐
│ Viewing Rptables table: Record 1 of 12                            Main    │
│                                                                           │
│ RPTABLES┬──Name──┬──────────Description──────────┬──Date──               │
│       1 │ Customer │ Raspberry Patch customer list    │ 8/23/89          │
│       2 │ Detail   │ Line items for orders in ORDERS table │ 8/23/89     │
│       3 │ Inventry │ All items with descriptions, prices  │ 8/16/89       │
│       4 │ Invrpt   │ Table to hold invoice report      │ 8/20/89         │
│       5 │ Orderlet │ Table to hold order confirmation report │ 8/14/89   │
│       6 │ Orders   │ Order info: order#, date, cust#, slsprsn │ 8/23/89  │
│       7 │ Phonebk  │ Kiki's phonebook                  │ 8/14/89         │
│       8 │ Projects │ Project list: who, target dates   │ 8/14/89         │
│       9 │ Projhrs  │ Project hours: who, date, hours   │ 8/02/89         │
│      10 │ Slsprsn  │ List of sales people: DOH, rate   │ 7/29/89         │
│      11 │ Stmnts   │ Table to hold statements report   │ 8/20/89         │
│      12 │ Trans    │ Transactions: sales, pymnts, returns │ 8/20/89      │
│                                                                           │
└─────────────────────────────────────────────────────────────────────────┘
```

Figure 9.3 RPTABLES, "table of tables" information

```
┌─────────────────────────────────────────────────────────────────────────┐
│ Viewing Struct table: Record 1 of 10                              Main    │
│                                                                           │
│ STRUCT┬────────Field Name────────┬─Field Type─┐                          │
│     1 │ Customer #                │ S*          │                         │
│     2 │ Last Name                 │ A20         │                         │
│     3 │ First Name                │ A15         │                         │
│     4 │ Company Name              │ A25         │                         │
│     5 │ Street Address            │ A25         │                         │
│     6 │ City                      │ A20         │                         │
│     7 │ State                     │ A2          │                         │
│     8 │ Zip                       │ A10         │                         │
│     9 │ Phone Number              │ A12         │                         │
│    10 │ Balance                   │ $           │                         │
│                                                                           │
└─────────────────────────────────────────────────────────────────────────┘
```

Figure 9.4 STRUCT resulting from **Tools/Info/Structure**/CUSTOMER

Add-on products are available to help you keep track of what's in your Paradox database. See Appendix G for more information. Paralex is especially popular.

Taking Care of Families

As was mentioned in Chapter 1, Paradox uses "families" to organize tables and their associated reports, forms, and other files such as indexes. There are restrictions on moving family members. This section outlines rules for working with families and offers a workaround solution for restoring part of a family without its corresponding table.

You can check a table's current family using **Tools/Info/Family**. Paradox will display all family members for the specified table in a temporary table called FAMILY. The FAMILY table for CUSTOMER is shown in Figure 9.5.

```
┌──────────────────────────────────────────────────────────────────────┐
│                                                                        │
│   Viewing Family table: Record 1 of 11                         Main    │
│                                                                        │
│   FAMILY┌──────────────────────Name──────────────────────┐┌────Date───┐│
│       1 │ Customer                                        ││  8/23/89  ││
│       2 │ Settings SET                                    ││  8/27/89  ││
│       3 │ Validity VAL                                    ││  8/27/89  ││
│       4 │ Form F1                                         ││  8/20/89  ││
│       5 │ Form F2                                         ││  8/20/89  ││
│       6 │ Form F3                                         ││  8/20/89  ││
│       7 │ Report R1                                       ││  8/20/89  ││
│       8 │ Report R2                                       ││  8/20/89  ││
│       9 │ Report R3                                       ││  8/20/89  ││
│      10 │ Report R4                                       ││  8/20/89  ││
│      11 │ Report R5                                       ││  8/20/89  ││
│                                                                        │
└──────────────────────────────────────────────────────────────────────┘
```

Figure 9.5 FAMILY table for CUSTOMER

You can rename FAMILY using **Tools/Rename/Table**, restructure the new table to add a description field, and add notes about each report and form. Using PAL, you can write a program to retrieve this information from the descriptions which are displayed for each form or report as you move the cursor through the form and report lists.

Copying Family Members

Paradox maintains control information on when each member of a table's family is copied. For this reason, *you should not use DOS to copy family members without copying the table (the .DB file) as well*. It is all right to copy a table and its entire family using the DOS command, **COPY CUSTOMER.***, but Paradox will not let you use family members which have been copied to a table by themselves. You will get a message which says that the object you are trying to use is obsolete, out-of-date or corrupt.

To copy a report from one table to another, use **Tools/Copy/Report /Different**Table. When you use the Tools commands to copy objects, Paradox updates its date and time information and you will not have problems. You can also use **Tools/Copy/Form**, or **Tools/Copy /JustFamily**, to copy a family of forms, reports, and other objects, from one table to another table which has exactly the same structure.

Backing Up Families

It is advisable to back up your database regularly, just in case you may have unexpected problems. How often you should back up information depends upon how much information you are willing to have at risk. If you enter much information into your tables, or make substantial changes to existing records on a daily basis, then you should probably back up your database every day. If you don't add much information each day, it may be sufficient to perform a back up every few days or even once a week.

Whenever you back up tables, be sure to back them up with their entire families. For example, if you use the DOS BACKUP command, type **BACKUP TABLE.* A:** where *TABLE* is the name of the table being backed up. Paradox looks at families as a group, and keeps track of when individual members were copied or changed. If you back up a table, the .DB file, by itself, you will not be able to use it with family members which were not backed up at the same time.

Restoring Paradox Objects

When you restore tables from a backup, be sure to restore any family members with them. If you don't, you will have problems when you try to use "old" family members with the newly restored table. Paradox will tell you that the family member which you are trying to use is corrupt or out-of-date.

Restoring a Table Without its Family

To restore a table, without overwriting current family members, follow these steps:

1. Rename the current table and its family on the hard disk. Use **Tools/Copy/Table** to do this. Paradox renames the specified table along with any family members for that table, automatically.
2. Restore the "old" table from your backup.
3. Use **Tools/Copy/JustFamily** from the renamed table to the restored table.

Restoring Family Members Without a Table

There are times when you may want to restore a family member, such as a form or a report, without restoring the underlying table. To do this, use the following instructions:

1. Rename the table whose family member which you want to restore using **Tools/Rename/Table**.
2. Restore the same table from the backup, along with any family members you want to restore.
3. Use **Tools/Copy** to copy the family report or form from the restored table to the renamed table.

4. Give the table renamed in Step 1 its original name using **Tools /Rename/Table**.

 For emergencies such as this, you may want to keep an empty table to "hold" any important forms or reports for use as a backup. Then, in case of damage, you can use **Tools/Copy/Report/DifferentTable**, or **Tools/Copy/Form/DifferentTable**, to copy a report or form from the "holding" table to the permanent table.

Taking Care of Indexes

See Chapter 14 for more information on table indexes.

When you create a primary index for a table, Paradox creates a file with the name TABLE.PX where *TABLE* is the name of the table being indexed. The index file is built according to the sort order which corresponds to the country code you chose during installation. If you copy a table and its index to another computer which is using a different Paradox sort order, you will get an error message indicating the index file has the wrong sort order.

To solve this problem, delete the .PX file for the problem table. Then, on the new computer, restructure the table using **Modify /Restructure** and re-specify the key field(s). Paradox will build a new primary index which will work with the new sort order.

Another problem which you may run across is an out-of-date index. If you restore a table without restoring its index, you will have problems when Paradox tries to use the index. Deleting the index and rebuilding it to add back the key fields will solve the problem.

Using Tools

The use of some Tools commands has already been shown in this chapter and in Chapter 7 "Putting Queries and Reports to Work." The Tools Menu gives you access to several other commands which you will find useful. This section outlines the complete Tools Menu and offers notes on each command.

The Tools Menu

The Tools Menu has two parts. The first menu is shown in Figure 9.6. The second menu, displayed by choosing More on the first menu, is shown in Figure 9.7.

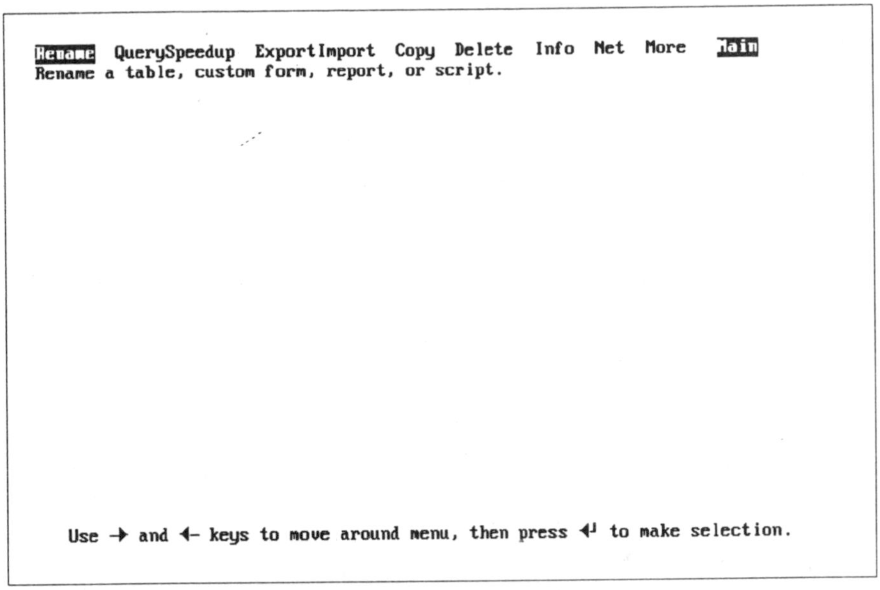

```
Rename  QuerySpeedup  ExportImport  Copy  Delete  Info  Net  More   Main
Rename a table, custom form, report, or script.
```

```
Use → and ← keys to move around menu, then press ↵ to make selection.
```

Figure 9.6 First Tools Menu

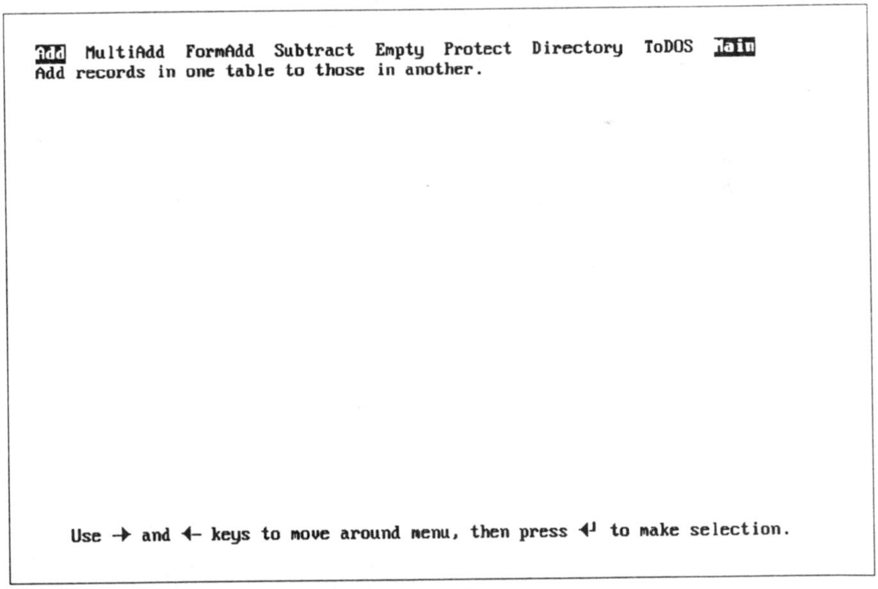

```
Add  MultiAdd  FormAdd  Subtract  Empty  Protect  Directory  ToDOS   Main
Add records in one table to those in another.
```

```
Use → and ← keys to move around menu, then press ↵ to make selection.
```

Figure 9.7 Second Tools Menu

- **Rename** lets you change the name of a table, form, report, script or graph.
- **QuerySpeedup** is used to generate a secondary index for a table.

- `ExportImport` has tools for creating Paradox tables from other file formats and vice-versa.
- `Copy` lets you copy a table, report, form, graph, script, or an entire family.
- `Delete` is used to delete a table, form, report, script, graph, Query-Speedup index, valcheck file, or settings file.
- `Info` can be used to inventory files, list a table's structure or family members, or list network users.
- `Net` lets you change network options such as the private directory, the AutoRefresh interval and your username; you can also lock or unlock tables using this command.
- `More` gives you access to additional `Tools` commands.

These additional commands are:

- `Add` lets you add together tables with compatible structures.
- `MultiAdd` adds tables using a source and a map table.
- `FormAdd` uses a multi-table form to add tables.
- `Subtract` lets you subtract one table from another table with the same structure.
- `Empty` deletes all records from a table.
- `Protect` gives you access to Password mode in which you can assign passwords to tables and scripts.
- `Directory` is used to change the current directory or disk drive.
- `ToDOS` temporarily suspends Paradox so that you can use DOS to execute commands or run other programs.

You can also use Ctrl-O or Alt-O to go to DOS.

Rename

Using **Tools/Rename** is simple. Choose `Table, Form, Report, Script` or `Graph` from the menu which is displayed and type the new name when prompted. If you specify the name of an existing table, Paradox will give you a chance to `Cancel` or `Replace` the operation.

When you `Rename` a table, Paradox also renames all of its family members. If you specify the name of an existing table, that table, and all of its family members, will be deleted. Because of this, be careful not to rename ANSWER tables with the name of a table which holds a report or form you want to use. Instead, use **Tools/Copy** to copy the desired reports or forms to ANSWER.

QuerySpeedup

Chapter 14 has more information on secondary indexes.

`QuerySpeedup` is used to generate a secondary index for a table. Secondary indexes are special files which Paradox uses during queries and other operations to speed up searches for specific records. Unlike primary indexes, secondary indexes do not require unique key values and they do not impose a sort order on the indexed table.

To create a secondary index, place a query image on the workspace for the table which you want to index. Then, enter search criteria into all fields you want to index and use Tools/QuerySpeedup. Paradox will display the message, "Processing query speedup," while it is generating the secondary index files. A separate secondary index is created for each field, except primary index fields, containing search criteria. For each secondary index, Paradox creates two files: TABLE.X## and TABLE.Y## where ## is the hexadecimal number corresponding to the field that the index is for.

Figure 9.8 shows a query image for CUSTOMER with search criteria in City and State. After using F10/Tools/QuerySpeedup with this query on the workspace, Paradox generates two secondary indexes, one for City and one for State. You can see these indexes listed in the FAMILY table for CUSTOMER in Figure 9.9.

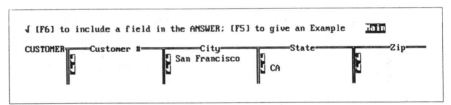

Figure 9.8 Query to generate `QuerySpeedup` for CUSTOMER

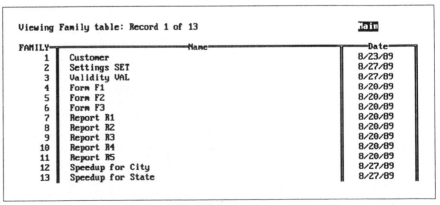

Figure 9.9 FAMILY listing for CUSTOMER

Sometimes Paradox will display the message, "No speedup possible." This means that Paradox has determined it will not save query processing time to generate a secondary index. You can force Paradox to generate a secondary index using the PAL INDEX command. More information about how secondary indexes are maintained, and the INDEX command itself, is included in Chapter 14, "Performance Tips."

ExportImport

`ExportImport` converts Paradox tables into other file formats and vice-versa. A few general notes on using this `Tools` command:

- You do not need to use the file extension when specifying the name of a file to import, unless (as with ASCII files) it can be different from the default.

- When you import a file, Paradox creates a new table except for delimited ASCII files where you can append records to an existing table.

Paradox tables will sometimes be larger than the files they are imported from because of Paradox's fixed file format.

- Be sure you have enough disk space for Paradox to complete the import or export; usually twice the size of the table or file involved is enough.

- If you have problems, make sure the source file or table you are working with is not damaged.

- For fixed-length ASCII files, use the FLIMPORT program included with Paradox instead of using **T**ools/**E**xportImport. (See details on FLIMPORT below.)

When you choose `ExportImport` on the Tools Menu, Paradox shows another menu with the choices `Export` and `Import`. To create a Paradox table from one of the supported file formats, choose `Export`. To create a new file from a Paradox table, choose `Import`. After making your choice, you will see another menu with the following choices:

- `Quattro`
- `1-2-3`
- `Symphony`
- `Dbase`
- `Pfs`
- `Reflex`
- `Visicalc`
- `Ascii`

You can convert files between Paradox and any of the above formats by choosing the desired file format and entering the new file or table name when prompted. Paradox will look in the current directory for the file or table to be converted. If necessary, you can use a pathname to specify files or tables in other directories. Notes on each type of file transfer follow:

Quattro

You can use Quattro Pro to create or link to Paradox tables.

When you import a Quattro spreadsheet into Paradox, each row in the spreadsheet becomes a record in the Paradox table and each column becomes a field. Paradox imports only the values in each row and column, not the formulas which are part of the spreadsheet. The field types used for the new Paradox table are based on *all* information in each column. If you have Alphanumeric labels in a column, that column will become an Alphanumeric field in the Paradox table.

Sometimes, you may have to "clean up" a spreadsheet before importing it into Paradox. It is usually preferable to do this before you use **Tools/ExportImport/Import**. Otherwise, you may have to edit and restructure the resulting Paradox table to get it into the form you want.

When you export a Paradox table to a Quattro spreadsheet, each record becomes a row in the spreadsheet and each field becomes a column. The Paradox field names are used as labels in the first row of the spreadsheet. If the Paradox field is longer than the maximum column width allowed by Quattro, the entire value will be exported but it will be partially hidden in the spreadsheet.

1-2-3 and Symphony

Paradox uses the same conventions for converting files between Paradox and 1-2-3 or Symphony. Any spreadsheet column with an Alphanumeric string will be imported as an Alphanumeric field in Paradox, so be sure to edit the spreadsheet to remove extraneous labels or hyphens before you import it.

Dbase

Paradox can work with dBASE II, dBASE III, dBASE III PLUS, or dBASE IV files. If you are importing a dBASE file with memo fields, Paradox will import only the first 255 characters of the memo field.

Pfs

You can export a Paradox table to a PFS:File or an IBM Filing Assistant file. The file extension .PFS will be used unless you specify another one. When you import a PFS file, Paradox will use only the first 255 characters of any attachment pages.

Reflex

Reflex files are easily converted into Paradox tables and vice-versa. Just specify the version of Reflex file you are using from the menu and give the appropriate file or table name when prompted. Note that any "untyped" fields in a Reflex file will not be included in the new Paradox table. Paradox does not know what field type to use and so eliminates the field.

Visicalc

There are many types of DIF files. If you have problems, check your file format.

When you use the Visicalc menu choice, Paradox uses the .DIF (Data Interchange Format) for working with files. The .DIF format which Paradox uses is the format defined by the DIF Clearinghouse. This file format is not always the same for different programs. If you have problems, see if you can convert the .DIF file to another format with which Paradox is compatible.

When you import .DIF files, Paradox uses each *tuple* in a .DIF file as a record and each *vector* as a field. If the DIF LABEL feature has been used to name a vector, Paradox will use the label for the field name.

Ascii

When you choose Ascii from the Export or Import menu, you will see additional choices. Using **Export/Ascii**, you can create an ASCII delimited file or an ASCII text file. You can also Import a delimited or an ASCII text file, optionally appending delimited records to an existing table.

You can check for the CR/LF using the DOS DEBUG command—the hex representation of these characters is ØD/ØA.

Text Files: ASCII text files are simply lines of information with no special characters between values. When you import these files into Paradox, Paradox expects there to be a CR/LF (Carriage Return/Line Feed) code at the end of each record in the ASCII text file. Each record in the text file becomes a record in the new Paradox table. The table which is created has one field, up to 132 characters long.

You can use **T**ools/ExportImport/Export to create an ASCII text file from a one-field Paradox table. Each record in the table becomes a separate line in the ASCII file.

Delimited ASCII Files: Delimited ASCII files have a format different from text files. While each record is still on a separate line in the file, field values are separated by special characters. In addition to field separators, all field values, or only Numeric field values, are optionally delimited by a special character.

Figure 9.10 shows a delimited ASCII file exported from the CUSTOMER table. Here the field separator is a comma and the delimiter is a double quotation mark , ". These are the default field separators and delimiters used when Paradox works with delimited ASCII files. You can change the separator or delimiter using the Custom script. It is also possible to specify whether Paradox should export a blank as *0* and whether all values, or only non-Numeric values, should be delimited. Details on changing these options will be found in Chapter 13, "Customizing Your Paradox System."

```
1,"D'Inos","Doug","No Grownups!","5487 - 145th St. N.W.","Seattle","WA","98999"»
2,"Dominicelli","Angelina","Bambini Time","525 Cambridge Street","Los Angeles",»
3,"Holly","Deirdre","Love Bundles","45 Thornhill Ave.","Venice","CA","90291","2»
4,"Michaels","Monique","Pour Les Enfants","1775 Terrace Drive","Belmont","CA","»
5,"Mitchinson","Coco","Tops to Bottoms","999 Golden Lane","San Francisco","CA",»
6,"Packwald","Vanessa","A to Z","927 Iris Ave.","Redwood City","CA","94061","41»
7,"Robinson","Ray","Little Stuff","200 W. 90th Street","New York","NY","10024",»
8,"Sizemore","Nick","Kidstuff","1 June Way","Marysville","WA","98270","206-659-»
9,"Gaines","Gloria","PlayGear","580 Skokie Ave.","Highland Park","IL","60035","»
10,"Tanner","Madonna","PlayGear","10050 Pacific Avenue","Beachtown","CA","90001»
11,"August","Ana Marie","Pour Les Enfants","1021 Summertime Lane","Rock Island"»
12,"Dominicelli","Angelina","Pour Les Enfants","999 Main Street","Santa Monica"»
13,"Michaels","Monique","Bambini Time","15 El Camino Real","San Mateo","CA","94»
14,"Dominicelli","Angelina","Brown Berries","5757 Ocean Drive","Malibu","CA","9»
15,"August","Ana Marie","Bambini Time","9001 Broadway","New York","NY","10024",»
16,"Pasquesi","Dominic","Grandpa's Place","720 Pieve Way","Chicago","IL","60000»
17,"Goldberg","Agnes","Grandpa's Other Place","131 High Way","Evanston","IL","6»


Line=18    Col=1          C:PATCHWRK\DELASCII.TXT        Insert   WW=Off
```

Figure 9.10 Delimited ASCII file

Paradox normally imports files into new tables. With delimited ASCII files, you can optionally append the new records to an existing table. If the existing table is unkeyed, the new records will be added to the end of the table. If you use **I**mport/**A**scii/**A**ppendDelimited to add records to a keyed table, Paradox will display another menu with the choices `NewEntries` and `Update`.

`NewEntries` is used only to add new records to the existing table. If key violations are detected, Paradox places the offending records into a temporary table called KEYVIOL. Chapter 2 had information on how to handle KEYVIOL tables. Briefly, you can edit the records in KEYVIOL to eliminate the conflicting key values and then use **T**ools/**M**ore/**A**dd to add KEYVIOL records to the target table.

`Update` lets you update existing records in the target table using information in the delimited ASCII file which is being imported. When Paradox finds a record with a duplicate key in the ASCII file, it replaces the existing record in the target table with the new record. The entire record, not just new field values, is replaced.

When you append ASCII records to an existing table, Paradox places any problem records in a temporary table called PROBLEMS. PROBLEMS has three fields: one for the record number, a second with the first 80 characters of the offending record, and a third field with a message about the source of the problem. Common problems are:

- Missing separators
- Missing delimiters
- Hex 00 null characters, or "garbage" characters, in the records

After the original ASCII file is edited to eliminate the problems, try the import operation again.

Fixed-Length ASCII Files

Fixed-length ASCII files, such as the one shown in Figure 9.11, have no special separators or delimiters to indicate field values. Instead, field values start at specific positions in each record, creating an ASCII file with a column for each field of values. There is no way to import or export these files using **T**ools/**E**xportImport. But don't try to get your file into another format without reading on!

```
  1    D'Inos          Doug          No Grownups!           5»
  2    Dominicelli     Angelina      Bambini Time           5»
  3    Holly           Deirdre       Love Bundles           4»
  4    Michaels        Monique       Pour Les Enfants       1»
  5    Mitchinson      Coco          Tops to Bottoms        9»
  6    Packwald        Vanessa       A to Z                 9»
  7    Robinson        Ray           Little Stuff           2»
  8    Sizemore        Nick          Kidstuff               1
  9    Gaines          Gloria        PlayGear               5»
 10    Tanner          Madonna       PlayGear               1»
 11    August          Ana Marie     Pour Les Enfants       1»
 12    Dominicelli     Angelina      Pour Les Enfants       9»
 13    Michaels        Monique       Bambini Time           1»
 14    Dominicelli     Angelina      Brown Berries          5»
 15    August          Ana Marie     Bambini Time           9»
 16    Pasquesi        Dominic       Grandpa's Place        7»
 17    Goldberg        Agnes         Grandpa's Other Place  1»
```

Figure 9.11 Fixed-length ASCII file from CUSTOMER

Check for your Install diskette for Flimport if it is not on Pprog disk 6.

There is a utility program called FLIMPORT included with Paradox which can be used to create Paradox tables from fixed-length files. The program is in the \UTIL directory of the Personal Programmer, Disk 6. The program is run from the DOS prompt and works by letting you create a "table specification" which is then used to import the fixed-length ASCII file. There is a documentation file for the program on the same diskette. For programmers, note also that you can optionally pass a file name and a table specification to FLIMPORT on the command line, making it possible to create tables "on-the-fly" using the PAL RUN command. Use RESET before RUN if you do this.

To create a fixed-length ASCII file from a Paradox table, use the following steps:

1. Use **R**eport/**D**esign/**T**abular to create a new Tabular report specification for the table which you want to export.

2. Use Ctrl-Y to delete all lines, except the line of field masks between the table lines, from the report specification. A sample report specification for CUSTOMER is shown in Figure 9.12.

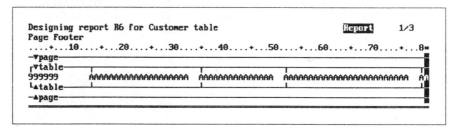

Figure 9.12 Report specification to get fixed-length ASCII file

3. Set the Paradox pagelength to **C** for Continuous using **S**etting/**P**ageLayout/**L**ength from the Report Menu. That way, Paradox will not include any extra line feeds in the report specification.

4. Save the report by pressing F2.

5. Send the report to a file using **R**eport/**O**utput/**F**ile, specifying the table name and report number used in Step 1.

Copy

Copy lets you make a copy of a table, form, report, script, graph, or entire family of a table. After choosing one of these options from the Copy Menu, you will be prompted for the name of the object to be copied. After entering a name, you will be prompted for a new name or see another menu as indicated below.

Table

When you use **T**ools/**C**opy to copy a table, Paradox copies the specified table and its entire family. The original table stays as it was. To rename a table, use **T**ools/**R**ename rather than **T**ools/**C**opy. When you give the new table name, Paradox will give you the option to cancel the operation if the new name is already in use. If you tell Paradox to go ahead, it will delete the existing table and its family.

Form or Report

You can copy an individual form or report using **T**ools/**C**opy/**F**orm or **T**ools/**C**opy/**R**eport. When you use either choice, Paradox displays a menu with the choices `SameTable` or `DifferentTable`. `SameTable` is used to copy a form or report to a new form or report in the same table. `DifferentTable` lets you copy a form or report to a different table. Whether you choose `SameTable` or `DifferentTable`, Paradox will display the list of available forms or reports to copy, and a second list where you pick which number to copy the form or report to.

Script or Graph

Scripts and graph settings can also be copied freely with DOS.

Paradox makes a copy of the script or graph settings file you specify and names the file with the new name you type. Scripts have the file extension .SC and graph settings have the file extension .G.

JustFamily

`JustFamily` is used to copy a table's family, without copying the table itself, to another table. The tables involved must have exactly the same structure. Paradox will prompt you for source and target table names, giving you the option to cancel the operation before the copy is performed. Any forms or reports in the target table which have the same number in the source table will be replaced by the source table file. Other files, such as settings or valchecks, will be replaced if they exist in the source and in the target table.

Delete

`Delete` allows you to delete a table, form, report, script, graph, QuerySpeedup index, ValCheck file, or KeepSet settings file. Paradox will prompt for the name or number of the object to be deleted and give you a chance to cancel the operation before the specified file is deleted.

When you delete a table, the table and its entire family are deleted. There is no way to get these files back, with the possible exception of a program such as the Norton Utilities. Be careful when you delete objects, and make sure you have adequate backup before you start any extensive housekeeping.

Info

The `Info` command gives you information about files, tables and Paradox network users. Choosing `Info` from the Tools Menu displays another menu:

- `Structure` shows the specified table's structure in a temporary table called STRUCT.
- `Inventory` displays another menu where you can tell Paradox to list `Tables`, `Scripts` or `Files`; the lists are displayed in a temporary table called LIST.
- `Family` creates a temporary table called FAMILY with information about the specified table's family members.
- `Who` displays a temporary LIST table showing who on a network is currently using Paradox.
- `Lock` creates a temporary LIST table of all locks on the specified table; it also lists form locks.

When you use the `Info` command, Paradox prompts for the name of a table, a directory, or a file pattern, depending on what you choose from the `Info` menu. We have already shown examples of the FAMILY, LIST, and STRUCT tables which are generated using **Tools/Info**.

Net

`Net` allows you to change some network options and also to lock or unlock tables. When you choose `Net` from the Tools Menu, another menu is displayed:

- `Lock` is used to explicitly lock or unlock a table with a `FullLock` or a `WriteLock`.
- `PreventLock` is used to explicitly lock or unlock a table with a prevent `FullLock` or prevent `WriteLock`.
- `SetPrivate` lets you change your private directory.
- `UserName` lets you change or set your Paradox username.
- `AutoRefresh` sets the AutoRefresh interval.

Lock and PreventLock

These commands let you lock or unlock a table so long as there are no conflicting locks already placed on a table. Paradox normally locks and unlocks tables with appropriate locks as needed so you don't need to place locks yourself. However, there may be times when you want to explicitly control the locks on a table. Chapter 15, "Networking With Paradox," contains more information about how Paradox locks tables.

The Private Directory

The Paradox private directory (which can be separate from a network private directory) is where Paradox creates its temporary files for each user. You can specify any directory on any drive for the private directory. Just make sure there is enough room in the private directory for Paradox's temporary work files. The rule-of-thumb is that you need two to three times the size of the tables in use available in free disk space.

The location of the private directory can also impact performance when you are on a network. If you have enough room on a local drive, it is preferable to have your private directory there. That way, Paradox does not have to go to the network to work with its temporary files.

You can specify a default private directory using the Custom script. See Chapter 13 for information about doing this. If you don't use Custom to specify a private directory in your PARADOX3.CFG file, Paradox attempts to make the current directory the private directory. If the current directory is on a network drive, Paradox writes a special lock file to the private directory. This ensures that the directory is not used as a shared directory or for another user's private directory. Because of this, make sure not to start Paradox from a shared directory if you don't have a private directory set using Custom.

UserName

Usually Paradox takes your Username from your network Username. Some networks do not support Usernames, though. If you are using such a network, or if you want to change your Username, use **T**ools/**N**et/**U**serName. The first 15 characters of the name you type will be used to identify you on a shared Paradox system. Paradox uses the Username when it lists who has placed locks on a table and when it gives messages about who has locked particular records. You can also specify a Username using the Custom script.

AutoRefresh

While you are using a shared table, Paradox periodically updates your screen with changes made by other users of the same table. The interval between such refreshes is called the AutoRefresh interval. The default interval is three seconds. You can change this value to anything between 1 and 3,600 seconds. You can also leave it blank to disable AutoRefresh.

Once again, a default for this option can be set using the Custom script. Any changes you make with the **Tools/Net** commands override the settings in your PARADOX3.CFG file created with the Custom script.

More

Choosing **More** on the Tools Menu gives you access to the second menu of **Tools** commands. Descriptions of these commands follow:

Add

Add lets you add records of one table to another table with a compatible structure. The tables do not need to have exactly the same structure since Paradox can add any kind of number field (N, S, or $) to each other. Alphanumeric fields can be truncated if they don't fit into the target table field. When you choose **Add** from the **Tools/More** menu, Paradox prompts for a source table and for a target table.

If the target table is keyed, you will see a menu with the choices **NewEntries** and **Update**. **NewEntries** tells Paradox to place records in the target table only if there are no conflicting key values. Records with conflicting key values are placed into a temporary KEYVIOL table. If you use **Update**, Paradox replaces any records in the target table which have duplicate key values with records from the source table.

To add records from one table to another table that has a different structure, use an Insert query. See Chapter 5 for details on setting up an Insert query.

MultiAdd

See Chapter 4 for information on setting up multi-entry source and map tables.

MultiAdd is used to add records from a table with the structure of a multi-entry source table to several target tables. Let's say that you want to edit records in tables into which you entered information using **MultiEntry**. You can perform a query which results in an ANSWER table which has the same structure as your multi-entry source table. Then, if you choose **Tools/More/MultiAdd**, Paradox will prompt for a source table and for a map table. The records in the specified source table, which could be ANSWER, will be added to the target tables using the specified map table.

After specifying a source table and a map table, Paradox will display the **NewEntries** or **Update** menu. If you choose **NewEntries**,

Paradox will place any source table records which duplicate key values in the target tables into a temporary KEYVIOL table, *but only if the rest of the record is different from the matching target table record.* If there is a key violation for any of the target tables, fields from the corresponding record in the source table will not be added to any of the target tables. When a KEYVIOL table results, you can edit it and then use Tools/More/Multiadd, specifying KEYVIOL as the source table, to add the records into the final table.

FormAdd

You can use `FormAdd` to add records from one group of related tables to another group of tables which are linked with a multi-table form. When you choose `FormAdd` from the **Tools/More** menus, Paradox will prompt for the name of the master target table and for the number of the multi-table form linking it to other tables. The records will be added to the target table and the linking tables defined with the multi-table form.

After specifying the master table and form, Paradox displays another menu with the choices `EntryTables` and `AnyTables`. Choose `EntryTables` to add records from ENTRY, ENTRY1, and so on, to the target tables. (These ENTRY tables are created when doing DataEntry using a multi-table form and use the `KeepEntry` option.) When you use `EntryTables`, Paradox assumes that the records in the ENTRY tables are new records. If records with duplicate keys are found, they are placed into KEYVIOL tables (KEYVIOL, KEYVIOL1, etc.). A temporary LIST table is also created which shows the KEYVIOL table corresponding to each target table. You can edit the KEYVIOL tables and use FormAdd /AnyTables to add their records to the target tables.

If you want to add a set of KEYVIOL tables, or another set of related tables, to the target tables, use FormAdd/AnyTables. The set of related source tables must, of course, be compatible with the structures of the target tables. Paradox will prompt whether the records are `NewEntries` or `Updates`. If you choose `NewEntries`, Paradox will create KEYVIOL tables containing any records in the source tables which duplicate keys in the target tables. After you choose `NewEntries` or `Update`, Paradox will prompt for the name of a source table for each target table on the multi-table form.

When you use `FormAdd`, Paradox will add records to the master target table, even if there are no corresponding detail records. Any detail records which do not share linking values with a master table record will not be added to the target detail tables. They will remain in the source detail tables, however.

Subtract

Tools/More/Subtract lets you subtract records in one table from records in another table which has a compatible structure. Paradox prompts for the name of a source table (the table with the records to be subtracted) and a target table (the table from which the records are to be subtracted). When records are subtracted from a target table, they remain in the source table.

Paradox subtracts records using these rules:

- If both the target and source tables are unkeyed, Paradox subtracts only those records from the target table which entirely match records in the source table.
- If the target table is unkeyed, and the source table is keyed, Paradox subtracts records from the target table which match key values in the source table.
- If the target table is keyed, Paradox subtracts records from the target table which have matching key values in the source table.

Empty

`Empty` is used to delete all records from a table. *There is no way to get these records back, not even with file-recovery utilities.* If you decide you really want to empty a table, choose **Tools/More/Empty**. Paradox will prompt for the name of the table to empty, and give you a chance to cancel the operation. Once you tell Paradox `OK`, the records are gone forever.

Protect

Tools/More/Protect gives you access to Paradox's Password mode. Password mode lets you assign passwords to tables and scripts. You can assign an owner password and auxiliary passwords for tables which then can be used to control access to a table, the table's fields, and its family members. You can also use `Protect` to write-protect a table without placing a password on it. The last section of this chapter will explain how to use Password mode.

Directory

Tools/More/Directory lets you change the working directory. The working directory is where Paradox looks for all objects, unless you specify them with a pathname. When you change directories using

Tools/More/Directory, Paradox clears the workspace and deletes any temporary tables which exist. Be sure to rename any temporary tables you want to save *before* you press Tools/More/Directory, specify a new directory, and give Paradox the OK.

ToDOS

The ToDOS menu choice on the Tools/More menus works the same as Ctrl-O, the DOS key in Paradox. When you use this menu choice, Paradox is suspended and you go to the DOS prompt from which you can execute DOS commands. To return to Paradox, type **EXIT** at the DOS prompt.

When Paradox is suspended, using ToDOS or Ctrl-O, the program still takes up about 420K of your computer's memory. This limits the type of commands or programs which you can run. If you need more memory while Paradox is suspended, you can use Alt-O, the DOS BIG key, to go to DOS and have more memory available. Paradox will take about 100K so the balance of memory will be available for use with other commands or programs. With DOS BIG, you can usually run word processing programs, spreadsheets, or other programs, depending upon how much memory was available before you loaded Paradox.

There are some things to be careful about when you suspend Paradox and go to DOS:

- Never delete, rename, or change any Paradox objects which were in use during the suspended Paradox session.

- Don't load RAM-resident software while Paradox is suspended; load RAM-resident *before* you load Paradox.

- Don't use the DOS PRINT or MODE commands unless you loaded them before you started Paradox.

- If you were using a floppy disk with Paradox before going to DOS, make sure that diskette is in the floppy disk drive before you exit from DOS.

- Make sure that you return to Paradox before turning off your computer.

Using Tools/More/Protect

You may want to protect your Paradox tables and scripts from unauthorized access. With Tools/More/Protect, you can place passwords on tables and scripts. Then, if an attempt is made to use a password-protected table or script, Password will prompt for the password. The password must be given before Paradox will grant access to the protected object. Paradox will remember the password you submit for the remainder of the current Paradox session or until you use **Tools/More/Protect/ClearPasswords** to clear all passwords which have been submitted.

 When you place a password on a table or a script, Paradox encrypts the protected object so it cannot be read, even using DOS. It is very important to remember any passwords that you assign using Protect. *There is no way to get back a protected object if you forget the password.* Even the Paradox Technical Support Department will be unable to help you retrieve a protected table or script, so write down your passwords and keep them secure.

Types of Protection

There are different types of protection which you can set up using **Tools/More/Protect.** For tables, you can assign passwords or write-protect the table. Table passwords are divided into master passwords and auxiliary passwords. You must have the master password to be able to set up auxiliary passwords. Auxiliary passwords are optional passwords which can be assigned to a table to limit rights to a table, a table's fields, or its family members.

For scripts, there is just an owner password. When a script is password-protected, it can be played without Paradox prompting for a password. The script itself cannot be accessed through the Script Editor, though, without the proper password submitted.

The Protect Menu

When you choose **Tools/More/Protect,** Paradox displays another menu with these choices:

- `Password` lets you assign or remove passwords.
- `ClearPasswords` is used to "unsubmit" all passwords.
- `Write-protect` sets, or clears, write-protection for a table.

Assigning Table Passwords

To assign table passwords, choose **Password/Table** from the Protect Menu. Type the desired table name when prompted. You are now in Password mode and can assign an owner and optional auxiliary passwords to the table.

Owner Passwords

Passwords are case-sensitive.

After you type a table name, Paradox will prompt for a new owner password. The password can be up to 15 characters long. Paradox will prompt a second time for the new password to confirm it. *Be sure to write down the password and keep it secure.*

The next screen you will see is the auxiliary password screen. The auxiliary password screen for CUSTOMER is shown in Figure 9.13. If you don't want to assign auxiliary passwords, press F2. Paradox will record the owner password and return you to Main mode.

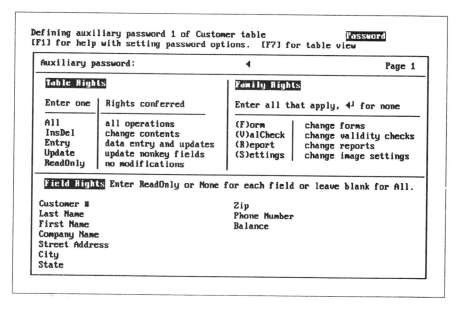

Figure 9.13 Auxiliary password form for CUSTOMER

Auxiliary Passwords

Auxiliary passwords are set up using an auxiliary password table created by Paradox. The table is edited using the form shown in Figure

9.13. You can use the Enter, Tab, and the arrow keys to move around the fields on the form. To enter a field value, you need only to press the first letter of your choice. Paradox will fill in the rest of the password right. There is one record in the auxiliary password table for each auxiliary password which you assign to a table.

You can see that there are four different areas of the auxiliary password form.

- The Auxiliary password field is used to enter or change the auxiliary password.
- The Table Rights area is used to select an overall level of access to the table for the specified password.
- The Family Rights area lets you control access to family members.
- The Field Rights area is used to control whether a field can be seen or changed.

Table Rights: There are five possible levels of Table Rights:

1. All is the same as having an owner password; the user can restructure or delete the table, as well as make any other changes; you may want to give a user an auxiliary password with All rights if your owner password grants you access to other tables which you want to protect.
2. InsDel gives a user Entry rights, as well as the ability to change fields, insert records, delete records, and empty the table.
3. Entry allows a user to add records using **Modify/DataEntry** or **Tools/More/Add**; Update Rights are also included.
4. Update lets a user change only non-key fields in existing records; no insertion or deletion of records is allowed.
5. ReadOnly prevents a user from making changes to a table.

Protecting Family Members: You can grant a user access to different types of family members using this part of the auxiliary password form. Type the first letter of each command below to give the user the listed rights:

- (F)orm lets a user design, change, or delete forms.
- (V)alCheck lets a user add, change, or delete valchecks.
- (R)eport lets a user design, change, or delete reports.
- (S)ettings lets a user add, change, or delete settings.

Protecting Fields: This part of the auxiliary password form is quite useful. You can use it to prevent users from changing selected non-key fields without restricting access to the entire table. There are three levels of Field Rights:

Unlike a display only field on a form, ReadOnly *protects field values in table view as well as form view.*

1. Leaving the Field Right blank lets a user view and change the field, the same as All.
2. ReadOnly lets a user see, but not change, the field values.
3. None keeps a user from seeing or changing a field's contents.

Fill in the desired Rights for each auxiliary password. If all of a table's fields will not fit onto one form, Paradox will create additional pages for each form. You can use the PgUp and PgDn keys to move through these pages. Press F2 to save your changes and return to Main mode.

The Password Menu

While you are entering auxiliary passwords, you can access the Password mode Menu by pressing F10. The choices on the menu are: Undo, Help, DO-IT! and Cancel. These choices work as they do on other Paradox menus.

Changing and Removing Passwords

It is easy to change or remove a password from a Paradox table. Choose **Password/Table** from the Protect Menu and specify the name of the desired table when prompted. Paradox will prompt for the table's master password if you have not already submitted it during the current session. Since the table is already protected, Paradox assumes that you want to change or remove the password. There are no special menu choices for this.

After the password has been entered, Paradox displays a menu with the choices Owner and Auxiliary. To change the owner password, choose Owner and type the new password, as prompted, twice. Paradox then displays the auxiliary password form where you can change auxiliary passwords, if you want to. When you have finished, press F2 to finalize the password changes.

To change only auxiliary passwords, choose Auxiliary from the Owner Auxiliary menu. Make your changes and then press F2 to exit from Password mode.

To remove an owner password, choose **Tools/More/Protect** **/Password/T**able from the Main Menu. Type the desired table name and the owner password when prompted. Choose `Owner` from the next menu and press Enter both times that you are prompted for a new password. All auxiliary passwords are also removed.

Individual auxiliary passwords can be removed using **Tools/More/Protect/P**assword/**T**able from the Main Menu. Specify the desired table and owner password when prompted. Choose either `Owner` or `Auxiliary` depending on whether you need to change the owner password, from the next menu. Paradox will then display the auxiliary password table. You can page through this table and use the Del key to delete any auxiliary passwords you don't need.

Clearing Passwords

There is a `ClearPasswords` choice on the Protect Menu. That choice is used to "clear" or "unsubmit" all passwords which have been submitted during the current session. It does not remove the passwords from a table. When you use `ClearPasswords`, Paradox also clears the workspace. Paradox will give you a chance to cancel the operation by displaying a `Cancel OK` menu.

Passwords on a Network

Paradox has a special program called the "Protection Generator" which you can use to protect an entire database used on a network. See Chapter 15, "Networking With Paradox," for details about how to use this program. This program can be optionally installed when you install Paradox.

Using Script Passwords

To place a password on a script, use **Tools/More/Protect** **/Password/S**cript. Paradox will prompt for a script name and a password. You will be prompted twice for the password.

To remove a password from a script, go through the above steps, giving the current password when prompted. Paradox will prompt for a new password. At this point, you can either type a new password or press Enter to remove the password. In both cases, you will be prompted twice for the new password.

Using Write-Protect

When you choose `Write-protect` from the Protect Menu, Paradox prompts for a table name and then displays a menu with the choices `Set` and `Clear`. When you use `Set` to write-protect a table, Paradox does not encrypt the object or ask you for a password. Paradox simply does not allow you to edit or delete the write-protected table until **Tools/More/Protect/Write-protect/Clear** is used to remove write-protection. The advantage is that you must go through an extra step before you can change, or inadvertently delete, a table.

Summary

This chapter gave you tips to keep your databases organized and showed you how to use the `Tools` commands. These are the important things to remember:

- Use subdirectories to stay organized.
- Keep directories compact.
- *BACK UP REGULARLY!!!*
- Be careful when copying, or moving, individual family members.
- Document what your tables and other Paradox objects are used for; you can use the **Tools/Info** commands to make this task easier.
- `Tools` contains several time-saving commands; take the time to be familiar with what is in the extensive Tools menus.
- Use passwords to protect your tables and scripts when it makes sense to do so.
- You can use auxiliary passwords to limit access to a table, individual fields, and family members.

Using Scripts and PAL

Scripts

This chapter will show you how to create and use scripts to save time. Using the `Scripts` menu command you can:

- Create scripts
- Play scripts
- Edit scripts
- Play scripts a specified number of times or continuously
- Tell Paradox to show what is happening while a script is playing

Information is also included on other ways to create and play scripts. In addition to the `Scripts` command, you can use Alt-F3 (the "Instant Script Record" key), the PAL Menu `MiniScript` command, or the Personal Programmer to create scripts.

What Are Scripts?

Script files are ASCII text files. You can use any ASCII text editor with scripts.

Scripts are files which contain Paradox commands. You can create a script and play it later when you want to have Paradox execute the same commands without your typing them. Using scripts to automate any processes that you do repetitively can save you a significant amount of time.

There are several different types of scripts. You can "record" your keystrokes, creating a script such as the one shown in Figure 10.1. (In the illustration, the script is being viewed with the Script Editor.) This script tells Paradox to:

- Query the ORDERS and DETAIL tables for orders placed within the last seven days

```
Changing script C:\patchwrk\instant                           Script

....+...10....+...20....+...30....+...40....+...50....+...60....+...70....+...80
{Ask} {orders} Right Check Example  "o" Right Check  ">today"
 "-7" Right Check Right Check Right Right Right Menu {Ask} {detail}
Right Example  "o" Right Check Right Check Right Check Right
Check Right Do_It! Menu {Tools} {Copy} {Report} {DifferentTable}
{orderlet} {R} {answer} {R} Menu {Report} {Output} {answer}
{R} {Printer}
```

Figure 10.1 Recorded keystroke script

- Copy the order-confirmation report from INVRPT to ANSWER
- Print order-confirmations from ANSWER, using the copied report specification

The commands in the script execute the steps which were outlined in Chapter 7, "Putting Queries and Scripts to Work," to generate order-confirmations. The difference is that in Chapter 7, the steps were done interactively, that is, using the menu commands one-by-one. By playing the script, you can tell Paradox to do these same steps with just two commands: **Scripts/Play**.

You can see that each menu command in the script is surrounded by curly braces *{ }* and the commands are listed, one after the other, without special formatting.

You can write your own scripts using the Script Editor (or a text editor of your choice). While you can write a script using the format shown in Figure 10.1, you can save time by using PAL abbreviated menu commands. The script shown in Figure 10.2 tells Paradox to do the same things as does the script shown in Figure 10.1. The difference is that PAL commands, instead of recorded keystrokes, are used.

You can see that the script shown in Figure 10.2 is easier to follow than the first version. This is just one advantage of using PAL, instead of recording scripts. PAL is a complete programming language. It allows you to do many things which are not possible interactively with Paradox. But more about that at the end of this chapter. The main point here is that there is more than one way to create a script.

How to Create Scripts

Appendix G has information on add-on editors for Paradox. Chapter 13 shows how to tie your own text editor into Paradox.

There are several ways to create scripts:

- **Scripts/Editor/Write** gives you access to the Paradox Script Editor where you can type commands; you can use any other text editor, optionally tying it into Paradox using the Custom script.

- Alt-F3, the "Instant Script Record" key, lets you record keystrokes and save them in a script called *Instant*.
- **Scripts/B**eginRecord lets you save keystrokes into a script which you name.
- **Scripts/Q**uerySave saves a query on the workspace to a script.
- The MiniScript command on the PAL menu can be used to execute scripts up to 175 characters long; these scripts are not saved.
- The Personal Programmer lets you create a simple application without having to write PAL code.

Regular scripts can have up to 132 characters per line.

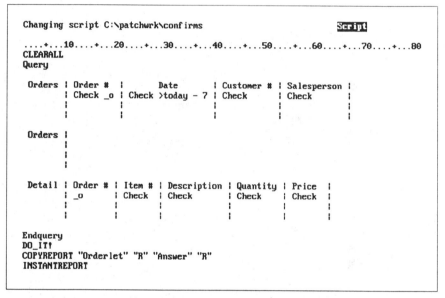

```
Changing script C:\patchwrk\confirms                              Script

....+...10....+...20....+...30....+...40....+...50....+...60....+...70....+...80
CLEARALL
Query

   Orders │ Order # │         Date        │ Customer # │ Salesperson │
          │ Check _o │ Check >today - 7 │ Check      │ Check       │
          │          │                     │            │             │
          │          │                     │            │             │

   Orders │
          │
          │
          │

   Detail │ Order # │ Item # │ Description │ Quantity │ Price │
          │ _o       │ Check  │ Check       │ Check    │ Check │
          │          │        │             │          │       │
          │          │        │             │          │       │

Endquery
DO_IT!
COPYREPORT "Orderlet" "R" "Answer" "R"
INSTANTREPORT
```

Figure 10.2 PAL script

Each option is described below. The examples in this chapter use a minimal amount of PAL code, only enough to illustrate the differences between recorded and typed scripts. If you are interested in learning more about PAL, see Chapter 11, "Introduction to PAL."

 Script files created by Paradox always have the extension *.SC* to distinguish script files from other files. If you create a script using your own editor outside of Paradox, be sure to add the *.SC* extension so you can play the script once it has been written.

Instant Scripts

The easiest way to create a script is with Alt-F3, the "Instant Script Record" key. When you press Alt-F3, you will see R in the upper-right corner of the screen. R will remain on the screen until you stop recording your keystrokes.

To stop recording, press Alt-F3 again. Paradox will save the recorded keystrokes in a special script called *Instant*. If you already have a script called "Instant," it will be overwritten. To save an *Instant* script as a permanent file, use **T**ools/**R**ename/**S**cript to rename it.

You can play an Instant script by pressing Alt-F4, the "Instant Script Play" key. An Instant script can be edited in the same manner as any other script. The script shown in Figure 10.1 was recorded using Alt-F3, and is shown as it is displayed using the Script Editor.

Scripts/BeginRecord

The Scripts Menu is shown in Figure 10.3 You can use **Scripts** /**B**eginRecord to tell Paradox to record your keystrokes and save them in a script file which you name. When you choose **Scripts/B**eginRecord from the menus, Paradox will prompt for a script name. Script names can be up to 8 characters long. Be careful to follow all DOS conventions for file names. After you type a file name, Paradox will return you to the Main Menu and begin recording your keystrokes. R will be displayed in the upper-right corner of the screen to indicate recording.

To stop recording, press F10 to access the Main Menu and choose Scripts. You will see a different menu from the one shown in Figure 10.3. Check Figure 10.4 again to see the differences. Instead of BeginRecord, you will see End-Record. There is also a Cancel choice which allows you to quit recording without creating a new script file.

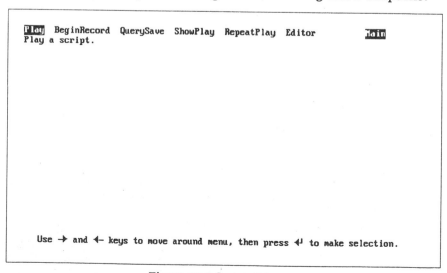

Figure 10.3 Scripts Menu

QuerySave

In Chapter 5, "Queries: The Exciting Part of Paradox," an example of how to save a query to a script was included. The process is simple. Place a query on the workspace, press F10 to access the Main Menu, and choose **S**cripts/**Q**uerySave. Paradox will prompt for a filename and save the query, in a special format, to a script with the specified name.

A script which is created with **S**cripts/**Q**uerySave can be played in the same way as any other script. Note that when you save a query to a script using **S**cripts/**Q**uerySave, Paradox does not include a "Do-It!" command in the script. To process the query when the `QuerySave` script is played, you must edit the script and add the "Do-It!" command. See Chapter 5 for complete instructions.

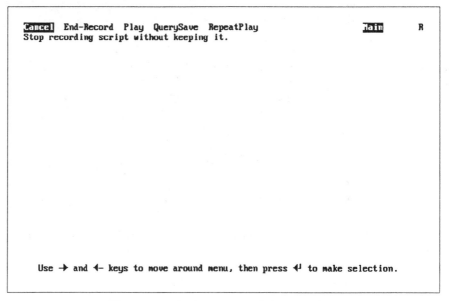

Figure 10.4 Scripts Menu while recording

The Script Editor

Paradox has its own Script Editor which you access by choosing **S**cripts/**E**ditor from the Main Menu. You can use the Script Editor to create or modify your scripts. You can also use it to modify Instant scripts, or scripts created using **S**cripts/**B**eginRecord.

When you choose `Editor` on the Scripts Menu, Paradox will display another menu with the choices `Write` and `Edit`. `Write` is used to create a new script. `Edit` allows you to change an existing script.

Detailed instructions on how to use the Script Editor are included in a separate section below.

Optionally, you can tie a text editor of your choice into Paradox using the Custom script. See Chapter 13 for details.

MiniScript

MiniScripts are not permanent scripts, but information on them is provided here so that you know about them. They are useful for those times when you want to execute a few commands quickly without having to leave current mode and go into the Script Editor.

To create a MiniScript, press Alt-F10 to display the PAL menu shown in Figure 10.5. Choose MiniScript and type the commands which you want Paradox to execute. You can enter a string of PAL commands up to 175 characters long. As soon as you press Enter, Paradox will execute the commands.

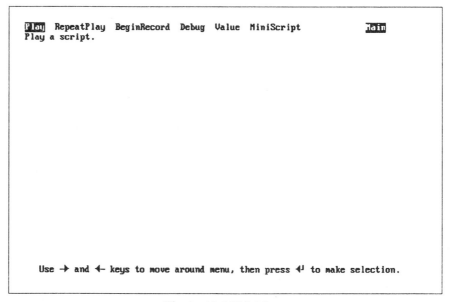

Figure 10.5 PAL Menu

 The scripts which you create in this way are not saved to disk for later access. MiniScript is used only to relay a few commands to Paradox without having to go through the process of using the Script Editor to create a new script file. Another important thing to know about MiniScripts is that you cannot use the Paradox Debugger with them.

(The Debugger, a tool for solving script problems, will be explained in Chapter 12, "Using PAL Features.") If the string of commands you want to enter is so long that you don't want to type them again *and* you are not entirely sure of the correct syntax, it is best to use the Script Editor to save the commands in a script file. Then, if Paradox has problems executing the commands, you can use the Debugger, make any necessary changes, and play the script again.

The Personal Programmer

There is another way to create scripts without recording your keystrokes or using PAL. You do it by using a special program, called the Personal Programmer, nicknamed *Pprog*, which is included with Paradox. The Personal Programmer is an *application generator*.

Some people use Pprog to "prototype" applications. It is just as easy to learn enough PAL to create your own menus.

The application generator creates a custom program based on the actions and tables which you specify. When you use the Personal Programmer, you are prompted for information about the type of program to create. The program asks you to define the tables, menus, actions, forms, and reports to be used in the application, and then generates a PAL program.

More information on how to use the Personal Programmer is included in a separate section at the end of this chapter.

Using the Script Editor

The Script Editor is easy to use. It lacks features such as block copies, and the ability to open more than one file at a time, but it is adequate if you are not trying to develop an entire application. As noted before, you can tie in the text editor of your choice if you want access to a more powerful editor while working with PAL.

Creating a New Script

To create a new script, use **Scripts/Editor/Write**. Paradox will prompt for a script name. You can use any 8-character name conforming to DOS rules for naming files. Paradox will append the .SC file extension automatically.

After you specify a file name, Paradox will bring you into the Script Editor. The screen you will see looks like the one shown in Figure 10.6. The cursor will be at the beginning of the first blank line under the horizontal ruler. This is where you start typing your commands.

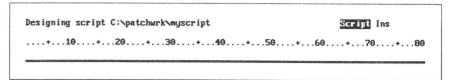

Figure 10.6 Paradox Script Editor

The first line contains status information such as the name of the script being designed, a reminder that you are in Script mode, and an insert mode indicator `Ins` is displayed when you are in insert mode. Below this line is a horizontal ruler which is useful for seeing where you are on each line. The display acts as a window on your script, which may be wider and/or longer than the screen.

Getting Around in the Script Editor

Moving the cursor in the Script Editor is similar to moving the cursor in the Report Generator. Here are some of the commands which you can use:

- Ctrl-Y deletes from the cursor to the end of the line.
- Enter creates a new line in insert mode.
- Ctrl-V displays a vertical ruler.
- Ctrl-left-arrow moves the cursor left half a screen.
- Ctrl-right-arrow moves the cursor right half a screen.
- PgUp moves the cursor up half a screen.
- PgDn moves the cursor down half a screen.

The Quick Reference Card contains complete information on how the numeric keypad functions in the Script Editor.

The Script Editor Menu

The Script Editor has its own menu, shown in Figure 10.7, which is displayed when you press F10. The choices on this menu are:

- `Read` is used to insert another script into the script being edited.
- `Go` saves any changes which you have made, returns to Main mode, and plays the script being edited.
- `Print` sends the script to the printer.

- Help gives you access to information about how to use the Script Editor.
- DO-IT! saves the script and returns you to Main mode.
- Cancel cancels any changes which you have made since entering the Script Editor and returns you to Main mode.

```
Read  Go  Print  Help  DO-IT!  Cancel                    Script  Ins
Read contents of another script into this script starting at the cursor.
....+...10....+...20....+...30....+...40....+...50....+...60....+...70....+...80
```

Figure 10.7 Script Editor Menu

The Read and Go commands are described below. The rest of the commands, Print, Help, DO-IT! and Cancel work the same as they do in the rest of Paradox.

Reading in a Script

To insert another script, place the cursor at the line just before the location where you want the new script inserted. Press F10 and choose Read from the menu. Paradox will prompt for the name of the script to "read" in. Type the name of the desired script and press Enter. Paradox will insert the specified script, starting at the line directly below the cursor.

Using Go

Choosing Go from the Script Editor menu is the same as using F2 to save the script and using **Scripts/P**lay to play it. Go is simply a shortcut which can save a few keystrokes.

Saving a Script

To save a script, press F2 or choose DO-IT! from the Script Editor Menu. Paradox will save the script with any changes made since you entered the Script Editor.

Using Another Editor

If you have tied another editor into Paradox using the Custom script, that editor is called whenever you use **Scripts/E**ditor or choose Debug from the Debugger menu. Paradox is suspended and you are under the control of the auxiliary editor until you complete your editing session. At that point, you are returned to Paradox.

There are editors which have been designed specifically to work with Paradox. For details, see the section in Appendix G listing add-on products for Paradox.

Playing Scripts

There are several different ways to play a script once it has been created. We have already mentioned most of them, such as using Alt-F4, the "Instant Script Play" key, to play an Instant script. There are other options, ShowPlay and RepeatPlay, which we have not yet covered. They are described here, along with notes on the other Play commands.

The Play Command

Before playing a script from the PAL Menu, make sure you are in the right mode.

The Play command is available on two menus, the Scripts Menu and the PAL Menu. In Main mode, press **S** while the Main Menu is displayed to access the Scripts Menu. To display the PAL Menu, press Alt-F10. The PAL Menu is available from anywhere in Paradox, except while you are using the Debugger in Help mode, or recording a script. The advantage of playing a script from the PAL Menu is that you don't have to return to Main mode first. (There may be times when you want to play a script while you are designing a report or editing a table.)

RepeatPlay

RepeatPlay is a command which is on the Scripts Menu as well as on the PAL Menu. This command lets you play a script repeatedly. When you choose RepeatPlay, Paradox prompts you to enter a number or to press **C** and then press Enter if you want the script played continuously. A script playing continuously can be stopped by pressing Ctrl-Break.

ShowPlay

Normally when you play a script, you do not see anything on the screen until Paradox has executed all of the commands in the script. ShowPlay shows you what Paradox is doing while it plays a script. When you choose ShowPlay from the Scripts Menu, Paradox will prompt for a script name and then display a menu with the choices Fast and Slow. Fast plays a script quickly. Slow is used to show what is happening at a slower pace.

The PAL PLAY Command

There is also a PAL command, PLAY, to play a script. We will not use the command in this chapter, but it is useful to know about. For example, instead of using Read from the Script Editor Menu to insert one script into another, you can add a line that says **PLAY "SCRIPTNAME"** where *SCRIPTNAME* is the name of the script which you would have inserted.

Playing a Script from DOS

You can easily tell Paradox to play a script from DOS by including the script name on the command line when you start Paradox. To do this, type **PARADOX3 SCRIPTNAME** at the DOS prompt or include this line in the batch file which you use to start Paradox. The script called *SCRIPTNAME* will be played automatically when Paradox is started if Paradox finds it in the directory which is current *after* Paradox is loaded. If you have specified a default directory in your PARADOX3.CFG file or with an Initial script, this directory may be different from the directory from which you start Paradox.

Problems Playing a Script

Once you have created a script, hopefully it will run to completion when you play it. However, you can have problems even if you recorded the script using **Scripts/BeginRecord**. Paradox may be unable to find a file which it needs, or may not be able to complete playing a script if a file is damaged. When this happens, Paradox displays an error message and a menu with the choices Cancel and Debug. See Figure 10.8 for an illustration of this menu.

At this point, you can choose to cancel script play or access the Debugger. The Debugger is a powerful part of Paradox and has many features to assist you in debugging problems with PAL code. If you choose Debug, additional information about the current script problem will be displayed as shown in Figure 10.9. Chapter 12 contains details on all Debugger features and how to use them. One of the nicest features is that you can press Ctrl-E to go into Edit mode on the problem script. Paradox will bring you to the line which caused the problem. You can then change your code and re-execute the script.

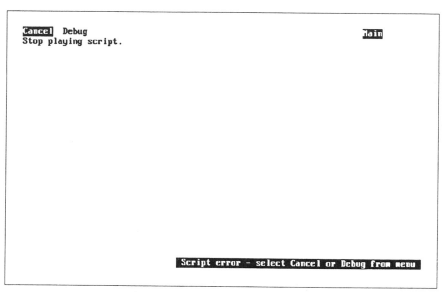

Figure 10.8 Cancel or Debug Menu

Using the Personal Programmer

The Personal Programmer is an optional program which you can install using the Paradox Install program. As mentioned, it is an application generator. You can use the Personal Programmer to create a complete Paradox application without writing any PAL code yourself.

What It Does

You are limited to using 15 tables in a Pprog application. To get around this, tie multiple applications together by playing one application as an action for a higher menu.

The Personal Programmer prompts you for the menus, actions, tables, forms, and reports to be included in your application. When you have finished defining your application, the Personal Programmer creates PAL scripts and procedure libraries which contain the code necessary for the user, even someone who doesn't know how to use Paradox, to "play" your application. Pprog creates a "driver" script (a script which starts the application) and special files, called procedure libraries, which contain the application program. The scripts containing the source code for the libraries are also saved by Pprog.

The application which is created can be run using Paradox or *Runtime*. Runtime is a special, inexpensive, version of Paradox which will run a PAL application but which cannot be used to access Paradox interactively. More information on Runtime is included in Chapter 12, "Using PAL Features."

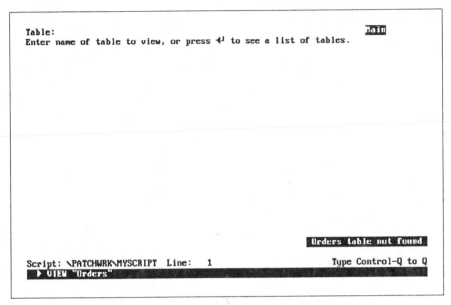

Figure 10.9 Debugger screen

When to Use It

Another limitation of Pprog is that you cannot change the structure of your tables in most cases.

The Personal Programmer can be useful to create a fairly simple application if you do not want to learn how to use PAL. Be aware, however, that you cannot do anything with it which you cannot do interactively. For example, the program can't automatically increment a number as records are entered. What the Personal Programmer does offer, though, is the ability to view selected records from one or more related tables, edit the tables, use DataEntry mode on them, and report on them. You can also optionally tie your own scripts into the application, specifying that a script be played when a certain menu choice is picked.

If your application fits within these limitations, then the Personal Programmer may be a good tool to use. If you want to create a highly-customized application, with special DataEntry routines or complex manipulation of tables, then that program cannot generate what you need. It is possible to modify the PAL programs which are generated, but it is usually not worthwhile doing so if you have to make substantial changes. If your modifications involve more than a few lines of code, it is probably best to take the plunge and learn enough about PAL to create the entire application on your own. You can write code which is more efficient since your code does not have to be generalized.

Making Your Own Changes

If you do create a Personal Programmer application, and choose to modify the scripts which are generated yourself, (*not* using the program's Modify command), be sure to update the procedure libraries for your application, as well. To do this, play the script called *APPNAMELIB.SC* where *APPNAME* is the name of your application.

Changing the Personal Programmer scripts alone will not change the application. That is because the program generates scripts, and then builds procedure libraries from them. The procedure libraries are used to run the application. The only script which is necessary, once the application is complete, is the "driver" script, the script which starts the application. The driver script always has the same name as the name of the application.

Paradox can "swap" procedures, but not scripts, out of memory.

Procedure libraries are special files which contain "proceduralized" PAL scripts, that is, scripts written to a procedure library in a special format which is ready for execution. Normally, each command in a script is interpreted by Paradox and then executed, one command at a time. When you proceduralize a script, it will normally execute more quickly. Paradox is also better able to manage its use of memory. Information about how to create and use procedure libraries is included in Chapter 12, "Using PAL Features."

When to Use PAL

Note: Even if you are not a programmer, and think that you don't want to use PAL, read this section. You may be surprised at some of the things you can do easily with just a little PAL code.

The **S**cripts/**B**eginRecord and "Instant Script" commands are a great way to automate any tasks which you do interactively with Paradox. Many times, you can create scripts which require no modification to do a job, such as generating The Raspberry Patch order-confirmations, but, other repetitive tasks may require changes each time that they are run.

Take, for example, the task of generating statements for The Raspberry Patch which was included in Chapter 7, "Putting Queries and Reports to Work." The first query in that example queried the TRANS table for all transactions which were posted in August. Recording this query will not, in itself, be useful because the query contains selection criteria for a specific month. (Note: ⟩=*today – 30* was *not* used as a selection criteria because not all months have 30 days. Even if they did, using ⟩=*today – 30* would not provide any flexibility as to when the query could be run.)

In a case such as this, you need to be able to use a variable in the query to make it usable in more than one month. Here is a typical case where PAL can be of help. Even if you have never programmed before, learning how to use PAL to place a variable as selection criteria in a query is not difficult. Chapter 11, "Introduction to PAL," will show you how to do this. It will also show you how to write utilities to change tables in ways not possible with queries.

Sometimes it takes just a few lines of PAL code to do something you thought was impossible with Paradox. So, if you have come across some things which you would like to do in Paradox and which aren't possible through menu commands, be sure to read the next chapter. You may find a solution available with PAL, the Paradox Application Language. PAL is easy to learn and it is built on the Paradox menu system. So, if you have gotten this far in the book, you are familiar with a fair amount of PAL commands already.

Summary

Scripts can be used to automate any repetitive work which you do in Paradox. There are several different ways to create and play scripts:

Rename your Instant script if you don't want it to be deleted next time you use Alt-F3.

- Alt-F3 is the "Instant Script Record" key. Use it to record your keystrokes to a script called *Instant*.

- Alt-F4 is the "Instant Script Play" key. Use it to play your Instant script.

- You can also record your keystrokes using **Scripts/BeginRecord**. Paradox will prompt for the name of the file in which to save your keystrokes.

- A Script Editor is included with Paradox. You can use this to create or modify scripts. Access it by using **Scripts/Editor** from the Main Menu.

- You can optionally tie your own text editor into Paradox using the Custom script.

- Scripts can be played using **Scripts/Play**, **Scripts/RepeatPlay**, or **Scripts/ShowPlay** from the Main Menu. You can also play scripts from the PAL Menu which is displayed when you press Alt-F10.

- You can tell Paradox to execute a string of PAL commands up to 175 characters long using the MiniScript command on the PAL Menu. A MiniScript is not saved.

- The Personal Programmer is an application generator which is included with Paradox. It is a menu-driven program which will create a PAL program based on tables, actions, reports, and forms which you specify.

- Sometimes, PAL code is needed to fully automate a script or a series of scripts. Chapter 11 will give you an introduction to PAL and will include examples of how to use PAL to modify your saved scripts.

Introduction to PAL

This chapter contains introductory information about PAL, the Paradox Application Language. The basic elements of PAL are described and there are sample scripts which show you how to use many PAL commands and functions. The sample scripts include:

- Querying the user for a value and using it in a query
- Building a Paradox-like menu using SHOWMENU
- Changing the format of field values
- Allowing the user to change a table under script control
- Using a variable with a report
- Using SETKEY to increment a field value
- Calculating elapsed time
- Using a non-displaying password

There is also a section which shows how PAL can be used to put together a complete system for The Raspberry Patch tasks which were discussed in Chapter 7. The system is built on the queries, forms and reports which were created interactively, and is tied together using PAL. It illustrates the practical use of many PAL commands and functions and also serves as the basis for the discussion in Chapter 12 about using PAL procedures.

The information to be presented in this chapter does not cover PAL completely. (Hundreds of PAL commands and functions are available.) The purpose of this chapter, then, is to familiarize you enough with PAL to be able to write simple scripts which will expand the capabilities of your Paradox system. Even if you have never programmed, you can easily learn enough about PAL to build on your interactive Paradox system.

What Is PAL?

PAL commands and functions can be used to create programs which tell Paradox what to do. At the simplest level, you can use PAL programs to automate repetitive tasks such as querying tables and reporting on ANSWER tables. It is also possible to use PAL to create a program which can be used by someone who is not at all familiar with Paradox. PAL includes commands which allow you to format your own screens, create Paradox-like menus, and guide the user through the steps which are necessary to use a database effectively.

See Appendix G for add-on editors.

PAL programs are created by typing commands into a Paradox script file. You can use the Paradox Script Editor, as was explained in Chapter 10, "Scripts," or your own text editor. When you create a script by using Paradox, Paradox automatically appends the .SC extension to the name of the script file. If you use a different editor to create scripts, be sure to include the .SC extension in the names of script files so that Paradox can recognize them.

PAL and Paradox's Menu Structure

PAL is built on the Paradox menu structure. If you look at the PAL commands listed in Appendix D, you will see that many of them will produce the same action as Paradox menu commands or special keys such as F2 or PgDn. You use these PAL commands to tell Paradox to perform the same tasks you would do interactively.

Additional PAL commands let you perform actions which are not possible with interactive Paradox. A combination of these special commands, and menu and key commands, makes it possible to create the building blocks of your Paradox system interactively. Then you can use PAL to add functionality and to automate tasks.

The PAL "Environment"

PAL is only part of what's available to you as a PAL programmer. Paradox also includes:

- An interactive Debugger to help you debug your scripts and get them running quicker
- The PAL Menu, which is available almost anywhere in Paradox
- The Script Editor with its links to the Debugger

Together, these features provide the means to write, test, and update scripts easily. How to use the Debugger will be covered in Chapter 12.

Advanced PAL Features

Procedure Libraries

PAL has special commands which allow you to create *procedure libraries*. A procedure library is a file which contains PAL procedures you write. A procedure can be called from a script or from another procedure. There are advantages to using procedures instead of scripts. How to create procedures, and why to use them, will be explained in Chapter 12, "Using PAL Features."

The Data Entry Toolkit

For the applications developer, Paradox has a special set of programs called *The Data Entry Toolkit*. The Data Entry Toolkit enables the experienced PAL programmer to write procedures which can control data-entry down to the keystroke level. The Toolkit is quite powerful and adds enhanced capability to the commands and functions which are available with PAL. This book does not include information about The Data Entry Toolkit. It is an advanced PAL programming tool beyond the scope of the examples which are included here.

The Runtime Version

The Runtime version of Paradox lets someone run a PAL program without giving them access to interactive Paradox. Runtime is very inexpensive. It allows you to make your PAL program available to personal computer users who do not own Paradox. Details on using Runtime will be included in Chapter 12.

You can see that there is much possible using PAL. Don't get overwhelmed, though, and think that PAL is only for the person who wants to develop Paradox applications. You can use PAL to automate your queries and reports. This chapter will show you how. We'll look at how to automate some of the tasks for The Raspberry Patch which were discussed in Chapter 7, "Putting Queries and Reports to Work."

PAL Basics

Using any programming language is easy once you know the rules or "syntax." This section covers the basic elements of PAL with which you should be familiar in order to understand the sample scripts included later in this chapter.

Syntax

Every programming language has its own "syntax." Syntax is the rules for using and organizing program commands. There are not many rules for using PAL, but the few that there are can cause problems if you are not aware of them. This section describes the rules to which you must adhere and offers general advice on using comments and naming conventions.

Format

PAL lets you type most script commands using any format that you like. You can place multiple commands on the same line, as in a recorded keystroke script, or you can use separate lines for each command. It is even possible to enter a command and its arguments on multiple lines as long as you don't split keywords, names, or values. Script lines can be up to 132 characters long.

Remember, Appendix D is a partial reference of PAL commands and functions.

The exceptions to these rules are the RETURN, STYLE, SETKEY, ?, ??, and TEXT commands. See Appendix D for notes on the proper syntax for these commands.

Although not necessary, it is a good idea to use indentation to show different command levels in scripts. The examples shown in this chapter use indentation to make it easier to follow the flow of logic in a script. This can speed up the debugging process if you have problems with a script which contains several control structures.

Comments

You can enter comments into your PAL scripts by preceding them with a ;. Paradox ignores any text after a ; (unless it is in a quote string) on any script line. The examples shown in this chapter use comments to help explain why certain commands and functions are used. You can use comments in your own scripts to remind you what the script is for, when it was created, and when it was last updated. Blank lines are also permissible. You don't have to precede them with a ;.

Case Sensitivity

Whether you use upper- or lowercase letters to enter commands, functions, or variable names is not important. Case *does* matter for strings, however. For example, "abc" is not the same as "ABC" to Paradox. The SHOWMENU command, and the CASE keyword of the SWITCH command, are also case-sensitive. See Appendix D for notes.

Referring to Literals and Variables

In general, when you refer to a literal value in a PAL script, it must be enclosed within quotation marks, as in "Tom Cat." When quotation marks are part of the value being referred to, precede the quotation marks with a backslash. For example, to refer to the literal value or string *The "Secret" Getaway* in a script, type *"The \"Secret\" Getaway"*. The backslash tells Paradox to take the next quotation mark in the value literally. Similarly, to use a backslash in a literal value, precede it with another backslash as in *\\PARADOX3*.

In most cases, Paradox assumes that Alphanumeric strings, not surrounded by quotes, are variables. The exceptions are when the string is a Paradox keyword or a PAL command, or if the string does not conform to the rules, outlined later in this chapter, for naming variables.

There are different ways to refer to blank values, depending upon the data type of the field or variable being checked. Blank Alphanumeric strings are represented in a script by " ". To check whether Number or Date fields are blank, you must use the PAL BLANKNUM() and BLANK-DATE() functions, respectively. More information about PAL functions is contained in the next section.

Commands

PAL consists of commands and functions, and rules, or syntax, for using them. Commands are used to tell Paradox what action to take. There are four basic types of PAL commands:

- Abbreviated menu commands
- Keystroke commands
- QuerySaves
- Programming commands

Let's look at the sample script shown in Figure 11.1 to see how these different types of commands are used.

Abbreviated Menu Commands

PAL has commands which can be used in place of certain Paradox menu choices. They are referred to as "abbreviated menu commands." On Line 1 in Figure 11.1, the abbreviated menu command VIEW is used. This command, like F10/View, places a table on the workspace.

```
Changing script C:\patchwrk\neworder                          Script

....+...10....+...20....+...30....+...40....+...50....+...60....+...70....+...80
VIEW "Orders"                          ;place ORDERS on workspace
FORMKEY                                ;toggle to multitable form F
COEDITKEY                              ;go into Coedit mode
END                                    ;move to last record in ORDERS
PGDN                                   ;Bring up new blank form
[Order #] = CMAX ("Orders","Order #") + 1  ;Assign next # to [Order #]
[Date] = TODAY()                       ;Assign today's date to [Date]
MOVETO [Salesperson]                   ;move cursor to [Salesperson]
```

Figure 11.1 Sample script

Some abbreviated menu commands take longer to execute than the equivalent menu commands. Put PARADOX3 at the beginning of your path to minimize the difference.

You may recall from the recorded keystroke script shown in Chapter 10 that menu selections are noted in curly braces when they are recorded. While you can type them this way, using an abbreviated menu command saves time. There are abbreviated menu commands for many of the commonly used strings of menu commands. They are listed in Table 11.1.

Table 11.1 Abbreviated Menu Commands

Abbreviated Menu Command	Paradox Menu Commands
ADD	Tools/More/Add
CANCELEDIT	Cancel/Yes
COEDIT	Modify/CoEdit
COPY	Tools/Copy/Table/**Replace**
COPYFORM	Tools/Copy/Form/**Replace**
COPYREPORT	Tools/Copy/Report/**Replace**
CREATE	Create
DELETE	Tools/Delete/Table/**OK**
EDIT	Modify/Edit
EMPTY	Tools/More/Empty/**OK**
EXIT	Exit
INDEX	Tools/QuerySpeedup
LOCK	Tools/Net/Lock or **Tools**/Net/PreventLock
PICKFORM	Image/PickForm

(continued)

Table 11.1 (continued)

Abbreviated Menu Command	Paradox Menu Commands
PLAY	Scripts/Play
PROTECT	Tools/More/Protect/Password/Table
RENAME	Tools/Rename/Table/Replace
REPORT	Report/Output/Printer
SETDIR	Tools/More/Directory/OK
SETPRIVDIR	Tools/Net/SetPrivate
SETUSERNAME	Tools/Net/UserName
SORT	Modify/Sort
SUBTRACT	Tools/More/Subtract
UNLOCK	Tools/Net/Lock or Tools/Net/PreventLock
UNPASSWORD	Tools/More/Protect/ClearPassword
VIEW	View

Many of these commands are used with one or more *arguments* which tell Paradox how to use the command. For example, in the sample script shown in Figure 11.1, Line 1 appears as VIEW "Orders". In this case, "Orders" is the argument for the VIEW command. More information about arguments is included in a later section of this chapter.

Keystroke Commands

The second group of PAL commands are keystroke commands. These are commands which do the same thing as your pressing a key or key combination when using Paradox interactively. There are three main categories of keystroke commands:

- Menu selections in a script are represented in curly braces.

- Special key commands work the same as pressing a key such as F2 or PgUp; they are listed in Appendix D.

- Literals are any strings of information which you type, such as selection criteria in a query; literals are always surrounded by quotation marks, ", in a script.

ClearAll, for Alt-F8, works a little differently in a script than interactively. It will clear the workspace in a script, but not flush the buffers to the disk. Use RESET to update the disk.

In Figure 11.1, you can see examples of several PAL commands used for special keys. FORMKEY is used in place of F7 to toggle to the standard form; COEDITKEY is the same as pressing Alt-F9 to go into Coedit mode; END moves the cursor to the end of the table; and PGDN brings up a blank form.

Other Commands

The remaining PAL commands are used to do things which cannot be done interactively. These commands fall into several groups:

- Commands to create handle input and output
- Control structures for branches, loops, and switches
- Workspace commands
- Variable and array commands
- Procedure library commands
- System commands
- Multi-user commands

The MOVETO command, shown on Line 8 of Figure 11.1, is an example of a workspace command. MOVETO lets you move the cursor to a specific field, record, or image without having to use the cursor movement keys. The = sign on Line 7 is used to assign the value of the function, TODAY(), to the field, Date. More about functions will be covered in the next section.

A list of commonly used PAL commands, along with notes on syntax and purpose, can be found in Appendix D. If you don't see commands in this chapter which will accomplish what you need, be sure to review Appendix D for additional commands.

Functions

Functions are special PAL procedures which you call by name. They return a specific value, such as today's date as in the example, or the Logical value of True or False, based upon whether a certain condition is met. Functions are used in conjunction with commands either to assign a value to a variable or a field, or to compare the returned value to another value. A common mistake for new PAL users is to refer to a function by itself, without using a command to tell Paradox what use to make of the returned value.

You can see an example of the TODAY() function used in the script shown in Figure 11.1. The last line of the script uses the TODAY() function, along with the = sign, to assign the value of today's date to the field called Date. The sample scripts in this chapter will show how to use several other functions. Appendix D contains a list of commonly used functions.

Arguments

Many commands and functions require *arguments*. An argument is a required or optional parameter which passes information to Paradox for use with a command or function. In the example shown in Figure 11.1, "Orders" is the argument for the VIEW command. In this case, the argument is a literal value. Arguments also can be variables.

In Line 6 of Figure 11.1, you can see an argument used with a function. The CMAX function is used to assign a new order number to the Order # field of a new record. CMAX requires two arguments, a table name and a field name. Once again, because the arguments used are literal values, they appear within quotation marks.

The listing of commands and functions in Appendix D will show you the arguments for each command.

Expressions

An expression is a way of referring to a specific value. (Arguments for commands and functions also can be called expressions.) You can create expressions using the following elements:

These elements are described in separate sections below.

- Constants, such as a number or a name
- Variables and array elements
- PAL functions
- Field specifiers
- Operators

Data Types

These elements can be combined to form an expression as long as the data types of the elements are compatible. The data types of expressions are the same as those of field types (Alphanumeric, Number, Short number, Currency, Date) with one addition. Logical. Logical data types always evaluate to True or False. An example of a Logical value is the expression x>0 where x is a Number-type variable. If x is greater than 0, the expression evaluates to True; if x is equal to or less than 0, the expression evaluates to False.

Variables and Arrays

A variable is a placeholder to which, using PAL, you can assign different values. You don't need to define variables and their data types explicitly. Paradox does this automatically when you first assign a value to a variable. The way to do this is with the = command, as in "x=123" or *x* = "*Cat*". In the first case, *x* is a Number-type variable. In *x* = "*Cat*", *x* is an Alphanumeric value.

There is a special variable called "retval." Paradox assigns a value to retval during certain operations. This is illustrated in the examples later in this chapter.

When you first assign a value to a variable, you name it like *x* in the above example. Follow these rules when naming a variable:

- Variable names can be up to 132 characters long.
- The first character must be an upper- or lowercase letter.
- Other characters can be letters, numbers, ., $, !, or __.
- A variable name cannot contain spaces.
- Don't use any of the Paradox reserved words listed in Appendix H.

When you refer to a variable, it doesn't matter whether you use upper- or lowercase letters. Paradox will recognize the variable, even if it was first assigned using different case letters.

Paradox distinguishes between variables and literal values through the use of quotation marks. Remember to use quotation marks around any Alphanumeric literals assigned to a variable. If you don't, Paradox will think you are referring to another variable.

An array consists of variables which you can work with as a group. Each variable in an array is called an array *element*. Unlike a variable, before you can use an array, you must use the ARRAY command to define it. An ARRAY command looks like *ARRAY x[7]*.

This command creates an array called *x* with seven elements. You can use an expression, instead of a constant, for the number of array elements. This allows you to create an array with a varying number of elements as in *ARRAY x[NRECORDS("TABLE")]*. In this case, the array, *x*, is created with the number of array elements equal to the number of records in the table, *TABLE*. (NRECORDS() is a special PAL function which returns the number of records in the specified table.)

The first element of an array created using COPYTOARRAY is reserved for the table name. Field values are assigned to the remaining array elements consecutively.

The one exception to the rule about defining an array before you can use it is the COPYTOARRAY command. This special PAL command allows you to assign all values from a table record to an array which Paradox creates "on-the-fly." The name used for an array created in this way is taken from the argument specified with the COPYTOARRAY command. There is a corresponding COPYFROMARRAY command which lets you copy an entire array of values from a specified array to a table record.

Once an array has been defined, you can assign values to the individual elements. You use the array name with the number, or *subscript*, of a specific array element to refer to it. For example, *x[1]* = "*Cat*" assigns the literal string *Cat* to the first array element of array *x*. Different array elements in the same array can have different data types. The data type of each element depends upon the value which is first assigned to the element.

Field Specifiers

Field specifiers are the way you refer to fields in a table on the workspace. When you use a field specifier, Paradox assumes that you are referring to the current field, current record, and current image unless otherwise noted. Here are the field specifiers which you can use:

- *[ ]* refers to the current field of the current image.
- *[#]* refers to the current record number of the current image.
- *[Field]* refers to the named field of the current record of the current image.
- *[Table-)]* refers to the current field of the named table.
- *[Table-)Field]* refers to the named field of the named table.
- *[Table(n)-)]* refers to the current field in the nth image of the named table.
- *[Table(n)-)Field]* refers to the named field in the nth image for the named table.
- *[Table(Q)-)]* refers to the current field in the query image of the named table.
- *[Table(Q)-)Field]* refers to the named field in the query image of the named table.

Table and Field in the above examples stand for the literal table and field names to which you are referring. This is the one place where you do not need quotation marks around a literal value. To use a variable for a table or field name in one of the above specifiers, use the EXECUTE command. See Appendix D for an example.

Operators

You can use "operators" in expressions to create a value from one or more data elements. There are three types of operators: Arithmetic, Comparison, and Logical.

Arithmetic Operators: The Arithmetic operators you can use with PAL are the same as those available in queries and reports:

- + adds values together.
- − subtracts one value from another or negates a value if used with a value by itself.

- * multiplies values.
- / divides one value into another.

The rules for using arithmetic operators with different data types are the same as they are in queries and reports. Using + with Alphanumeric values concatenates the values into one string. You can add a number to a date. A number or a date can be subtracted from another date. Only Numeric data types can be used with * and /.

Comparison Operators: Comparison operators compare two values and return a Logical value of True or False. You can use these comparison operators:

- = checks whether two values are equal.
- ⟨⟩ means *not equal*.
- ⟨ means *less than*.
- ⟨ = means *less than or equal to*.
- ⟩ is the symbol for *greater than*.
- ⟩ = is the symbol for *greater than or equal to*.

When you compare numbers, larger numbers are greater than smaller numbers, as you would assume. For dates, earlier dates are less than later dates. When Comparison operators are used with Alphanumeric values, Paradox uses the sort order specified at installation to determine how values compare. For the ASCII sort order, which is the sort order if you chose U.S. for the country code at installation, *A-Z* comes before *a-z*. With other sort orders, Paradox uses a "dictionary"-type sort, where upper- and lowercase versions of the same letter are used together. You can refer to Appendix J to see how Paradox sorts values for each sort order.

Logical Operators: There are three Logical operators, AND, OR, and NOT. AND and OR allow you to check more than one expression when evaluating a logical expression. NOT negates the Logical value of an expression. The operators work as follows:

- *AND* returns True only if *both* expressions are True, as in *x*⟩5 *AND x*⟨ =10.
- *OR* returns True if *either* expression is True, as in *x*⟩5 *OR x*⟨0.
- *NOT x* returns True if *x* is False, and vice-versa.

Order of Operations: You can combine different types of operators in the same expression. Paradox observes the following order when evaluating an expression:

- Anything within () is evaluated first, and inner parentheses are evaluated before outer parentheses.
- * and / are evaluated next.
- + and −
- Comparison operators =, ⟨⟩, ⟨, ⟨=, ⟩, ⟩=
- NOT
- AND
- OR

When operators have equal precedence in an expression, they are evaluated from left to right.

Loops and Other Control Structures

PAL has commands which allow you to create control structures in your scripts. IF, WHILE, and FOR control the order of execution of script commands. SWITCHCASE and SCAN are other control statements. Additional commands let you return to a script which called another script, exit from a loop, or stop playing a script. These commands are outlined briefly here. The examples later in this chapter will show you how to use some of them. Appendix D contains more information about these commands.

IF Statements

You can use AND, OR and NOT in the expression after IF. If the expression evaluates to True, Paradox executes the command(s) after THEN.

IF statements tell Paradox to execute commands only if certain conditions are met. The IF statement has two required keywords and an optional ELSE keyword. A typical IF statement looks like this:

```
IF [Name] = "Tony Tomcat"
    THEN QUIT
    ELSE PLAY "ScriptA"
ENDIF
```

THEN and ENDIF are required keywords for the IF command. Paradox will display an error message if it does not find both required keywords. ELSE, the optional keyword, lets you specify the action to take place if the IF condition is not met. You can *nest* IF statements (use them one within another) to create different logic flows in your scripts.

WHILE Loops

The WHILE command tells Paradox to execute a sequence of commands as long as certain conditions are met. The WHILE command must be used together with the ENDWHILE command, as in:

```
WHILE x <= 5
   Play "ScriptA"
   x = x + 1
ENDWHILE
```

In this example, Paradox will play ScriptA as long as the value of x is less than, or equal to, 5. As soon as that condition is no longer satisfied, Paradox will exit from the loop and execute the next command after ENDWHILE. If there are no other commands in the script, Paradox will stop script execution, or return to the script which called the current script (if there are any commands left to execute in that script).

You can create an arbitrary WHILE loop by using a Logical True as the condition. If you do this, you must provide the means, within the WHILE loop, to exit from the loop. Here is an example:

WHILE True is commonly used with the WAIT command to give a user access to a table until a certain key is pressed.

```
x = 1
WHILE True
   x = x + 1
   IF x = 10
      THEN QUITLOOP
   ENDIF
ENDWHILE
```

This script serves only to illustrate the use of the Logical True as a condition for a loop. Paradox will execute the command which increments the value of x by 1 until x = 10. Then, Paradox will exit from the loop.

FOR Loops

You can use the FOR command to set up yet another type of loop. The FOR command executes a specified set of commands a certain number of times. It uses a *counter* which is incremented on each pass through the loop. The FOR command is used with the keyword ENDFOR like this:

```
FOR x FROM 1 TO 10
   INSTANTREPORT
ENDFOR
```

The counter is x. The starting and ending numbers are 1 and 10, respectively. This PAL code will print the Instant Report for the current table 10 times. Paradox automatically assigns the value 1 to x and increments x by 1 each time through the loop. When x has a value of 10, the commands in the loop are executed the last time and then Paradox exits from the loop.

You can use variables for the starting and ending counter values. These values are optional. If you do not specify an ending value, Paradox will continue to execute the commands in the loop until it encounters a quit command. If the starting value is not specified, Paradox uses the current value of x as the starting value.

The optional keyword, STEP, can be used to change the value which is used to increment the counter. STEP can be used with either a positive or a negative number. (If STEP is negative, the starting value must be larger than the ending value.)

FOR loops execute one or more commands a varying number of times without checking other conditions. For example, to move through all of the fields within a record in CUSTOMER, you can use a FOR loop such as the following:

```
FOR x FROM 1 TO NFIELDS ("Customer")
   MESSAGE []
   SLEEP 1000        ;keeps message on screen for one second
   RIGHT
ENDFOR
```

Assuming that you started with the cursor in the first field of a record, each pass of this FOR loop displays the contents of the current field in the message window and moves the cursor one field to the right. The loop will execute as many times as there are fields in the table.

SWITCH and CASE

The SWITCH command branches to different commands when certain conditions are met. SWITCH uses the keyword CASE to define the conditions, and ENDSWITCH to indicate the end of the SWITCH. Here is a typical SWITCH command:

You can also use the optional OTHERWISE keyword before ENDSWITCH to specify an action for any conditions not specified with CASE.

```
SWITCH
   CASE [Field] = 0 : PLAY "Closeact"
   CASE [Field] <= 100 : PLAY "Smallint"
   CASE [Field] > 100 : PLAY "Bigint"
ENDSWITCH
```

CASE statements are case-sensitive. If you check for CASE [Field] = ''ABC'', and [Field] is ''abc'', the command specified with the CASE statement will not be executed.

The SCAN Command

Be careful about using commands to move to another record in a SCAN loop.

The SCAN command lets you move through all records in a table, executing a set of commands for each one only when certain conditions are met. SCAN is especially useful because you don't have to write code to move from record to record within a table. SCAN automatically moves the cursor to the next record after the commands within the SCAN loop have been executed. SCAN is used like this:

```
EDIT "Table"
SCAN FOR [Date] = BLANKDATE()
[Date] = 1/1/89
ENDSCAN
DO_IT!
```

The FOR keyword is optional; you can use SCAN alone to perform actions for every record in a table.

This script puts TABLE onto the workspace in Edit mode and assigns the value, *1/1/89*, to the Date field for any record in which that field is blank. (BLANKDATE() is a PAL function which checks for a blank Date-type value.)

SCAN loops are an easy way to make table changes which are not possible with queries. Many of the sample scripts shown later in this chapter use SCAN, along with PAL functions, to standardize the case of an Alphanumeric field or to change a date format.

Playing a Script from Another Script

You can nest scripts by using the PLAY command in a script. There is no limit to the number of scripts which you can nest in this way. When Paradox encounters a PLAY command in a script, it plays the new script. It then returns to the ''calling'' script if there are more commands there to be executed. You don't need a special command to return to the calling script.

Exiting from Loops and Scripts

There are special commands to exit from arbitrary loops and scripts.

- QUITLOOP exits from the current loop; Paradox executes the next command after the ENDWHILE, ENDFOR, or ENDSCAN which marks the end of the current loop.

- QUIT exits from script play, including exiting from any calling scripts which are still active.
- EXIT exits from script play to DOS.
- RETURN exits from the current script and returns to the calling script, optionally returning a value.

Problems with Loops

In debug, the worksapce is visible on the screen.

It is common to have problems with scripts which include complicated control structures. The best tool for working out these problems is the PAL Debugger. The Debugger can be used to examine what Paradox is doing with a script one step at a time. At each step, you can look at the workspace to see what is happening and use the Debugger menu to execute commands, skip over commands, "pop up" a script level, or to check the value of expressions, variables, and PAL functions. Sometimes, what you think you are telling Paradox to do is not the same as what Paradox is really doing. The Debugger quickly can make this clear. Information about using the Debugger will be found in Chapter 12.

The Canvas vs. the Workspace

When you use Paradox interactively, what you see on the screen is what is on the workspace. When you play a script, you usually don't see what is happening on the workspace (unless you use **Scripts/ShowPlay**) until the script is over. Paradox displays a blank screen, called the "canvas," during script play. When the canvas is in place, you see the cursor in the upper-left corner of the screen. Then, when script play has been completed, the final state of the workspace is visible.

With PAL, you can "paint" the canvas using the special commands SHOWMENU, TEXT, ?, and ??. You can control what the user sees during script play with the optional ECHO command to display the workspace instead of the canvas. More information on these commands is included in Appendix D. Examples are included in the sample scripts shown later in this chapter.

Interacting with the User

All scripts shown so far have included only commands to tell Paradox to take some action on a table or a variable. Recorded keystroke scripts are like this. They command Paradox to follow exactly what you have done while recording. This is sufficient to use a script to automate tasks in which the steps are always exactly the same.

Sometimes, though, you may want to repeat tasks with different query selection criteria or use a different table or report as we did in generating statements for The Raspberry Patch. The steps outlined in Chapter 7 showed how to create statements for the month of August. To use this process for any month, the saved query needs to be modified.

You need a script which will ask for the month for which you want to create statements, save the value you type, and use it to generate the desired report. PAL has special commands which let you do this, as well as create menus, wait for the user to type a character, or allow the user to access a table.

- ACCEPT is used to accept a value typed by the user and assign it to a variable.

- SHOWMENU places a Paradox-style menu on the screen (with choices you define) and waits for the user to make a choice. The choice is assigned to a variable which determines the next action.

- SHOWFILES, SHOWTABLES, and SHOWARRAY work similarly to SHOWMENU, and use specified files, tables, or array elements for menu choices.

- WAIT passes control to the user until a specified key is pressed. WAIT automatically restricts the user to a specified field, record, or table.

- The GETCHAR() function reads a key from the keyboard buffer and returns the ASCII code of that key; if there is no key waiting, GETCHAR() waits for the user to press a key.

The ACCEPT Command

ACCEPT is used, along with the *?* or *??* command, to prompt the user to enter a value. The value entered is then assigned to a variable. Typically, ACCEPT is used like this:

Be sure to use "" around the S for the datatype since it is a literal, not a variable.

```
CLEAR                          ;clears the screen
@ 5,0                          ;positions the cursor
? "Enter number of month to use in query: "
ACCEPT "S" MIN 1 MAX 12 TO x
```

ACCEPT waits for the user to type a value. The value is assigned to the variable x named at the end of the ACCEPT statement. The "S" after ACCEPT tells Paradox to create a Short number-type variable in which to store the response. You must specify the data-type this way when you use ACCEPT.

The system variable retval is assigned False if Esc is pressed after ACCEPT.

The optional keywords PICTURE, MIN, MAX, LOOKUP, DEFAULT, and REQUIRED used with ACCEPT place limits on what can be entered. These keywords act like valchecks on the value which is typed. Paradox will not accept a value which does not conform to the keyword used. If you press Esc, the variable used with ACCEPT remains unchanged or unassigned if it does not already contain a value.

Using the WAIT Command

Two WAITs are used in the example below: one for each table on the multi-table form.

The WAIT command is used to stop script play and let the user view, or make changes to, a table. After the specified key is pressed, control is returned to Paradox and script play resumes. Listing 11.1 shows a sample script which lets the user post payments to the TRANS table.

Listing 11.1 Script using WAIT command

```
COEDIT "Customer"              ;Places CUSTOMER on workspace in
                               ;Coedit mode
PICKFORM 3                     ;Toggles to multi-table form 3 with
                               ;embedded TRANS table
WAIT TABLE                     ;Lets user move only through CUSTOMER
                               ;portion of form
   PROMPT "Use Ctrl-Z or PGDN to find a customer",
          "Press F2 to select customer or press Esc to quit"

UNTIL "F2", "Esc"              ;Lets user press F2 or Esc to return to
                               ;script control
IF retval = "Esc"             ;retval contains key trapped by
                               ;UNTIL
   THEN DO_IT!                 ;return to Main mode
   MESSAGE "Posting Complete"
   SLEEP 2000                  ;Pauses for two seconds
   QUIT                        ;Stops playing script
ENDIF

DOWNIMAGE                      ;Moves to TRANS portion of multi-table
                               ;form
WAIT TABLE                     ;Lets user move freely through TRANS
                               ;records for selected customers only
   PROMPT "Enter payment information. Press F2 when finished."
```

```
UNTIL "F2"
DO_IT!                        ;returns to Main mode after F2 is
                              ;pressed
```

In this example, WAIT is used with the TABLE keyword. The user is given free access to the table until one of the keys specified with the UNTIL keyword is pressed. (You can limit the part of a table to which a user has access by using the keywords FIELD or RECORD, instead of TABLE.) Paradox automatically limits the cursor movements possible based on the keyword used.

WAIT often is used in a WHILE loop to let the user enter one record at a time. Other commands can be included within the loop to assign a calculated value to a field, or to have Paradox do other tasks. Listing 11.2 is a modification of the script shown in Figure 11.1. The new script shows how to use WAIT with a WHILE loop to add records to TRANS for multiple customers.

Listing 11.2 Script using WAIT in WHILE loop

```
COEDIT "Customer"            ;Places CUSTOMER on workspace in
                             ;Coedit mode
                             ;Coedit is faster than Edit for
                             ;Zooming to find customer
PICKFORM 3                   ;Toggles to multi-table form 3 with
                             ;embedded TRANS table
WHILE True                   ;Sets up loop to enter payments for
                             ;multiple customers
WAIT TABLE                   ;Lets user move only through CUSTOMER
                             ;portion of form

   PROMPT "Use Ctrl-Z or PGDN to find a customer",
          "Press F2 to select customer or press Esc to quit"

UNTIL "F2", "Esc"            ;Lets user press F2 or Esc to return
                             ;to script control
IF retval = "Esc"            ;Retval contains key code trapped by
                             ;UNTIL
   THEN DO_IT!               ;Returns to Main mode
   MESSAGE "Posting Complete"
   SLEEP 2000                ;Pauses for two seconds
   QUIT                      ;Stops playing script
ENDIF
```

```
                          ;Next section of script played only if
                          ;F2 is used above to select customer
DOWNIMAGE

                          ;Moves to TRANS portion of multi-table
                          ;form
WAIT TABLE                ;Lets user move freely through TRANS

    PROMPT "Enter payment information. Press F2 when finished."

UNTIL "F2"                ;Checks for F2 to exit from WAIT
UPIMAGE                   ;Returns to CUSTOMER part of form
ENDWHILE                  ;Marks end of WHILE loop
```

The SHOWMENU Command

SHOWMENU creates a Paradox-style menu without your having to
write the code needed to format the screen. You provide SHOWMENU
with the desired menu choices and descriptions. Paradox takes care of
the rest. Listing 11.3 shows a typical SHOWMENU command. Figure
11.2 shows the resulting menu.

Listing 11.3 SHOWMENU command

```
SHOWMENU                                              ;Places menu
                                                      ;on screen

  "Customers" : "Add or change CUSTOMER records",
  "Orders"    : "View or enter orders",
  "Shipments" : "Update ship amounts, post sales",
  "Payments"  : "Post payments",
  "Statements": "Generate statements",
  "Leave"     : "Go back to interactive Paradox"     ;No comma here
TO choice                                             ;Assigns menu
                                                      ;choice to
                                                      ;variable
                                                      ;called
                                                      ;choice

SWITCH
    CASE choice = "Customers" : PLAY "Customer"
    CASE choice = "Orders"    : PLAY "Orders"
    CASE choice = "Shipments" : PLAY "Ship"
    CASE choice = "Payments"  : PLAY "Pmnts"
    CASE choice = "Statements": PLAY "Stmnts"
ENDSWITCH
```

```
Customers  Orders  Shipments  Payments  Statements  Leave
Add or change CUSTOMER records
```

Figure 11.2 Menu produced by SHOWMENU

SHOWMENU is usually used with the SWITCH command as shown. SWITCH lets you assign an action to each menu choice specified with SHOWMENU. If the user presses Esc when the menu is displayed, Paradox assigns "Esc" to the SHOWMENU variable. Because of this, you can use SWITCH to specify an action to take place when Esc is pressed as well as for the menu choices.

Using Variables

We have already seen how to assign a value to a variable or to an array element. Most times, you can simply use the name of a variable in order to refer to it. There are a few special cases, though. Read on to see how to use a variable as a menu choice, in a query, or in a report.

Variables as Menu Choices

It is possible to use a variable as a menu choice through the use of the SELECT command. All you do is to substitute SELECT x (or whatever your variable is named) for the bracketed menu choice in a script. Look at this line of code:

```
MENU {REPORT} {OUTPUT} SELECT x {R} {FILE} {MYREPORT.RPT}
```

These PAL commands tell Paradox to send the R report for the table name contained in variable x to the file called MYREPORT.RPT.

Variables in Queries

Variables can be used in queries as long as they are preceded by the tilde symbol, ~. The tilde tells Paradox that the string which follows is a variable and *not* a literal selection criteria. When the query is processed, Paradox uses the current value of the variable for selection criteria.

Listing 11.4 shows a script which can be used to generate Raspberry Patch statements for any month. It does so by using a tilde variable in a query. The first part of the script uses the ? and ACCEPT commands to prompt the user for a value which is then assigned to the variable called x. The variable x is then used in a query like the one shown in Chapter 7 to select records from TRANS for statements. Finally, the Statement report is copied from STMNTS to ANSWER and the statements are printed.

Listing 11.4 Script using a variable in query

```
CLEAR                                              ;Clears screen
CLEARALL                                           ;Clears
                                                   ;workspace
a 5,0                                              ;Positions
                                                   ;cursor on
                                                   ;screen
? "Enter month for which to generate statements:" ;Prompts user
                                                   ;to enter month
ACCEPT "S" MIN 1 MAX 12 TO x                       ;Assigns month
                                                   ;to variable x

Query                                              ;Query TRANS
                                                   ;for month in x
Trans | Cust # |    Date    | Type  | Charge | Payment/Credit |
      | Check  | Check ~x.. | Check | Check  | Check          |
      |        |            |       |        |                |
      |        |            |       |        |                |
Trans | Order # |
      | Check   |
      |         |
      |         |
Endquery
DO_IT!                                             ;Note
                                                   ;Underscore and
                                                   ;not hyphen

COPYREPORT "STMNTS" "R" "ANSWER" "R"               ;Copies
                                                   ;Statement R
                                                   ;report from
                                                   ;STMNTS to
                                                   ;ANSWER
CLEAR
a 5,5
? "Printing statements..."
```

```
INSTANTREPORT                                    ;Can use
                                                 ;INSTANTREPORT
                                                 ;because ANSWER
                                                 ;is current
                                                 ;image
MESSAGE "Statements Complete"
SLEEP 2000
```

This script is a good example of how to use just a bit of PAL code to extend the usefulness of a `QuerySave`. Just follow these steps:

1. Use **ASK** to place a query, such as the one in Listing 11.4, on the workspace. Be sure to use a tilde ~ in front of the variable x.
2. Save the query to a script using **Scripts/QuerySave**.
3. Use **Scripts/Editor/Edit** to edit the script created in Step 2. At the beginning of the script, add the lines above "Query" from Listing 11.4. These lines prompt the user to enter the month to be used in the query.
4. Type **DO__IT!** after the line which says Endquery.
5. Add the PAL commands, COPYREPORT and INSTANTREPORT, as shown in Listing 11.4. These commands tell Paradox to copy the Statements report specification from STMNTS to ANSWER and print statements from ANSWER.

When you use ACCEPT, and the user presses Esc instead of entering a value, the variable x will remain unassigned and the system variable retval is assigned False. Paradox will process the query, looking for all records in which the field has no value. It is easy to test for this condition with just a few PAL commands. See Listing 11.21 for an example.

Variables in Reports

There is no feature which lets you use a variable in a report the way you can do in a query. However, you can use the TYPEIN command to add a variable to a report specification just before the report is printed. See Listing 11.5 for an example of how to place a variable title into a report on CUSTOMER before it is printed.

Listing 11.5 Using a variable to change a report

```
CLEAR
@ 5,0
```

```
? "Enter a report title for CUSTOMER of up to 60 characters:"
a 7,0
ACCEPT "A60" to title
Menu {Report} {Change} {Customer} {R} Enter
FOR x FROM 1 TO 5                     ;lets up loop to move down 5
                                      ;lines
DOWN
ENDFOR
DELETELINE                            ;Erases current title line
INS                                   ;Goes into insert mode
ENTER                                 ;Creates new blank line
UP                                    ;Moves back up to new blank line
TYPEIN FORMAT ("W79,AC",title)        ;Centers title in 79 character
                                      ;Space
DO_IT!
REPORT "Customer" "R"                 ;Sends R report to printer
```

Sample Scripts

This section will show you how to use PAL commands and functions to create several utility scripts. The examples do not have code for error checking; they are kept simple to illustrate the basics of using different PAL commands and functions.

Standardizing Case

It is important to enter Alphanumeric values into tables using one standard for upper- or lowercase since Paradox is case-sensitive while doing queries or lookups in reports. You can always use a valcheck to control this as values are typed, but there is no interactive way to standardize the case of records which already exist. You need to use a PAL script to do that.

Only a few commands, and the FORMAT function, are necessary to format a field to all initial caps. See Listing 11.6 for an example. In that script, the Last Name and First Name fields of CUSTOMER were reformatted to initial caps only.

It's even easier to reformat a field to upper- or lowercase. For uppercase, substitute the UPPER function for FORMAT like this: [Last Name] = UPPER ([Last Name]). Similarly, LOWER is used to produce a value which is in lowercase letters.

Listing 11.6 Standardizing case

```
EDIT "Customer"                          ;Places CUSTOMER on
                                         ;workspace in Edit mode
SCAN                                     ;Uses SCAN to go through
                                         ;each record
[Last Name] = FORMAT ("CC",[Last Name])  ;Uses
                                         ;FORMAT with CC
                                         ;for initial caps
[First Name] = FORMAT ("CC",[First Name])
ENDSCAN
DO_IT!                                   ;Saves changes
```

Incrementing a Field Using SETKEY

Paradox does not have a command to increment a field interactively. You can add this capability easily, though, by using the SETKEY command in your INIT.SC. *Init* is a special script which Paradox plays when it is started if Init is found in the private directory or in the working directory specified in the .CFG file. See Chapter 13 for more information about Init scripts.

The SETKEY command lets you attach one or more commands to a key or to a key combination. For example, SETKEY "DEL" BEEP, tells Paradox to beep whenever the Del key is pressed. To reset a key back to its original action, use SETKEY and the desired key name again, but this time with no command specified (as in SETKEY "DEL").

SETKEY is one of the few commands which have a restriction on how they must be entered into a script. You must enter all commands to be invoked by SETKEY on the same line as "SETKEY". If your string of commands won't fit onto one 132-character line, you can use SETKEY with the PLAY command like this:

```
SETKEY 20 PLAY "ScriptA" ;20 is the keycode for Ctrl-T
                         ;Any keycode recognized by Paradox can
                         ;be substituted for the 20
```

To use SETKEY to increment a field *in a non-shared table*, you can use one of several approaches. The first example below makes the following assumptions:

- You are in Edit or Coedit mode in form view on a new record.
- The field to be incremented is a Numeric key field; you can then assume that the last record for that field has the highest value.

- The cursor will be in the field to be incremented when the key specified with SETKEY is pressed. The "magic" key here is Ctrl-N.

```
SETKEY 14 CTRLPGUP x=[] CTRLPGDN []=x+1
```

The commands after the 14 are executed when Ctrl-N is pressed. They tell Paradox to go to the preceding record (PGUP can be used if the form is a single-page form), assign the value of the current field to the variable x, move back to the original record and assign x, incremented by 1, to the current field.

If you increment a field which is not keyed, you cannot assume that the last record in the table has the highest value for the field. You can use CMAX with SETKEY instead. The only disadvantage is that CMAX will take a bit of time to calculate the maximum value in the table if there are several records in the table. If you don't mind waiting, the next line will work for you:

```
SETKEY 14 [] = CMAX ("Table","Field") + 1
```

In this case, *Table* is the name of the table, and *Field* is the name of the field, to be incremented. Be sure to use quotation marks around these names unless you are really using variables for the table and field names.

For incrementing a field value in a shared table, you have to use a different approach. You cannot just move to the last record because another user may try to do it at the same time. Remember, your record is not posted until you leave it or use Alt-L to lock it. Thus, it is possible for more than one user to go to the "last" record in the table and increment the same value.

Use MOVETO or UPIMAGE to move to the desired table.

The safest multi-user solution is to create a one-field, one-record, table which contains the last number used. SETKEY has to play a script, or call a procedure which moves to the table holding the number and attempts to place a full lock on it. You can put the LOCK command in a WHILE loop to handle a situation where the table is already in use. When the table is successfully locked, the script can increment the number in the table by one, unlock the table, and move back to the original table using the new value from the number table.

Changing a Date Format

When you import information from another file format into Paradox, your date fields may be imported as Number or Alphanumeric fields, depending upon the date format of the incoming file. Listing 11.7 shows how to reformat a date from the format *yymmdd* into the format *mm/dd/ yy*. For this script to work, the field must be Alphanumeric so it can accept the slashes in the new format. If the field to be changed is a Number field, it can be changed with **Modify/Restructure** prior to playing the script. After the script has been played, use **Modify/Restructure** to change the Alphanumeric field to a Date-type field and the process will be complete.

Listing 11.7 Script to change date from *yymmdd* to *mm/dd/yy*

```
EDIT "Newdata"
SCAN
    [Date] = SUBSTR([Date],3,2) + "/" +
    SUBSTR([Date],5,2) + "/" +SUBSTR([Date],1,2)
ENDSCAN
DO_IT!
```

Top 10 Records in a Table

Although the Paradox query mechanism is quite powerful, there is no easy way to query for a fixed number of the highest or lowest values in a table. Let's say you want to see only the top 10 records in a table. You can use the following steps, along with the script in Listing 11.8, to get the table you need.

1. Do a query on the desired table using Ctrl-F6, Check Descending, in the field(s) to be used for the comparison. Use Ctrl-R to move that field to the first position. If the desired field(s) is not in the first position, Paradox will not use it to sort the table except in the case of a tie in the field directly to the left of it. Check all other fields which you want included in ANSWER.

The QueryOrder() function will return "ImageOrder" or "TableOrder."

Also, make sure that `QueryOrder` is set to `ImageOrder` in the configuration file. You can check the setting of `QueryOrder` by pressing Alt-F10, choosing `Value` and typing **QueryOrder()** at the expression prompt.

Then press F2 to process the query.

2. Play the script in Listing 11.8 to add the first 10 records from ANSWER to TEMP. TEMP is a table, created in the script, with the same structure as ANSWER. TEMP is used to "hold" the top 10 records. This script uses the COPYTOARRAY and COPYFROMARRAY commands. Those commands let you move records between tables easily.

Listing 11.8 Script to copy records from one table to another

```
CREATE "TEMP" LIKE "ANSWER"     ;Creates TEMP table with same
                                ;structure as ANSWER
VIEW "TEMP"                     ;Places TEMP on workspace
COEDIT "ANSWER"                 ;Places ANSWER on workspace in Coedit
                                ;mode
FOR x FROM 1 TO 10             ;FOR loop to copy first 10 records
                                ;from ANSWER
   COPYTOARRAY A                ;Copies record from ANSWER to an
                                ;array called A
   MOVETO [Temp->]             ;Moves cursor to TEMP table
   COPYFROMARRAY A             ;Copies record from array A to TEMP
   DOWN                        ;Moves cursor down to new blank
                                ;Record in TEMP
   MOVETO [Answer->]           ;Move cursor back to ANSWER table
   DOWN                        ;Moves to next record in ANSWER to be
                                ;copied
ENDFOR                         ;Quits loop after 10 records have
                                ;been copied
DO_IT!                         ;Saves changes to TEMP
```

Another approach to this problem, not requiring PAL, involves adding a dummy field to the table. You can then type a one-character "flag" in the dummy field of all records which you want to see, and use a query to select only the flagged records.

Query a Variable Table

You cannot use a variable name in a query saved with **S**cripts /**Q**uerySave. You must use the SELECT command with a recorded keystroke script. First, record your keystrokes while you create the desired query. Then, use the Script Editor to substitute SELECT x (or any other variable containing the name of the table to be queried) for the name of the table in curly braces. The script in Listing 11.9 shows a recorded keystroke script which will query a variable table, such as CUSTOMER, with #s greater than 100 in the first field, after prompting the user for that name of the table to query.

Listing 11.9 Script to query a variable table

```
CLEAR                          ;Clears the canvas
CLEARALL                       ;Clears the workspace
@ 0,5                          ;Positions the cursor
```

```
? "Enter name of table to query: "     ;Prompts for a table name
ACCEPT "A8" TO x                        ;Assigns the table name
                                        ;to variable x

MENU {ASK} SELECT x CHECK RIGHT ">100"  ;Uses SELECT to
                                        ;specify table name
DO_IT!                                  ;contained in variable x
```

Split Name into Separate Fields

There may be times when you need to split one field into separate fields. Look at the table COMPANY shown in Figure 11.3. This table has just one field for name. To allow for more flexibility with queries, it's best to have the First and Last Names in separate fields. To do this, first restructure COMPANY and add two new fields, Last Name and First Name. (You could actually add just one field and rename the original field.) After you have the new fields, use the script in Listing 11.10 to assign names to the appropriate fields.

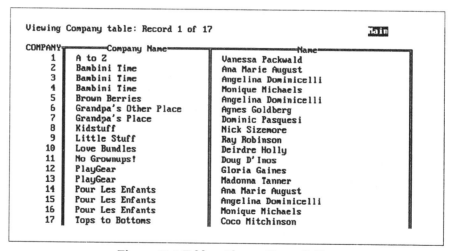

Figure 11.3 Table with one Name field

Listing 11.10 Script to separate field values

```
COEDIT "COMPANY"                        ;Places COMPANY on workspace
                                        ;in Coedit mode

SCAN                                    ;Uses SCAN to check every
                                        ;record in table

IF MATCH ([Name],".. .. ..",a,b,)       ;For names with two words
   THEN [First Name] = a                ;Assigns first word to
                                        ;First Name
```

```
        [Last Name] = b                        ;Assigns second word to
                                                ;last Name


ENDIF
ENDSCAN
DO_IT!
```

This script shows how to use the MATCH() function to look for patterns in field values. As written, the script looks first for values which have at least one blank space. It assumes that the first part is the first name and the second part is the last name. To account for first names with more than one word, or entries with middle initials, you will need a series of MATCH statements.

Calculate Elapsed Time

Paradox does not have a time function. To do calculations using time values, you must use a PAL script. The script in Listing 11.11 assumes that you are calculating the elapsed time between the values in *[Start Time]* and *[End Time]* and assigning the difference to a field called *[Length Of Time]*. The example also assumes that times are entered into an Alphanumeric field using the format hh:mm:ss. All times are entered in military format (where the hour is represented by a number from 00 to 23) and do not span greater than 24 hours. If it is possible for the times to span more than 24 hours, additional commands (to check date differences) would have to be included.

Listing 11.11 Script to calculate elapsed time

```
COEDIT "CALLS"
SCAN
IF MATCH ([Start Time],"..:..:..",a,b,c) AND
MATCH ([End Time],"..:..:..",d,e,f)
    THEN [Minutes] = (NUMVAL(d)*60 + NUMVAL(e) + NUMVAL(f)/60)
    - (NUMVAL(a)*60 + NUMVAL(b) + NUMVAL(c)/60)
ENDIF
IF [Minutes] < 0                                ;where End
                                                ;Time is
                                                ;after midnight
                                                ;and Start
                                                ;Time is before
    THEN [Minutes] = [Minutes] + 1440           ;Adds 24
                                                ;hours to get
```

```
                                        ;accurate
                                        ;minutes
        ENDIF
        ENDSCAN
        DO_IT!
```

There are several ways to calculate elapsed time. The example uses the MATCH() function to parse the hours, minutes and seconds, and uses the values individually to calculate the total minutes between *Start Time* and *End Time*. The final result is stored in a field called *Minutes*. The script checks for the case where the *Start Time* is before midnight and the *End Time* after midnight by checking for a negative value for *Minutes*. 1440, the number of minutes in 24 hours, is then added to show the true elapsed minutes.

Using Text Files for Notes

Although Paradox does not support the use of memo fields directly, you can attach a note file to a record using the RUN command. This is how you do it:

1. Create an "A8" or "A12" field called [*Notes*] in your table to contain the name of a text file to hold notes.

2. Place a SETKEY in your init script which will go to DOS and bring up your text editor with the note file specified in [*Notes*]. That SETKEY command looks like this:

The EXECUTE command is used to tell Paradox to create a command by concatenating expressions.

```
SETKEY 1 EXECUTE "RUN + \"EDITOR " + [Notes] + "\""
```

Substitute the command to start your editor for *EDITOR* in the above line. This example uses 1, the ASCII code for Ctrl-A.

3. To use the SETKEY, press Ctrl-A with the cursor in the record with the entry for the note field you want to edit. Paradox will suspend itself and take you to DOS and into your text editor. When you have finished using the editor, use the usual commands to exit and you will be returned to Paradox where you left off.

A Non-Displaying Password

When you use **Tools/More/Protect/Password** to protect a script, the password is not needed to play the script. The password is required only to read the script using the Script Editor. To prevent a user from playing a script without a password, you can write a script incorporating GET-CHAR(). Listing 11.12 shows an example of how to do this.

Listing 11.12 Script for non-displaying password

```
CLEAR                                    ;Clears the screen
@ 5,0                                    ;Positions the cursor
? "Enter secret code and press Enter: "  ;Prompts for password
secret = ""                              ;Initializes variable
                                         ;secret to "nothing"
y = 1                                    ;Sets counter y to
                                         ;use for three tries only
WHILE y <= 3                             ;Starts WHILE loop for
                                         ;three tries
WHILE True                               ;Starts WHILE loop to
                                         ;accept characters
x = GETCHAR()                            ;Uses GETCHAR() to get
                                         ;key; no display
IF x = 27                                ;Checks to see if key
                                         ;pressed is Esc
   THEN RETURN                           ;If so, quits script play
ENDIF
IF x = 13                                ;Checks if key pressed is
                                         ;Enter
   THEN QUITLOOP                         ;If so, quits inner loop
                                         ;for GETCHAR()
   ELSE secret = secret + CHR(x)         ;Adds new character to
                                         ;variable secret
ENDIF
ENDWHILE
y = y + 1
IF secret <> "Abracadabra"               ;Increments counter y
   THEN
   IF y <= 3                             ;Checks for number of
                                         ;tries <= 3
     THEN MESSAGE "Incorrect password, try again"
     SLEEP 1000
     ELSE MESSAGE "That was your last chance - Goodbye!"
     SLEEP 1000
     QUIT
   ENDIF
   ELSE
   MESSAGE "You got it!"
   SLEEP 1000
```

```
        RETURN
ENDIF
ENDWHILE
```

Two WHILE loops were used in this example. The first, or outer-most WHILE loop, gives the user three tries in which to enter the correct password. The second WHILE loop increments a variable with the characters typed from the keyboard before Enter was pressed. That variable is then compared to the actual password, in this case *Abracadabra*.

The script which actually contains the password can be password-protected to prevent anyone from being able to read the password from the script. Or, the script can be proceduralized, that is, written to a PAL procedure library and called from a script when needed. Chapter 12 will explain how to use this PAL feature. While scripts are ASCII text files, procedures are stored in a format which is not understandable to humans. You can give the user a small "driver" script which calls your procedures and eliminates the need to distribute copies of your source code. The password is then protected.

The Raspberry Patch Application

Chapter 7 outlined the steps necessary for doing the following tasks for The Raspberry Patch:

- Producing order-confirmation letters
- Updating shipment information
- Generating invoices from shipped orders
- Posting sales and payments to a transaction table
- Generating statements

Some of these steps could be automated using recorded scripts, but you would still have to be very careful to execute all necessary queries and reports in the right order. You can use PAL to put together an application which automatically ties certain tasks such as shipping orders, creating invoices, and posting sales together, eliminating the risk of forgetting to do a necessary update before or after reports are run. Here is an example of how it can be done, making use of several of the commands and functions described in this chapter.

The Main Menu Script

We looked at an example of the SHOWMENU command in Listing 11.3. The menu choices in the example generally correspond to The Raspberry Patch tasks in the above list. This SHOWMENU, with the addition of a WHILE loop, can be used as the Main Menu for The Raspberry Patch application. Placing the SHOWMENU in a WHILE loop, as shown in Listing 11.13, allows the user to return to the menu instead of playing the menu script repeatedly, after completing a task. Choosing Leave from the menu, or pressing Esc, allows the user to exit from the loop and return to Paradox.

Listing 11.13 Main Menu script

```
CLEAR                                                   ;Clears the
                                                        ;screen
CLEARALL                                                ;Clears the
                                                        ;workspace
WHILE True                                              ;Puts menu in
                                                        ;a loop
SHOWMENU                                                ;Places menu
                                                        ;on the screen
   "Customers" : "Add or change CUSTOMER records",
   "Orders"    : "View or enter orders",
   "Shipments" : "Update ship amounts, post sales",
   "Payments"  : "Post payments",
   "Statements": "Generate statements",
   "Leave"     : "Go back to interactive Paradox"  ;No comma here
TO choice                                          ;Assigns menu
                                                   ;choice to
                                                   ;variable
                                                   ;called choice

SWITCH
   CASE choice = "Customers" : PLAY "Customer"
   CASE choice = "Orders"    : PLAY "Orders"
   CASE choice = "Shipments" : PLAY "Ship"
   CASE choice = "Payments"  : PLAY "Pmnts"
   CASE choice = "Statements": PLAY "Stmnts"
   CASE choice = "Esc"       : QUIT
   CASE choice = "Leave"     : QUIT
ENDSWITCH
ENDWHILE                                                ;Closes WHILE
                                                        ;loop
```

Changing CUSTOMER Information

The script played by the menu choice `Customers` is shown in Figure 11.14. This is a simple script which uses the WAIT TABLE command to let the user change or add records to CUSTOMER. Because WAIT TABLE instead of WAIT RECORD is used, the user can take advantage of Alt-Z for "Zoom," Ctrl-U for "Undo," the Edit Menu and all cursor movement keys, without the need for any special commands in the script. This is an easy way to give the user full access to a table.

Listing 11.14 Script to change CUSTOMER

```
COEDIT "Customer"    ;Coedit mode for better performance while
                     ;"Zooming" on key field
FORMKEY              ;Toggles to form F
WAIT TABLE           ;Gives user free access to table
   PROMPT "Use Ctrl-Z or PgDn to find customer, F2 to save",
        "End there PgDn to add customer, Ctrl-U to Undo"
UNTIL "F2"
DO_IT!
CLEARIMAGE           ;Clears CUSTOMER table from workspace
                     ;Returns to PATCHWRK.SC when played from that
                     ;script
```

Entering Orders

The second menu choice, `Orders`, plays the script called *Orders* shown in Listing 11.15. That script shows a more complex use of the WAIT command on a multi-table form. When you use WAIT with a multi-table form, cursor movement is restricted to one part of the form at a time, even with the WAIT TABLE command. It is necessary to "trap" the F3 and F4 keys, using the UNTIL statement, and write PAL commands which let the user move between multiple images on the same form.

Listing 11.15 Script to add orders

```
COEDIT "Orders"      ;Puts ORDERS on workspace in Coedit mode
FORMKEY              ;Toggles to multi-table form F including
                     ;CUSTOMER and DETAIL
END                  ;Moves to last order in ORDERS
WHILE True           ;Sets up WHILE loop to enter more than one
                     ;new order
```

```
x = [Order #]                 ;Assigns highest Order # to variable x
PGDN                          ;Brings up new blank order
[Order #] = x + 1             ;Assigns new order number,
                              ;incrementing x by 1
[Date] = TODAY()              ;Assigns today's date to Date field
MOVETO [Salesperson]          ;Moves cursor to the Salesperson field


WHILE True                    ;WHILE loop to move between ORDER and
                              ;DETAIL tables on same record
WAIT RECORD                   ;Allows the user to change ORDER portion
                              ;of order
   Prompt "Enter Customer # and Salesperson. Press F1 for help",
        "F4 to enter detail, PgDn for new order, Esc to quit"

UNTIL "F2","F4","PGDN","Esc"

IF retval = "F4"              ;If user presses F4, moves to DETAIL part
   THEN DOWNIMAGE
   DOWNIMAGE
   WAIT TABLE                 ;Allows user to enter multiple line items

       Prompt "Enter detail info. Press F1 for help in [Item #].",
             "Press F3 to move to top of form, F2 to finish."

   UNTIL "F2","F3"
   UPIMAGE
   UPIMAGE                    ;Moves to ORDER even if F2 pressed
   IF retval = "F2"           ;Del below to discard order if DETAIL
                              ;empty
      THEN QUITLOOP           ;If user presses F2, quits editing this
                              ;record
   ENDIF
   ELSE QUITLOOP              ;If user presses PGDN, F2, or Esc in
                              ;top of
ENDIF                         ;form, stops editing current record
ENDWHILE                      ;Closes loop to edit current record
IF retval = "PGDN"            ;If PgDn is pressed in ORDER part of
                              ;form,
   THEN LOOP                  ;goes to top of loop and brings up new
                              ;order
ENDIF
DEL                           ;Del discards order only if DETAIL
                              ;empty
DO_IT!                        ;Saves changes after pressing F2 or
                              ;Esc in
```

```
      QUITLOOP                    ;top of form, quits outer loop
      ENDWHILE                    ;Closes loop for adding orders
      CLEARIMAGE                  ;Clears workspace
      RELEASE VARS x
      PLAY "Letters"              ;Generates order-confirmations
```

Order-Confirmation Letters

PLAY "Letters" can be changed to a procedure call if you proceduralize your scripts.

Instead of doing a query for the last week's orders as we did in Chapter 7, we can use PAL to generate order-confirmation letters for each group of orders as they are entered. The last line of Listing 11.15 tells Paradox to play a script called *Letters*. That script is shown in Listing 11.16.

Listing 11.16 Order-Confirmation Letter Script

```
CLEAR                          ;Clears screen
CLEARALL                       ;Clears workspace
a 5,0
? "Generating order-confirmation letters..."

Query                          ;Selects records where letter has not been sent

Orders ¦ Order # ¦ Date  ¦ Customer # ¦ Salesperson ¦ Letter Sent ¦
       ¦ Check _o ¦ Check ¦ Check      ¦ Check       ¦ blank       ¦
       ¦         ¦       ¦            ¦             ¦             ¦
       ¦         ¦       ¦            ¦             ¦             ¦

Orders ¦
       ¦
       ¦
       ¦

Detail ¦ Order # ¦ Item # ¦ Description ¦ Quantity ¦ Price ¦
       ¦ _o      ¦ Check  ¦ Check       ¦ Check    ¦ Check ¦
       ¦         ¦        ¦             ¦          ¦       ¦
       ¦         ¦        ¦             ¦          ¦       ¦

Endquery
DO_IT!

COPYREPORT "ORDERLET" "R" "ANSWER" "R"
INSTANTREPORT                  ;Prints order confirmations
```

```
CLEARALL                      ;Clears old query and images from workspace
                              ;Updates [Letter Sent] field in ORDERS
Query
  Orders |    Letter Sent            |
         | blank, changeto today     |
         |                           |
         |                           |
         |                           |
Endquery
DO_IT!
CLEARALL
```

First, the script queries ORDERS and DETAIL for all orders where the *[Letter Sent]* field is blank. Then, a report specification is copied from ORDERLET to ANSWER and the letters printed from ANSWER. Finally, a Changeto query is done on ORDERS to update the *[Letter Sent]* field with today's date for all records where that field is empty. Including these steps in the order entry script eliminates the possibility of forgetting to send letters. It also saves going through the interactive steps necessary to produce the letters.

Shipments, Invoices, and Posting Sales

The script in Listing 11.17 corresponds to the Shipments menu choice. It is used to do three tasks:

- Update the ORDERS and DETAIL tables with shipment dates, costs, and amounts
- Print invoices
- Post the final sales amounts to the transactions table (for use later in statements)

Listing 11.17 Ship script

```
COEDIT "Orders"             ;Places ORDERS on workspace in Coedit
                            ;mode
WHILE True                  ;Sets up loop to update multiple orders
CLEAR                       ;Clears screen

a 5,0                       ;Positions cursor
? "Enter number of order to update with shipping info: "
ACCEPT "S" to ordernum      ;Assigns Order # to variable called
                            ;ordernum
```

```
      IF retval = False            ;If Esc was pressed, retval = False
         THEN DO_IT!               ;Returns to Main mode
            CLEARIMAGE
            RETURN
      ENDIF

      MOVETO [Order #]             ;Moves to Order # field to do
                                   ;LOCATE for ordernum
      LOCATE ordernum
      IF retval = False OR NOT ISBLANK ([Ship Date])
                                   ;retval True if order was
                                   ;found
         THEN MESSAGE "Order not found or already filled"
            SLEEP 2000
            LOOP                   ;Goes to top of WHILE loop
      ENDIF
      PICKFORM 1                   ;Toggles to multi-table form
      WAIT RECORD                  ;Allows user to update shipping date
                                   ;and cost

         PROMPT "Enter ship date/cost, F2 to enter amounts, Esc quits"

      UNTIL "F2","Esc"

      IF retval = "Esc"
         THEN DO_IT!
            RETURN
      ENDIF

      DOWNIMAGE
      DOWNIMAGE                    ;Moves cursor to DETAIL part of form
      WAIT TABLE                   ;Allows user to enter shipping amounts

         PROMPT "Enter ship amounts, press F2 when finished"

      UNTIL "F2"
      UPIMAGE
      UPIMAGE                      ;Moves back to ORDER part of multi-
                                   ;table form
      LOCKKEY                      ;Posts record to allow toggle to table
                                   ;view
      FORMKEY                      ;Toggles to table view so LOCATE on
                                   ;Order # will
                                   ;work, Order # is Display-only on form 1
```

```
    ENDWHILE                    ;Closes WHILE loop for entering
                                ;shipping information

    CLEARIMAGE

    PLAY "Invoices"             ;Plays script to generate invoices for
                                ;newly shipped orders
    PLAY "Postsale"             ;Plays script to post total sale
                                ;amount, including shipping cost,
                                ;to TRANS table
                                ;TRANS table used later to generate
                                ;statements
```

The first part of the script uses several PAL commands which we have already seen. ACCEPT is used to prompt the user for an Order # to update. WAIT is used to let the user update the ORDER and DETAIL tables. There are several new commands shown as well:

- *MOVETO* moves the cursor to the specified field. It also can be used to move to tables or record numbers.
- *LOCATE* is used to find the Order # entered with ACCEPT.
- *ISBLANK()* is a PAL function which is used to see if the *[Ship Date]* field is blank.
- *LOCKKEY* posts the current record in ORDERS so that it is possible to toggle to table view.

The last two lines in the script play the scripts which print invoices and post the sales amounts. These scripts are shown in Listings 11.18 and 11.19, respectively. They exactly duplicate the steps shown in Chapter 7, with the addition of a few screen messages.

Listing 11.18 Invoices script

```
CLEAR
@ 5,0
? "Generating invoices for orders shipped today..."

Query                                 ;Select newly shipped
                                      ;orders for invoicing
```

Orders	Order #	Date	Customer #	Salesperson	Ship Date
	Check _o	Check	Check	Check	today

```
Orders | Ship Cost |
       | Check     |
       |           |
       |           |

Detail | Order # | Item # | Description | Ship Qty          | Price |
       | _o      | Check  | Check       | Check as Quantity | Check |
       |         |        |             |                   |       |
       |         |        |             |                   |       |

Detail |
       |
       |
       |
       |

Endquery
DO_IT!
COPYREPORT "INVRPT" "R" "ANSWER" "R"    ;Copies invoice report
                                        ;from INVRPT
INSTANTREPORT                           ;to ANSWER and reports on
                                        ;ANSWER

CLEAR
CLEARALL
```

Listing 11.19 PostSale script

```
CLEAR
@ 5,0
? "Posting total sales amounts to TRANS table..."

CLEARALL              ;Makes sure the workspace is clear

Query                 ;Query to calculate extended prices for
                      ;orders shipped today
                      ;(shipping amount may vary from order amount)
Orders | Order # | Ship Date |
       | _o      | today     |
       |         |           |
       |         |           |

Detail | Order # | Price | Ship Qty      |
       | Check _o| _p    | _q,calc _p*_q |
       |         |       |               |
       |         |       |               |

Endquery
```

```
DO_IT!

Query                    ;Query to calculate sum of extended prices
                         ;for each order
  Answer | Order # | Price * Ship Qty |
         | Check   | calc sum         |
         |         |                  |
         |         |                  |

Endquery
DO_IT!

Query                    ;Query to insert total sale amount for each
                         ;order into TRANS table
                         ;(used later for statements)
  Trans | Cust # | Date  | Type |       Charge       | Order # |
  insert| _c     | today | S    | _shipcost+_ordsum  | _o      |
        |        |       |      |                    |         |
        |        |       |      |                    |         |

  Orders | Order # | Customer # | Ship Cost |
         | _o      | _c         | _shipcost |
         |         |            |           |
         |         |            |           |

  Answer | Order # | Sum of Price * Ship Qty |
         | _o      | _ordsum                 |
         |         |                         |
         |         |                         |

Endquery
DO_IT!
CLEARALL
CLEAR
```

Posting Payments

Listing 11.20 shows another example of the WAIT command with a multi-table form. The main table here is CUSTOMER. TRANS is the linked table on the form. The first WAIT TABLE allows the user to select a customer record to update. The second WAIT gives access to the TRANS table so that payments can be entered. Both WAIT are in a WHILE loop so that payments can be entered for multiple customers.

Listing 11.20 Script to post payments

```
COEDIT "Customer"              ;Places CUSTOMER on workspace in
                               ;Coedit mode
                               ;Coedit is faster than Edit for
                               ;"Zooming" to find customer
PICKFORM 3                     ;Toggles to multi-table form 3 with
                               ;embedded TRANS table

WHILE True                     ;Sets up loop to enter payments for
                               ;multiple customers
WAIT TABLE                     ;Lets user move freely only through
                               ;CUSTOMER portion of form

    PROMPT "Use Ctrl-Z or PGDN to find a customer.",
           "Press F2 to select customer or Esc to quit"

UNTIL "F2", "Esc" ;Lets user press F2 or Esc to return to script
                  ;control

IF retval = "Esc"              ;retval contains key trapped by
                               ;UNTIL
   THEN DO_IT!                 ;Returns to Main mode
   MESSAGE "Posting Complete"
   SLEEP 2000                  ;Pauses for two seconds
   QUIT                        ;Stops playing script
ENDIF
                               ;Next section of script played only if
                               ;F2 is used above to select customer
DOWNIMAGE                      ;Moves to TRANS portion of multi-table
                               ;form
WAIT TABLE                     ;Lets user move freely through TRANS

    PROMPT "Enter payment information. Press F2 when finished."

UNTIL "F2"
UPIMAGE                        ;Returns to CUSTOMER part of form
ENDWHILE                       ;Marks end of WHILE loop
```

Generating Statements

The system variable retval is assigned False if Esc is pressed after ACCEPT.

The script in Listing 11.21 is used to generate statements for the **Statements** menu choice. It uses the ACCEPT command to prompt the user for a month on which to report as shown earlier in this chapter. The query is then processed. A few simple commands are all that are needed to copy the report specification to ANSWER and print the statements.

Listing 11.21

```
CLEAR                                         ;Clears the screen
CLEARALL                                      ;Clears the
                                              ;workspace
a 5,0                                         ;Positions cursor
                                              ;on the screen
? "Enter month to generate statements for: "  ;Prompts user to
                                              ;enter month
ACCEPT "S" MIN 1 MAX 12 TO x                  ;Assigns month to
                                              ;variable x
IF retval = False                            ;Checks to see if
                                              ;Esc was pressed
   THEN RETURN                                ;If so, return to
                                              ;menu
ENDIF

CLEAR                                         ;Clears the screen
a 5,0                                         ;Positions the
                                              ;cursor
? "Processing statements..."                  ;Displays message

Query                                         ;Query TRANS for
                                              ;month in x
 Trans | Cust # |    Date    | Type | Charge | Payment/Credit |
       | Check  | Check ~x.. | Check| Check  | Check          |
       |        |            |      |        |                |
       |        |            |      |        |                |

 Trans | Order # |
       | Check   |
       |         |
       |         |

Endquery
DO_IT!

COPYREPORT "STMNTS" "R" "ANSWER" "R"          ;Copies Statement
                                              ;report from
                                              ;STMNTS to ANSWER
```

```
CLEAR
@ 5,5
? "Printing statements..."

INSTANTREPORT                              ;Can use
                                           ;INSTANTREPORT
                                           ;since ANSWER is
                                           ;current image

MESSAGE "Statements Complete"
SLEEP 2000
```

You can use PAINTCANVAS with question marks to create more interesting messages.

This small group of scripts greatly simplifies the steps shown in Chapter 7. PAL tells Paradox what to do and asks you only for pertinent information. Using the scripts saves time and also eliminates the possibility of forgetting some important steps.

The Tip of the PAL Iceberg

The information presented in this chapter was a very small part of all that is possible through PAL. You can create sophisticated applications which allow the user who has no knowledge of Paradox to utilize a database effectively. It is also possible to write multi-user applications which let several network users share the same database. PAL has special commands for multi-user applications which make it easy to develop an application for network use. That topic, and The Data Entry Toolkit, are not covered in this book.

The next chapter contains information about using some of the other features of the PAL environment. Chapter 12 will show you how to use the Debugger, create procedure libraries, and use Runtime. If you plan to use PAL at all, be sure to review Chapter 12 for information about the Debugger. Even if you are not an applications developer, you can use the Debugger to make writing scripts easier. You may also decide to use the Runtime version of Paradox to share your work with PC users who do not own Paradox.

Summary

PAL is the Paradox Application (programming) Language. Even if you are not a programmer, you can learn enough about PAL to expand the capabilities of your interactive system fairly easily. PAL is a high-level language which is built on the Paradox menu system so if you know how to use Paradox, you are already familiar with some PAL commands. Here are some basics about PAL:

- PAL has a free-form syntax; there are no rules for indenting and, usually, you can place as many commands as you like on a line.
- There are hundreds of PAL commands and functions. Commands tell Paradox what to do; functions return a value.
- There are four types of PAL commands: QuerySaves, keystroke commands, abbreviated menu commands, and other programming commands.
- You create expressions for use with commands by combining constants, PAL functions, operators, variables, and field specifiers.
- PAL has special commands, IF, SWITCH, SCAN, FOR, and WHILE, for branching and looping.
- You can use a variable in a query by preceding it with a tilde ~.
- Scripts can be played by other scripts.

Using Advanced PAL Features

This chapter contains information about three topics related to PAL:

- The Debugger
- PAL procedures
- Paradox Runtime

If you are going use PAL at all, you should read the section on the Debugger. The Debugger is a tool for debugging your scripts and quickly getting them running. It has its own menu and provides a link to your text editor. This makes the process of changing code, and testing it, less time consuming.

The other topics in this chapter are optional. If you use PAL only for one-time tasks which are not part of your normal Paradox work, you probably won't have much need for using procedures or for the Runtime version. But, if you use PAL to develop applications for your own use, or to distribute to others, you should be familiar with procedures and Runtime. The benefits of using procedures and the Runtime version are outlined in the respective sections below.

Using the Debugger

Writing scripts is usually an iterative process of testing, rewriting, and testing again until the script works the way you want it to. Sometimes, the problems encountered relate to using the right commands and logic structures which tell Paradox what to do. Your script may run to completion, but may not accomplish what you expect of it. Other problems result from improper syntax in a script, missing files, or other unexpected situations which cause Paradox to give a "Script error" or "Run error" message. The Debugger can help you solve both types of problems.

The Debugger has several features. It has its own menu with commands which let you:

You can see what is happening on the workspace while the Debugger is active.

- Check the value of variables, functions, and other expressions
- Step through scripts one command at a time
- Skip commands or "pop up" a level when you are using nested scripts or procedures
- Execute commands or play scripts "on-the-fly"
- See which scripts and procedures are active, how they are nested, and which procedures are swapped out of memory
- Go into the Script Editor (or your own text editor) directly to the line which caused a script error

Entering the Debugger

There are several ways to enter the Debugger. Paradox gives you the option to enter it when a script error or run error is encountered; you can use the PAL DEBUG command; you can use Debug from the PAL Menu; or you can press Ctrl-Break while playing a script.

Script Errors and Run Errors

If you have started writing scripts, you have probably come across the Cancel Debug menu shown in Figure 12.1. When Paradox encounters a problem while playing a script, it stops script play and displays that menu. At this point, you can choose Cancel to quit script play or choose Debug to enter the Debugger.

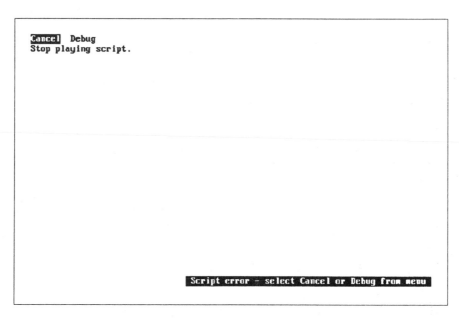

Figure 12.1 `Cancel Debug` menu

If you choose `Debug` from the menu shown in Figure 12.1, you will see a screen like the one shown in Figure 12.2. In that example, the workspace is empty and the information on the screen comes only from the Debugger. You see several elements while using the Debugger:

- The current state of the workspace, instead of that of the canvas, is shown on the screen.
- The second-from-the-bottom line shows the current script and the current line number.
- The bottom line shows the current script line with the Debugger cursor (a triangle) pointing to the next command to be executed.
- An error message is displayed on the right side of the screen.

At this point, you have access to the Debugger Menu and several special keys which correspond to Debugger commands. The Debugger Menu is described below with the shortcut keys for each command listed.

When you press Ctrl-Break while playing a script, Paradox stops playing the script and gives the script error menu. This is one way to force Paradox to display the `Cancel Debug` menu so that you can enter the Debugger at will.

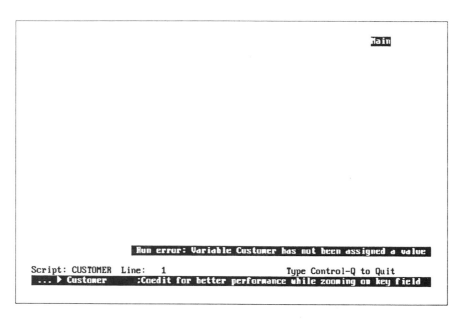

Figure 12.2 Screen after entering the Debugger

The DEBUG Command

The Debugger is great for unraveling logic problems.

There may be times when you want to use the Debugger even if you have not encountered a script or run error. For example, your script may play through to completion but not give the intended result. The Debugger is very useful for solving such problems.

There are two ways to call the Debugger explicitly. You can choose `Debug` from the PAL Menu and specify the name of a script to debug. Paradox will enter the Debugger and stop before executing the first command in the specified script. Or, you can place the PAL DEBUG command into your script. As soon as it encounters the DEBUG command, Paradox will stop playing the script and enter the Debugger. Whether you enter the Debugger using the PAL Menu or the DEBUG command, you can press Alt-F10 at this point to display the Debugger Menu.

The Debugger Menu

The Debugger Menu is shown in Figure 12.3. The choices are:

MiniScript can be used to reassign a value to a variable or field on-the-fly before resuming execution.

- `Value` lets you check the current value of any valid PAL expression.
- `Step` executes the current command in the current script.
- `Next` skips the current command and executes the one following.

- `Go` resumes script play.
- `MiniScript` lets you execute a short string of PAL commands "on-the-fly."
- `Where?` shows the current nesting of scripts and procedures.
- `Quit` exits from the Debugger.
- `Pop` moves up one level of script play.
- `Editor` takes you to the current line in the current script under editor control.

There are also shortcut keys for accessing most of these commands while under Debugger control:

Table 12.1 Debugger Shortcut Keys

Key	Debugger Command
Ctrl-S	Step
Ctrl-N	Next
Ctrl-G	Go
Ctrl-W	Where?
Ctrl-Q	Quit
Ctrl-P	Pop
Ctrl-E	Editor

Except in the case of a syntax error, these commands are available while you are in the Debugger. When you go into the Debugger after a syntax error, Paradox will not let you use `Step`, `Next`, or `Go`. The syntax error must be resolved before you can continue script play.

A Quick Trip Through the Debugger

Let's take a quick trip through the Debugger to see how some commands are used. The error message seen in Figure 12.2 occurred when a script, which attempted to put the CUSTOMER table on the workspace in Coedit mode, was played. The message tells us that Paradox is looking for a variable named *customer* which has not been assigned a value. To go into the script and see what is wrong, press Ctrl-E. Paradox will take you directly to the line where the error occurred, as shown in Figure 12.4. Here you can see that there are no quotation marks around the table name *CUSTOMER*. Because Paradox looked for a variable called *cus-*

tomer, instead of for a table named *CUSTOMER*, that caused a script error. The correction can be made quickly and the script played again using F10/Go if you are using the Paradox Script Editor.

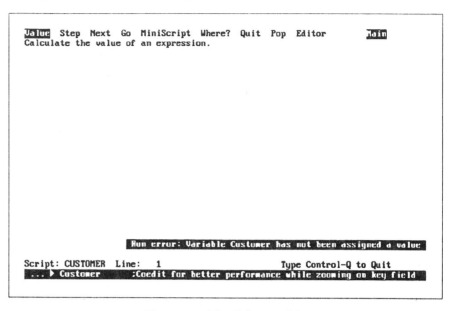

Figure 12.3 The Debugger Menu

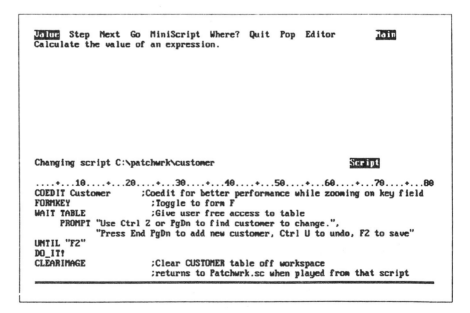

Figure 12.4 Screen after entering Script Editor with Ctrl-E

The last example was quite simple. Let's look at a different problem to see how some of the other Debugger commands work. Assume that you have played the menu script for The Raspberry Patch, chosen Shipments from the menu, updated orders with shipping information, and waited for invoices to print. Nothing happened after you updated ORDERS and you were returned to The Raspberry Patch menu.

Using the DEBUG command can be useful here. You know that you were able to update ORDERS successfully, so the error occurred after that point. The next command in the SHIP script is PLAY "Invoices." We can put a DEBUG command in INVOICES.SC, as shown in Figure 12.5, to step through the script one command at a time, hopefully discovering the source of the problem along the way.

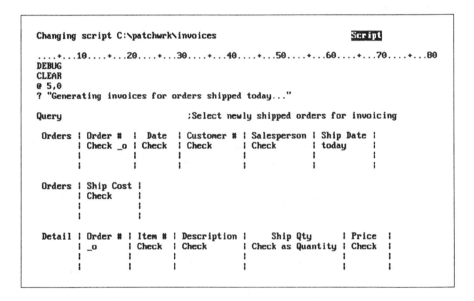

Figure 12.5 DEBUG in INVOICES script

Ctrl-W is useful for narrowing-down memory problems as it indicates which procedures are swapped out.

When the SHIP script is played next, it executes normally until it calls the INVOICES script. At this point, Paradox stops script play and enters the Debugger. The current command is the first command in INVOICES.SC as shown in Figure 12.6. That screen does not tell much about the problem. The first thing we can check is where we are in terms of script play. Pressing Ctrl-W displays the screen shown in Figure 12.7 which shows that the current script is *INVOICES.* It also shows that INVOICES has been called by SHIP.SC, which in turn has been called by MAINMENU.SC.

```
View Ask Report Create Modify Image Forms Tools Scripts Help Exit
View a table.
```

```
Script: INVOICES  Line:   2                    Type Control-Q to Quit
  ▶ CLEAR
```

Figure 12.6 Screen after entering Debugger

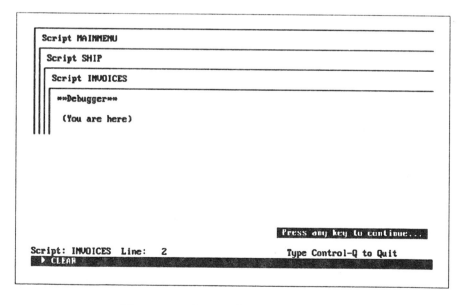

Figure 12.7 Screen after pressing Ctrl-W

In this case, it makes sense to execute some commands in the current script until we can see something which may illuminate the problem further. Pressing Ctrl-S steps through the commands in the script one at a time, showing the current state of the workspace after each command. Figure 12.8 shows how the workspace appears after processing the DO_IT! command for the query in the INVOICES script. You can see that the ANSWER table is empty. That is why no invoices were printed.

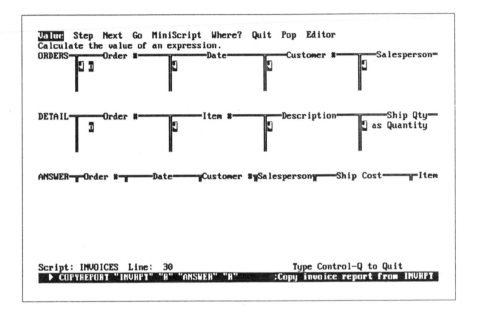

Figure 12.8 Screen after DO_IT! in query

You can manipulate the workspace freely under the Debugger. Just be sure to leave it in the necessary state before resuming execution.

The problem has been discovered but is unresolved. The Debugger can still help. Since the query in the INVOICES script checks for orders which have today's date in the *[Ship Date]* field, let's look at the ORDERS table. You can do this without leaving the Debugger. Press Alt-F10 to access the Debugger Menu and choose MiniScript. On the command line, type **View "Orders"**. The ORDERS table will be displayed on the workspace as shown in Figure 12.9.

The orders in question here are Numbers 6 and 7. Both of these orders were updated with a Ship Date of *8/13/89*. Assuming that 8/13/89 is today's date, the INVOICES script should successfully query out these records and print invoices for them. Now we can use another Debugger feature to do more investigative work. Press Alt-F10 to display the Debugger Menu and choose Value. Type **TODAY()** at the expression prompt and press Enter to see what Paradox thinks today's date is. The answer is displayed near the lower-right corner of the screen shown in

Figure 12.10. Surprise! The date shown is **8/12/89**. Paradox takes the value of TODAY() from the system clock which must have been set incorrectly.

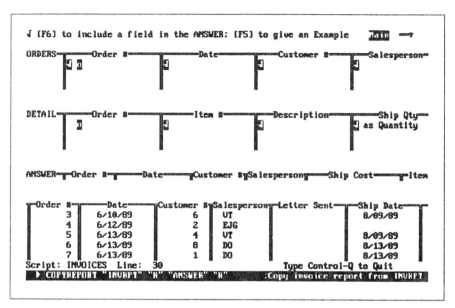

Figure 12.9 ORDERS placed on workspace with Debugger

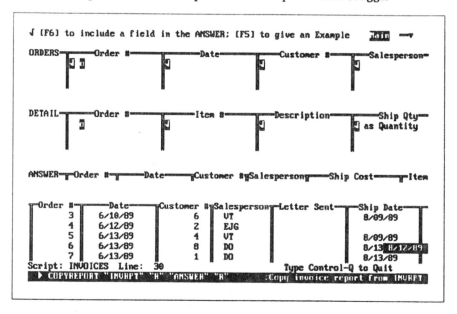

Figure 12.10 Value of TODAY() displayed

After changing the system clock to the current date, the query will run successfully. You can make this change, and replay the script as well, without leaving the Debugger. Press Alt-F10 to access the Debugger Menu and choose MiniScript. Type **RUN "DATE 8/13/89"** at the command prompt and press Enter. The RUN command tells Paradox to send the command within quotation marks to DOS for execution. Then, press Ctrl-P twice to "pop up" two levels of script play to MAINMENU.SC. From here, you can press Ctrl-G, choose Shipments from the menu and generate the invoices.

Debugger Tips

Paradox will make its best guess about the cause of a problem, but this guess is not always correct. If the message from the Debugger is not clear, look at the previous line which was executed. Sometimes, there is a problem such as a missing keyword or a punctuation mark. Paradox may not notice the problem until it tries to execute the following command and cannot interpret it correctly.

The Debugger is also quite helpful for debugging logic problems. Sometimes, it can be confusing to work with nested IF statements, WHILE loops, and other control structures. Use the Debugger to trace your scripts one step at a time to see what Paradox is *really* doing, instead of what you *think* it is doing.

The Next command is useful if you want to resume script play from the current point. First, use Alt-F10/MiniScript to reenter the correct command and use Ctrl-S to execute it. Then, use Ctrl-N to skip over the problem command. At this point, you can press Ctrl-G to resume normal script play.

When used effectively, the Debugger can save you hours trying to figure out what is happening behind the scenes when you have script problems. You can use it to "see" what Paradox is doing. You can enter corrections "on-the-fly" and use the MiniScript command to test them. When you make corrections in this way, be sure to update your original script to avoid encountering the problem again.

Using Procedures

If you are writing PAL scripts which you will use regularly, consider using PAL procedures. There are important benefits that you should be aware of before you say "it's too complicated" or "I'm not a programmer." This section explains procedures, the benefits they provide, and how to use them.

What Is a Procedure?

A procedure is a set of PAL commands grouped together under one name. The procedure can be executed by calling the procedure name in a script or from another procedure. A procedure is different from a script in these ways:

- A procedure must be "defined" (resident in memory) before you can call it.
- A procedure definition creates commands which are ready to be executed by the computer; they do not need to be interpreted one command at a time as commands in a script must be.
- You can pass values to a procedure.
- A procedure can return a value to another procedure or to a script.
- Procedures can be swapped in and out of memory by Paradox as needed.

Benefits of Procedures

There are several benefits to using procedures instead of scripts:

- There is a performance benefit. Procedures are resident in memory in executable form and do not need to be interpreted one command at a time.
- Paradox makes better use of memory when procedures are used. Unlike scripts, procedures can be swapped in and out of memory.
- Procedures can save time in writing code for similar tasks; you can write generalized procedures which act on arguments passed to the procedure.

When you create procedures, you are expanding the available PAL commands and functions. In some ways, procedures are similar to PAL functions. You can use arguments with procedures, and return values from them, as you can with functions. Once you create procedures, you can save them in libraries for repeated use.

Defining a Procedure

A procedure is created or defined in a script by using the PROC command and the ENDPROC keyword. Look at Figure 12.11. The script shown creates a procedure called MYPROC which has just two commands; MESSAGE and SLEEP. The end of the procedure is indicated by the ENDPROC keyword.

```
Designing script C:\patchwrk\myproc                              Script

....+...10....+...20....+...30....+...40....+...50....+...60....+...70....+...80
PROC Myproc()

MESSAGE "This is my first procedure!"
SLEEP 2000

ENDPROC
```

Figure 12.11 Simple procedure

When you define a procedure in a script, the procedure is then resident in memory. A procedure definition in a script is useless by itself, though. As soon as the script is over, the procedure is no longer resident in memory. To use it, you must call the procedure before the script is over.

Calling a Procedure

To call a procedure, you use the procedure name followed by parentheses. The parentheses tell Paradox that you are calling a procedure and not referring to a variable. In addition, the parentheses can be used to pass any arguments to the procedure. See the example shown in Figure 12.12. On the last line, the procedure is called with the expression Myproc(). That procedure does not use any arguments.

Creating a Procedure Library

As mentioned above, you cannot call a procedure unless it is currently "defined," or resident in memory. When you define a procedure in a script, it is resident in memory only as long as the script is active. As soon as the script is over, any procedure which was defined in the script is released from memory. You may wonder, then, what is the advantage of using procedures if you have to type the entire procedure into a script every time you want to use it.

The solution is to use a procedure library. You can create a procedure library and use it to store procedure definitions until they are needed. Creating a procedure library is easy. You use the PAL command CREATELIB as follows:

```
CREATELIB "Raspbrry"
```

This line creates a procedure library called *Raspbrry* which can store up to 50 procedures. A library name can be up to 8 characters long, must conform to DOS rules for naming a file, and it cannot be one of Paradox's reserved words. When you create a procedure library, Paradox creates a file with the name which you specify and the file extension .LIB. You can write a one-line script to create a procedure library or, easiest of all, use MiniScript on the PAL Menu.

Optionally, you can use the SIZE keyword with CREATELIB to allow up to 300 procedures to be stored in the same library. There is some overhead associated with library size, though. In general, try to keep procedure libraries to 50 entries or less.

```
Designing script C:\patchwrk\myproc                          Script

....+...10....+...20....+...30....+...40....+...50....+...60....+...70....+...80
PROC Myproc()

MESSAGE "This is my first procedure!"
SLEEP 2000

ENDPROC

Myproc()
```

Figure 12.12 Procedure definition and call

Using a Procedure Library

Once you have created a procedure library, you can use it to store your procedures. Then you can call them as needed. This section outlines how to do this.

Writing Procedures to a Library

Once a procedure library has been created, you write procedures to it by using the WRITELIB command. See Figure 12.13 for an example. You first define the procedure in a script using the PROC command and then use WRITELIB *in the same script* to write the procedure to the named library. In the example, the last line of the script writes the procedure called *Myproc* to the library named *Raspbrry*.

```
Changing script C:\patchwrk\myproc                          Script

....+...10....+...20....+...30....+...40....+...50....+...60....+...70....+...80
PROC Myproc()

MESSAGE "This is my first procedure!"
SLEEP 2000

ENDPROC

WRITELIB "Raspbrry" Myproc
```

Figure 12.13 Writing a procedure to a library

Using Procedures from a Library

A procedure in a library must be read into memory before it can be called. There are three ways to read a procedure from a library into memory. First, you can use the READLIB command like this:

```
READLIB "Raspbrry" MYPROC
```

READLIB loads the specified procedure into memory so it is available when you want to call it. If you choose this method, you must remember to execute a READLIB command before you try to call a procedure. You can specify a list of procedures with one READLIB command.

A better way to read procedures from a library is to let Paradox read in the procedures as needed. There are two ways to facilitate this. One involves naming your procedure library *Paradox*. Whenever a procedure that is not currently defined in memory is called, Paradox looks for a procedure library called *Paradox* in the working directory. If it is there, Paradox will see if the called procedure exists in that library. If so, Paradox will read the desired procedure into memory automatically and execute it.

Paradox will look in all the libraries specified with Autolib the way DOS uses the PATH to look for files.

There is a second way to have Paradox automatically load procedures into memory as they are called. *Autolib* is a special Paradox variable which you can use to specify the name of one or more libraries where Paradox should check for procedures which are not already defined. See Figure 12.14 for an example of using *Autolib*. In that script,

Autolib is assigned the value "raspbrry". When the Mainmenu() procedure is called, Paradox will read Mainmenu() in from the Raspbrry library if it is not already in memory.

```
Changing script C:\patchwrk\driver                              Script

....+...10....+...20....+...30....+...40....+...50....+...60....+...70....+...80
CLEAR
CLEARALL
@ 0,0
TEXT



                   Welcome to The Raspberry Patch Paradox System!


ENDTEXT
Autolib = "raspbrry"
Mainmenu()
RELEASE VARS ALL
CLEAR
CLEARALL
```

Figure 12.14 Using the Autolib variable

Autolib is like any other variable. It is released if you use a RELEASE VARS ALL in a script or procedure so be careful to reassign it if you need to.

Releasing Procedures from Memory

You can release procedures from memory explicitly by using the RELEASE PROCS command. This command can be used with the keyword ALL or with a list of procedure names. Once a procedure is released from memory, it must be defined again before it can be called.

You may need to experiment to determine the proper SETSWAP amount for various operations. This is only necessary if Paradox is running out of memory at certain spots in your program.

Execute disable swapping.

There really is no need to use the RELEASE command, though. Paradox swaps procedures out of memory if memory is needed for another procedure or for the next command. You can set the amount of memory which Paradox will attempt to keep free with the SETSWAP command. After each command is executed, Paradox looks at the current SETSWAP amount. If memleft() (the workspace memory variable) is less than the SETSWAP amount, Paradox will try to swap procedures out of memory to free up memory for the workspace.

There are a few restrictions on which procedures can be swapped out of memory. Only procedures which were read into memory with the READLIB command, the Autolib variable, or automatically from PARADOX.LIB can be swapped. A procedure which is defined and called in a script cannot be swapped out of memory. Also, a procedure which calls another procedure used as an argument for a command, or as part of an expression used on the right side of an = sign, cannot be swapped out of memory. (If the procedure is the sole element of an expression used with =, however, swapping is not prohibited.) Usually you can code around this type of procedure call to eliminate a problem in which swapping is prevented.

Maintaining a Procedure Library

This section contains notes on how to manage a procedure library. You should be aware of how Paradox adds entries to libraries and how you can keep track of them.

INFOLIB

You can check to see which procedures are stored in a library using the INFOLIB command like this:

```
INFOLIB "Raspbrry"
```

Press Alt-F7 while viewing LIST to send the procedure information to the printer.

INFOLIB produces a temporary LIST table which has an entry for each procedure in the specified library. You can see the LIST generated by the above command in Figure 12.15. The size, in bytes, of each procedure in the library is shown in LIST.

Procedure Size

You may run into problems if you go more than about 20 levels deep in procedure calls. Avoid this by using a different logic structure.

A good rule-of-thumb is to keep procedures as small as possible. This gives Paradox more flexibility in managing memory. In general, try to keep procedures less than 8K in size. This should not be a problem because there is no limit on the number of procedures which you can use.

Library Size

As you write new versions of your procedures to a library, you may notice that the library is growing in size. That is because Paradox does not reclaim space within a procedure library. Old entries are flagged as being out-of-date and new entries are added to the library. The only way to release space from a library is to delete the library. Thus, it is a good idea to recreate a library using CREATELIB and then write the desired procedures to it once they have been debugged.

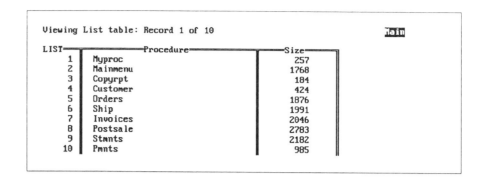

```
Viewing List table: Record 1 of 10                        Main

LIST                    Procedure                 Size
      1    Myproc                                  257
      2    Mainmenu                               1768
      3    Copyrpt                                 184
      4    Customer                                424
      5    Orders                                 1876
      6    Ship                                   1991
      7    Invoices                               2046
      8    Postsale                               2783
      9    Stmnts                                 2182
     10    Pmnts                                   985
```

Figure 12.15 LIST generated by INFOLIB

Using Arguments with Procedures

As mentioned before, you can define a procedure with arguments. The values passed as arguments to a procedure can be constants, variables, or individual array elements. Here is a simple example of defining a procedure which uses arguments:

```
PROC COPYRPT(a,b,c,d)
COPYREPORT a,b,c,d
REPORT c d
ENDPROC
```

When this procedure is called, it expects four arguments to be passed. They can be variables, as in *COPYRPT(w,x,y,z)*, or constants, as in *COPYRPT("Invrpt","R","Answer","R")*. Note that the arguments which are specified when the procedure is called are substituted for the parameters *a,b,c,* and *d,* used in the procedure definition. The parameters *a,b,c,* and *d* are special variables within the procedure *COPYRPT()*. They are private to the procedure which uses them as parameters. Even if they have already been assigned values outside of the procedure *COPYRPT()*, those values will be ignored inside the procedure. Only the arguments passed with the procedure call will be used as values for their corresponding parameters.

Private Variables

You can also define private variables to be used within a procedure by using the PRIVATE keyword in a procedure definition. PRIVATE must be the first line in the procedure definition and must be followed by the variables being declared private. Variables which are private to a procedure are also private to any procedures called by that procedure. This is called "dynamic scoping" of variables.

Global Variables

Any variables which are used in a procedure, other than parameter variables or PRIVATE variables, are called *global variables*. You can refer to these variables from any script or procedure as long as they are assigned a value. The value of a global variable is the same inside or outside of any particular procedure, except in the case where the global variable is the same as one of the parameters used in a procedure definition. Take the COPYRPT() example above. If *a* had been assigned a value before the call to COPYRPT(), that value will be unchanged after COPYRPT() executes. However, while COPYRPT() is being executed, *a* will have the value of the first argument passed with the procedure call.

Look at the lines of code below for an illustration of this:

```
a="Tom Cat"
PROC COPYRPT(a,b,c,d)
COPYREPORT a b c d
REPORT c d
MESSAGE a        ;displays value of first argument
SLEEP 1000
ENDPROC
COPYRPT("Invrpt","R","Answer","R")

MESSAGE a                ;displays the value "Tom Cat"
SLEEP 1000
```

While COPYRPT() is being executed, any reference to it returns the value "Invrpt". As soon as the procedure has been completed, a reference to *a* returns the value "Tom Cat".

Returning a Value

You can use a procedure to return a value to a script or to another procedure by using the RETURN command. Look at this example:

```
PROC PERCENTCALC(a)
z = (a/[Total Sales])*100
RETURN z
ENDPROC
```

This procedure returns the value of z which the procedure has calculated. You can use a procedure which returns a value in the same way as you use a PAL function. It can be used as part of any PAL expression as in:

```
[Percent of Total] = PercentCalc(a)
```

You are limited to passing back one value from a procedure. The value to be returned must be on the same line as the RETURN command.

CLOSED Procedures

CLOSED procedures are used to improve Paradox's memory utilization.

You can create CLOSED procedures by using the CLOSED keyword immediately after the PROC command in a procedure definition. A CLOSED procedure is different from regular procedures in these ways:

- A CLOSED procedure must be called from a library, preferably by using Autolib.
- All previously defined procedures and variables are unknown to a CLOSED procedure, unless you use the USEVARS keyword.
- A variable used within a CLOSED procedure is available to all procedures called by the CLOSED procedure.
- All memory used by variables, arrays, and procedures in a CLOSED procedure is freed up when the CLOSED procedure has finished executing; there is no need to use RELEASE VARS or RELEASE PROCS; variables specified with USEVARS will still be available outside of the CLOSED procedure.
- You can nest up to six CLOSED procedures.

A CLOSED procedure definition looks like this:

```
PROC CLOSED MYPROC()
USEVARS Autolib
x = Amounts()
[Field] = x * [Price]
ENDPROC
```

Debugging Procedures

When you use the Debugger with procedures, Paradox looks for the source scripts in the directory which they were in when the procedures were written to the library. If you move the source scripts to another directory, Paradox will not be able to find them and will give you an error message. Be sure to keep your source scripts in a directory with the proper name if you want to debug procedures.

Using Runtime

To distribute a PAL program which you have written to other users, you can use the Runtime version of Paradox. This is an inexpensive way to make your PAL program available to users who do not own Paradox.

You can make an unlimited number of copies of Runtime to distribute with your PAL application. Runtime can even be installed on a network, providing multi-user capabilities. If you are a registered user of Paradox, Runtime can be ordered from Borland International.

What is Runtime?

Runtime is a special version of Paradox which can run PAL programs but which cannot be used interactively. When you start Runtime, you must specify the name of a PAL script on the command line like this:

```
PDOXRUN3 "myscript"
```

Runtime then plays the named script and returns to DOS when the script has been completed.

Differences Between Paradox and Runtime

There are two other differences between Paradox and Runtime. Runtime does not support the use of the ECHO NORMAL, ECHO SLOW, or ECHO FAST commands. These commands are used by The Data Entry Toolkit. A special version of TOOLKIT.LIB is distributed with Runtime for use with applications developed using The Data Entry Toolkit. The other difference is that, under Runtime, you cannot use the PAL WAIT command on a query image. These differences ordinarily do not limit the type of application which you can distribute with Runtime. It is easy to code around these restrictions and to use Runtime to do anything else possible with interactive Paradox.

The hard disk can be a network drive.

Runtime requires the same amount of memory as Paradox does to load and can be used only on a system with at least one hard disk. It can be installed on a network server and allow network users to share tables, the same as with interactive Paradox.

How to Create a Runtime Application

Any application which you create using PAL can be run under Runtime, with the exception of the differences noted above. You need to provide the Runtime user with the following:

You can copy PARADOX3.CFG to PDOXRUN3.CFG rather than play the custom script with Runtime.

- An installed copy of Runtime
- The proper PDOXRUN3.CFG file
- A script to start the application (a "driver" script)
- Any other scripts played by the application
- Any procedure libraries which contain procedures called by the application
- All Paradox objects, such as tables and reports, that are used by the application.

If you don't want the user to see your source code, you can create a driver script which sets the Autolib variable appropriately and makes a call to the procedure which starts the rest of the application. Figure 12.14 showed an example. That script displays a brief message and then calls the MAINMENU() procedure. When the user exits from the Main Menu, control is returned to the driver script. That script, in turn, clears the screen and the workspace before returning the user to DOS. These last commands are necessary only when playing the application under interactive Paradox. When it is played using Runtime, the user is automatically taken to DOS when the application has finished running.

Summary

This chapter showed you how to use the Debugger, procedure libraries, and the Runtime version of Paradox. These are the important things to remember:

- The Debugger is useful when writing PAL scripts; it has a direct link to the Script Editor and can shorten the time needed to get a script running.

- The Debugger lets you check the value of any valid PAL expression; step through script commands one at a time; skip commands or pop up a level in script play; see where you are in script play; execute MiniScripts; and go into the Script Editor at the problem line.

- A PAL procedure is a set of PAL commands which you define. It is called by a name that you give it.

- Using procedures results in better Paradox performance and in better memory utilization.

- You can use procedures to return a value to another procedure or a script (similar to using a PAL function).

- You can pass arguments to a procedure. This gives you the ability to write generalized code which can be used repeatedly with different values.

- Runtime is a special version of Paradox which lets the user who does not own Paradox play your Paradox application; it is inexpensive and has multi-user capabilities.

Getting the Most
Out of Paradox

Customizing Your Paradox System

After you are familiar with Paradox, you may want to spend some time customizing your system. You can use the Custom script or an Init script to change default settings. You can also use a DOS batch file to send special command line options to Paradox when you start the program, or to start Paradox from a certain directory. These options can be combined to customize Paradox for your particular needs. This chapter will give you information about using these three options.

If you are using Paradox on a network, be sure to read carefully the notes for network users. When you are working on a network, you have additional factors which affect whether Paradox finds the right .CFG file or Init script. You may be using a network login script, and possibly a batch file, to start Paradox. All of these things must be considered together when you decide where to put your .CFG file and the Init script, if you use one. Chapter 15, "Networking With Paradox," also has information about this topic.

The Paradox Configuration File

Paradox uses the DOS path to find the .CFG if it is not in the current directory when Paradox is started.

When you start Paradox, there are default values used for report and graph settings, working and private directories, network options, and various other parts of your Paradox work environment. Paradox keeps default settings information in a file called PARADOX3.CFG, the Paradox configuration file. Every time you load Paradox, it looks at the .CFG file to set the defaults.

The Custom Script

The default settings can be changed using a special script called Custom. The Custom script is copied into your \PARADOX3 directory, along with the library of PAL procedures it uses, when you install Paradox. These files are called CUSTOM.SC and CUSTOM.LIB. The Custom script is password-protected so you cannot view it, but you can play it by using **Scripts/Play**.

With the Custom script, you can change these, and other options:

- Video attributes
- Report and graph settings
- Default working and private directories
- QueryOrder for ANSWER tables
- Expanded memory allocation for caching
- ASCII file delimiters and separators
- Your script editor
- Various network settings

A large part of this chapter will be devoted to a description of all options in the Custom script and how they can be set. In addition to the Custom script, there are other options which you can utilize to customize your Paradox system.

Init Scripts

You can create a special Init script to tell Paradox to execute certain commands as soon as you start the program. INIT.SC works in Paradox similarly to the way an AUTOEXEC.BAT file works in DOS. When you load Paradox on a standalone system, it looks for this script in the private directory specified in the .CFG file. If INIT.SC is found, Paradox plays the script *after* setting itself up according to the PARADOX3.CFG file. If no private directory was specified (as is the case for most standalone computers), Paradox looks for INIT.SC in the working directory.

You can include any Paradox command in an Init script. It is commonly used to change the working directory or to tie scripts to keys using the PAL SETKEY command. See the section on "Using Init Scripts," later in this chapter, for examples.

Batch Files

It is also possible, to some extent, to use a DOS batch file to customize your Paradox system. Various command line options can be used to tell Paradox to play a script or change settings when it is loaded. Information about these command line options is included in the section, "Using Batch Files With Paradox," later in this chapter.

Using the Custom Script

The Custom script, and the library it uses, were copied into the \PARADOX3 directory when you installed Paradox. To play the Custom script, first make sure that the working directory is \PARADOX3 (or the directory in which you keep your Paradox system files). If necessary, you can change the working directory, by using **T**ools/**M**ore/**D**irectory from the Main Menu. Then, choose **S**cripts/**P**lay from the Main Menu, type **Custom** at the script prompt, and press Enter.

What you see next depends on whether your computer has a color/graphics card. If it does, Paradox will ask whether you are using a black and white monitor. Press **Y** if you are using a black-and-white monitor. This will cause Paradox to change the configuration file so that you can see highlighted text. If you are using a monochrome or a color monitor, press **N**. Paradox will then display the Custom Script Menu shown in Figure 13.1.

```
Video Reports Graphs Defaults Int'l Net PAL Ascii Help Do-It! Cancel
Monitor, Snow, Colors, NegativeColors, and FormPalette.
```

Figure 13.1 Custom Script Menu

The Custom Script Menu

The Custom Script Menu is used to access dozens of different options. They are organized as follows:

- Video lets you change screen attributes.
- Reports is used to change report settings.

- **Graphs** has choices for graph settings, printers, and screen type.
- **Defaults** groups together several miscellaneous settings.
- **Int'l** is used to change date and number formats.
- **Net** lets you change network options.
- **PAL** is used to change the script editor and specify when secondary indexes are to be updated.
- **Ascii** lets you specify how delimiters, separators, decimal characters, and zero-fill should be handled.
- **Help** gives you help on using Custom.
- **Do-It!** saves your changes, writes them to the .CFG file in the directory you specify, and returns you to DOS.
- **Cancel** exits from the Custom script and returns you to Paradox.

The menu trees for some of these choices are quite extensive. The main branches for each choice are described below. The menu tree for the Custom script is shown in Appendix A.

Changing Video Attributes

When you choose **Video** from the Custom Script Menu, you will see another menu with these choices:

You may not be able to eliminate all the snow on some machines.

- **Monitor** is used to specify whether you are using a monochrome, color, or black-and-white display.
- **Snow** tells Paradox to try to eliminate screen interference, if possible.
- **Colors** accesses the Color subsystem with its own extensive set of menus.
- **NegativeColors** lets you specify whether only negative numbers, only negative currency, or both, should be displayed in a different color.
- **FormPalette** is used to tell Paradox whether it should automatically display the color palette on the screen during form design.
- **Return** takes you back to the Custom Main Menu.

Most of these menu choices are self-explanatory. The only one which is a bit complicated is **Colors**. When you choose **Colors** from the Video menu, Paradox will load special files which are used during the color definition process, into memory. You will then see a menu with these choices:

- ExistingSettings is used to select, rename, or delete a color setting.
- Modify is used to change the current color setting.
- Help provides assistance while using the Color subsystem.
- Return returns you to the previous menu.

To change a particular color setting, use ExistingSettings/**S**elect to make that setting current, if it is not already current. Then use the Modify command to change it. After you choose Modify, Paradox will display a form which looks like the Paradox workspace, with a color palette on the right side of the screen. To change the color of individual elements of the workspace, choose an element from the menu at the top of the screen, when prompted, and use the arrow keys to change the colors. You can use PgDn and PgUp to move through separate forms for different types of Paradox screens. Each can be modified separately.

When you have finished changing the colors, press F10 to access the Color subsystem Menu. You can use this menu to save your work or to cancel any changes which you have made. If you save the color changes, Paradox will ask whether you want to save them to the same setting or to a new color setting. When you save the setting to a new name, the old setting, and its name, are retained.

Changing Report Settings

You can also use Report/SetPrinter /Override/Setups to change the setup string for a report temporarily.

The Custom script can be used to change several of the default report settings. When you create a new report specification, Paradox uses the current report settings in the .CFG file as the defaults. If you use Custom to change these settings, note that *the changes you make will affect only new reports which are created*. Existing report specifications are not changed. Existing report specifications must be changed using **R**eport /**C**hange.

Choosing Report from the Custom Menu displays a menu similar to the Setting Menu in Report mode:

- PageWidth lets you change the default number of characters across a page.
- LengthOfPage is used to specify the number of lines per page.
- Margin sets the default left margin.
- Wait tells Paradox whether to wait for a keystroke before printing a new page.
- GroupRepeats is used to tell Paradox whether to retain or suppress repeated group values in a Tabular report.

- `Setups` lets you define an entire group of setup strings, including a default, and also sets the default printer port.
- `FormFeed` can be used to send a form-feed to the printer.

More information on each choice was included in Chapter 6, "Using the Report Generator." The one difference with using Custom for this is when you choose `Setup`.

When you choose `Setup` from the Custom Report Menu, Paradox will display a table called PRINTER as shown in Figure 13.2. This table can be edited in the same way as any other table. You can use it to:

- Add setup strings
- Change setup strings, names, or printer ports
- Delete setup strings
- Designate a default setup string

To designate a default setup string, type an asterisk after the desired setup string name in PRINTER. In Figure 13.2, you can see the asterisk after the first name. To include a non-printable character, such as Esc, in a setup string, use the ASCII code for the character and precede it by a backslash. For example, to place Esc into a setup string, type \027. A listing of ASCII codes for the IBM character set is included in Appendix C.

Changing Graph Settings

The `Graph` choice on the Custom Menu is used to define the default graph settings such as type, colors, and titles, as well as to tell Paradox the type of screen and printer(s) that you are using.

When you choose `Graph`, you will see a menu with these choices:

- `GraphSettings` lets you specify defaults for the settings you can change using Image/Graph/Modify.

You define printers here; they cannot be defined using Image/Graph.

- `Printers` is used to define up to four printers for use with Graph.
- `Screen` lets you tell Paradox the type of screen that you are using.
- `Return` takes you back to the Custom Main Menu.

If you choose `GraphSettings`, you will see a menu similar to the one which is available through Image/Graph/Modify/F10. You can change the graph type, overall settings such as titles, colors, axes, grids, printer layout, and the device for graph output. For more information about these settings, see Chapter 8, "Graphs."

```
Press: [F1] - Help; [F2] - save changes; [F7] - Form Toggle; [Esc] - cancel.
To choose a default, place an asterisk at the end of name of desired string.
PRINTER          Name              Port                      Setup String
   1      StandardPrinter*         LPT1
   2      Small-IBMgraphics        LPT1    \027W\000\015
   3      Reg-IBMgraphics          LPT1    \027W\000\018
   4      Small-Epson-MX/FX        LPT1    \015
   5      Small-Oki-92/93          LPT1    \015
   6      Small-Oki-82/83          LPT1    \029
   7      Small-Oki-192            LPT1    \029
   8      HPLaserJet               LPT1    \027E
   9      HP-Portrait-66lines      LPT1    \027E\027&l7.27C
  10      HP-Landscape-Normal      LPT1    \027E\027&l1O
  11      HP-Compressed            LPT1    \027E\027(s16.66H
  12      HP-LandscpCompressed     LPT1    \027E\027&l1O\027(s16.66H
  13      Intl-IBMcompatible       LPT1    \027\054
  14      Intl-IBMcondensed    ◄   LPT1    \027\054\015
```

Figure 13.2 PRINTER table

Defining Printers for Graphing

Custom also is used to tell Paradox which printer or plotter you want to use with graphs. You can define up to four printers. To define a printer, choose `Printers` from the Custom Graph Menu, select a printer (1, 2, 3, or 4) and choose `TypeOfPrinter` from the next menu. Paradox will display a form on which you can select a printer manufacturer and model. First, use the arrow keys to move the cursor to the desired manufacturer and press Enter. Then, use the same method to indicate the model of printer which you are using.

To specify a device for the selected printer, choose **S**ettings/**D**evice from the Custom Graph Menu. Paradox displays a listing of the possible devices for each printer: Parallel1, Parallel2, Serial1, LPT1, and so on. Select the device which corresponds to the DOS device name associated with the printer which you are defining. If you select a port which is not a parallel port, Paradox will display another menu which can be used to set the baud rate (speed), parity, and stop bits for serial communications. These settings must be the same as your printer settings if you use a serial port.

`PrinterWait` is another choice on the Graph/Printers Menu. You can use it to tell Paradox to pause after each graph page is printed. The default is `No`.

Changing the Graphs Printer

Once you have defined your printers, you can select them while using Paradox. The commands for changing the default graph printer are: **I**mage/**G**raph/**M**odify/F10/**O**verall/**D**evice/**P**rinter. You can then choose the 1st, 2nd, 3rd, or 4th printer from the list displayed. To change the characteristics of any of these printers, you must use the Custom script again.

Defining Your Screen for Graphs

When you send a graph to the screen, Paradox will check to see what type of graphics adapter is installed. It will use the highest resolution possible for displaying graphs on the screen. Normally, you don't need to do anything for this to work. The choice called `Screen` on the Custom Graphs Menu can be used to change the screen type if you have problems. When you choose `Screen`, Paradox displays a listing of the graphics adapters with which it will work. The default is `Auto`. `Auto` is used to let Paradox select the graphics adapter type. To select another type, use the arrow keys to move the cursor through the list and press Enter to make a selection.

Changing the Working Directory

Normally, when you start Paradox, it uses the current directory as the working directory. You can change this using the Custom script. Choose **Defaults/SetDirectory** from the Custom Menu. Type a directory name, optionally including a drive letter as in C: \ MYDIR and press Enter. The next time you load Paradox, the specified directory will be the working directory unless you are using an Init script to change it.

Setting the QueryOrder

When you process a query which generates an ANSWER table, its structure is normally taken from the structure of the table(s) being queried. Even if the query images have been rotated, the ANSWER table will reflect the true underlying structure of the query table(s).

This setting can affect whether scripts run properly.

You can change this by using **Defaults/QueryOrder** in the Custom script. Two choices are displayed: `ImageOrder` and `TableOrder` (the default). If you choose `ImageOrder`, Paradox will create ANSWER tables using the structure of the query images, rather than the structure of the table.

You can compare Figures 13.3 and 13.4 to see an illustration of this. Figure 13.3 shows a query on CUSTOMER and the resulting ANSWER table with `QueryOrder` set to `TableOrder`. Note that in the query image for CUSTOMER, the fields have been reordered using Ctrl-R. In Figure 13.4, the same query has been processed with `QueryOrder` set to `ImageOrder`. You can see that ANSWER has a different structure than that shown in Figure 13.4. The second ANSWER table reflects the structure of the query image instead of that of the table structure.

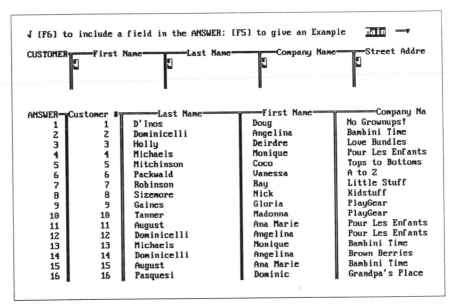

Figure 13.3 ANSWER using `TableOrder`

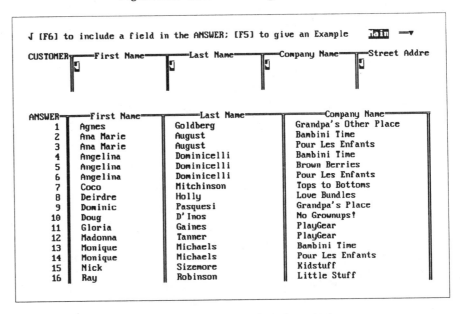

Figure 13.4 ANSWER using `QueryOrder`

Using Blanks in Calculations

If calculations use fields which have one or more blank values, Paradox will return a blank for the result. In some cases, this is not desirable. You can tell Paradox to use a *0* for any blanks it finds during calculations by using **D**efaults/**B**lank = 0 from the Custom Menu. When you choose **No** for **B**lanks=0, Paradox will not substitute 0s for blanks. **No** is the default. Selecting **Yes** tells Paradox to use *0* for blanks in calculations. If you don't get the results you expect from queries or reports which do calculations where blanks are involved, be sure to check this setting in your .CFG file.

Changing Expanded Memory Allocation

Paradox will use expanded memory automatically if it is available. With the Custom script, however, you can change the way in which Paradox uses expanded memory. Before you experiment with the setting, it might be useful to know a bit about what Paradox does with expanded memory.

Paradox will allocate the first 48K of expanded memory to its Virtual Memory Manager. About two-thirds of this amount is used to augment the workspace. The balance is used for other memory management purposes. Of the expanded memory over 48K, 192K is used for temporary storage of Paradox overlay files and procedures. If there is any expanded memory left, 25% of it is allocated to the temporary storage area, and 75% of it is used for caching other data usually stored on your hard disk.

If you are using QEMM, Quarterdeck's Expanded Memory Manager 386, Paradox can use up to 208K for the Virtual Memory Manager. You can also get this amount using some other EEMS drivers. That way, you can get a substantial boost in performance from the large addition to the workspace. This can also solve memory problems if you are running on a network or running a large application.

The Custom script lets you change the percentage of expanded memory used for caching through the menu choices, **D**efaults/**E**MS. You can specify any number from 0 to 100. If you specify *0*, Paradox will not do disk caching. If you are using another caching program, you will probably want to turn off the Paradox cache. Two cache programs running at the same time can cause problems and actually decrease performance if they work against each other. When you specify a number other than the default, Paradox will not use the 192K for the temporary storage area. Instead, it will use the remaining memory not used for the disk cache.

Usually, you will not need to change the expanded memory allocation. If your application has many often-used procedures, you may want to decrease the percentage used for caching so that the temporary storage area is increased. Or, if you are using tables only from a server, you may want to decrease the disk cache. (Paradox will not cache data from a server, anyway.) In this case, you might want to leave some expanded memory only for caching information in your private directory if it is on a local drive. See Chapter 14, "Performance Tips," for more information about using expanded memory with Paradox.

Using AutoSave

Paradox's `AutoSave` feature periodically saves the changes which you make during editing or data-entry sessions to disk. You can adjust the frequency of this save activity using **D**efaults/AutoSave from the Custom Menu. There are two choices: `No` and `Yes`. `No` minimizes the `AutoSave` activity. Specifying `Yes` makes more frequent saves adjusted to your typing rate. The default setting for `AutoSave` is `Yes`.

Disabling Ctrl-Break

Pressing Ctrl-Break usually cancels the current operation and returns you to the previous operation. This can be useful in canceling queries or sorts if you don't want them to run to completion. At other times, it can be a nuisance to cancel what you are doing, especially if Ctrl-Break is sent accidentally. With some keyboards which use European keyboard drivers, this key combination can be sent inadvertently if the special key sequences are not used completely. In this case, it is nice to be able to turn off Ctrl-Break. (If you used a European country code during installation, Ctrl-Break is disabled automatically.)

You can disable the Ctrl-Break action for some operations using **D**efaults/**D**isableBreak from the Custom Menu. If you choose `Disable` from the menu, Paradox will not respond to any Ctrl-Breaks which would cause you to exit from a subsystem and return to Main mode. Ctrl-Break will still work, however, for canceling queries and sorts.

International Formats

The format for displaying dates and numbers on the screen and in reports is based on the country code you specified when you installed

Paradox. You can change this format by using `Int'l` from the Custom Menu. For dates, there are three formats available:

- mm/dd/yy
- dd-Mon-yy
- dd.mm.yy

For numbers, you can choose `USFormat` or `InternationalFormat`. In `USFormat`, a period, ., is used to separate whole numbers from decimal digits. A comma, ,, is used to separate groups of thousands like this: **51,419.57**. The `InternationalFormat` reverses the use of commas and periods so the number in the last sentence would appear as **51.419,57**. You can also use Image/Format to change the appearance of values seen on the screen and Field/Reformat to change the format of dates and numbers used in a report.

Network Options

There are three network-related options, your username, private directory, and the AutoRefresh interval, which you can change using the Custom script. To change any of these, choose `Net` from the Custom Main Menu.

User Name

Your username is usually taken from your network (if it supports the use of usernames). You can change your username or add one if your network doesn't use one, by typing a name of up to 15 characters at the `UserName` prompt. When using Paradox, you will be identified with the name you specify.

The Private Directory

If you are working on a network, the location of your private directory is important. The private directory is where Paradox keeps your temporary tables. No one else can have access to this directory. Paradox ensures this by writing a special lock file to your private directory if it is on a network drive. This can cause problems if it is a directory which is shared with other users. Other users will be denied access to a shared directory if it is in use as your private directory.

If you are on a network, always specify a private directory in the .CFG to be safe.

To ensure that Paradox does not use a shared directory as your private directory, a private directory location should be specified in your .CFG file. If there is no private directory specified in the .CFG file,

Paradox will attempt to use the current directory as your private directory. As long as that directory is not in use by anyone else, Paradox will write a lock file indicating that the directory is in use by you and cannot be used by anyone else. To avoid this problem, use Net/SetPrivate from the Custom Menu to specify a private directory, preferably a directory on a local drive, which will not be used by another user. If you use a local drive, you will get better performance because Paradox will not have to go over the network to write and read temporary tables.

PAL Options

There are two settings which you can change using the `PAL` choice on the Custom menu:

- `MaintainIndexes` tells Paradox when to update secondary indexes.
- `Editor` can be used to tie a text editor of your choice to use in place of the Paradox Script Editor.

Secondary Indexes

You can choose whether a secondary index on a keyed table should be updated incrementally (after each change to the table) or only when the index is needed. The default is for these indexes to be maintained incrementally. You can change this by using **PAL/MaintainIndexes** on the Custom Menu. Choose `No` if you want Paradox to update secondary indexes on keyed tables only when it needs to use the index and sees that it is out-of-date. If you choose `No`, you can override this in Paradox by using the PAL INDEX command with the optional MAINTAINED keyword. This option is available only for a secondary index on a keyed table. Secondary indexes on non-keyed tables cannot be maintained incrementally.

Changing the Script Editor

You may want to save different versions of PARADOX3.CFG under different names and copy them as needed rather than play custom again.

The Paradox Script Editor is suitable if you write simple scripts which don't need much editing. It also enables you to play a script without going back to the Paradox Main Menu and using the **Scripts/Play** command. However, if you regularly program in PAL, you may want to use your own editor instead.

You can tie your own text editor into Paradox using **PAL/Editor** from the Custom script menu. The editor you specify will be called whenever you use **Scripts/Editor** or press Ctrl-E to enter the Script Editor from the Debugger. After making the choices in Custom, first type the

DOS command which starts your editor at the Editor Command prompt. You also need to make sure that the directory in which your editor resides is on the DOS path so it can be found when called.

To be able to pass the script file name and line number when the editor is invoked (if, indeed, your editor can accept this information), there are parameters you must specify with the command which starts the editor. To pass a script name, use an asterisk to represent the file name. Use two asterisks to represent the line number, such as: **EDIT-CMD * **** where *EDITCMD* is the command to invoke your editor. You can also add an ! before the command to invoke the editor with extra memory available, just as you would use Alt-O, instead of Ctrl-O, to go to DOS.

Script files are simply ASCII text files. Make sure that any editor you tie-in to Paradox works with that type of file. You cannot use an editor which inserts special control codes into the text or you will have problems later in trying to play your scripts.

Delimited ASCII File Options

One file format which you can use with the Paradox `ExportImport` command is delimited ASCII. In a delimited ASCII file, a record is represented by a line of field values separated by some special character, most often a comma. In addition, some or all of the fields may be delimited, that is surrounded, by another special character. A line from a typical delimited ASCII file is shown below (but would appear on the screen as one line):

```
1,"D'Inos","Doug","No Grownups!","5487 - 145th St. N.W.",
"Seattle","WA","98999"
```

When Paradox works with delimited ASCII files, the default separator is a comma ,. The default delimiter is a quotation mark ". You can change the default separator and delimiter, and other options, by choosing `Ascii` from the Custom Menu. A menu will be displayed with these choices:

- `Delimiters` lets you change the delimiter character and specify whether all fields, or only Alphanumeric fields, should be delimited.

- `Separator` lets you choose the character to be used to separate field values.

- `ZeroFill` is used to specify if blank Numeric fields should be exported as blanks or zeros.

- ChooseDecimal lets you choose a period or a comma as the decimal separator in Numeric fields.

 The ChooseDecimal option is necessary only if you are importing ASCII, PFS or IBM *Filing Assistant* files which have a comma as the decimal separator. For other file formats, Paradox recognizes Numeric fields even if they have comma separators in numeric values. One other thing to watch out for when working with files which use a comma for the decimal separator is to make sure that all fields are delimited. Otherwise, Paradox may interpret the decimal separator as a field separator.

Saving Your Changes

After you have made the desired changes to your default Paradox settings by using the Custom script, press F2 or choose Do-It! from the Custom Main Menu. Paradox will display a menu with two choices, HardDisk and Network. If Paradox is installed on your hard disk, choose HardDisk. Paradox will write the PARADOX3.CFG file to the directory which contains your Paradox system files.

If you will be loading Paradox from a network server, choose Network. Paradox will display the specified directory as your default private directory if you used the Net/SetPrivate option. You can change this location if you want to. Press Enter to tell Paradox to write the .CFG file to the specified directory.

If You Are on a Network

If you are using Paradox on a network, you need to take precautions to be sure that Paradox finds your .CFG file, and not the default, when you start the program. Just placing the PARADOX3.CFG file in your private directory does not ensure that it is the .CFG file which Paradox will find when it is loaded. For example, if you start Paradox from the directory on the server which contains the Paradox system files, Paradox will find the default .CFG file before it finds your customized .CFG file in your private directory. One way to prevent this is to delete the default .CFG from the PARADOX3 directory.

Do some tests of certain options to make sure Paradox is finding the right .CFG file when you are on a network e.g., Use Tools/Net/SetPrivate to see what the private directory is set to.

Another way to ensure that Paradox finds your .CFG file is to place that file in your private directory *and* start Paradox from that directory. As long as the directory containing the Paradox files is on your path (or, on some networks, set up as a search drive), you will be able to start Paradox from any directory. Since Paradox first looks in the current directory for any files it needs, the proper .CFG file will be found by using this approach.

Using Init Scripts

Although there are many settings which you can change with the Custom script, you may want to have Paradox execute other commands as soon as the program is started. You can do this by creating an Init script and placing it into your private directory. If you do not have a private directory, place it in the default working directory. Paradox will play Init when you start the program before turning control over to you.

This feature is useful for two reasons: you can include key definitions, created with the PAL SETKEY command, in Init. You also can tell Paradox to play a script or execute other PAL commands automatically to set up your Paradox work environment. Look at this sample Init script for an example:

```
SETKEY 20 TYPEIN TIME()          ;Lets you press Ctrl-T to enter time
SETKEY 14 PGUP x=[] PGDN []=x+1 ;Uses Ctrl-N to increment field
COEDIT "Orders"                  ;Puts "Orders" on workspace
FORMKEY                          ;Toggles to entry form
END                              ;Goes to last record
PGDN                             ;Brings up new blank record
```

When Paradox is started, the Init script above sets up two key definitions and places a new blank order on the workspace. This could be useful for someone who uses Paradox predominantly for entering orders. They could turn on their computer, load Paradox manually, or through the DOS AUTOEXEC.BAT file, and immediately get to work.

How to Create INIT.SC

Creating an Init script is easy. First, change your working directory to the private directory. Then, use **S**cripts/**E**ditor/**W**rite and type **Init** when prompted for a script name. Type the commands, press F2 to save the script, and that's it. Next time you start Paradox, the Init script will be played automatically.

Creating Key Definitions

SETKEY can be used with any PAL commands, including the PLAY command. The only restriction is that the commands used with SETKEY must be on the same script line as SETKEY. This means you need to work within the limit of 132 characters per script line. If the commands which you want to tie to a key don't fit onto one line, type them into a separate script file and use SETKEY with the PLAY command. Instead of including the commands to bring up a new blank order every time Paradox is started, the above Init script could assign the same group of commands to a key combination such as Alt-C for a new order.

The sample key definitions in the example above work as follows: The first line tells Paradox to "timestamp" the current field whenever Ctrl-T is pressed. SETKEY 14 instructs Paradox to go to the preceding record, capture the current field value, assign it to the variable x, move back to the original record and assign a new value to the field using the value of x incremented by 1. This is an easy way to increment the key field in a table using a one-page form.

You can create many key definitions for use as shortcuts in your work. SETKEY, used in your Init script, can be one of the most helpful Paradox features.

Where to Put INIT.SC

If you start Paradox from the \PARADOX3 directory on a local drive, you can place INIT.SC into that directory. If you start Paradox from another directory, and have specified a private directory, put INIT.SC into your private directory. If you don't, Paradox will not be able to find the script. If you have no private directory specified, place INIT.SC into the default working directory specified in your .CFG file. If there is no working directory specified in the .CFG file, place INIT.SC in the directory that is current when you start Paradox.

Using Batch Files with Paradox

You can create a DOS batch file using the DOS COPY CON command or any text editor.

You can also use DOS batch files to control what happens when you start Paradox. The simplest case is using a batch file to determine the working directory after you start Paradox. To do this, you must follow these steps:

1. Make sure that the directory with the Paradox system files is on your path.
2. Play the Custom script, choose **D**efaults/**S**etDirectory, and press Ctrl-Backspace to delete any default directory setting.
3. Create a batch file to start Paradox from the desired working directory.

An example of this is:

```
PATH = \PARADOX3;\MYEDITOR
CD\ACCOUNTS
PARADOX3
```

You can use this approach with different batch files to start Paradox from different directories for particular tasks. You can optionally pass Paradox a script name on the command line as in *PARADOX3 MYSCRIPT*. Paradox will look for the specified script in the working directory.

Command Line Options

There are several command line options which you can use when you start Paradox to control expanded memory utilization, video attributes, and so on.

Display Command Line Options

The display-related command line options are useful if Paradox does not properly detect the kind of display you are using. (See Chapter 16, "Troubleshooting," for more details on solving this problem. These options are:

- *-mono* tells Paradox that you are using a monochrome display with a monochrome adapter.
- *-b&w* is used for a monochrome or black-and-white display with a colors/graphics or an Enhanced Graphics Adapter.
- *-color* is used for a color monitor with a color/graphics adapter or an Enhanced Graphics Adapter.
- *-snow* eliminates interference caused by some color graphics adapters.

The command line options are typed as: **PARADOX3 -B&W**. Be sure to leave a space between PARADOX3 and the option you choose.

Expanded Memory Command Line Options

Through the use of command line options, you also can control the way Paradox uses expanded memory.

- *-emk n* tells Paradox to use n Kilobytes of expanded memory. For example, **PARADOX3 -EMK 0** tells Paradox not to use expanded memory.

- *-emp* n tells Paradox to use n% of expanded memory for file caching; this command is similar to using **Defaults/EMS** in the Custom script.
- *-ems* 3 tells Paradox you are using LIM 3.2. Try this if you are having problems using Paradox with your expanded memory.

The first option can be useful if you suspect problems with memory conflicts. Use *-emk 0* to tell Paradox not to use any expanded memory which is present. If Paradox then runs successfully, your suspicions are confirmed. See Chapter 16, "Troubleshooting," for more information about solving these problems.

Summary

You can customize your Paradox system using the Custom script, an Init script, or a DOS batch file. This chapter showed how each option can be used. Here are the important points about customizing your system:

- Paradox keeps information on the default settings for reports, graphs, and network options in the PARADOX3.CFG file. Each time you load Paradox, it looks at this file for the default settings.
- You can change the settings in the PARADOX3.CFG file with the Custom script. The Custom script is in the PARADOX3 directory. Make that directory the current directory and use **Scripts /Play/Custom** to play the script.
- Any changes you make with Custom for reports and graphs affect only *new* reports and graphs which you create. Existing report specifications and graph settings are not changed.
- If you start Paradox from a network server, be sure to save any changes to your PARADOX3.CFG to a directory which Paradox can find.
- You can create an Init script; if Paradox finds it, it is played every time you start Paradox.
- The Init script should be in your private directory if you have one; otherwise, it should be in the working directory.
- You can start Paradox with a DOS batch file to control the Paradox working directory or just for convenience.
- It is possible to specify a script name on the command line when you start Paradox; this script must be in the working directory for Paradox to find it.

- There are command line options which tell Paradox what kind of display you are using, and how to utilize expanded memory.

If you use Paradox on a network, see Chapter 15, "Networking with Paradox," for more information about this topic. If you have problems starting Paradox, read Chapter 16, "Troubleshooting."

Performance Tips

Paradox is known for its overall good performance. It is especially quick when working with indexed tables. There are other factors, too, such as memory and table structure, which significantly affect performance. This chapter contains information on these topics and tips to maximize the performance of your Paradox system.

Table Structure

Having a fast hard disk can help performance significantly.

Paradox uses a virtual memory management system which enables it to work with tables that are much larger than the amount of memory in your computer. When you place a table onto the workspace, Paradox puts only a limited number of records into your computer's memory. As the table is used, additional records are read into memory from the disk as they are needed. This is part of the reason you may notice frequent disk activity while you are using Paradox. Paradox frequently moves groups of records back and forth from the disk to memory as they are needed.

Width

Because accessing information in your computer's memory is much faster than reading records from a disk, you will get better performance from Paradox if it can find needed records in RAM (Random Access Memory) rather than on disk. The probability of Paradox finding what it needs in RAM, of course, is greater when there are more records in memory than when there are fewer. You can maximize the number of records which can be kept in RAM by keeping tables as narrow as possible. The rule-of-thumb is that you should limit the number of fields in a table to 15 or 20 in order to get the best performance.

This rule is rather general, though. If the table has very wide fields, performance will not be as good as when you work with narrower fields. The overall width of your table, not just the number of fields, is what impacts performance. If you work with wide tables, Paradox will have to go to the disk much more frequently to find needed records.

Using a disk optimization program usually results in better performance.

Another thing to consider when designing a table is that Paradox allocates space for records on disk using 1K, 2K, 3K, or 4K blocks. Depending upon the width of a record, and how many records Paradox can pack into a block, you will have a varying amount of "dead" space in your disk file. Sometimes, taking just a few bytes off a record will allow Paradox to squeeze more records into each block. This will give you better disk space utilization. Conversely, you can sometimes add several bytes to a record without impacting the number of records which will fit into a block. This is why the change in disk space after restructuring a table is not always proportional to the changes made to a table. See the Section below on "File Fragmentation" for more information about this topic and how it can affect performance.

Key Fields

Creating the proper indexes for your tables is one of the most important ways to improve performance. When you create a table, look at which fields you will be using to search for information, link tables, or do sorts. If possible, make those fields key fields so that Paradox will create a primary index for the table.

Using Indexes

Information about how to create a primary index was included in Chapter 2. This section will provide further information about how primary indexes are used. It will also discuss secondary indexes.

Primary Indexes

Paradox creates a primary index using key fields which you specify when a table is created or restructured. A primary index is a special file which is a subset of the original table. It has an entry for each unique key value in the table, and a pointer to the location of the corresponding record. When Paradox searches for a specific value, it first checks the primary index to see where the desired record is located. Thus, Paradox does not have to search an entire table for records which match the search value.

Primary indexes are incrementally maintained. This means that as you make changes to a table, Paradox automatically updates the primary index file.

If you get a message indicating that an index is out-of-date, it may be because you used DOS to copy a table (the .DB file only) without also copying the table's family. The primary index file has a .PX extension after the table name. To solve this problem, use DOS to delete the .PX file. Then reindex your table by choosing the **Modify/Restructure** menu choices and place asterisks after the Field Type of key fields. If you don't remember which fields were indexed, be sure to check the table's structure with **Tools/Info/Structure** before deleting the .PX file. Key fields will be indicated with asterisks in the STRUCT table which is displayed.

Secondary Indexes

It is also possible to set up secondary indexes for tables. Secondary indexes are used to speed searches for values in non-key fields. While a table can have only one primary index, which may be based on one or more fields, a table can have multiple secondary indexes. A secondary index always corresponds to one field. The values in that field do not have to be unique, and no sort order is imposed on the table by using a secondary index.

There are two ways in which you can request Paradox to create a secondary index. The first is to create a query and place search criteria into each field for which you want Paradox to create a secondary index. Then, before you process the query, press F10 and choose **Tools /QuerySpeedup** from the menus. If you get the message, "No speedup possible," Paradox has determined that there would be no performance benefit to be gained from creating a secondary index.

The PAL INDEX command will force Paradox to create a secondary index. There are two ways to have Paradox execute the INDEX command. You can create and play a script which includes the INDEX command or you can use Paradox's MiniScript capability. If you are creating several secondary indexes, you may want to write a script. To create a secondary index on just one field, a PAL MiniScript will work nicely. Press Alt-F10 to access the PAL menu. Choose **MiniScript** and type the following line at the Command prompt:

```
INDEX "TABLE" on "FIELD"
```

where *TABLE* is the name of the table to be indexed, and *FIELD* is the name of the desired field.

The optional keyword, MAINTAINED, for the INDEX command causes Paradox to incrementally maintain a secondary index. This means that Paradox will make changes to the secondary index file as changes are made to the table. The MAINTAINED option can be used only on a table which has a primary key. It is usually desirable to use this option whenever possible. A secondary index created without the MAINTAINED option will be updated in a batch mode. Paradox will wait until the next time it needs to use the index for a search. If the index is marked as out-of-date, Paradox will regenerate it at that time. For a large table, this will take a significant amount of time.

Using Indexes with Edit and Coedit Modes

As soon as you go into Edit mode on an indexed table, Paradox marks the index as being out-of-date for the duration of the editing session. This means that if you use "Zoom" or LOCATE to try to find a value while you are editing, Paradox will not use a primary index if one exists. In contrast, Paradox will use indexes in Coedit mode. Because each record is posted to the table when it is unlocked or moved off of, Paradox makes a permanent change to the index file at the same time. If you use "Zoom" or LOCATE in Coedit mode, you will get the performance benefit of any indexes which are on the table. Thus, it may be worthwhile to use Coedit, instead of Edit mode, even if you are not sharing tables on a network.

Paradox and Memory

Adding memory to your computer will also make a big improvement to performance, but memory has to be the right kind of memory. Paradox will use all memory (up to 640K) it finds on your computer. Beyond that, Paradox will use memory which is configured as *expanded memory*. Adding expanded memory to your computer can make a vast difference in the performance you get from your Paradox system.

RAM disks can help performance, too.

Paradox will take the first 48K of expanded memory and use it for the VMM, Virtual Memory Manager. About two-thirds of this amount is used for the workspace. Of the remainder, 192K is used for temporary storage of Paradox overlay files and procedures. If there is any memory remaining, Paradox will use 25% for temporary storage and 75% for disk caching of your data. This percentage can be changed using the

Custom script. See Chapter 13, "Customizing Your Paradox System," for details.

Note that the amount of memory actually added to the workspace will vary depending on your particular configuration. If you have excluded any address ranges from use by your expanded memory driver, Paradox will not be able to allocate the maximum possible amount of expanded memory to the workspace. Still, the expanded memory which is used for storage and caching will give you a performance benefit.

There is one exception. If you are using QEMM, *Quarterdeck's Expanded Memory Manager 386*, Paradox can use up to 208K of expanded memory for the VMM. This means that you can get up to 150K added to your workspace. If you are running on a network which takes up a considerable amount of your computer's memory below 640K, this addition to the workspace can allow Paradox to do more than just simple tasks. Besides solving memory problems, adding this much memory to the workspace greatly improves performance. The more memory available for the workspace, the less often Paradox has to go to disk. And this, of course, means that it will take less time to complete tasks.

A note to network users: Paradox does not cache information from a network drive. This is to ensure that information on a shared drive is current. If Paradox used data cached in your expanded memory which originated from a server, other users could be changing the records with which you are working. To prevent this, Paradox will cache information only from local drives in expanded memory.

Directories and Files

While having enough memory and using the proper indexes are probably the most important ways you can increase performance, there are factors, such as directory size and fragmented files, which can affect performance adversely. These can cause software problems in general, not just with Paradox. With Paradox, though, the problems may be noticed quicker because of the amount of disk accessing Paradox does. Remember, Paradox constantly creates and deletes temporary work files, and pages records to and from the disk, when you work with tables which do not fit into available memory. Keep this in mind if you suddenly experience performance problems. It could be that your system has reached the problem threshold for file fragmentation and/or directory size and is displaying the symptoms.

If you are working on a network, the location of your private directory is also important. See the appropriate section below for details.

Directory Size

If you are working with a directory of about 100 or more files, Paradox can start to slow down. When you have this problem, it is not sufficient just to erase files from the problem directory. When you erase files, DOS still keeps an entry in the File Allocation Table for the directory. And when the File Allocation Table gets really large, Paradox will slow down.

The solution is to create a new directory and copy to it only those files which you need. This will give you a fresh File Allocation Table which will be more compact and easier to search. Paradox will then require less time to access the files it needs.

File Fragmentation

When DOS writes information to a file, it does not always place the file sectors contiguously on your disk. It takes space wherever it can and keeps track of which blocks belong to each file. Ordinarily, this does not cause problems. However, if a file gets too fragmented on disk, it can degrade performance significantly. There are a couple of steps which you can take to solve this problem.

One way to "compact" a table is to restructure it by using **Modify /Restructure**. You don't need to make actual changes to the table's structure; just press F2 and Paradox will write the table to the disk. Paradox will squeeze out any empty space which it can. Also, the table will usually end up in more contiguous blocks on the disk.

Sometimes a restructure alone is not enough to fix the problem, though. If most of your disk is fragmented, rewriting the table will not help because there may not be any contiguous space left to use. In this case, you need to use a utility program, such as Disk Optimizer, to reorganize the information on your disk. There are several programs like this one available. Keeping your disk optimized with one of these tools can make a big improvement in system performance.

Private Directories

Paradox uses your private directory to store temporary tables and other work files. Quite a number of these files may be created, depending on the operation which Paradox is doing. Because of this, it is best to keep your private directory on a local hard disk whenever possible. If you are sharing tables from a server, this will minimize the amount of information which Paradox has to move over a network.

At times, you may not be able to use a local drive for your private directory because of space requirements. You need two to three times the size of the tables with which you are working available in free disk space. When you are working with large tables on a server, you may need to use a network drive for your private directory just to have enough space for temporary tables.

Paths

Some Paradox users have found that the position of Paradox on their DOS path makes a difference in performance when starting the program from a directory other than the \PARADOX3 directory. Because of this, it is advisable to keep your \PARADOX3 directory as close to the beginning of your path statement as possible.

Paradox 386 and Paradox OS/2

A few notes are included on Paradox 386 and Paradox OS/2 (even though they are compatible with Paradox 2.0) because of the performance benefit which they can provide. If you do not need the Paradox 3.0 features and are working with very large tables, it may be advantageous to use Paradox 386 or Paradox OS/2. Appendix K has detailed information about the system requirements for these products and how they differ from Paradox 3.0.

One of the biggest improvements these products offer is their ability to use up to 16Mb of extended, not expanded, memory. This means that Paradox can keep more tables in your computer's memory. When you are working with very large tables, say 30,000 records or more, the use of extended memory can make a vast difference in performance. This performance benefit has to be weighed, of course, against the disadvantage of not having certain Paradox 3.0 features available.

Summary

If you want better performance from your Paradox system, check these points:

- Keep the width of tables to a minimum. Paradox can fit more records in memory when you work with narrow tables. This results in less disk activity.

- Make sure your tables are indexed appropriately. You can create primary or secondary indexes for tables. Paradox uses indexes to speed up searches for specific field values.
- Use expanded memory if you can. Paradox will use it to supplement the workspace, for temporary storage, and for caching.
- Do regular housekeeping on your hard disk. Make sure that directories are not too big and that files are not fragmented.

Networking with Paradox

Paradox includes multi-user capabilities which allow you to share tables with other network users. This chapter contains information about:

- The types of networks supported by Paradox
- How to install Paradox on a network
- Starting Paradox on a network
- How Paradox ensures data integrity on a network
- Common problems in networking with Paradox
- Performance on a network
- The Protection Generator
- Using different versions of Paradox on a network

What is "Multi-user"?

There are many different types of computer systems which can be classified as multi-user systems. Some systems use "dumb" terminals which are attached to a computer and software which lets more than one person run programs at the same time. Other configurations use special hardware and software which enable users to share each others' computing resources. Paradox works with the latter type of system.

Local Area Networks

The type of network which Paradox works with is called a *Local Area Network*. There are many hardware and software combinations which can be put together in a LAN (Local Area Network), but they have one thing in common. Each user has their own computer or workstation on the network and uses the network to share resources with other network users. Typically, LAN users share hard disks and printers.

The equipment which facilitates such sharing is called a network server. On some networks, servers are separate from the workstations. On other networks, each network workstation can act as a server for other network users. Paradox can work with both types of networks.

Networks Paradox Works With

Paradox is designed to work with networks which run under DOS version 3.1 or higher and which are compatible with one of the following LANs:

- 3Com 3 + network with 3Com + software (Version 1.0 or higher)
- Novell network with Advanced Netware (Version 2.0A or higher)
- IBM Token Ring or PC Network with IBM PC Local Area Network Program (Version 1.12 or higher)
- Torus Tapestry II (Version 1.0 or higher)
- AT&T Starlan Network (Version 1.1 or higher)
- Banyan Vines Network (Version 2.10 or higher)

How Paradox Supports Multiple Users

The Paradox LAN Pack

Paradox's multi-user capabilities are built into every package of Paradox 3.0. You can use individual versions of Paradox 3.0 to share information on a network by installing each copy on a workstation and pressing **Y** at installation when asked if you want to share information on a network.

This approach facilitates information-sharing using workstations which have installed Paradox locally.

There is another option, the LAN Pack, which you can use to provide Paradox access to network users. The LAN Pack is separate from Paradox 3.0 but needs to be installed with at least one copy of Paradox 3.0 in order to work. The LAN Pack provides an additional five user counts on a server. It is used with a copy of Paradox 3.0 which is installed on a network server.

The User Count

When you install Paradox on a network server, you are prompted for all Paradox 3.0 serial numbers which you want to use on the network. Paradox writes this information to the .SOM file. This number is referred to as the *user count* and is used to limit the number of users who can access Paradox from the server at one time. The LAN Pack serial number will add five user counts to your Paradox system.

Any workstation can load Paradox from the server as long as there is an available "user count." Users who start Paradox from their own workstation, instead of from the server, can share tables with LAN Pack users but do not decrement the user count. When you install Paradox on a server, serial numbers from the LAN Pack and from Paradox 3.0 can be used in any combination. The total number of users is realistically limited by the number of users your network can support.

The .NET File

As mentioned above, people using Paradox from a server can share information with each other *and* with users who have installed Paradox on their own workstation. The key to doing this is the .NET file, a special file which Paradox creates to keep track of which users have access to shared directories. When you install Paradox for network use, the program will prompt for the location of the .NET file. The location which you specify needs to be the same for users who will be sharing information, whether they load Paradox from the same copy on a server or whether they use their own copy of Paradox. This ensures that Paradox will use the same .NET file to control all access to shared directories. More information about how to specify the location of the .NET file is included in the installation instructions below.

Installing Paradox for Networking

On a Server

Follow these general steps to install Paradox on a server:

1. First, create a "read only" directory on the desired network drive for Paradox3 files.

2. Create at least one directory on the server for information which will be shared. Users will need read, write, and create network rights for this directory. This directory is often called \ PDOXDATA and also is used for the location of the .NET file. *Each user needs to have the same logical drive linked or mapped to* \ *PDOXDATA.* This logical drive is then used to specify the location of the .NET file.

3. Install Paradox in the read only directory created in Step 1: Make that directory the current directory, place the Paradox installation diskette into drive A: and type **A:INSTALL**. Select `Network Installation` from the menu which is displayed.

Paradox will then prompt for the destination drive and directory, and the country code, before copying the Paradox files to the server. You will also be prompted for any serial numbers which you want to use for your user count, the type of network you will be using, and the location of the .NET file. Be sure to specify the logical drive which will be linked or mapped to \ PDOXDATA in each user's network login script or in the batch file used to start Paradox.

A note for Novell users: Even if your users will have a drive letter, like H:, mapped to \ PDOXDATA, it is not sufficient just to specify H: as the location of the .NET file. You must specify H: \ PDOXDATA (or give the name of your shared directory). Otherwise, Paradox will usually look in the root directory of the drive which contains \ PDOXDATA. This will work if you have sufficient network rights in that directory, but it will not result in the .NET file being written to the desired location.

Follow the rest of the instructions as prompted. You can install optional software on the server after the Paradox3 installation has been completed.

On a Workstation

See note for Novell users above.

You can install Paradox on a workstation and use it to share information with other users. Follow the instructions in Appendix D making the following change: when you are asked whether you want to access data on a network, press **Y**. Paradox will then prompt for the location of the .NET file. Be sure to specify the logical drive which you will have linked to ＼PDOXDATA (or whichever directory contains the shared information). You and all other users must have the same logical drive linked or mapped to this directory. All other installation steps are the same.

Changing Installation Information

NUPDATE is a special program which you can use to change serial numbers, the network type, the Network Administrator's name, or the location of the .NET file without going through the entire installation process. To run NUPDATE, make sure that no one on the network is using Paradox and log on as the network supervisor so you have the network rights required to make changes in the read-only directory where the Paradox files are located. Make the directory containing the Paradox files the current directory and type **NUPDATE** at the DOS prompt. Paradox will prompt you through making the changes.

Before You Can Start Paradox

There are other tasks which you must do before you can use Paradox successfully on a network.

The CONFIG.SYS File

If you have installed Paradox on a server, you must make sure that the CONFIG.SYS file for each workstation which will use Paradox includes these commands:

```
FILES=20
BUFFERS=20
```

If you are not familiar with how to create or modify a CONFIG.SYS file, see Chapter 16 for details. This file must be in the root directory of the boot disk for every workstation which will start Paradox from the server. Otherwise, Paradox will display an error message saying that the parameters in the CONFIG.SYS file are not set up correctly and won't load.

The Private Directory

It is extremely important for each network user to have their own private directory. This directory can be specified in the PARADOX3.CFG file by using the Custom script. If no directory is specified, Paradox will attempt to use the current directory as the private directory. A special lock file is written to the private directory to prevent anyone else from accessing it. If this directory is a shared directory, it can cause problems for anyone else trying to use Paradox.

The best way to avoid this problem is to start Paradox from the desired private directory *and* make sure that Paradox finds the right .CFG file for each user. Paradox uses the DOS path to find PARADOX3.CFG files, if they are not in the current directory. It is possible for Paradox to find the wrong .CFG file specifying a different private directory. If you are not sure of what is happening "behind the scenes" when you start Paradox, use **T**ools/**N**et/**S**etPrivate after Paradox is loaded to see what the private directory was set to.

Setting Up the Path and Logical Drives

There are two more tasks to check before you try to start Paradox on a network. They are related to your software setup. First, for users who load Paradox from a server, a logical drive must be linked or mapped to the directory containing the Paradox3 files. Assuming that Paradox is not started from this drive, this logical drive must be included on the DOS path or as a search drive.

Second, all users, whether they start Paradox from a server or from a workstation, must have the same logical drive linked or mapped to the shared directory which is used for the .NET file. If different directories are linked or mapped to the drive specified for the .NET file when Paradox was installed, each user may end up using a different file. This will work only until the user tries to use a table controlled by another .NET file. Paradox will permit only users accessing the same .NET file to share tables.

Memory Requirements

Memory is more of a concern on a network workstation because of the added overhead of network drivers.

There is an additional requirement which must be satisfied before you can start Paradox on a network. Your computer must have adequate memory to start the program. The memory requirements are the same as when you start Paradox on a standalone computer (see Chapter 16 for details). Without expanded memory on your workstation, you will need about 450K of free memory to start Paradox, preferably more.

With the overhead of network software, it can be difficult to have 450K free. Expanded memory helps, because you can load Paradox with slightly less memory. If you are using QEMM, the *Quarterdeck Expanded Memory Manager 386*, you can actually load Paradox with available memory as low as 350K, depending on your configuration. The results you experience will depend on whether you have excluded address ranges from use by your expanded memory driver and the amount of memory taken by any RAM-resident software.

Once you have Paradox properly set up, and enough memory available, you can start the program.

Starting Paradox for Use on a Network

To start Paradox when it was installed on a workstation, you can use your normal method. You may want to place the network commands to set up any of the logical drives needed for the shared directory in a batch file. Also, place \PARADOX3 on your path if you start Paradox from a different directory and type **PARADOX3** to start the program. Be sure that Paradox finds the proper .CFG file. This is easy to control if you are loading Paradox from a local drive. Simply place the .CFG file in the directory which is current when you start Paradox.

When you start Paradox from a server, there are other considerations. You may use a network login script to start Paradox every time you log onto the network or you may use a separate batch file which sets up the necessary logical drives and then starts Paradox. Also, make sure that each user has their own private directory. There are several ways to do this. The easiest method is to place each user's .CFG file in their private directory *and* start Paradox from that directory. This ensures that Paradox will use the desired private directory and not cause conflicts for other users.

You may need to use the DOS SUBST command to assign a logical drive letter to the hard disk of a non-dedicated server.

If you are using Paradox on a network which uses non-dedicated servers (servers which can be used as workstations, at the same time they are providing network services), you may need to start Paradox with a command line which tells Paradox you are loading it from a shared drive. To do so, type **PARADOX3 -SHARE** when you start Paradox.

How Paradox Controls Sharing

Paradox facilitates information-sharing by restricting use at three different levels: directories, tables, and records. The reasons for each level of locking are discussed below.

Directory Locking

Paradox needs to control directory access on a network to ensure that each user's temporary tables cannot be accessed by another user. It is easy to understand why this is necessary. Imagine doing a query which generates an ANSWER table at the same time that another user does a similar operation. Unless the ANSWER table for each user is stored in its own directory, the first ANSWER table would be overwritten as soon as the second query was completed. To prevent this, Paradox uses each user's private directory to store temporary tables and other work files.

When a user starts the program, Paradox writes a lock file in the private directory which was specified in the .CFG file (or in the current directory if there is no default) *only when the private directory is on a shared drive.* This lock file tells Paradox that no other user can access information in that directory. If your private directory is on a local drive which can be accessed by other users, make sure that you use a directory which no one else will use.

Similarly, Paradox writes a lock file in any shared directory when it is in use to indicate that the directory cannot be used exclusively by any other user. This is another reason why it is important to specify a private directory in the .CFG file. If a user starts Paradox from the shared directory, and has no private directory specified in the .CFG file, Paradox will attempt to make the shared directory the private directory. If that directory is in use, Paradox will fail in its attempt to write the lock file.

Table Locking

Once a directory is flagged as a shared directory, further controls are necessary to make sure that tables are protected from changes which could cause problems for other users. For example, you would not want Paradox to allow another user to restructure a table while you are editing it. This would cause horrendous problems. Paradox prevents this by placing different types of locks on tables which reside in a shared directory for different operations.

These are the types of locks which can be placed on tables:

- `FullLock` puts a complete lock on a table; if a user places a full lock on a table, no one else can use the table.
- `WriteLock` lets only the user who placed the lock change the table; other users can use the table but not change it.
- `PreventFullLock` prevents any other user from placing a full lock on a table.

- `PreventWriteLock` prevents any user from placing a write lock on a table.

During operations, Paradox automatically places the necessary table locks to prevent tables from being damaged or experiencing other problems. The locks which are placed are always the least restrictive possible. This maximizes the amount of sharing possible between users. The locks which are placed by different operations are listed in Table 15.1.

You can also place locks explicitly on a table by using **T**ools/**N**et/**L**ock or **T**ools/**N**et/**P**reventLock while you use Paradox interactively. For applications developers, there are PAL locking commands which are useful in preventing script errors. You can attempt to lock a table and then check the value of *retval* to see if the lock was placed successfully. Retval returns True if a lock was placed and False if locking was not possible.

Table 15.1 Locks Placed by Paradox Commands

Command(s)	Lock
View	PFL*
Ask (except Insert, Delete, or Changeto queries)	PFL
Ask (Insert, Delete, or Changeto queries)	FL
Report	PFL on table; FL on reports being designed or changed
Create	FL
Borrow	PFL on table being borrowed
Sort (different tables)	WL on source table; FL on target table
Sort (same table)	FL
Coedit	PFL, PWL while any record is locked
Edit	FL
DataEntry	PFL on source table; PWL at DO-IT!
MultiEntry	WL on source table; WL on map table; PWL on target tables
Restructure	FL
ValCheck/TableLookup	PFL on lookup table
Image/KeepSet	FL on table during creation
Image/Graph/CrossTab	PFL
Image/Graph/View	PFL

(continued)

Table 15.1 (continued)

Command(s)	Lock
Forms	PFL on table; FL on forms being designed or changed
Tools/Rename	FL
Tools/QuerySpeedup	PFL
Tools/ExportImport/Export	WL on source table
Tools/ExportImport/Import	FL on target table
Tools/Copy/Table	WL on source table; FL on target table
Tools/Copy (other than table)	WL on source table; FL on target table
Tools/Copy/JustFamily	PFL on source table; WL on source family; FL on target family
Tools/Delete/Table	FL
Tools/Delete/Report or Form	FL on report or form; PFL on table
Tools/Delete/Settings or ValCheck	FL on .SET or .VAL; FL on table
Tools/Info/Structure	PFL
Tools/Info/Family	WL on table and family
Tools/Add	WL on source table; PWL on target table
Tools/MultiAdd	WL on source and map table; PWL on target tables
Tools/FormAdd	PFL on source and target tables. For update: WL on source and target tables. For new entries: WL on source tables; PWL on target tables
Tools/Subtract	FL on source and target tables
Tools/Empty	FL
Tools/Protect	FL

*Key: FL = FullLock; PFL = PreventFullLock; WL = WriteLock;
  PWL = PreventWriteLock

Record Locking

Paradox allows more than one user at the same time to edit a table through Coedit mode. Coedit places a `PreventFullLock` on a table so that no user can lock other users out. It also places a `PreventWriteLock` on the table while any record is being changed so that no user can prevent other users from updating the table.

Coedit works by using record locking. This topic was discussed in some detail in Chapter 4, "Modifying Your Paradox Tables," in the section on Modify/Coedit. Basically, in Coedit mode each user has free access to the table *except for records which are locked by another user.*

Records are locked by Paradox only when a user starts to change a record. At that point, the record is locked and cannot be changed by any other user. If another user attempts to change the record, Paradox will display a message that the record is locked by and give the other person's username.

You need to use Alt-L before you can toggle to table view while on an unposted record.

Paradox ordinarily handles all record locking automatically. You can explicitly lock a record by using Alt-L, the "Lock key," a toggle key which will lock or unlock a record. If you are changing a record, it is usually not unlocked and posted to the table until you leave the record. You can unlock the record before you leave it by pressing Alt-L and make the record available to other users for further changes.

Problems on a Network

It is possible to experience many different problems while working with Paradox on a network. Sometimes, it is difficult to sort out the cause. There are many factors at work: the network hardware and software, the workstation and its operating system, memory and other device drivers, Paradox itself, and the tables with which you are working. Here are a few tips on common problems which you can fix easily. For additional information on possible causes of problems, review Chapter 16, "Troubleshooting."

"Access denied..."

You will get the "Access denied" message when you try to start Paradox if there is a conflicting lock file either in your private directory or in the directory specified for the .NET file. For example, if no private directory was specified in your .CFG file, and you start Paradox from the shared directory, Paradox will try to write a lock file to the shared directory to make it your private directory. If the directory is already in use, Paradox will display the "Access denied" message. The solution is to specify a different private directory in the .CFG file. See Chapter 13, "Customizing Your Paradox System," for information about how to do this.

If you are trying to access a table in a shared directory, and you get the "Access denied" message, it may be that someone else is using the directory for their private directory. Another possibility is that there are leftover .LCK files in the directory from a network crash or some other problem. To see if this is the problem, have all other users exit from Paradox and try to access the table again. If your problem persists, exit from Paradox yourself and delete any files with the .LCK extension in the shared directory. You may need to use a utility, such as XTreePro, to do this. On some networks, you cannot delete a file using DOS if it thinks the file is in use.

"Can't record lock/unlock in…"

This message appears when Paradox cannot write to the .NET file upon startup. This can happen if you have insufficient network rights in the shared directory specified for the location of the .NET file at installation time. This directory should have read, write, and create rights. If you are on a Novell network, be sure that the logical drive *and* the name of the shared directory is specified for the location of the .NET file. Otherwise, Paradox may try to write or update the .NET file in the root directory of the logical drive.

If you are certain that Paradox is looking in the right directory for the .NET file, check for leftover .LCK files. Delete any which exist and try to start Paradox again. If all else fails, have all users exit from Paradox and delete the .NET file if it exists. (Paradox creates this file only if it does not already exist in the specified directory.)

Performance on a Network

The biggest factor affecting network performance is the network itself. The first thing to check if you are having performance problems is your network setup. You may need to change some network software parameters to alleviate bottlenecks in buffers or elsewhere.

There also are other ways to improve performance. Check the items which were discussed in Chapter 14, "Performance Tips," and also see if any of the following suggestions will work for you.

Private Directories

Placing your private directory on a local drive will make a big improvement in performance. Doing so minimizes the number of times Paradox will have to use the network to get information. Keep your private directory on a network drive only if you have insufficient space on your local drive or do not have a local drive.

Moving the Paradox System Files

If you are using Paradox from a server, you can place all system files, except PARADOX3.EXE and PARADOX3.SOM in a directory on your local drive. Then, place this directory on your path ahead of the network directory for the Paradox files. This will allow Paradox to read overlay files from the local disk when they are needed. This also cuts down on network delays.

Queries

When you perform a query on a shared table, Paradox takes a "snapshot" of the table and then starts to process the query. If a change is made to the table, Paradox starts the process again. When frequent changes are being made to a query table, this can cause the query process to take a long time. To get around this problem, try to perform queries when activity on the tables involved is low. Also, you may want to consider copying the table to a local drive and then doing the query. Copy puts a write lock on the source table so that you may be able to get a copy even if other people are using the table.

The Protection Generator

What it Does

The Protection Generator lets you give each user one password which grants access to whichever tables are needed. The tables associated with the password can have different levels of protection. In this way, each network user has to remember only one password to access the necessary tables.

How it Works

The Protection Generator prompts you to enter password and user information into tables. Using this information, the Protection Generator writes a login script for each user which prompts them for their password when they start Paradox.

Using the Protection Generator

To use the Protection Generator, follow these steps:

1. First, install the Protection Generator using the `Optional Software` portion of the Paradox installation program.

2. Decide where you want to keep the files to be generated by Protect. You must have read, write, and create network rights in this directory.

3. To start the Protection Generator, play the *Protect* script using **S**cripts/**P**lay. This script is in the Protect subdirectory of the PARA-DOX3 directory.

4. Enter a password when prompted and write it down. You cannot get back into the Protection Generator without this password.

5. Enter the *logical drive* linked or mapped to the directory which you want to protect.

6. Follow the menus to create your protection system. When you have finished, choose `Exit` from the Protection Generator Menu to save your work.

After you have set up a password system, and generated the necessary login script, you need a command in each user's Init script which will play the login script when Paradox is started. The command should look like this:

```
PLAY "G:\\DIRNAME\\LOGIN"
```

where G: is a logical drive and DIRNAME is the subdirectory in which the login script resides. This drive and directory is the one which was chosen in Step 2 above. Specifying the full pathname of the login script is not necessary if that directory is the working directory when Paradox is loaded.

You also can include PLAY "Login" as the first command in an application program. This will cause Paradox to prompt users for their name and password before continuing with the application program.

Sharing with Different Paradox Versions

All versions of Paradox from 2.0 on have multi-user capabilities. This means that you can share information among users of:

- Paradox 2.0
- The Paradox Network Pack (2.0)
- Paradox 386
- Paradox OS/2
- Paradox 3.0
- Paradox LAN Pack installed with Paradox 3.0

The only requirement is that the same location be specified for the location of the .NET file when Paradox is installed. Remember to use the logical drive with which each user is linked or mapped to the shared directory. As long as that requirement is satisfied, users of these different versions of Paradox can share information.

Summary

Paradox includes multi-user capabilities which allow users to share information on a Local Area Network. You must have a network compatible with one of the networks which Paradox supports. The key points about using Paradox on a network are:

- Paradox works with 3Com, Novell, AT&T Starlan, Torus Tapestry, Banyan, and IBM Local Area Networks.
- Each copy of Paradox 3.0 provides one "user count." You can purchase the LAN Pack for use *with* Paradox 3.0. The LAN Pack adds 5 to your user count and must be installed on a server with Paradox 3.0. You can add multiple LAN Packs to get the count you need.
- Users can start Paradox from a server or from their own workstation and share information with other Paradox users, as long as they are using the same .NET file.
- Paradox uses the .NET file to keep track of who is using tables in shared directories.
- Paradox implements three levels of locking, directory locking, table locking, and record locking, to insure data integrity and to avoid other problems.
- Temporary tables are kept in each user's private directory; this directory must be unique for each user. It cannot be the shared directory.

- Paradox places four kinds of locks on tables and their family members depending on the operation being done. The types of locks are `FullLock`, `WriteLock`, `PreventFullLock`, and `PreventWriteLock`.

- When you use Coedit mode to edit a table concurrently with other users, Paradox places a lock on a record when you attempt to change it; if the record is locked by another user, Paradox will notify you of the username if it is available.

- The location of your private directory significantly impacts Paradox performance; keep it on a local drive if you can.

- Problems can be caused by insufficient network rights or conflicting locks in directories; if you are the Network Administrator, make sure you know where each user's private directory is.

- You can use the Protection Generator to create one password for each network user which grants them the desired level of access to different tables. The Protection Generator creates a login script which must be played by each user when Paradox is started; the "PLAY login" command can be included in each user's login script or as the first command of an application.

Troubleshooting

All computer users encounter software and hardware problems at one time or another. These problems can be frustrating, especially if the source of the problem is not recognized quickly. This chapter presents information to help you solve some problems you may have in using Paradox. The first section offers general tips for narrowing down the source of problems. The remaining sections offer specific suggestions for dealing with two different problem symptoms which you may encounter.

General Troubleshooting Guidelines

When you have a problem, the first thing to do is see if it can be re-created. Most computers have problems at some time or another due to power fluctuations, damaged files, or hardware failures. Sometimes these problems occur once and are not repeated. So, the first step in troubleshooting is trying to re-create the problem.

Once you have re-created the problem, the next step is to try and determine the source. There are several elements which work together in your computer. It can be difficult to see which one is behind a particular problem. In general, you should start from the specific and work toward the general when trying to pinpoint the source of a problem.

When you work with Paradox, you can try to re-create the problem by using a different table, or a different form or report with the same table. This will tell you whether the problem is related to a specific Paradox object, or if it lies elsewhere. If the problem occurs while doing the same operation on different tables, there may be a problem with your

457

Paradox files. One section below tells you how to check your files. Once you know that your Paradox files are OK, you can look for problems with your hardware. If it appears that all is well with your system, there may be a conflict between Paradox and any RAM-resident software which you may be using. Loading Paradox by itself will usually show whether this is the source.

As a last resort, it is sometimes very useful to try and re-create your problem on another computer which is configured differently. If the problem disappears, you can assume that there may be a hardware problem or an incompatibility on the first system tested.

Problems Starting Paradox

Sometimes you can have problems just trying to get to the Paradox Main Menu. In some cases, Paradox will give you useful messages which indicate the source of the problem. At other times, it may appear that your computer has "died" once you type **PARADOX3** at the DOS prompt. This section offers information on both situations.

"Can't start Paradox: not enough memory"

Paradox displays this message when you don't have enough conventional RAM available to load Paradox. "Conventional RAM" here refers to memory below 640K. It does not include expanded or extended memory.

You must have a minimum of 512K of RAM to use Paradox. In reality, the number that matters is the amount of memory that is available when you try to start Paradox. If you do not have expanded memory, Paradox will need approximately 450K of RAM to load. You may have more than this amount of RAM installed, but it may be in use by DOS, network software, device drivers, or other RAM-resident software.

You cannot use CHKDSK on a network drive.

You can check to see how much memory is available by using the DOS CHKDSK command from a non-network drive. Type **CHKDSK** at the DOS prompt. Information about your current drive and the amount of conventional RAM will be displayed. The last line shows how much memory is available, as shown in Figure 16.1. This number must be approximately 450K to load Paradox.

If you have expanded memory, you will be able to load Paradox with less conventional RAM available. How much less, though, depends on your system configuration. In any case, it will not be a large amount. Most likely, it will be a difference of about 20K.

```
C:\>chkdsk

  21204992 bytes total disk space
     40960 bytes in 2 hidden files
    159744 bytes in 68 directories
  17758208 bytes in 1511 user files
     47104 bytes in bad sectors
   3190976 bytes available on disk

    655360 bytes total memory
    455872 bytes free

C:\>
```

Figure 16.1 Display after using DOS CHKDSK command

An exception to this rule occurs if you are using Quarterdeck's Expanded Memory Manager 386, QEMM. Paradox users who are using QEMM as their expanded memory driver will be able to load Paradox with much less conventional memory available, perhaps as little as 350K. Once again, the exact amount of memory you need depends on your system configuration.

If you have close to the required amount of memory, you may be able to disable an unneeded device driver, or unload some RAM-resident software, to gain conventional RAM. Then, try again to load Paradox.

A note for all users: if you start Paradox with only a minimum amount of memory available, it is likely that you will run out of memory while you are doing anything more than the simplest tasks. You may even be unable to view a very wide table. Information about memory requirements was included in Chapter 14, "Performance Tips." More will be found in the section below on the "Not enough memory to complete operation" message.

"Can't start Paradox: file limit in CONFIG.SYS too low"

This message may be displayed when you try to start Paradox. It indicates that the commands FILES = 20 and BUFFERS = 20 were not found in CONFIG.SYS.

When you install Paradox, it writes these commands to your CONFIG.SYS file, or creates a CONFIG.SYS file if it does not exist. The CONFIG.SYS file will be written to the root directory of the drive from which Paradox assumes you boot your computer. If you boot your computer from another drive, the CONFIG.SYS, with the FILES = 20 and

BUFFERS = 20 commands, may not be found. Paradox will then give the above message when you try to start the program.

To fix the problem, you can:

- Find the CONFIG.SYS file which Paradox wrote and copy it to the root directory of your boot disk
- Edit your CONFIG.SYS file and add the commands *FILES = 20* and *BUFFERS = 20* if they are not in the file
- Use a text editor to create a CONFIG.SYS file with the FILES = 20 and BUFFERS = 20 commands; place that file in the root directory of your boot disk
- Use the DOS COPY command to create a CONFIG.SYS file in the root directory of your boot disk

For the last approach, change to the root directory of your boot disk. At the DOS prompt, type **COPY CON CONFIG.SYS** and press Enter. The cursor will be at the beginning of a blank line. Type **FILES = 20** and press Enter. Then type **BUFFERS = 20**, press Enter, and then press F6. You will see a carat (^) and a "Z" displayed as shown in Figure 16.2. This is an end-of-file marker. At this point, press Enter. You will see the DOS prompt displayed again.

If you are using a computer that runs DOS under some other operating system, put CONFIG.SYS in the root directory of the disk that DOS is booted from.

After making sure that the necessary commands are in the CONFIG.SYS file, reboot your computer and start Paradox. You should see the Main Menu shortly.

This message can also indicate that you forgot to reboot your computer after you installed Paradox. (You must reboot your computer in order to execute the commands in the CONFIG.SYS file.) If this was the case, reboot and restart Paradox. It should load successfully.

Machine "Hangs" with No Message

Memory Conflicts

If you are using a LIM 3.2 EMS driver, you may need to start Paradox with the command line option -ems3. Try this if you are having problems.

If you have expanded memory, it is possible for a memory conflict to "hang" your computer when you try to start Paradox. These conflicts can occur if Paradox attempts to use expanded memory through an EMS driver, using an address which is in use by another board in your computer. To see if the problem is due to a memory conflict, start Paradox with the command-line option which tells Paradox not to use any expanded memory which may be present. To do this, type **PARADOX3 -EMK 0** at the DOS prompt.

```
C:\>copy con config.sys
files=20
buffers=20
^Z
        1 File(s) copied

C:\>
```

Figure 16.2 Creating CONFIG.SYS using DOS COPY CON command

If Paradox loads successfully, you can safely assume that the problem was due to a memory conflict. Resolving the conflict is the next task. This can take a little more time than the last step. You need to figure out which board in your computer is the source of the conflict. Usually, it is either an EGA or a network board. These devices often have addresses in the same range as the addresses used by EMS drivers to map out the use of expanded memory.

If you have an EGA board or a network board in your computer, find out the address being used by the device. Sometimes this information is included in the documentation for the device; otherwise, you may need to check with the manufacturer's Technical Support Department. Once you have the address range, try excluding it from use by your EMS driver.

Most EMS drivers have a parameter which allows you to exclude address ranges. You will need to review the documentation for the EMS driver to get the proper syntax for the exclusion parameter. It typically looks like "EXCLUDE D000-DFFF" or "/x = D000-DFFF," where *D000-DFFF* is an address range.

The expression *D000-DFFF* is a hexadecimal number which represents an address range in your computer's memory. Addresses which you may need to exclude generally will fall between A000 and FFFF. You may need to exclude one range for an EGA board and another range for a network board. If you have to exclude more than two, you may have problems. The EMS driver may indicate that it does not have enough contiguous memory. In that case, you may not be able to use expanded memory with Paradox and your current configuration. This is rare, though. It may take a bit of trial-and-error to find the proper address ranges to exclude, but once you find them, Paradox should run without a hitch.

If you still cannot load Paradox, use the "-emk 0" command-line option.

Display Problems

See Appendix B for more information on display problems.

If you get a blank screen after trying to start Paradox, you may have a configuration problem. Paradox will usually detect the type of display which you are using and adjust appropriately. On occasion, this does not work as expected. Paradox may load into memory, and be ready for use, but you may not be able to see anything on the screen. To see if this is the problem, press **E** and then **Y**. Assuming Paradox is active, but just not visible, this will cause you to exit from the program.

If you return to the DOS prompt, you can start Paradox again using a command-line option to tell Paradox which kind of display is in use. The options are *-mono*, *-color*, and *-b&w*. Use the command-line option which is right for your display. If Paradox starts successfully, you can change this permanently by playing the Custom script and using the **V**ideo/**M**onitor menu choices.

If you don't return to the DOS prompt after pressing **E** and **Y**, there may be a memory conflict as described in the previous section. Or, there may be a conflict due to RAM-resident software.

Using Paradox with RAM-Resident Software

Paradox runs successfully with many RAM-resident programs. These programs can sometimes cause problems, though, especially if you are using them in combination. To see if there is a conflict between Paradox and RAM-resident software, try to load Paradox with only your operating system active. If Paradox starts successfully, the next step is to determine the source of the conflict.

If you are not familiar with how your computer is configured, you may need assistance from the person who set it up to determine the source of the conflict. Because it is not always possible to contact that person, some information is included here which may be useful if you face this task alone and are not very knowledgeable about DOS.

If you are not familiar with your computer setup, check with someone more knowledgeable if possible.

The next several paragraphs contain information for new computer users on the AUTOEXEC.BAT and CONFIG.SYS files. These special files are used by DOS. The files are located in the root directory on your boot disk. (For new computer users: the boot disk is where your computer looks to find the start-up DOS files it needs.) These files may or may not be present on your disk.

If you are not familiar with your computer's setup, please be careful. It can take many hours to set up a system which has been extensively customized. Use the following information cautiously, if at all. You may want to back up your AUTOEXEC.BAT and CONFIG.SYS files before making any changes to them.

The AUTOEXEC.BAT File: The AUTOEXEC.BAT file contains commands which are executed when you turn on your computer or reset it. These commands may be as simple as the DOS DATE and TIME commands or they may invoke a menu program which is used to control access to your system. The AUTOEXEC.BAT file may also contain commands which start programs such as Paradox automatically. You can view the contents of the AUTOEXEC.BAT file by using the DOS **TYPE** command.

First, make the drive from which you boot the current drive. Then type **CD ** and press Enter to make the root directory the current directory. Type **TYPE AUTOEXEC.BAT** at the DOS prompt and press Enter. The AUTOEXEC.BAT file, if it exists, will be displayed. You can check the file for commands which start any RAM-resident software. If there are commands present which you suspect may be causing a conflict, you can temporarily rename the AUTOEXEC.BAT file and reboot your computer. Then, see if Paradox will load successfully.

The CONFIG.SYS File: To check the contents of your CONFIG.SYS file, type **TYPE CONFIG.SYS** at the DOS prompt in the root directory of your boot disk and press Enter. The file's contents will be displayed. You should see the commands `FILES=20` and `BUFFERS=20,` as a minimum. These commands were written to the CONFIG.SYS file when you installed Paradox. In the CONFIG.SYS file, you may also see commands which load device drivers for expanded memory or other devices. These device drivers sometimes can conflict with Paradox. You can edit the CONFIG.SYS file and "comment out" any drivers which you think might be causing a problem by typing a colon in front of the lines to be excluded. Then reboot your computer and try again to start Paradox.

If Paradox still will not start, and you have checked for a memory conflict and for a display problem, your Paradox files may be damaged.

Damaged Paradox Files

If you think your Paradox files are damaged, reinstall Paradox and try to re-create your problem. In most cases of damaged files, this will solve the problem. In the case where the files on your diskettes are damaged, you can get new diskettes from Borland.

Problems Starting Paradox on a Network

Many problems can occur while trying to start Paradox from a network workstation. These problems were covered in Chapter 15, "Networking With Paradox."

Machine "Hangs" While Using Paradox

Damaged Tables

If your computer "hangs" while you are using a table, it may indicate that the table is damaged. A table can become damaged if the computer's power supply is interrupted while the table is in use. Common causes are power failures, power surges, and rebooting your computer while Paradox is in use.

Damaged tables can also result from hardware problems, especially memory problems. Paradox, unlike some other programs, will use all available memory. A memory problem may go undetected until you use Paradox. Memory problems can cause tables to be damaged repeatedly. If you experience this problem, you may want to have diagnostic tests run on your computer's memory.

When a table becomes damaged, it may or may not be detected by Paradox. If Paradox catches the damage, it will flag the table and not allow access to it. Many times, though, Paradox does not know that a table is damaged. Your first indication that something is wrong may be when you attempt to query or sort a table and the process never completes. Your computer may "hang" completely, or the disk light may flicker, showing that Paradox is still hard at work. It is possible for Paradox to get stuck in an endless loop while working with a damaged table.

When this happens, you will need to reboot your computer to exit from Paradox. Don't worry about damaging the tables which were in use; most likely, the table or tables are already damaged. This is what may have caused the problem in the first place. After rebooting your computer, use the Tutility program.

Tutility

Use COPY A:TUTILITY.* if TUTILITY is on your Install diskette.

Tutility is included with your Paradox files. If you have Paradox Version 3.01 or higher, it is in the \UTIL directory of Personal Programmer disk 6. In earlier Paradox versions, Tutility is included on the Installation diskette. Tutility can be used to check for damaged tables and, in most cases, rebuild them. To run Tutility, first copy it to your hard disk using the DOS COPY command. Put the diskette with the Tutility program into drive A:, make the Paradox directory your current directory, type **COPY A:\UTIL\TUTILITY.*** at the DOS prompt, and press Enter. If your Paradox directory is on your DOS path, you will be able to start Tutility from whatever directory your table is in.

To start Tutility, type **TUTILITY** at the DOS prompt and press Enter. You will see a menu which looks like a Paradox menu. It is shown in Figure 16.3.

```
Verify  Rebuild  Directory  Monitor  Exit
Verify table structure
═══════════════════════════════════════════════════════════════════

                 ▓▓▓▓▓▓▓ PARADOX TABLE UTILITIES ▓▓▓▓▓▓▓

              In the event of power failures or other
              problems with your computer system, you
              can use the VERIFY option of this program
              to make sure that your Paradox tables have
              not been damaged.  In many cases, you can
              repair a damaged table by using the program's
              REBUILD option


                            Release 3.0
              Copyright (c) 1985, 1986, 1987, 1988 by Borland International
                        All Rights Reserved


   Use ← and → to highlight selection          Press ↵ to make selection

   Paradox Table Utilities                          Press F1 for Help
```

Figure 16.3 Tutility Menu

- `Verify` is used to check for damaged tables.
- `Rebuild` will repair damaged tables, if that is possible.
- `Directory` allows you to change the working directory.
- `Monitor` sets video display attributes.
- `Exit` returns you to the DOS prompt.

If you choose `Verify` from the Tutility Menu, you will be prompted for a table name. You can press Enter to get a list of the tables in the current directory, as you can when you are using Paradox. The table you choose will be checked for damage. If `Verify` detects a problem, you will see a message that the table should be rebuilt; otherwise you see a message, as shown in Figure 16.4, that the table is OK.

A note on using `Verify`: if you think that a table may be damaged, use `Rebuild` without using `Verify` first. `Verify` does not always detect problems in a table. It is possible to get a "Table OK" message and still have problems with a table. On the other hand, rebuilding a table unnecessarily will not hurt the table. It will just cost you time. This may be better than losing important information later.

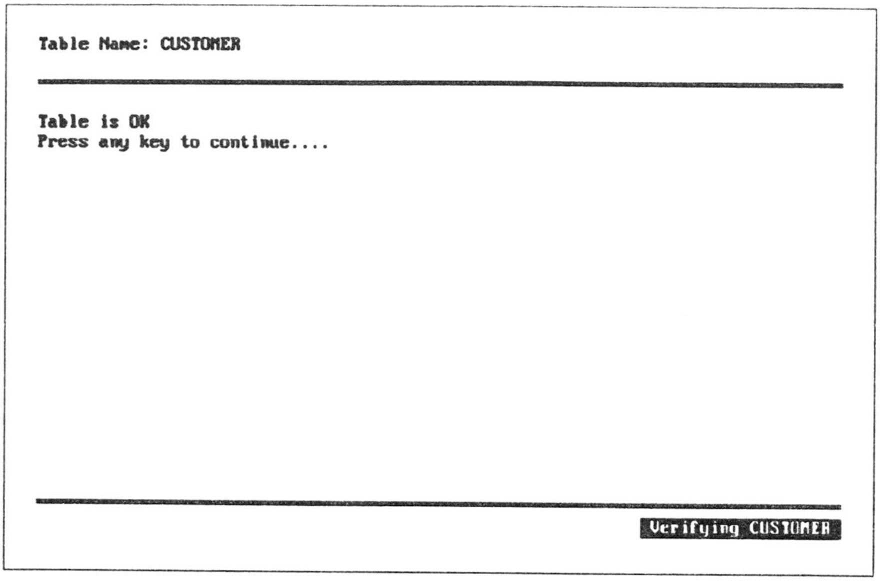

```
Table Name: CUSTOMER
_____

Table is OK
Press any key to continue....




                                                    Verifying CUSTOMER
```

Figure 16.4 Table OK message using Tutility Verify option

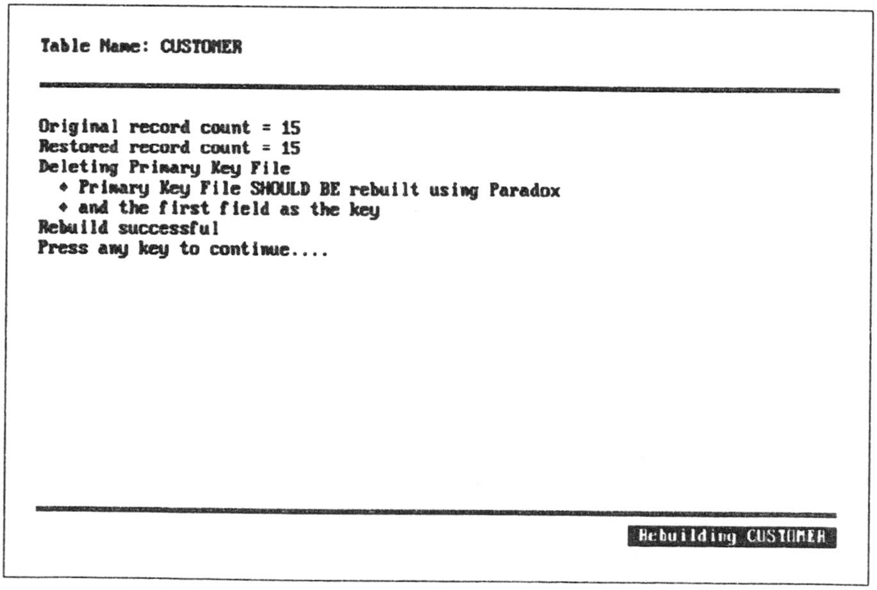

```
Table Name: CUSTOMER
_____

Original record count = 15
Restored record count = 15
Deleting Primary Key File
   • Primary Key File SHOULD BE rebuilt using Paradox
   • and the first field as the key
Rebuild successful
Press any key to continue....




                                                    Rebuilding CUSTOMER
```

Figure 16.5 Rebuild successful message using Tutility

When you choose `Rebuild` on the Tutility Menu, you will be prompted for a table name. Type a table name or press Enter to see a list of tables in the current directory. Tutility will ask you whether it should proceed with the rebuild. Press **Y** to continue. `Rebuild` will rewrite the table, if possible, making corrections where necessary. You will see the message shown in Figure 16.5, when the rebuilding has been completed.

`Rebuild` will delete the primary index for a table. If your table was indexed, you will need to re-create the primary index by using Paradox's **M**odify/**R**estructure commands. After specifying the rebuilt table's name, type asterisks after the desired key fields in the STRUCT table and press F2 to "Do-It!." Chapter 2 contained more information on keying tables.

Usually, `Rebuild` will successfully recover all information in a damaged table. There are times, though, when you may not get all of your records back after using `Rebuild`. Your results from using Tutility depend on the extent to which the table was damaged. Check a table carefully, especially near its end, after it has been rebuilt to see if you need to re-create any records.

Sometimes, problems with a damaged table may persist even after `Rebuild` says it has rebuilt a table successfully. This situation is rare, but it can happen. Usually, it is due to damage to the header of the original table which Tutility does not detect. In this case, export your Paradox table to an ASCII file using **T**ools/**E**xportImport/**E**xport/**A**scii/**D**elimited. Then, import the ASCII file into a new Paradox table using **T**ools/**E**xportImport/**I**mport/**A**scii/**D**elimited. This will force Paradox to create a new table with a new header. Your problem should be solved.

At times, a table may be too damaged for `Rebuild` to work at all. The message, "Table descriptor is damaged beyond repair," means that Tutility cannot read the essential information about the table's structure needed to do its job. There is no way to recover a table when this happens. You will have to rely on your backup which, hopefully, is current. This is why it is important to back up your valuable information. There was a section on backing up information in Chapter 9, "Managing Your Paradox System," which you may find useful.

Leftover .LCK Files

Does your machine "hang" when you try to use Paradox on a network? If so, you may be having problems trying to use tables in a shared directory due to "leftover" .LCK files. .LCK files are special lock files which Paradox creates to control access to tables and directories on a network. Paradox normally deletes its .LCK files when they are no longer needed. After a network crash, or some other abnormal termination of Paradox, though, out-of-date .LCK files may remain. These "leftover" .LCK files can cause problems when the next attempt is made to access the table or directory the .LCK files are for.

To see if this is the problem, ask all users to exit from Paradox. Then, check the shared directory where the table is located for files with the .LCK extension. You can use the DOS DIR command to do this by typing **DIR *.LCK** at the DOS prompt. Delete any .LCK files.

Depending on the network, you may see a message saying that you cannot delete a file when you attempt to do so. Some network software will not allow you to delete a file if it thinks the file is in use. In that case, you will need to use a utility program such as XTreePro to delete a .LCK file. Or, you may be able to use special network commands to delete the file. Once the .LCK files have been deleted, restart Paradox and see if you can access the tables you need.

As with many problems, there is no way to check whether the .LCK files are the real source of the problem. You will know for sure only after you have tried the possible solution. If the problem disappears, you know that the .LCK files were to blame. If the problem persists, you may have lost a little time, but you have narrowed the problem down a bit further.

Other Causes of Computer "Hanging"

Damaged tables and "leftover" .LCK files are two of the more common causes of your computer "hanging" while you use Paradox. There are many other possibilities. You may need to do a little investigation if neither of the two suggestions above solves your problem. Things to look for:

- Conflicts with RAM-resident software
- Hardware problems, especially with memory
- Damaged Paradox system files

For more information on narrowing-down problems in these areas, review the earlier sections in this chapter on problems in trying to start Paradox.

"Resource Limit Exceeded–not enough memory"

Remember, Paradox needs a certain amount of conventional RAM free to work.

You may come across the message, "Resource Limit Exceeded–not enough memory to complete operation," which indicates that there is not enough RAM available for Paradox to complete the current task. The memory referred to in the message applies only to the Paradox workspace, the area in your computer's memory which Paradox uses to do its work.

Although Paradox can use up to 8 megabytes of expanded RAM to enhance its performance, only a relatively small part is actually used for the workspace. So, even if your computer has expanded memory, you may encounter this message when you try to add another table to the workspace, process a query which links many tables, work with very wide tables, or do some other task, after loading Paradox with limited memory below 640K.

Complex queries and sorts require more memory free than simpler tasks.

When you get this message, the source of the problem may be immediately obvious. Perhaps the workspace is cluttered with too many tables. In this case, you can clear unnecessary images off the workspace using F8, the "Clear Image" command. Or, you may be trying to link very wide tables with a query which would result in an excessively wide ANSWER table. If you are having problems trying to process a query, you may need to divide the query into smaller tasks.

Checking Your Computer's Available Memory

There is no formula for determining exactly how much memory Paradox needs for its workspace to complete a given task. You will need to use trial-and-error to determine this. The first step is to check how much memory is currently available for the workspace. You can check this in two ways. You can press Alt-= and look at the number listed near the bottom of the display after the expression "kLeftGetm( )." This number approximates the amount of RAM, in kilobytes, available for the workspace.

Alternatively, you can check the value of the PAL function MEM-LEFT( ) which returns the amount of free RAM that can be used for the workspace. To check the current value of MEMLEFT( ), press Alt-F10. This will display the PAL menu as shown in Figure 16.6. Choose Value from the menu, type **MEMLEFT( )** at the expression prompt as shown in Figure 16.7, and press Enter. Paradox will display the current MEM-LEFT( ) amount in the lower-right corner of the screen.

The typical MEMLEFT( ) result, after loading Paradox on a stand-alone computer (one which is not on a network) with nothing on the workspace, is usually 125–150K. This assumes there is 640K of RAM in a computer with no expanded memory and DOS version 3.2 is the operating system. Also, there are no device drivers or RAM-resident software loaded. How much MEMLEFT( ) you see depends on the version of DOS you are using, the amount of RAM free before you load Paradox, and whether any expanded memory is available. This amount can vary greatly, especially if you are on a network and/or using expanded memory.

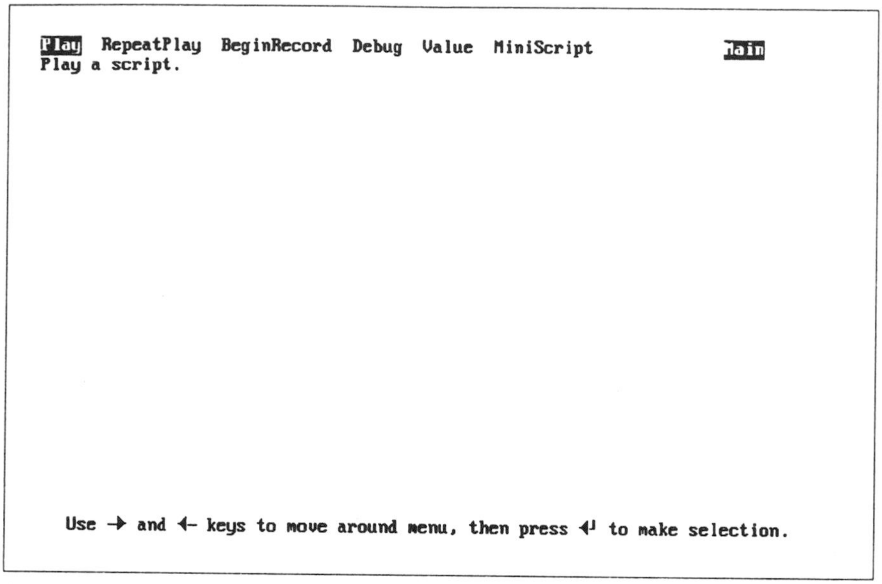

```
Play  RepeatPlay  BeginRecord  Debug  Value  MiniScript              Main
Play a script.














Use → and ← keys to move around menu, then press ↵ to make selection.
```

Figure 16.6 PAL Menu

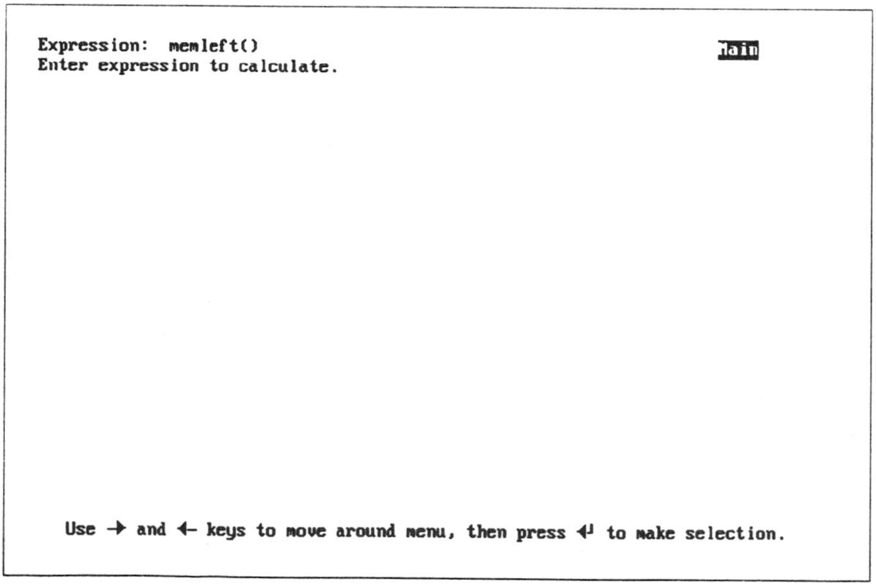

```
Expression:  memleft()                                               Main
Enter expression to calculate.














Use → and ← keys to move around menu, then press ↵ to make selection.
```

Figure 16.7 MEMLEFT( ) at expression prompt

In the special case where Quarterdeck's Expanded Memory Manager 386, QEMM, is the expanded memory driver being used, Paradox can add up to 200K to its workspace. How much is actually used for the workspace depends on the overall system configuration. Take the example of a workstation with 640K of RAM on a 3Com 3Plus network. If there are no device drivers other than QEMM and the network drivers, and no RAM-resident software besides the network programs loaded, you can have a MEMLEFT( ) greater than 150K. This assumes that you are using DOS 3.2 and that there are no memory conflicts due to EGA or network boards.

Please do not take these numbers as guaranteed MEMLEFT( ) amounts. They are offered only as an example of what is possible with various configurations. What you experience is dependent on several factors:

- The amount of RAM in your computer
- Whether or not you are using expanded memory
- Any device drivers and/or RAM-resident software, especially network software, in use
- The version of DOS which you are using

Once you know what your MEMLEFT( ) is, you can get an idea of whether you are trying to do something that is just too big a task or whether you may be running under memory constraints. How much memory you should have available for MEMLEFT( ) depends on the nature of what you are using Paradox for. If you will use only Paradox for simple tasks, you may be able to operate with a MEMLEFT( ) of 40- to 50K, or even less if you don't try to do anything complicated. This is not recommended, though. The typical user should probably try to have a MEMLEFT( ) figure of at least 100K or 125K to allow the workspace to take full advantage of Paradox's capabilities.

"Not enough disk space"

You may see the message "Not enough disk space to complete operation" during queries, sorts, or other operations in which many temporary files are created. There are three common reasons for this message.

The most common is that you don't have enough disk space for Paradox to do what it needs. The rule-of-thumb is that you should have two to three times the size of the tables being used available in free disk space. For example, if you are trying to join two tables in a query, add the sizes of the tables and multiply the sum by two (or three if you are performing a complicated query). This is the amount of free disk space you should have available to perform the operation.

Private Directories and Free Disk Space

Remember that Paradox needs this space on the disk where your private directory is located. If you are on a network, you may be working with a table on a huge network drive with megabytes of free disk available. Your private directory, though, may be on a local drive with much less free space.

You can find out the location of your private directory by using **Tools/Net/SetPrivate**. The location of your current private directory will be displayed as shown in Figure 16.8. If nothing is displayed, the current directory is your private directory. At this point, you can change the private directory. Simply erase the current location using Ctrl-Backspace. Then type the new location and press Enter. Paradox will change the location of your private directory. (Remember that when you change the private directory, all temporary tables will be deleted.)

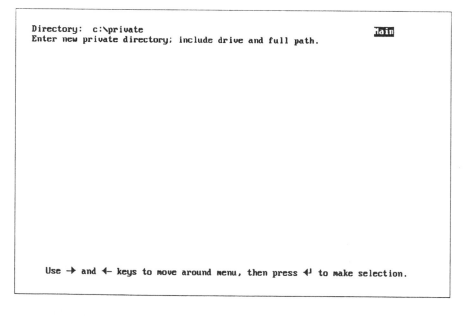

Figure 16.8 Private directory displayed using **Tools/Net/SetPrivate**

Damaged Tables and Disk Space

You may also get the "Not enough disk space" message if you work with a damaged table. Paradox may loop and create temporary files until your disk is full. If this happens, rebuild your table using Tutility and retry the failed operation.

If your original table is empty or missing records, check the temporary work tables before you delete them.

Paradox usually deletes all temporary files which it has created. Occasionally, Paradox will leave these files intact if it has a problem completing the operation normally. Delete them if you are sure you have all your information in your original table. If some information is missing, though, you may be able to recover it from the temporary files. These files will have names such as TEMP.001. If you rename them with the .DB extension, you can view them as you can other Paradox tables. Your missing information may be in one of these temporary tables. If it is, rebuild the table using Tutility and rename it with the original table name.

"Cross-Product" Queries

Sometimes people run out of disk space performing queries because they unknowingly ask Paradox to create a huge ANSWER table. If you run out of disk while doing a query which links tables, see if you are linking the tables on values which are non-unique *in both tables*. Paradox creates ANSWER table records based on all possible linking values. If you link tables on values which are not unique in at least one table, you may create an ANSWER table which is much larger than you expect.

For an example, look at the tables, SHIPMENT and DETAIL, displayed in Figure 16.9. They have the Order # field in common. Note that there may be more than one record for a particular Order # in both tables. This is true for Order #5, which is listed twice in SHIPMENT and five times in DETAIL. Figure 16.10 shows a query which links SHIPMENT and DETAIL on the Order # field. The resulting ANSWER table is shown in Figure 16.11. You can see that Paradox created 10 records for Order #5 in ANSWER.

In this example, you see that Paradox created records in the ANSWER table which are based on every possible match on the linking values. The query is obviously useless. However, you may do this with a query on large tables and not be aware of it. If many records are involved, Paradox may not have enough disk space for all the records in the ANSWER table.

You can check for duplicate records in tables using a Count All > 1 query. See the query in Figure 16.12 and the resulting ANSWER table. All records in ANSWER are non-unique in the original table. The same query is shown for the SHIPMENT table in Figure 16.13.

You can use the Count All > 1 query on DETAIL, rename ANSWER, execute the second query on SHIPMENT, and compare the ANSWERs using a third linking query. Or, you can link the first ANSWER to SHIPMENT as shown in Figure 16.14. This is an easy way to check for duplicate records in linking tables.

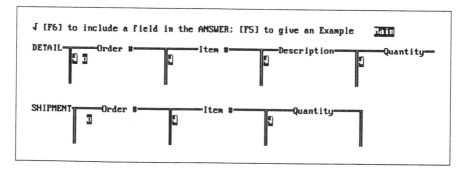

```
Viewing Detail table: Record 27 of 34                          Main

DETAIL┬─Order #─┬─Item #─┬──────Description──────┬─Quantity─┬──────Price─
    11 │    2   │  603   │ Red/White Overalls    │    5     │    8.00
    12 │    3   │  801   │ Red Stripe Tank Suit  │    5     │    6.00
    13 │    3   │  802   │ Red Stripe Tank Suit  │    5     │    6.00
    14 │    3   │  803   │ Red Stripe Tank Suit  │    5     │    6.00
    15 │    3   │  901   │ Cobalt Stripe Bikini  │    5     │    6.00
    16 │    3   │  902   │ Cobalt Stripe Bikini  │    5     │    6.00
    17 │    3   │  903   │ Cobalt Stripe Bikini  │    5     │    7.50
    18 │    4   │  901   │ Cobalt Stripe Bikini  │   12     │    6.00
    19 │    4   │  902   │ Cobalt Stripe Bikini  │   12     │    6.00
    20 │    4   │  903   │ Cobalt Stripe Bikini  │   12     │    7.50
    21 │    5   │  901   │ Cobalt Stripe Bikini  │   12     │    6.00
    22 │    5   │  902   │ Cobalt Stripe Bikini  │   12     │    6.00
    23 │    5   │  903   │ Cobalt Stripe Bikini  │   12     │    7.50
    24 │    5   │  904   │ Cobalt Stripe Bikini  │   12     │    7.50
    25 │    5   │  905   │ Cobalt Stripe Bikini  │   12     │    7.50
    26 │    6   │  601   │ Red/White Overalls    │   20     │    8.00
    27 │    6   │  602   │ Red/White Overalls    │   20     │    8.00


SHIPMENT┬─Order #─┬─Item #─┬──Quantity─
      1 │    5    │  904   │    12
      2 │    5    │  905   │    12
```

Figure 16.9 SHIPMENT and DETAIL

```
√ [F6] to include a field in the ANSWER; [F5] to give an Example    Main

DETAIL────────Order #───────────Item #─────────Description────────Quantity─
      │✓ ✓│             │✓│            │✓│              │✓│


SHIPMENT┬──────Order #───────────Item #─────────Quantity─
        │✓│            │✓│            │✓│
```

Figure 16.10 Query linking SHIPMENT and DETAIL on non-unique field

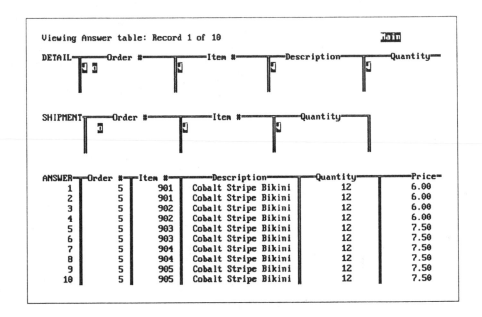

Figure 16.11 ANSWER from query in Figure 16.10

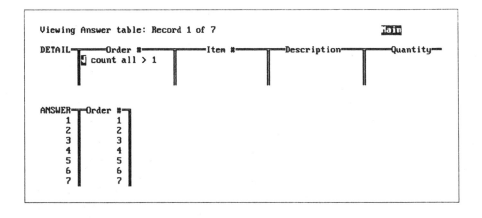

Figure 16.12 Query for non-unique records in DETAIL

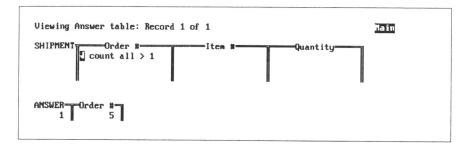

Figure 16.13 Query for non-unique values in SHIPMENTS

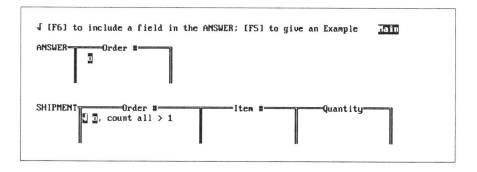

Figure 16.14 SET Query for non-unique values

Usually if you are creating a query which is linking on values that are non-unique in all of the involved tables, you really intended to ask a different question. Look at what you want to see in your ANSWER table and consider whether you are using the correct query to get the desired result.

"Unexpected Conditions"

Paradox has a family of error messages which are referred to as "Unexpected Conditions." This is because these messages usually appear as "Unexpected Condition" followed by an error code and the message "Leaving Paradox." At that point, you are returned to the DOS prompt with no further warning.

There are several types of unexpected conditions. The error code after "Unexpected Condition" usually indicates what caused the problem. You will see something like *File Read (I113)* or *File Open (I104)*. The words in these error messages are more important than the numbers. The words often indicate that Paradox has attempted to do something but been unable to complete the task. Several error codes for unexpected conditions are listed below, along with descriptions of the typical causes.

File Open (I104). This message appears when Paradox is unable to open a new file, usually a temporary file, it needs. Paradox may be unable to open a file because it is already open. Check your private directory for temporary files which may have been left behind if the prior session was ended without exiting properly from Paradox. Delete files with names such as TABLE.ED and restart Paradox.

You may also see the *File Open* message if you do not have enough network file handles available. In that case, consult your Network Administrator. He or she may be able to adjust the number of files which can be open at any one time.

File Read (I113). This message will be displayed if Paradox is unable to read information from the disk. It usually indicates a bad sector on the disk. Be sure to check your disk for problems. Back up the information you can, and use a utility program to check for bad sectors. Flag them as unusable before doing anything else with your computer.

If a table is on the part of the disk which has the bad sector, you may lose some information. You will not be able to copy or back up the table. Try to query out these records if you can. First, find the bad spot in the table by paging through it. When Paradox attempts to read a record from the problem area, it will "crash" and display the *File Read* message. You will not be able to get this record back. If your table is keyed, though, you can use appropriate search criteria to query out records from either side of the problem record(s). Good Luck!

File Create (I112). Paradox will display this message if it attempts to create a new file and it cannot do so. On a network, this may happen if you have insufficient rights in a shared directory or in your private directory for temporary files. Make sure that your rights are set so that you can create new files and try the operation again.

This problem can also occur if you attempt to write a file to the root directory of a disk which is at its file limit. While there is no limit on the number of files which can be created in a subdirectory, limits do apply to root directories. The limit for the root directory on a two-sided, low-density floppy disk is 112 files. If you try to copy a table to the root directory of a disk which is at its file limit, you will see the *File Create* message. Erase some files or change the target directory and try again.

File Seek (I114). This message appears while you are using a damaged table. It is also possible to see a *File Seek* message if you are having disk problems. Damaged FATs (File Allocation Tables) or other problems can cause Paradox to get "lost" while it is looking for information on a disk. If you see this message, check your disk for problems and run Tutility against your tables.

File Delete (I117). Paradox displays this message when it cannot delete a file, usually one of its temporary files, from your disk. Possible causes are insufficient network rights, RAM-resident software which does not allow the deletion of files without confirmation, or file attributes which prevent a file from being deleted. Because Paradox creates and deletes many files, your computer must allow for this. If you are on a network, make sure your rights allow you to delete files in any shared directories and in your private directory. If you were using a RAM-resident utility program which does not allow you to delete files, disable it while you use Paradox.

HFree (L5). This infrequent message usually results from hardware problems. Use Tutility to rebuild the table you were using when the problem occurred. Then try to duplicate the problem. If the problem recurs, check your Paradox files and then your hardware for possible damage.

Table Buffer (L8). You may see this message if you try to use Paradox with a damaged table. When you see a *Table Buffer* message, rebuild your table using Tutility. If the message persists when you try to use the table, try exporting your table to an ASCII file using **T**ools/**E**xportImport/ **E**xport/**A**scii/**D**elimited. Then, import the same file into a *new* Paradox table using **T**ools/**E**xportImport/**I**mport/**A**scii/**D**elimited. Sometimes this solves the problem if it was due to a damaged table header. Importing records into a new table forces Paradox to create a new table header which should alleviate the problem.

You can also see a *Table Buffer* message if you attempt to perform a query which would result in a table having more than 255 fields. The workaround is simple–use fewer checkmarks.

Report Get String.... Paradox displays this message when it has a problem reading a report specification. It means that the report specification is damaged. Unfortunately, there is no program to recover damaged reports or forms. You have to delete the problem report specification and restore it from a backup or re-create it.

See Chapter 9 for more information on managing tables and their families.

If you restore a report or form from a backup, remember that Paradox keeps track of when all family members are copied. You cannot simply restore a family member without also restoring the table, .DB file. Before you restore the .DB file, rename the existing copy of the table so it is not overwritten. Then restore the backup copy of the .DB file along with the desired family members. Do a **T**ools/**C**opy/**J**ustFamily or **T**ools/**C**opy /**R**eport from the restored table to the renamed table. Finally, give the renamed table its original name.

Other Damaged Table Problems

As discussed earlier, damaged tables can cause your computer to "hang" while running Paradox. There are other symptoms which indicate table damage. They include:

- Random ASCII characters in the table
- Records "disappearing" from the screen as you page through a table
- Losing records from a table
- Mixed-up information in records
- Queries give wrong results

These occurrences show that your table should be rebuilt using Tutility. Instructions for using Tutility were included earlier in this chapter.

Query Problems

Queries allow you to be quite flexible in the questions which you can ask about your information. At the same time, you have to abide by certain syntax rules. Otherwise Paradox will not be able to make sense of your requests.

Chapter 5 covers all the basics of queries.

Query problems can be divided into two main categories. The first group involves syntax errors detected when you pressed F2 to "Do-It!" These are usually fairly easy to solve. A few of the messages generated by syntax problems are listed below, along with suggestions for solutions.

The other type of query problem usually requires a little more "think time" to solve. Such is the case where you create a query, press F2 to "Do-It!," and get an ANSWER table (or a CHANGED, INSERTED, or DELETED table) without any error messages. However, the result is not what you expected to see. Queries can be tricky to set up, especially when you first get familiar with them. Some of the more common query setup problems are also discussed in this section.

"Query asks two unrelated questions"

Paradox always tries to use all query images on the workspace when it processes a query. If there are multiple query images present, Paradox looks for example elements which show how the tables should be related. Example elements are the only way to tell Paradox how to use the tables together.

This message is displayed when you try to "Do-It!" with query images on the workspace which are not related by example elements. The solution is to place example elements as needed or to clear unnecessary query images from the workspace using F8.

Sometimes the problem may not be obvious. If you have several query images and table images on the workspace, you may not be able to see all of them at once. A query image may have scrolled off the screen as more images were added to the workspace. When it starts processing your query, Paradox will use query images which may not be visible on the screen. The "unrelated questions" message will then be displayed. You can tell if there are "hidden" images on the workspace by checking for the upward-triangle indicator in the upper right corner of the screen. If you have "leftover" query images, use F3 to move to them. Then, clear them from the workspace using F8.

Trying to use Calc in two different fields on different query lines will also generate the "unrelated questions" message. Paradox will not allow you you to use a multi-line query to do Calc in different fields of the same table, even if the same fields are Checkmarked on each query line.

"Query makes no sense"

Many users laugh when they first see this message, unless they are rushing to complete some project which involves queries that just won't work. Paradox displays this message when it can't guess what question you are trying to ask.

To eliminate the problem, look for Checkmarks in different fields on different lines or other "dangling" query elements. You may need to simplify your query and add to it, one step at a time, until the part causing the problem is apparent.

Blanks from Calculations

Use Alt-F10/Value and type QueryOrder( ) to check this setting without playing Custom.

When you are using a Calc query to get a calculated result from Number fields, you may sometimes get blanks, instead of numbers, for your answer. This occurs if there are blanks in any field being used in the calculation *and* `Blanks=Zero` is set to `No` in your PARADOX3.CFG file.

`Blanks=Zero` is an option set by using the Custom script. If it is set to `Yes`, Paradox will use 0 for any blank it comes across while doing calculations on Number fields in queries and reports. Otherwise, Paradox will display a blank as the result of any calculations on values which include blanks. You can check what Blanks=Zero is currently set to by playing the Custom script. Details were included in Chapter 13, "Customizing Your Paradox System."

Counts Do Not Add Up

There are some common mistakes trying to use Calc Count in queries. If you don't put the keyword All after your Calc Count expression, you will not get the results you want. Paradox will give a count of 1 for each unique value in a field, rather than a count of the number of records for each value.

Another problem trying to do counts is related to the use of Checkmarks. In a Calc query, Paradox uses Checkmarks as group operators, as well as indicators of which fields to include in the ANSWER table. If you Checkmark all fields, as shown in Figure 16.15, and try to get a count for each Part # in DETAIL, you will get an ANSWER table like the one displayed beneath the query. To get a count by Item #, you must check *only* the Item # field in the query image, as shown in Figure 16.16. The resulting ANSWER table is displayed in the same figure.

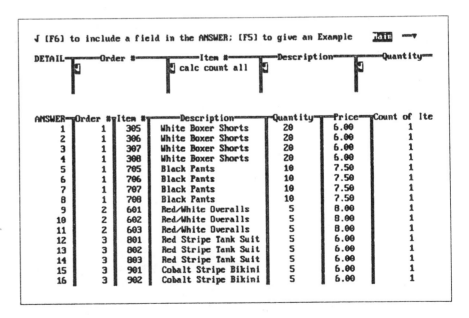

Figure 16.15 Incorrect Calc query

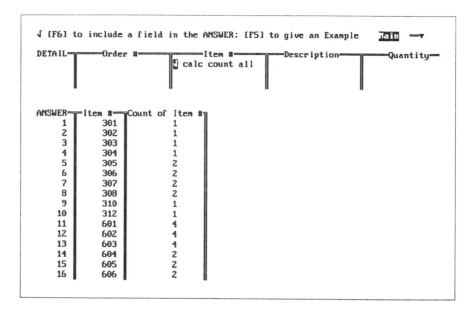

Figure 16.16 Correct Calc query

Records Are Not Changed After Changeto Query

There a few possibilities to look for when it appears that Changeto queries have not worked. After Paradox processes a Changeto query, a CHANGED table is created and becomes the current image on the workspace. CHANGED contains the old form of any records which have been changed by the query. You may be viewing the CHANGED table, instead of the original table, without being aware of it. If you experience this problem, make sure you are looking at the original table and not the CHANGED table.

Make sure OR changeto queries are set up correctly. See Chapter 5 for an example.

If you are sure that records were not changed as you expected, check to see if your query was correctly set up. When different criteria are used for different changes, they should be placed on separate query lines. Otherwise, Paradox will look for records which match *all* the criteria you have specified. Then unless a record matches the search criteria in every field, it will not be changed.

Records Don't Show Up in ANSWER Table

If you do not get records in the ANSWER table which you *know* should be there, check for the following things in your query:

- Mutually exclusive search criteria on the same line (creating an And query instead of an Or query. See Chapter 5 for examples)
- Using keywords without quotation marks as search criteria
- Search criteria not entered in the proper case (using the .. wild card will solve this problem)

If you still do not get the results you expect, try rebuilding your table using Tutility.

Report Problems

The Paradox Report Generator allows you much freedom in setting up the format for Tabular or Free-form reports. It is sometimes hard to sort out the effect of all the different commands along with your printer settings. The best approach here is to simplify your report specification as much as possible and then add options, one at a time, until you get the result you want.

First of all, go through your report specification and note the current settings for Pagelength, RemoveBlanks and SetUp. Then, see how many lines are in your headers and footers. If you are using a Free-form report, look at how many lines are contained in the form itself. While you are in the Report Generator, use Ctrl-V to display a vertical ruler. All lines, except the page, group, table, or form lines, are included when Paradox decides what to print.

If the file has "garbage," your table may be corrupted.

Once you have this information, you can start to sort out your report problem. If the problems persist, even after trying some of the suggestions in the following sections, send the report to a file. Look at the file with a text editor. Check to see if the file looks like the report which you want to be printed. If it does, you can assume the problem is with your printer. You may be sending incorrect printer control codes in a custom setup string or you may be having other printer problems.

If the viewed file has the same problems that the printed version does, you can assume that your report specification needs to be changed. The following sections have tips for solving some of the common report problems.

First Page Blank

Sometimes Paradox will print only a Report or Page Header and leave the rest of the first page blank. This can happen if you are using a Free-form report where the sum of the form length and any headers and footers exceeds the specified pagelength. After any headers are printed, Paradox looks to see whether it can fit a complete form onto the rest of the page. If not, it will go to the next page, even on the first page, before printing the next record.

One way around this problem is to set your pagelength to C for continuous. This will work if you don't need Page Headers and/or Footers. You can then place a Calculated field at the bottom of your form area to send a form feed to the printer after each form is printed. To do this, use the commands F10/Field/Place/Calculated. Type " \ **012** " when prompted for an expression. Place the field on a line by itself just above the bottom form line. Paradox will display two *As* to indicate where the field is placed.

Using PAGEBREAK will not work the same way. Usually, when Paradox encounters PAGEBREAK, it sends line feeds to get to the last line of the page. Then, it sends another line feed, or a form feed if `FormFeed` is set to `Yes` in the configuration file, to get to the first line of the next page. But, if the pagelength is set to C for continuous, Paradox ignores PAGEBREAK commands.

Blank Pages Between Printed Pages

This can happen if the report pagelength is not set correctly. The most common occurrence of this is when you are using a Hewlett-Packard LaserJet. Check to make sure that your Paradox pagelength is set to the default pagelength for your printer. For the LaserJet, this is usually 60 lines if you are printing in portrait mode and using standard-size print.

Pagelength Problems

This seems to be the most troublesome area when working with the Paradox Report Generator. There are several factors which determine the number of lines to be printed on each page:

- The Paradox pagelength setting
- The printer form length setting

- The number of lines in the Page Header and Footer of your report specification
- The number of lines in your Report Header and Footer of your report specification
- The use of embedded form feed characters or PAGEBREAKs in your report specification
- Any control characters sent to the printer to alter the margins, print size, or vertical spacing
- The form feed setting in your PARADOX3.CFG file

For the pagelength setting, Paradox takes into consideration any headers and footers in your report specification, the form length (if you are using a Free-form report) and figures out how many records to print on a page. After printing those records, and any Page or Group Footers, Paradox sends line feeds to move the printhead to the last line of the page. At that point, what happens depends on the `FormFeed` setting in the Custom script. If you have the `FormFeed` option set to `No`, Paradox will send another line feed to get the first line of the next page. If you have the `FormFeed` option set to `Yes`, Paradox will send a form feed to the printer.

If you have problems getting the pagelength you want actually printed, first look at the pagelength setting in your report specification. That number should match the number of lines per page that your printer will print. Most printers will print 66 lines using 8½″ × 11″ paper and a print size of six lines per inch. With some printers, though, there are default top and bottom margins which you have to take into account.

Pagelength Problems with a LaserJet

For the LaserJet, the default margins are 1/2" at the top and bottom of each page. This means you have to subtract three lines for each margin, or a total of six lines, from the number of lines which would ordinarily fit onto a page. If you are using a print size of six lines per inch, and printing in portrait mode on 8½″ × 11″ paper, set your Paradox pagelength to 60, instead of 66.

The general rule-of-thumb is to set your Paradox pagelength equal to the number of text lines that your printer is set to print on each page. This number includes any blank lines *other than the printer margin lines* which may be included in your Page Header and Footer. Figuring out the number of text lines per page is usually simple. Just subtract any printer-imposed margin lines from the total number of lines which will fit onto a page. In the example above, the number of text lines is 60 lines per page. This number will vary if you print in landscape mode or use a print size other than six lines per inch. It will also change if you alter the vertical spacing (VMI, or Vertical Motion Index) used by the printer.

If it seems impossible to get things working by changing the Paradox pagelength, try this approach to the problem.

1. Set up your report so that it does not have any Page Headers or Footers in the page band areas of the report specification. Use Group Headers or Footers instead. Or, if you are using a Free-form report, include the headers and/or footers in the form itself.

2. Change your Paradox pagelength to "C" for continuous.

3. To print each form on a separate page, place a Calculated field which sends a form feed to the printer on the last line of the form area in your report specification. Place the field using the commands F10/Field/Place/Calculated. Type "\012" when prompted for an expression. Place the field on a line by itself as the last line in the form area.

4. To start each new group of records on a new page, place the Calculated field described in Step 3 as the last line in your Group Footer.

When you print your report, Paradox will send an ASCII 12, a form feed character, to the printer after each form or group of records, depending on where you placed the Calculated field in the report specification. Paradox will make no assumptions regarding pagelength and will not send other line feeds or form feeds to move the printhead to the top of a page.

"Short" Forms

There are two approaches which can be used here. You can set the Paradox pagelength equal to the length of the form, taking into consideration the number of lines per inch which will be printed. For example, if you are printing forms which are 4" high and you are printing six lines per inch, set your Paradox pagelength to 24. If you are using a LaserJet, or another printer with default margins, be sure to subtract the number of lines for any margins imposed by the printer. This will work for most printers as long as FormFeed is set to No (the default) in your PARADOX3.CFG file. When FormFeed is set to Yes, you also have to send a control code which defines the form length to your printer.

The other option is to set the Paradox pagelength to C for continuous and make sure the form band is the same size as the real form. If you are not using the LineSqueeze option in a Free-form report, your forms will always be the same size. When you use LineSqueeze, be sure to specify LineSqueeze/Yes/Fixed. That way, Paradox appends any blank lines it squeezes out of a form to the end of the form. This ensures that all forms are the same length, even if the number of printed lines per form varies.

Envelopes

It may seem tricky to print envelopes using Paradox, but it is just a matter of getting your form and settings defined properly. The key is to make sure that none of the settings are in conflict. For example, if you are using a LaserJet, and sending margin settings to the printer in a setup string, *don't* include any margins in your report specification. The printer will take care of margins for you. Your report can be set up with all the envelope information in the upper-left corner of the form.

Set the pagelength to C and place a formfeed above the bottom form line.

Similarly, if you are manually feeding envelopes to the printer, make sure you have the Wait option in your report specification set to Yes and set the pagelength to the length of your envelopes. Make sure that the total number of lines in your form do not exceed the specified pagelength. You can check the number of lines quickly by pressing Ctrl-V when you are in the report specification. All lines between the form lines are used for the form. Paradox does not include the lines for page, group, table, or form when it determines how many lines to print.

Report Columns Do Not Line Up

One cause of this problem is using a proportional font for printing. The workaround for this problem is, of course, to use a font which has a fixed size for each character. The problem can also occur if you have included printer control codes in a Calculated field on the same line as field masks in the report specification. Although the Calculated field takes up room in the report specification, it does not take up room on the printed page. Make allowances in the report specification for these fields when you are aligning columns.

On occasion, this problem may occur if you are creating a report from a damaged table. Use Tutility to rebuild the table and try printing the report again.

Other Sources of Information

Appendix E contains information on "Getting Help" with your Paradox problems. Other users may have already experienced the same problems and will be happy to share their information and experience. So, if the information you need was not included here, don't be discouraged. There are several other sources of information to which you can turn before giving up!

Summary

Experiencing problems while using Paradox can be quite frustrating, especially if you don't know where to start looking for the source of trouble. Try these guidelines to get off to a good start:

- The first task in problem determination is to try to re-create the problem.
- If the problem can be duplicated, look up any error messages that you may receive for information on what might be causing the problem.
- Narrow down the problem by trying to re-create the problem with different files or hardware.
- If your computer "hangs" on loading or while using Paradox, review the sections in this chapter for possible causes.
- For problems with queries and reports, double-check to see that you are really telling Paradox to do what you want; review the chapters on queries and reports and the section in this chapter for common mistakes.
- If you are really stuck, get help. There are many Paradox users who are willing to assist you. Refer to Appendix E for other sources of help.

Menus

Main Menu

```
┌ View
├ Ask
├ Report ─┬ Output ─┬ Printer
│         │         ├ Screen
│         │         └ File
│         ├ Design ─┬ Tabular ──┐
│         │         └ Free-form ┴─ ▼ See Report Menu
│         ├ Change
│         ├ RangeOutput
│         └ SetPrinter ─┬ Regular
│                       └ Override ─┬ PrinterPort
│                                   ├ Setup
│                                   └ EndOfPage ─┬ Line Feed
│                                                └ Form Feed
├ Create
├ Modify ─┬ Sort        ▼ See Sort Menu
│         ├ Edit        ▼ See Edit Menu
│         ├ CoEdit      ▼ See CoEdit Menu
│         ├ DataEntry   ▼ See DataEntry Menu
│         ├ MultiEntry ─┬ Entry   ▼ See DataEntry Menu
│         │             └ SetUp
│         └ Restructure   ▼ See Restructure Menu
├ Image      ▼ See Image Menu   ▼ Graph Mode accessed through Image Menu
├ Forms ─┬ Design ┐
│        └ Change ┴ ▼ See Forms Menu
├ Tools      ▼ See Tools Menu   ▼ Password mode accessed through Tools Menu
├ Scripts    ▼ See Scripts Menu
├ Help
└ Exit
```

▼ Indicates entry into new mode from Main mode.

Report Menu

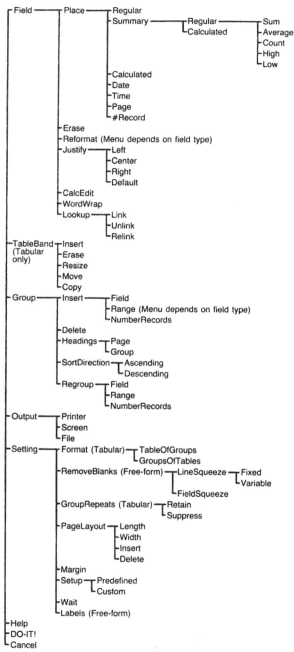

Create Menu and Restructure Menu

```
┌ Borrow
├ Help
├ DO-IT!
└ Cancel
```

Sort Menu

```
┌ Help
├ DO-IT!
└ Cancel
```

Scripts Menu

```
┌ Play
├ BeginRecord
├ QuerySave
├ ShowPlay ──────┬ Fast
│                └ Slow
├ RepeatPlay
└ Editor ────────┬ Write
                 └ Edit
```

Scripts Menu (while recording)

```
┌ Cancel
├ End-Record
├ Play
├ QuerySave
└ RepeatPlay
```

Edit Menu

```
┌ Image (See Menu below)
├ Undo
├ ValCheck ┬ Define ┬ LowValue
│          │        ├ HighValue
│          │        ├ Default
│          │        ├ TableLookup ┬ JustCurrentField ──────┬ PrivateLookup
│          │        │             │                        └ HelpAndFill
│          │        │             └ AllCorrespondingFields ┬ FillNoHelp
│          │        │                                      └ HelpAndFill
│          │        ├ Picture
│          └ Clear  └ Required
├ Help
├ DO-IT!
└ Cancel
```

CoEdit Menu

```
┌ Image (See Menu below)
├ Undo
├ AutoRefresh
├ Help
└ DO-IT!
```

DataEntry Menu

```
┌Image (See Menu below)
├Undo
├ValCheck (See Menu above)
├KeepEntry
├Help
├DO-IT!
└Cancel
```

Image Menu

```
┌TableSize (Table view only)
├ColumnSize (Table view only)
├Format (Menus depend on field type)
├Zoom──┬Field
│      ├Record
│      └Value
├Move (Table view only)
├PickForm
├KeepSet
└Graph     ▼ On Image Menu from Main mode only. See Graph Menu
```

Graph Menu

```
┌Modify/F10 ─┬Type (Stacked Bar, Bar, 3-D Bar, Rotated Bar, Line, Markers, X-Y,
│            │      Combined Lines & Markers, Pie Graph, Area Graph)
│            ├Overall ──┬Titles (Titles, Fonts, Sizes)
│            │          ├Colors (Screen, Printer, Copy)
│            │          ├Axes (Scaling, Ticks)
│            │          ├Grids (Line, Color, Frame line and Color)
│            │          ├PrinterLayout (Orientation, Margin, etc.)
│            │          ├Device ─┬Printer (1, 2, 3, or 4 defined with
│            │          │        │        Custom script)
│            │          │        └File ─┬CurrentPrinter
│            │          │               ├EPS
│            │          │               └PIC
│            │          └Wait ──┬KeyStroke
│            │                  └Duration
│            ├Series ──┬LegendsAndLabels
│            │         ├MarkersAndFills
│            │         └Colors ┬Screen
│            │                 ├Printer
│            │                 └Copy (Screen to Printer and vice-versa)
│            ├Pies (Label Format, Explode Slice?, Fill Pattern, Colors)
│            ├ViewGraph┬Screen
│            │         ├Printer
│            │         └File
│            ├Help
│            ├DO-IT!
│            └Cancel
├Load
├Save
├Reset
├CrossTab ──┬1) Sum
│           ├2) Min
│           ├3) Max
│           └4) Count
└ViewGraph ┬Screen
           ├Printer
           └File
```

Forms Menu

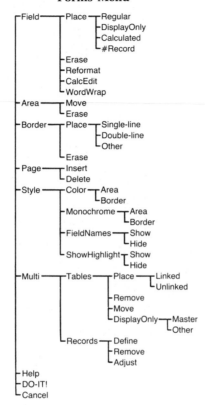

Password Menu

- Undo
- Help
- DO-IT!
- Cancel

Tools Menu

```
┌─Rename ─┬─Table
│         ├─Form
│         ├─Report
│         ├─Script
│         └─Graph
├─QuerySpeedup
├─ExportImport ─┬─Export ─┬─Quattro
│               └─Import ─┤─1-2-3
│                         ├─Symphony
│                         ├─dBase
│                         ├─Pfs
│                         ├─Reflex
│                         ├─Visicalc
│                         └─Ascii ─┬─Delimited
│                                  ├─AppendDelimited (Import only)
│                                  └─Text
├─Copy ─────┬─Table
│           ├─Form ─┬─SameTable
│           │       └─DifferentTable
│           ├─Report ─┬─SameTable
│           │         └─DifferentTable
│           ├─Script
│           ├─JustFamily
│           └─Graph
├─Delete ─┬─Table
│         ├─Form
│         ├─Report
│         ├─Script
│         ├─QuerySpeedup
│         ├─KeepSet
│         ├─ValCheck
│         └─Graph
├─Info ─────┬─Structure
│           ├─Inventory ─┬─Tables
│           │            ├─Scripts
│           │            └─Files
│           ├─Family
│           ├─Who ─┐
│           └─Lock ─┴─No information if not on network
├─Net ──────┬─Lock ─┬─FullLock ─┬─Set
│           │       └─WriteLock ─┴─Clear
│           ├─PreventLock ─┬─FullLock ─┬─Set
│           │              └─Writelock ─┴─Clear
│           ├─SetPrivate
│           ├─UserName
│           └─AutoRefresh
└─More ─────┬─Add
            ├─MultiAdd ──┬─NewEntries (If target table keyed)
            │            └─Update
            ├─FormAdd ───┬─EntryTables
            │            └─AnyTables ─┬─NewEntries (If target table keyed)
            │                         └─Update
            ├─Subtract
            ├─Empty
            ├─Protect ──┬─Password ─┬─Table ─┬─Master
            │           │           │        └─Auxiliary
            │           │           └─Script
            │           ├─ClearPasswords
            │           └─Write-protect ─┬─Set
            │                            └─Clear
            ├─Directory
            └─ToDOS
```

Custom Script Menu

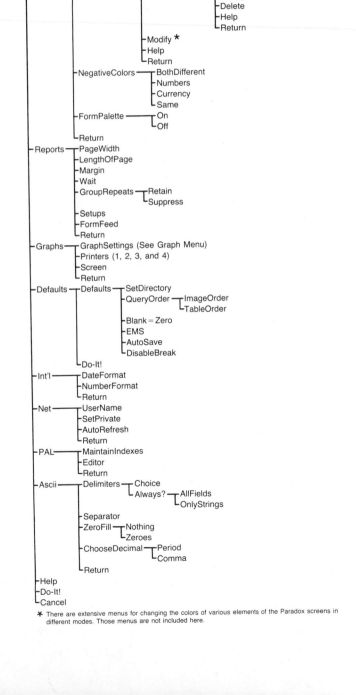

* There are extensive menus for changing the colors of various elements of the Paradox screens in different modes. Those menus are not included here.

appendix

Paradox 3.0 System Requirements & Installation Procedure

System Requirements

Paradox 3.0 has slightly different requirements for standalone and networked systems. "Standalone" here means a computer which is not being used on a network.

Standalone System Requirements

To run Paradox 3.0 on a standalone system, you must have the following hardware and operating software:

- IBM Personal System/2, PC, PC-XT, XT-286 or PC-AT or any 100% compatible computer
- One hard disk and at least one floppy disk drive
- At least 512K bytes of internal memory (RAM)
- DOS version 2.0 or higher
- A compatible monochrome or color monitor with adapter. (A CGA, EGA, VGA, or Hercules card is necessary to display graphics.)

- A compatible printer with adapter. (A graphics printer is needed to print graphics)

If you have only 512K bytes of RAM in your computer, you may run into problems in using wide tables or in trying to link several tables. It is recommended that you have at least 640K bytes of RAM in your computer for best results.

Paradox 3.0 will also use up to 8 megabytes of expanded memory which is compatible with the LIM (Lotus-Intel-Microsoft) expanded memory specification. If you use expanded memory, you can expect to get better performance from Paradox 3.0.

Network Workstation

If you are using Paradox 3.0 on a network workstation, you need one of the following networks:

- Novell network with Novell Advanced Netware, Version 2.0A or higher
- 3Com 3Plus network with 3Com 3Plus software, Version 1.0, 1.1 or higher
- IBM Token Ring or PC Network with IBM PC Local Area Network Program, Version 1.12 or higher
- Torus Tapestry network, Version 1.4 or higher
- AT&T Starlan, Version 1.1 or higher
- Banyan Vines, Version 2.10 or higher

You also need:

- One of the workstations listed above
- A disk drive (which may be a logical drive on the server)
- At least 640K bytes of RAM and perhaps EMS as well
- DOS version 3.1 or higher
- A compatible monitor as listed above
- A compatible printer (optional)

A Note on Paradox 3.0 Memory Requirements

 If you are using Paradox 3.0 on a network, you may need expanded memory in addition to 640K bytes of RAM. Whether you need this additional memory depends on how much RAM is available after load-

ing DOS and/or your network software. You can check how much RAM is available by using the DOS CHKDSK command on a non-network drive. The last line displayed will show you how much RAM is available.

If you do not have expanded memory on your computer, Paradox 3.0 will need about 450K available just to load. If you want to use Paradox 3.0 to do more than just view tables and perform other simple operations, you should have more memory available.

If you have expanded memory, you can load Paradox 3.0 with less than 450K of RAM available. How much is actually required depends upon the type of expanded memory which you are using and other aspects of your configuration. Usually, you will still need at least 430K available to load Paradox 3.0.

If you have less than 450K of RAM available before you load Paradox 3.0, you will need expanded memory in addition to 640K of RAM. If you have less than 430K of RAM available, you may not be able to load Paradox 3.0 even with expanded memory. Whether you can use Paradox 3.0 depends upon the type of expanded memory you are using.

If you have a 386 workstation and are using QEMM, Quarterdeck's Expanded Memory Manager, you can load Paradox 3.0 with much less conventional RAM available. The exact amount depends upon your configuration. In general, you can have as little as 370K free and still be able to load Paradox 3.0.

The numbers cited here are only guidelines. The actual amount of RAM you need to have free to load Paradox 3.0 is affected by the type of EMS you are using and other boards which may be installed in your computer. This information is presented as a cautionary note, not as a hard-and-fast rule.

Paradox 3.0 Disk Space Requirements

You need to have at least 2 megabytes of disk space available to install Paradox 3.0 and use the tutorial which is included with the software. The actual hard disk space requirements may be much greater. Paradox 3.0 creates many temporary files as it works. The rule of thumb is that you need two to three times the size of the tables with which you are working (at any one time) available in free disk space. Without this disk space, Paradox 3.0 will be unable to complete queries, sorts, reports, and other operations.

Installation Procedure

  The following steps show how to install Paradox 3.0 on a standalone computer, even if you intend to access tables on a server. If you want to install Paradox 3.0 on a network server, refer to Chapter 15, "Networking with Paradox."

If you are installing Paradox 3.0 on an IBM PS/2 or an AT&T 6300 (or any other computer with built-in color capability) *and* you are using a monochrome monitor, see the notes following this section before you continue.

1. Make sure that the hard drive on which you want to install Paradox 3.0 is the current drive. Usually, you can check the DOS prompt to determine the current drive. For example, if you are currently using your C: drive, the DOS prompt will be *C⟩*. If the current drive is not the desired drive, type **C:** (or the letter of desired drive) and press Enter to change to the desired drive.

2. If you are using the 5-1/4" diskettes, insert the Paradox 3.0 Installation/Sample Tables Disk into your floppy disk drive. If you are using the 3.5" diskettes, insert the Installation/Sample Tables Disk into the floppy disk drive.

3. At the DOS prompt, type **A:INSTALL** and press Enter.

4. Follow the instructions which will appear on the screen. You will be prompted to choose either:
   - Hard Disk Installation
   - Network Installation
   - Optional Software Installation

   Choose Hard Disk Installation. The Optional Software choice can be used later to install the Sample Tables, Sample Application, Personal Programmer, Protection Generator or Data Entry Toolkit without reinstalling Paradox 3.0.

5. When prompted, type the letter of the source drive. This is the drive, usually **A**, into which you inserted the Paradox 3.0 diskettes. Type **C** or the letter of the hard drive on which you are installing Paradox 3.0, for the destination drive.

6. Paradox 3.0 will display the name of the directory on which it will be installed. You can change this or use the default directory, ⟍ PARADOX3.

7. Paradox 3.0 will check your CONFIG.SYS file to make sure that it has *FILES = 20* and *BUFFERS = 20* commands. If you do not have a CONFIG.SYS file, Paradox 3.0 will create one. If your CONFIG.SYS file needs to be changed, Paradox will copy your CON-

FIG.SYS file to CONFIG.PDX and add the necessary lines to CONFIG.SYS.

You do not have to do anything during this part of the installation. It is mentioned only because you may have problems later if DOS does not find this CONFIG.SYS file in the root directory of the drive from which you boot. Paradox 3.0 will write the CON-FIG.SYS file to the root directory of drive C. If you boot from another drive, be sure to have the commands *FILES = 20* and *BUFFERS = 20* in the CONFIG.SYS file on that drive.

If you are using Paradox 3.0 in the Compatibility Box under OS/2, you may need to make some changes on your own. For OS/2 versions which read the CONFIG.SYS file when the computer is booted, Paradox 3.0 will run without any changes. But, if your version of OS/2 reads the CONFIG.OS2 file when you boot your computer, you will have to add the command *BUFFERS = 20* to that file. (The FILES = 20 command is not necessary here.)

8. You will be prompted to specify a country code. There are five codes from which to pick:
     • United States
     • English International
     • European
     • Swedish/Finnish
     • Norwegian/Danish

   The country code you choose determines how Paradox 3.0 will sort information and what format will be used for displaying dates and numbers. See Appendix J to see the sort orders corresponding to each country code.

   Type the number which corresponds to your selection and press Enter.

9. Paradox 3.0 will prompt you to insert System Disk 1. If you are using 3.5" diskettes, insert System Disk 1/2. Insert the appropriate diskette into the source drive and press Enter.

10. The next screen displayed is the "signature" information screen. You can enter this information only once. It is then written permanently to System Disk 1 or System Disk 1/2, as appropriate. If you must change this information in the future, contact Borland's Paradox Technical Support Department.

    The final question on this screen will ask whether you want to access data on a network. If you will not be using a network, type **N**. If you will be using Paradox 3.0 to access tables on a network, type **Y**.

If you specified *Yes*, you will be prompted for the network type and the location of the PARADOX.NET file. This location will be a logical drive on your network server. Contact your Network Administrator, or the person responsible for coordinating the use of Paradox 3.0 on the network, to learn what this location should be. All users who will be sharing tables must specify the same location for the PARADOX.NET file.

If you specified *No*, you will not be prompted for the network type and location of the PARADOX.NET file. Press F2 to complete entering the signature information.

11. As prompted, insert the required diskettes. At the end of the process, you will be prompted to enter the Installation/Sample Tables and the Data Entry Toolkit 1 diskettes. That step does not actually copy the files to your hard disk. It only updates these diskettes with information about the sort order you have chosen.

12. If Paradox 3.0 was installed successfully, you will see a screen listing the optional software which you can install. You can quit at this point by choosing 6 and pressing Enter.

13. Reboot your computer before attempting to start Paradox 3.0. This will ensure that your system is started with the parameters from the CONFIG.SYS file which are needed to run Paradox 3.0.

Note for IBM PS/2 and AT&T 6300 Users with a Monochrome Monitor

On some computers which have built-in color capability, you may not be able to read part of the installation text on a monochrome screen. At the bottom of the first installation screen, you should see the message, "Press Enter to continue." If you don't see this message, press Esc, type **Y**, and then press Enter to exit from the installation program.

Start the installation program again with the command line option, **A:INSTALL -B&W** to tell Paradox 3.0 that you are using a black-and-white monitor.

Problems Starting Paradox 3.0

If you have problems trying to start Paradox 3.0, refer to the section "Starting Paradox" in Chapter 16.

appendix

ASCII Codes
for the IBM
Character Set

ASCII Character Set

Code	Symbol	Keystroke
0	Blank (Null)	Ctrl-2
1	☺	Ctrl-A
2	●	Ctrl-B
3	♥	Ctrl-C
4	♦	Ctrl-D
5	♣	Ctrl-E
6	♠	Ctrl-F
7	·	Ctrl-G
8	▪	Ctrl-H, Backspace, Shift Backspace
9	○	Ctrl-I
10	◙	Ctrl-J
11	♂	Ctrl-K

(continued)

ASCII Character Set (continued)

Code	Symbol	Keystroke
12	♀	Ctrl-L
13	♪	Ctrl-M
14	♫	Ctrl-N
15	☼	Ctrl-O
16	►	Ctrl-P
17	◄	Ctrl-Q
18	↕	Ctrl-R
19	‼	Ctrl-S
20	¶	Ctrl-T
21	§	Ctrl-U
22	▬	Ctrl-V
23		Ctrl-W
24	↑	Ctrl-X
25	↓	Ctrl-Y
26	→	Ctrl-Z
27	←	Ctrl-[, Esc, Shift Esc, Ctrl Esc
28		Ctrl-\
29	↔	Ctrl-]
30	▲	Ctrl-6
31	▼	Ctrl--
32	Blank Space	Spacebar, Shift Space, Ctrl-Space, Alt-Space
33	!	!
34	"	"
35	#	#
36	$	$
37		%
38	&	&
39	'	'
40	(	(
41	)	)
42	*	*

ASCII Character Set

Code	Symbol	Keystroke
43	+	+
44	,	,
45	-	-
46	.	.
47	/	/
48	0	0
49	1	1
50	2	2
51	3	3
52	4	4
53	5	5
54	6	6
55	7	7
56	8	8
57	9	9
58	:	:
59	;	;
60	⟨	⟨
61	=	=
62	⟩	⟩
63	?	?
64	@	@
65	A	A
66	B	B
67	C	C
68	D	D
69	E	E
70	F	F
71	G	G
72	H	H
73	I	I
74	J	J
75	K	K
76	L	L
77	M	M

(continued)

ASCII Character Set (continued)

Code	Symbol	Keystroke
78	N	N
79	O	O
80	P	P
81	Q	Q
82	R	R
83	S	S
84	T	T
85	U	U
86	V	V
87	W	W
88	X	X
89	Y	Y
90	Z	Z
91	[	[
92	\	\
93	]	]
94	^	^
95	—	—
96	`	`
97	a	a
98	b	b
99	c	c
100	d	d
101	e	e
102	f	f
103	g	g
104	h	h
105	i	i
106	j	j
107	k	k
108	l	l
109	m	m
110	n	n
111	o	o
112	p	p

ASCII Character Set

Code	Symbol	Keystroke
113	q	q
114	r	r
115	s	s
116	t	t
117	u	u
118	v	v
119	w	w
120	x	x
121	y	y
122	z	z
123	{	{
124			
125	}	}
126	~	~
127	Δ	Ctrl-
128	ç	Alt-128
129	ü	Alt-129
130	é	Alt-130
131	â	Alt-131
132	ä	Alt-132
133	à	Alt-133
134	å	Alt-134
135	ç	Alt-135
136	ê	Alt-136
137	ë	Alt-137
138	è	Alt-138
139	ï	Alt-139
140	î	Alt-140
141	ì	Alt-141
142	Ä	Alt-142
143	Å	Alt-143
144	É	Alt-144
145	æ	Alt-145
146	Æ	Alt-146
147	ô	Alt-147

(continued)

ASCII Character Set (continued)

Code	Symbol	Keystroke
148	ö	Alt-148
149	ò	Alt-149
150	û	Alt-150
151	ù	Alt-151
152	ÿ	Alt-152
153	Ö	Alt-153
154	Ü	Alt-154
155	¢	Alt-155
156	£	Alt-156
157	¥	Alt-157
158	Pt	Alt-158
159	ƒ	Alt-159
160	á	Alt-160
161	í	Alt-161
162	ó	Alt-162
163	ú	Alt-163
164	ñ	Alt-164
165	Ñ	Alt-165
166	ª	Alt-166
167	º	Alt-167
168	¿	Alt-168
169	⌐	Alt-169
170	¬	Alt-170
171	½	Alt-171
172	¼	Alt-172
173	¡	Alt-173
174	«	Alt-174
175	»	Alt-175
176	░	Alt-176
177	▒	Alt-177
178	▓	Alt-178
179	│	Alt-179
180	┤	Alt-180
181	╡	Alt-181
182	╢	Alt-182

ASCII Character Set

Code	Symbol	Keystroke
183	⊓	Alt-183
184	╕	Alt-184
185	╣	Alt-185
186	║	Alt-186
187	╗	Alt-187
188	╝	Alt-188
189	╜	Alt-189
190	╛	Alt-190
191	┐	Alt-191
192	└	Alt-192
193	┴	Alt-193
194	┬	Alt-194
195	├	Alt-195
196	─	Alt-196
197	┼	Alt-197
198	╞	Alt-198
199	╟	Alt-199
200	╚	Alt-200
201	╔	Alt-201
202	╩	Alt-202
203	╦	Alt-203
204	╠	Alt-204
205	═	Alt-205
206	╬	Alt-206
207	╧	Alt-207
208	╨	Alt-208
209	╤	Alt-209
210	╥	Alt-210
211	╙	Alt-211
212	╘	Alt-212
213	╒	Alt-213
214	╓	Alt-214
215	╫	Alt-215
216	╪	Alt-216
217	┘	Alt-217

(continued)

ASCII Character Set (continued)

Code	Symbol	Keystroke
218	⌐	Alt-218
219	█	Alt-219
220	▄	Alt-220
221	▌	Alt-221
222	▐	Alt-222
223	▀	Alt-223
224	∝	Alt-224
225	β	Alt-225
226	Γ	Alt-226
227	π	Alt-227
228	Σ	Alt-228
229	σ	Alt-229
230	μ	Alt-230
231	τ	Alt-231
232	Φ	Alt-232
233	θ	Alt-233
234	Ω	Alt-234
235	δ	Alt-235
236	∞	Alt-236
237	ϕ	Alt-237
238	$\in$	Alt-238
239	$\cap$	Alt-239
240	$\equiv$	Alt-240
241	$\pm$	Alt-241
242	$\geq$	Alt-242
243	$\leq$	Alt-243
244	$\int$	Alt-244
245	$\int$	Alt-245
246	$\div$	Alt-246
247	$\approx$	Alt-247
248	$\circ$	Alt-248
249	·	Alt-249
250	·	Alt-250
251	$\sqrt{}$	Alt-251
252	n	Alt-252
253	²	Alt-253
254	∎	Alt-254
255		Alt-255

PAL Commands for Special Keys

Table D1. Function Keys

Function Keys	PAL Commands
F1	HELP
F2	DO__IT!
F3	UPIMAGE
F4	DOWNIMAGE
Alt-F4	INSTANTPLAY
F5	EXAMPLE
Alt-F5	FIELDVIEW
F6	CHECK
Alt-F6	CHECKPLUS
Ctrl-F6	CHECKDESCENDING
Shift-F6	GROUPBY
F7	FORMKEY
Alt-F7	INSTANTREPORT
Ctrl-F7	GRAPHKEY
F8	CLEARIMAGE
Alt-F8	CLEARALL

(continued)

Table D1. *(continued)*

Function Keys	PAL Commands
F9	EDITKEY
Alt-F9	COEDITKEY
F10	MENU

Table D2. Cursor Keys

Cursor Keys	PAL Commands
Home	HOME
End	END
PgUp	PGUP
PgDn	PGDN
Left-Arrow	LEFT
Right-Arrow	RIGHT
Up-Arrow	UP
Down-Arrow	DOWN
Ins	INS
Del	DEL
Backspace	BACKSPACE
Esc	ESC
Enter	ENTER
Tab	TAB
Shift-Tab	REVERSETAB
Ctrl-Break	CTRLBREAK
Ctrl-Home	CTRLHOME
Ctrl-End	CTRLEND
Ctrl-Left-Arrow	CTRLLEFT
Ctrl-Right-Arrow	CTRLRIGHT
Ctrl-Backspace	CTRLBACKSPACE
Ctrl-PgUp	CTRLPGUP
Ctrl-PgDn	CTRLPDN

Table D3. Other Keys

Other Keys	PAL Commands
Ctrl-D	DITTO
Ctrl-F	FIELDVIEW
Alt-K	KEYLOOKUP
Alt-L	RESYNCKEY
Ctrl-L	LOCKKEY
Alt-O	DOSBIG
Ctrl-O	DOS
Alt-R	REFRESH
Ctrl-R	ROTATE
Ctrl-V	VERTRULER
Alt-X	CROSSTABKEY
Ctrl-Y	DELETELINE
Alt-Z	ZOOMNEXT
Ctrl-Z	ZOOM

Commonly Used PAL Commands and Functions

This section contains a listing of commonly used PAL commands and functions grouped by the type of task for which they are used. Brief descriptions are included.

Following this information is an alphabetical listing of commands (except for those which correspond to special keys) showing the proper syntax and giving an example of how to use each command. A similar list is included for PAL functions.

NOTE: *This is only a partial list of PAL commands and functions. There are many more commands and functions available in PAL.*

PAL Commands by Type

Abbreviated Menu Commands

Table D4.

PAL Commands	Paradox Menu Choices
ADD	Tools/More/Add
CANCELEDIT	Cancel/Yes
COEDIT	Modify/Coedit
COPY	Tools/Copy/Table/Replace
COPYFORM	Tools/Copy/Form/Replace
COPYREPORT	Tools/Copy/Report/Replace
CREATE	Create/Replace
DELETE	Tools/Delete/Table/OK
EDIT	Modify/Edit
EMPTY	Tools/More/Empty/OK
EXIT	Exit/Yes
INDEX	Tools/QuerySpeedup
LOCK	Tools/Net/Lock or Tools/Net/PreventLock
PICKFORM	Image/Pickform
PLAY	Scripts/Play
PROTECT	Tools/More/Protect/Password/Table
RENAME	Tools/Rename/Table/Replace
REPORT	Report/Output/Printer
SETDIR	Tools/More/Directory/OK
SETPRIVDIR	Tools/Net/SetPrivate
SETUSERNAME	Tools/Net/UserName
SORT	Modify/Sort
SUBTRACT	Tools/More/Subtract
UNLOCK	Tools/Net/Lock or Tools/Net/PreventLock
UNPASSWORD	Tools/More/Protect/ClearPassword
VIEW	View

Special Key Commands

Table D5. Function Keys

HELP	F1. Accesses Paradox help system
DO__IT!	F2. Saves work; returns to Main mode
UPIMAGE	F3. Moves cursor up an image on the workspace
DOWNIMAGE	F4. Moves cursor down an image on the workspace
INSTANTPLAY	Alt-F4. Plays *Instant* script
EXAMPLE	F5. Places example element in a query
FIELDVIEW	Alt-F5. Lets you edit values inside a field
CHECK	F6. Places Checkmark in query image
CHECKPLUS	Alt-F6. Places Checkmark Plus in query image
CHECKDESCENDING	Ctrl-F6. Places Check Descending in query image
GROUPBY	Shift-F6. Places Check Groupby in query image
FORMKEY	F7. Toggles between form F (or Image/**P**ickform form) and table view for current table
INSTANTREPORT	Alt-F7. Prints report R for current table
GRAPHKEY	Ctrl-F7. Creates graph using current table and graph settings
CLEARIMAGE	F8. Clears current image from workspace
CLEARALL	Alt-F8. Clears all images from workspace
EDITKEY	F9. Goes into Edit mode from Main mode
COEDITKEY	Alt-F9. Goes into Coedit mode from Main mode
MENU	F10. Displays current menu

Table D6. Cursor Keys

HOME	Home
END	End
PGUP	PgUp
PGDN	PgDn
LEFT	Left-Arrow
RIGHT	Right-Arrow
UP	Up-Arrow
DOWN	Down-Arrow

(continued)

Table D6. (*continued*)

INS	Ins
DEL	Del
BACKSPACE	Backspace
ESC	Esc
ENTER	Enter
TAB	Tab
REVERSETAB	Shift-Tab
CTRLBREAK	Ctrl-Break
CTRLHOME	Ctrl-Home
CTRLEND	Ctrl-End
CTRLLEFT	Ctrl-Left
CTRLRIGHT	Ctrl-Right
CTRLBACKSPACE	Ctrl-Backspace
CTRLPGUP	Ctrl-PgUp
CTRLPGDN	Ctrl-PgDn

Table D7. Other Keys

DITTO	Ctrl-D. Copies field in prior record to same field in current record
FIELDVIEW	Ctrl-F. Goes into field view
KEYLOOKUP	Alt-K. Toggles between record with conflicting key and current record in Coedit mode
LOCKKEY	Alt-L. Locks or unlocks current record in Coedit mode
RESYNCKEY	Ctrl-L. Resynchs details records with master record while in a master table of a multi-table form
DOS	Ctrl-O. Goes to DOS
DOSBIG	Alt-O. Goes to DOS with more memory available
ROTATE	Ctrl-R. In table view, moves a column to end of image
REFRESH	Alt-R. Refreshes the screen with other users' changes while in Coedit mode
VERTRULER	Ctrl-V. Toggles the vertical ruler on and off in Report or Script mode
CROSSTAB	Alt-X. Generates CROSSTAB table from the current table
DELETELINE	Ctrl-Y. Deletes the rest of information on line in Report or Script mode
ZOOM	Ctrl-Z. Places "Zoom" prompt on the screen
ZOOMNEXT	Alt-Z. Looks for the next record containing a value found with "Zoom"

Table D8. Screen Commands

@	Positions the cursor on the screen
?	Places information on the screen on the line below the cursor
??	Places information on the screen starting at the cursor
CANVAS	Turns the canvas on or off
CLEAR	Clears the canvas
CURSOR	Turns the cursor on or off; changes the cursor type
ECHO	Shows or hides workspace on the canvas
MESSAGE	Places a message in the lower-right corner of the screen
PAINTCANVAS	Changes the attributes on part of the canvas
PROMPT	Places a prompt on the top two lines of the screen
SETMARGIN	Sets the left margin for displaying text
SHOWARRAY	Creates a Paradox-type menu using arrays
SHOWFILES	Creates a Paradox-type menu using a file list
SHOWMENU	Creates a Paradox-type menu
SHOWTABLES	Creates a Paradox-type menu using a table list
STYLE	Sets the attributes for ?, ??, and TEXT
SYNCCURSOR	Places the cursor on the canvas where it was on the workspace
TEXT	Displays text on the canvas

Table D9. Getting Information from a User

ACCEPT	Assigns the value the user types to a variable
SHOWMENU	Creates a menu and assigns selection to a variable
WAIT	Gives user access to a table, record, or field

See also GETCHAR() function

Table D10. Other Input/Output Commands

BEEP	Makes the computer beep
KEYPRESS	Passes a keycode to Paradox as if it were typed by the user
PRINT	Sends information to the printer or a file
PRINTER	Sends the screen output to a printer, or turns off this function
SELECT	Makes a menu selection; can be used with a variable
TYPEIN	Passes a string of characters to Paradox

Table D11. Moving the Cursor

LOCATE	Looks for value(s) in field(s); moves to a record if found
MOVETO	Moves cursor to a record, field, table, or query image

Also see Table D2 for commands for cursor movement keys

Table D12. Variable and Array Commands

=	Assigns a value to a variable, array element, or field
ARRAY	Defines an array with a specified number of elements
COPYTOARRAY	Copies table records to an array created "on-the-fly"
COPYFROMARRAY	Copies array elements to records in a table
RELEASE	Releases, all or by name, variables, arrays or procedures
SAVEVARS	Saves values of variables and arrays to a script

Table D13. Procedure Commands

CREATELIB	Creates a procedure library
INFOLIB	Creates LIST table with names of library entries
PROC	Defines a procedure
READLIB	Reads a procedure from a library into memory
RELEASE	Release procedures, all or by name, from memory
SETSWAP	Defines the minimum amount of memory Paradox will try to maintain by swapping procedures
WRITELIB	Writes a defined procedure to a procedure library

Table D14. Control Structure Commands

FOR	Tells Paradox to execute a group of commands a specified number of times using a counter
IF	Tells Paradox to execute commands if specified conditions are met
LOOP	Goes to the top of the current WHILE, FOR, or SCAN loop
QUIT	Quits all script play, returns to Paradox
QUITLOOP	Quits the current WHILE, FOR, or SCAN loop
RETURN	Returns from the current script or procedure

(continued)

Table D14. *(continued)*

SCAN	Moves through a table and executes a group of commands
SWITCH	Used with CASE, executes commands based on specified conditions
WHILE	Tells Paradox to execute a group of commands while specified conditions are met; can set up an arbitrary loop using WHILE TRUE

Table D15. Other Commands

DEBUG	Enters the Debugger
PASSWORD	Submits passwords to Paradox
UNPASSWORD	"Unsubmits" password
RESET	Clears the workspace, writes all changes to disk, and returns to Main mode
RUN	Suspends Paradox and executes a DOS command or program
SETKEY	Defines PAL commands to be executed when a key is pressed
SETQUERYORDER	Specifies `TableOrder` or `ImageOrder` for ANSWERs
SLEEP	Tells Paradox to stop script play for a specified period of time

PAL Functions by Type

Table D16. Table and Field Information

FIELD	Name of the current field
FIELDTYPE	Field type of the current field
FORM	What form is being used for the current table?
ISEMPTY	Is a table empty?
ISENCRYPTED	Is a table password-protected?
ISFORMVIEW	Is the current table in form view?
ISTABLE	Does a table exist?
NFIELDS	Number of fields in a table
NKEYFIELDS	Number of key fields in a table
NRECORDS	Number of records in a table
RECNO	Number of the current record
TABLE	Name of the current table

Table D17. Expression Information and Manipulation

ARRAYSIZE	Number of elements in an array
ASC	Returns the ASCII code for a character
BLANKDATE	Returns a blank Date-type value
BLANKNUM	Returns a blank Number-type value
CHR	Returns the character corresponding to the ASCII code
DATEVAL	Returns the date value of a string
FILL	Returns a string of specified fill characters
FORMAT	Formats a value
ISASSIGNED	Is a variable or an array element assigned?
ISBLANK	Is an expression blank?
LEN	Returns the length of a string
LOWER	Returns a string in lowercase letters
MATCH	Looks for patterns in a string, assigns matches to variables
NUMVAL	Returns the number value of a string
SEARCH	Looks for a substring
SPACES	Returns a string of spaces
STRVAL	Returns the string value of a number or date
SUBSRT	Returns a substring
UPPER	Returns a string in uppercase letters
TYPE	Data-type of an expression

Table D18. Input Functions

CHARWAITING	Checks for a character waiting in the keyboard buffer
GETCHAR	Takes, or waits for, a character in the keyboard buffer; the character is not displayed on the screen

Table D19. Date Functions

BLANKDATE	Returns a blank date
DATEVAL	Returns the date value of a string
DAY	Returns the number of day in date
DOW	Returns the name of day in date
MONTH	Returns the number of month in date
MOY	Returns the name of month in date
TODAY	Returns today's date
YEAR	Returns the year in date

Table D20. System Information

DIRECTORY	Name of the current directory
DIREXISTS	Does a directory exist?
DRIVESPACE	Amount of space, in bytes, on a drive
DRIVESTATUS	Is a drive ready?
FILESIZE	Size of a file in bytes
GRAPHTYPE	Current graph type
ISFILE	Does a file exist?
ISBLANKZERO	Is `BLANK=0` set to `Yes` in .CFG file?
MEMLEFT	Memory, in bytes, free for the workspace
PRINTERSTATUS	Is the printer ready?
PRIVDIR	Name of the private directory
QUERYORDER	`TableOrder` or `ImageOrder`?
SORTORDER	Sort order being used
SYSMODE	Current Paradox mode
VERSION	Current Paradox Version

Table D21. Mathematical Functions

ABS	Absolute value of a number
INT	Integer part of a number
MOD	Remainder after dividing one number by another
RAND	Returns a random number
ROUND	Rounds a number

Table D22. Statistical Functions

CAVERAGE	Average of the values in a column
CCOUNT	Count of the values in a column
CMAX	Maximum value in a column
CMIN	Minimum value in a column
CSUM	Sum of values in a column

PAL Command Syntax and Examples

This section lists selected PAL commands alphabetically. PAL commands and their keywords are shown in uppercase letters as in

IF...THEN...ELSE...ENDIF. The arguments, if any, for each command are indicated as follows:

- *ArrayA* is an array name.
- *Expression* stands for any valid PAL expression.
- *Field* is a field name.
- *Table* is a table name.
- *Variable* is a variable name.

 Optional arguments are shown in { }. The { } are not used in the actual code. If there is no syntax or example shown, you can assume that the command has no arguments. All special key commands, such as Left, Enter, or Ctrl-Backspace will be listed this way.

Multiple examples for the same example are separated by a blank line.

=

Assigns a value to a variable, array element, or field in an image on the workspace.

Syntax

Variable = Expression
Array[n] = Expression where *n* is the number of an array element
[Field] = Expression

Examples

```
x = 123
x = "Tom Cat"
A[5] = 123
[Name] = "Tom Cat"
```

??

Places information on the screen starting at the cursor.

Syntax

?? Expression(s); where expressions are separated by +

Examples

```
?? "Enter a name, please: "

?? "This is today's date " + TODAY()
```

?

Places information on the screen at the beginning of the line below the cursor.

Syntax

? Expression(s); where expressions are separated by +

Examples

See ?? above.

@

Positions the cursor on the screen.

Syntax

@ rownumber, colnumber

Example

```
@ 5,0 ;positions the cursor at the first column in the fifth row
```

ACCEPT

Assigns the value which the user types to a variable. Can be used with optional keywords to control what is entered. Retval is assigned False if the user presses Esc.

Syntax

ACCEPT datatype
    {PICTURE Picture}
    {MIN Value}
    {MAX Value}
    {LOOKUP Table}
    {DEFAULT Value}
    {REQUIRED}
    TO variable

Example

```
@ 5,0
?? "Enter a name, please: "
ACCEPT "A25" PICTURE "!*" TO name
```

ADD

Adds two tables with compatible structures together. Works the same as **Tools/More/A**dd.

Syntax

ADD Table1 Table2   ;*Table1* is the source; *Table2* is the
           ;target table.

Example

```
ADD "Customer" "Custhist"        ;Adds CUSTOMER to CUSTHIST.
```

ARRAY

Defines an array with a specified number of elements.

Syntax

ARRAY ArrayName[Number]   *ArrayName* is any valid variable name;
            Number is any number from 1 to 15,000.

Example

```
ARRAY MyArray[7]        ;Creates an array called MyArray
                        ;with seven elements.
```

BEEP

Causes computer to beep.

CANCELEDIT

This command works the same way as pressing F10 in Edit mode and choosing **Cancel/Y**es from the menus.

Example

```
EDIT "Table"
WAIT TABLE
     PROMPT "Press F2 to save, Esc to quit"
UNTIL "F2", "Esc"
IF retval = "Esc"
     THEN CANCELEDIT
     ELSE DO_IT!
ENDIF
```

CANVAS

Turns the canvas on or off. Lets you turn off canvas, "paint" the canvas with TEXT, ?, or ??, and then display the completed canvas. ON is the default.

Syntax

CANVAS ON or CANVAS OFF

CLEAR

Clears all or part of the canvas.

Syntax

```
CLEAR        ;Clears the entire screen when used alone
CLEAR EOL    ;Clears from the cursor position to the end
             ;of the line
CLEAR EOS    ;Clears a rectangle from the cursor position
             ;to bottom-right corner of the screen.
```

COEDIT

This command is the same as using **Modify/Coedit**.

Syntax

COEDIT Table

Examples

```
COEDIT x     ;Where x is a variable containing a table name

COEDIT "Customer"        ;Where Customer is a table name
```

COPY

Makes a copy of a table and its family. Works like **T**ools/**C**opy/**T**able/**R**eplace.

Syntax

COPY Table1 Table2

Example

```
COPY "Answer" "History"
```

COPYFORM

This command is the same as using **T**ools/**C**opy/**F**orm/**R**eplace.

Syntax

COPYFORM Table1 Form1 Table2 Form2

Examples

```
COPYFORM "Customer" "F" "Customer" "5"

COPYFORM "STMNTS" "F" "Answer" "F"
```

COPYFROMARRAY

Copies array elements to the current record in a table. The first array element is assumed to contain the table name. Array elements, starting with the second element, are assigned to fields until there are no more fields or no more array elements.

Syntax

COPYFROMARRAY ArrayName

Examples

```
COPYFROMARRAY x          ;x is a variable containing an array name.

COPYFROMARRAY "MyArray" ;MyArray is an array name.
```

COPYREPORT

This command is the same as using **T**ools/**C**opy/**R**eport/**R**eplace.

Syntax

COPYREPORT Table1 Report1 Table2 Report2

Example

```
COPYREPORT "Stmnts" "R" "Answer" "R"
```

COPYTOARRAY

Creates an array with one element more than the number of fields in the current record and copies the current record to the array. The table name is assigned to the first element of the array.

Syntax

COPYTOARRAY ArrayName

Example

```
COPYTOARRAY "MyArray"
```

CREATE

Works the same as **Create/Replace**.

Syntax

CREATE Table FieldName1 FieldType1 FieldName2 FieldType2 ....

CREATE Table LIKE Table2

Examples

```
CREATE "Newtable" LIKE "OldTable"

CREATE "NewTable" "Name" "A20"
                  "Street" "A20"
                  "City" "A15"
                  "State" "A2"
                  "Zip" "A10"
```

CREATELIB

Creates a procedure library. The name can be up to eight characters in length and must start with a letter. Paradox adds the file extension, .LIB. Default size is 50 procedures. Can be changed to up to 300 with the SIZE keyword.

Syntax

CREATELIB Name {SIZE Value}

Examples

```
CREATELIB "Raspbrry"        ;Default size of 50 procedures.

CREATELIB "Accting" SIZE 150  ;Can hold up to 150 procedures.
```

CURSOR

Turns canvas cursor on or off. Can also be used to change the cursor type.

Syntax

CURSOR BAR

CURSOR BOX

CURSOR NORMAL   ;Default.

CURSOR OFF

DEBUG

Enters the Debugger.

DELETE

Works the same as **Tools/Delete/Table/OK**.

Syntax

DELETE Table

Examples

```
DELETE "OldTable"

DELETE x  ;Where x is a variable which contains a table name.
```

ECHO

Shows the workspace on the canvas or hides the workspace action.

Syntax

ECHO FAST   ;Shows workspace action slowly.

ECHO SLOW   ;Shows workspace action very slowly.

ECHO OFF   ;Default.

ECHO NORMAL   ;Shows the workspace action on the screen at real ;speed.

EDIT

Works the same as **Modify/Edit**.

Syntax

EDIT Table

Example

```
EDIT "Customer"

EDIT z    ;Where z is a variable containing the name of a table.
```

EMPTY

This command is the same as **Tools/More/Empty/OK**.

Syntax

EMPTY Table

Example

```
EMPTY "Trans"
```

EXECUTE

Tells Paradox to execute a command parsed together from an expression.

Syntax

EXECUTE Command   ;Where command is an expression

Example

```
Execute "MOVETO [" + x + "]"   ;Where x is a variable
                               ;containing a field name.
```

EXIT

This is the same as using Exit/Yes from the Main Menu. It quits Paradox and returns the user to DOS.

FOR

Tells Paradox to execute a group of commands a specified number of times using a counter. You can use the STEP keyword to specify the number by which to increment the counter at each pass through the loop. The numbers used to specify the starting and ending counter values can be positive or negative numbers.

Syntax

```
FOR variable
      {FROM NUMBER1}
      {TO NUMBER2}
      {STEP NUMBER3}
      Commands....
ENDFOR
```

Example

```
FOR x FROM 1 TO 10     ;Prints Instant Report for the current
      INSTANTREPORT    ;table 10 times.
ENDFOR
```

IF

Tells Paradox to execute commands if specified conditions are met. The THEN keyword must be used; the ELSE keyword is optional.

Syntax

IF Condition
    THEN Commands...
    {ELSE Commands...}
ENDIF

Examples

```
IF retval = "Esc"
     THEN CANCELEDIT
     ELSE DO_IT!
ENDIF

IF x = 2 AND y <> 5
     THEN z = x + y
ENDIF
```

INDEX

This command is used, like **Tools/QuerySpeedup**, to create a secondary index for a table. The MAINTAINED keyword can be used to force Paradox to maintain the index incrementally *if the table is keyed.*

Syntax

INDEX Table ON Field {MAINTAINED}

Example

```
INDEX "CUSTOMER" ON "State" MAINTAINED
```

INFOLIB

Creates LIST table with names of library entries and procedure sizes in bytes.

Syntax

INFOLIB LibraryName

Example

```
INFOLIB "Raspbrry"
```

KEYPRESS

Passes a keycode to Paradox as if it were typed by the user. Must be used with recognizable keycode such as "F2" or ASCII code, such as 27 (for Esc).

Syntax

KEYPRESS Keycode

Examples

```
KEYPRESS 27

KEYPRESS "F2"

KEYPRESS " ~ "
```

LOCATE

Looks for value(s) in records, and moves to the record if the value(s) is found. If you are looking for one value, LOCATE is done on the current field. If you search on more than one value, LOCATE starts with the first field and matches the remaining values used with LOCATE with consecutive fields. Retval is True if LOCATE was successful.

The PATTERN keyword must be used if you are using a pattern for the search value.

To use LOCATE NEXT, first move down one record after successful LOCATE.

Syntax

```
LOCATE {PATTERN} Value(s)    ;Multiple values must be separated
                                      ;by commas.
LOCATE {NEXT} {PATTERN} Value(s)
```

Examples

```
LOCATE "Smith"            ;Looks for record with Smith in current field.
```

```
MOVETO [Last Name]        ;This example uses LOCATE NEXT.
LOCATE PATTERN "S.."      ;Looks for first record where the current field
                          ;starts with an S.
counter = 0               ;Sets variable named counter to 0
WHILE True
IF retval = True                  ;If prior locate was successful,
     THEN counter = counter + 1   ;increment counter or
                          ;performs some other action.
          DOWN            ;Moves the cursor down one record.
          LOCATE NEXT "S.."    ;Looks for the next record.
ENDIF
ENDWHILE

LOCATE a,b,c     ;Looks for values in variables contained in
                 ;a, b and c in first three fields.
```

LOOP

Goes to the top of the current WHILE, FOR, or SCAN loop.

MESSAGE

Places a message in the lower-right corner of the screen. Message is displayed only until the next command is executed. Usually used with SLEEP.

Syntax

MESSAGE Expression1 {+ Expression2 ...}

Examples

```
MESSAGE "Hi There!"
SLEEP 2000

MESSAGE "The amount is " + CSUM("Detail","Amount") + " dollars."
```

MOVETO

Moves the cursor to the specified record, field, table, or query image.

Syntax

MOVETO [Field]

MOVETO [Table->]

MOVETO [Table->Field]

MOVETO RECORD Number

MOVETO ImageNumber

MOVETO TableName

MOVETO FIELD FieldName

Examples

```
MOVETO [Last Name]             ;Moves to field Last Name in the
                               ;current table.

MOVETO [CUSTOMER->]            ;Moves to the CUSTOMER table.

MOVETO [CUSTOMER->Last Name] ;Moves to Last Name field in CUSTOMER.

MOVETO RECORD 100             ;Moves to record #100 in the current
                               ;table.

MOVETO 3                       ;Moves to the third image on the
                               ;workspace.

MOVETO Field "Date"           ;Moves to field Date in the current
                               ;table.
```

PAINTCANVAS

Changes attributes on part of the canvas, whether or not it has text on it. Used with BORDER keyword, affects a one-character border only. FILL is used to overwrite an area with a specified string of characters. ATTRIBUTE is used with a number to set colors. BACKGROUND is used to change the FILL string only.

Syntax

PAINTCANVAS {BORDER}
                {FILL Characters}
                {BLINK} or {INTENSE} or {REVERSE}
                {ATTRIBUTE Number}

{BACKGROUND}
Row1, Column1, Row2, Column2

Example

```
a 5,0
?? "Processing query..."
PAINTCANVAS BLINK 5,16,5,18     ;Makes dots blink.
```

PICKFORM

This command works the same as **I**mage/**P**ickForm.

Syntax

PICKFORM Number

Examples

```
PICKFORM "F"

PICKFORM 3
```

PLAY

This command works the same as **S**cripts/**P**lay.

Syntax

PLAY ScriptName

Examples

```
PLAY "MyScript"

PLAY x   ;Where x is a variable containing the name of a script.
```

PROC

Defines a procedure in a script. See Chapter 12 for more information.

Syntax

PROC {CLOSED} Procname ({Arguments})
        {USEVARS Variablelist}

```
{PRIVATE Variablelist}
Commands
ENDPROC
```

Example

```
PROC MyProc()
MESSAGE "HI!"
SLEEP 2000
ENDPROC
WRITELIB "MyLib" MyProc  ;Writes procedure MyProc to library
                         ;MyLib.
```

PROMPT

Places a prompt on the top two lines of the screen.

Syntax

PROMPT {STRING1{, STRING 2}}

Example

```
PROMPT "Press F3 to move to master portion of form.",
       "Press F2 to save work, Esc to quit."
```

QUITLOOP

Quits the current WHILE, FOR, or SCAN loop. Goes to the command following ENDWHILE, ENDFOR, or ENDSCAN.

QUIT

Quits all script play and returns to Paradox. Optionally, you can have Paradox display an expression. If you do, the expression must be included on the same script line as the QUIT command.

Syntax

QUIT {EXPRESSION}

Example

```
CASE retval = "Leave" : QUIT "Goodbye!"
```

READLIB

Reads a procedure from a library into memory. You can use the IMMEDIATE keyword to have Paradox load a procedure into memory right away. If there is not enough memory, a script error will occur. When IMMEDIATE is not used, Paradox will load only as many procedures into memory as there is room for.

Syntax

READLIB LibraryName [IMMEDIATE] ProcedureList

Examples

```
READLIB "Raspbrry" Mainmenu, Stmnts, Pymnts, Orders

READLIB "Raspbrry" IMMEDIATE Mainmenu, Stmnts, Pymnts, Orders
```

RELEASE

Releases variables, arrays, or procedures from memory. You can list them by name or use the keyword ALL.

Syntax

RELEASE PROCS {ALL} or {ProcedureNameList}

RELEASE VARS {ALL} or {VariableNameList}

Examples

```
RELEASE PROCS ALL

RELEASE VARS x,y,z
```

RENAME

This command works the same as **T**ools/**R**ename/**T**able/**R**eplace. The first table specified, and its family, are given the second name used with the command.

Syntax

RENAME Table1 Table2 ;Renames Table1 as Table2.

Example

```
RENAME "CUSTOMER" "CUSTHIST"
```

REPORT

This command is the same as using **R**eport/**O**utput/**P**rinter.

Syntax

REPORT Table ReportNumber

Example

```
REPORT "Customer" "5"
```

RESET

Clears the workspace, writes all changes to disk, and returns to Main mode. It should be used before suspending Paradox and going to DOS if you are going to use any files with DOS which Paradox may not have closed yet. Should be used after the EMPTY command to ensure that the emptied table is written to disk immediately.

RETURN

Returns from the current script or procedure. Optionally, can return a value which must be specified on the same line.

Syntax

RETURN {VALUE}

Examples

```
RETURN
```

```
RETURN x
```

RUN

Suspends Paradox and executes a DOS command or program. Can be used with the BIG keyword to provide more memory while in DOS. The

SLEEP keyword tells Paradox to pause before resuming script play. NOREFRESH leaves the PAL canvas displayed while Paradox is suspended; NORESTORE does not restore the canvas when Paradox resumes activity—the DOS screen output remains visible until a PAL command is used to show the workspace or to change the canvas.

Syntax

RUN {BIG} {SLEEP Number} DOSCommand {NOREFRESH}
{NORESTORE}

Example

```
RUN SLEEP 4000 "CHKDSK" ;Shows results of CHKDSK for four
                        ; seconds before returning to Paradox.
```

SAVEVARS

Saves the values of any defined variables and array elements to a script called *SAVEVARS*. This script can be played in another session to reassign the variables which were included. You can save the variables and array elements by name, or with the keyword, ALL.

Syntax

SAVEVARS {ALL} or {VariableNameList}

Examples

```
SAVEVARS ALL
```

```
SAVEVARS x,y,z,A[1],A[2],A[3]
```

SCAN

Moves through a table and executes a group of commands for each record. Optionally, you can use the FOR keyword to have Paradox execute only the commands for those records which meet the specified condition.

Syntax

SCAN {FOR CONDITION}
     Commands
ENDSCAN

Examples

```
EDIT "Table"
SCAN
[Record #] = RECNO()
ENDSCAN
DO_IT!

EDIT "Table"
SCAN FOR [Date] = BLANKDATE()
[Date] = TODAY()
ENDSCAN
DO_IT!
```

SELECT

Tells Paradox to use a specified expression for a menu selection; can be used to specify a variable for a menu choice. You do not need to use { } around the expression used for the menu choice.

Syntax

SELECT Expression

Example

```
MENU
ASK
SELECT x   ;Places a query image for the table name contained
           ;in variable x on the workspace
```

SETKEY

Defines PAL commands to be executed when key is pressed. See Chapter 11 for details on using SETKEY. Any commands which are tied to a keystroke with SETKEY must appear on the same script line which can total no more than 132 characters. SETKEY used by itself reinitializes a key to its normal action.

Syntax

SETKEY Keycode {Commands}

Examples

```
SETKEY 20 TYPEIN TIME()

SETKEY 14 PLAY "ScriptName"
```

SHOWMENU

Creates a Paradox-type menu using menu choices and descriptions which you specify. You can use the DEFAULT keyword to specify a default menu choice. Assigns the menu selection to a variable you name.

Syntax

```
SHOWMENU
    Choice1 : Description1
      ⋮
    Choice n : Description n
    {DEFAULT Choice}
    TO Variable
```

Example

```
SHOWMENU
     "Customers" : "Add or change CUSTOMER records",
     "Orders"    : "View or enter orders",
     "Shipments" : "Update ship amounts, post sales",
     "Payments"  : "Post payments",
     "Statements": "Generate statements",
     "Leave"     : "Go back to interactive Paradox"
TO choice
SWITCH
     CASE choice = "Customers" : PLAY "Customer"
     CASE choice = "Orders"    : PLAY "Orders"
     CASE choice = "Shipments" : PLAY "Ship"
     CASE choice = "Payments"  : PLAY "Pmnts"
     CASE choice = "Statements": PLAY "Stmnts"
ENDSWITCH
```

SLEEP

Tells Paradox to stop script play for a specified amount of time.

Syntax

SLEEP Number ;Where *number* is milliseconds.

Example

```
MESSAGE "Goodbye!"
SLEEP 2000              ;Shows the message for two seconds.
```

SORT

This command works the same as **Modify/Sort**. You can specify one or more fields on which to sort. The keyword D can be used to sort in descending order. You can use TO to sort an unkeyed table to a new table. TO must be used if you are sorting a keyed table.

Syntax

SORT Table1
{ON FieldNameList {D}}
{TO Table2}

Examples

```
SORT "Customer" ON "State" TO "Tempcust"

SORT "Answer" ON "Date" D ;Sorts ANSWER in descending date order.
```

SUBTRACT

This command works the same as **Tools/More/Subtract**. See Chapter 9 for more information.

Syntax

SUBTRACT Table1 Table2

Example

```
SUBTRACT "Answer" "Customer"
```

SWITCH

Used with CASE to execute commands based on specified conditions. See the example for SHOWMENU above.

TEXT

Displays text on the canvas, starting at the current cursor position. Can be changed with the STYLE command. TEXT and ENDTEXT must be on lines by themselves, except for comments.

Syntax

```
TEXT
:                    ;Include lines of text here
:
ENDTEXT
```

TYPEIN

Passes a string of characters to Paradox as if the string was typed from the keyboard.

Syntax

TYPEIN Expression

Example

```
MENU
{ASK} {ORDERS}
CHECK
MOVETO [Date]
TYPEIN ">=today - 30"
DO_IT!
```

VIEW

This command places a table on the workspace in Main mode the same as using F10/View.

Syntax

VIEW Table

Examples

```
VIEW x    ;Where x is a variable containing a table name.

VIEW "Orders"
```

WAIT

Gives the user access to table, record, or field until a specified key is pressed. TABLE, RECORD, or FIELD is used to automatically limit a user's movement through the table. The key which ends the WAIT is assigned to the system variable *retval*.

Syntax

WAIT {TABLE} or {RECORD} or {FIELD}
        {PROMPT Expression1{,Expression2}}
UNTIL KeyCode(s)

Example

```
EDIT "phonebk"
WAIT TABLE
      PROMPT "Press F2 to Save, Esc to Cancel"
UNTIL "F2", "Esc"
IF retval = "Esc"
      THEN CANCELEDIT
      ELSE DO_IT!
ENDIF
```

Note: For an example of using WAIT on a multi-table form, see Listing 11.15 in Chapter 11. That example uses both WAIT TABLE and WAIT RECORD.

WHILE

Tells Paradox to execute a group of commands as long as specified conditions are met. You can set up an arbitrary loop using WHILE TRUE. If you do, remember to provide a means of exiting from the loop by using QUITLOOP, EXIT, or QUIT.

Syntax

WHILE Condition
        Commands
ENDWHILE

Example

```
x=1
WHILE x<=5
      MYPROC ()##          ;call MYRPOC procedures 5 times
```

```
    x = x + 1
ENDWHILE
```

Note: For an example of an arbitrary WHILE loop, used with a WHILE loop based on a condition, see Listing 11.12 in Chapter 11.

WRITELIB

Writes a defined procedure to an existing procedure library created with CREATELIB.

Syntax

WRITELIB LibraryName ProcedureNameList

Example

```
PROC "MyProc"
MESSAGE "HI!"
SLEEP 2000
ENDPROC
WRITELIB "MyLib" MyProc
```

PAL Functions Syntax and Examples

This is an alphabetical list of commonly used PAL functions. Each entry contains notes on the use of the function, the proper syntax and an example of the function and the value it returns. Remember that functions are not used by themselves like commands are; functions are always used as an expression, or as part of an expression, to refer to a value for use with a command.

Many functions can be helpful in trying to debug script problems. You can use Alt-F10/Value when you are in the Debugger to check the value of any function.

The spaces between a function name and the () that follow are optional.

ABS

Returns the absolute value of a number.

Syntax

ABS(Number)

Example

```
x = ABS (-2)    ;Assigns value of two to variable x.
```

ASC

This function returns the ASCII code for a character.

Syntax

ASC (Character)

Example

```
x = ASC ("F2")    ;Assigns value of -60 to x.
```

BLANKDATE

Returns a blank Date-type value. Useful for checking if a date type field is blank.

Example

```
[Date] = BLANKDATE()      ;Assigns a blank value to [Date].
```

BLANKNUM

Returns a blank Number-type value.

Example

```
[Amount] = BLANKNUM()   ;Assigns a blank value to [Amount].
```

CAVERAGE

This function returns the average of the values in a table column. It uses only non-blank values, even if Blank=0 is set to Yes in the .CFG file. You can use CAVERAGE() only on a Number-type field.

Syntax

CAVERAGE (Table,Field)

Example

```
z = CAVERAGE ("Trans","Sales Amount")
```

CHR

This function returns the character corresponding to a specified ASCII code.

Syntax

CHR (AsciiKeycode)

Example

```
y = CHR(65)   ;Assigns "A" to y.
```

CMAX

This function returns the maximum value in a Number-type field in a table.

Syntax

CMAX (Table,Field)

Example

```
maxvalue = CMAX ("Orders", "Total Amount")
```

CMIN

CMIN( ) returns the minimum value from a Number-type field in a table.

Syntax

CMIN(Table,Field)

Example

```
smallest = CMIN("Babies","Weight")
```

CSUM

This function returns the sum of all values in a Number-type field in a table.

Syntax

CSUM (Table,Field)

Example

```
totalamt = CSUM("DETAIL","Quantity")
```

DIRECTORY

DIRECTORY( ) returns the name of the current directory. It is used by itself and returns a string such as "C:\\PARADOX3". If you display this value, the extra backslashes are removed.

FIELDTYPE

This function returns the field type of the current field. It takes no arguments and returns one of these values: "An","N", "S", "D" or "$".

FIELD

FIELD( ) takes no arguments and returns the name of the current field as a string such as "Last Name".

GETCHAR

GETCHAR( ) takes no arguments. It takes a character from the keyboard buffer and returns the ASCII code. If there is no character waiting, GETCHAR( ) will wait until a key is pressed. The character taken by GETCHAR( ) is not displayed on the screen. This makes GETCHAR( ) useful for accepting non-displaying passwords. See the example in Listing 11.12.

INT

INT( ) returns the integer part of a number.

Syntax

INT(Number)

Example

```
x=INT(123.45)   ;Assigns the value 123 to x.
```

ISASSIGNED

This functions returns *True* if a variable or an array element is assigned a value and *False* if it is not.

Syntax

ISASSIGNED (VariableName)

ISASSIGNED (ArrayElementName)

ISBLANKZERO

This function lets you check how `BLANK=0` is set in your .CFG file without having to play the Custom script. If `Blank=0` is set to `Yes`, the function returns *True*. If it is set to `No`, *False* is returned. The function takes no arguments and is specified as *ISBLANKZERO( )*.

ISBLANK

This function returns *True* if an expression is blank and *False* if it is not. A blank string value is denoted by " ". This is *not* the same as spaces. Blank Date- and Number-type values cannot be represented by " "; you must use *BLANKDATE()* and *BLANKNUM()*.

Syntax

ISBLANK (Expression)

Examples

```
x = ISBLANK ('''')    ;Assigns True to x.

y = ISBLANK (" ")    ;Assigns False to y.
```

ISEMPTY

This function lets you check if a table is empty. It returns *True* if a table contains no records and *False* otherwise.

Syntax

ISEMPTY (Table)

Example

```
IF ISEMPTY ("Answer")
    THEN MESSAGE "No records found"
         SLEEP 2000
         RETURN
ENDIF
```

ISFILE

You can use this function to see if a file exists. Returns True if the specified file exists and False otherwise.

Syntax

ISFILE (FileName)

Example

```
IF ISFILE ("C:\\MYDIR\\TEMP")
    THEN RUN "ERASE C:\\MYDIR\\TEMP"
ENDIF
```

ISFORMVIEW

Checks whether the current table is in form view. Returns *True* if current image is in form view and *False* if it is not.

Syntax

ISFORMVIEW( )

Example

```
IF NOT ISFORMVIEW()    ;Checks to see if a function returns False.
    THEN PICKFORM 3    ;If the function returns False,
                       ;brings up Form 3.
ENDIF
```

ISTABLE

This function is used to see if a table exists. If the specified table exists, the function returns True. If the table does not exist, the function returns *False*.

Syntax

ISTABLE (Table)

Example

```
IF NOT ISTABLE ("Sales")
    THEN CREATE "Sales" LIKE "Template"
ENDIF
```

LEN

Returns the length of a string. You can use any PAL expression with LEN( ).

Syntax

LEN (Expression)

Example

```
IF LEN ([Zip Code]) = 4  ;Checks for Zip Code with leading 0
                         ;truncated.
    THEN [Zip Code] = "0" + [Zip Code]
ENDIF
```

LOWER

Returns a string in all lowercase letters. Only letters in the specified string are affected.

Syntax

LOWER (Expression)

Example

```
EDIT "Dogs"
SCAN
[Breed] = LOWER ([Breed])   ;Changes all letters to lowercase.
ENDSCAN
DO_IT!
```

MATCH

The MATCH( ) function looks for substrings matching a pattern in a string and assigns any matches to variables. If a match is found, the function returns *True*. If no match is found, the function returns *False*.

Syntax

MATCH (String, Pattern, VariableList)

Examples

```
x = MATCH ("Deirdre Dryden",".. ..",a,b) ;Assigns True to x.
                                         ;Assigns "Deirdre" to a
                                         ;Assigns "Dryden" to b.

EDIT "Table"
SCAN
IF MATCH ([Name],".. ..",a,b)            ;Looks for a space in
                                         ;[Name].
     THEN [First Name] = a
          [Last Name] = b
ENDIF
ENDSCAN
DO_IT!
```

MEMLEFT

This function returns the memory, in bytes, available for the Paradox workspace.

Syntax

MEMLEFT( )

Example

```
MESSAGE "Memleft = " + MEMLEFT()
SLEEP 2000
```

MOD

The MOD( ) function returns the remainder after dividing one number by another.

Syntax

MOD (Number1, Number2)

Example

```
EDIT "Table"
SCAN
[Group #] = MOD (RECNO(),3)   ;Assigns 0, 1, or 2 to [Group #].
ENDSCAN
DO_IT!
```

NRECORDS

This function returns the number of records in a table.

Syntax

NRECORDS (Table)

Example

```
IF NRECORDS ("History") > 100,000
     THEN MESSAGE "History should be archived"
          SLEEP 3000
ENDIF
```

NUMVAL

Returns the number value of a string. This is useful for using a number in an Alphanumeric field in a calculation or assigning that number to a Number-type field. See the elapsed time script in Chapter 11 for another example.

Syntax

NUMVAL (String)

Example

```
IF MATCH ([Time], "..:..:..",a,b,c)
    THEN [Minutes] = NUMVAL (a) * 60 + NUMVAL (b)
ENDIF
```

QUERYORDER

This function returns `TableOrder` or `ImageOrder` depending on the current `QueryOrder` setting in the .CFG file. You can check the value of this function using Alt-F10/Value instead of playing the Custom script. The function takes no arguments.

Syntax

QUERYORDER( )

RECNO

RECNO( ) returns the number of the current record. The function takes no arguments.

Syntax

RECNO( )

Example

```
EDIT "Table"
SCAN
[Number] = RECNO()    ;Assigns the record number to the field called
                      ;Number.
ENDSCAN
DO_IT!
```

ROUND

Rounds a number to a specified number of places. The number of places can be any number from -15 to 15. Positive numbers are used to round a value to a number of decimal places; negative numbers are used to round a value to a number of whole digits.

Syntax

```
ROUND (Number1, Number2)  ;Number1 is the number to be rounded.
                          ;Number2 specifies the number of digits
                          ;for the rounded value.
```

Examples

```
x = ROUND (123.45,0)   ;Assigns 123 to x.

y = ROUND (123.45,-1) ;Assigns 120 to y.

z = ROUND (123.45,2)   ;Assigns 123.45 to z.
```

STRVAL

Returns the string value of a number or date. This is useful for assigning the result of calculation to an Alphanumeric field.

Syntax

STRVAL (Expression)

Example

```
x = STRVAL (14*2) ;Assigns "28" to the Alphanumeric variable x.
```

SUBSTR

Returns a substring of a specified string. *Number1* represents the starting position in the string. *Number2* represents the number of characters to be used for the substring.

Syntax

SUBSTR (String, Number1, Number2)

Examples

```
x = SUBSTR ("Hippopotamus",1,5)   ;Assigns "Hippo" to x.

y = SUBSTR ([Zip],7,4)            ;Assigns the last part of a
                                  ;two part Zip to y.
```

SYSMODE

This function returns the current mode. It is valuable in debugging to see what mode you are in if you get a message such as "Not an available menu choice." The function will return: "Main", "Create", "Edit", "Coedit", "DataEntry", "Form", "Graph", "Report", "Restructure", "Password", or "Script".

Syntax

SYSMODE( )

Example

```
MESSAGE SYSMODE()  ;Displays "Main" if you are in Main mode.
```

TABLE

This function returns the name of the current table. It takes no arguments.

Syntax

TABLE( )

Example

```
Edit "Phonebk"
x = TABLE()       ;Assigns "Phonebk" to x.
```

TODAY

Returns today's date. The date is taken from the current system date setting for your computer.

Syntax

```
TODAY( )
```

Example

```
EDIT "Table"
SCAN FOR
     [Date] = TODAY()
ENDSCAN
DO_IT!
```

TYPE

TYPE( ) returns the data-type of an expression. This is useful for debugging script problems if you get messages such as "Expression has wrong type."

Syntax

```
TYPE (Expression)
```

Examples

```
x = TYPE ("123")   ;Assigns "A3" to x.

y = TYPE (123)     ;Assigns "N" to y.
```

UPPER

Returns a string in uppercase letters. UPPER can be used with any type of PAL expression. However, only Alphanumeric characters are affected.

Syntax

```
UPPER (Expression)
```

Example

```
x = UPPER ("Big Time")   ;Assigns "BIG TIME" to x
```

Getting Help

Here are a few ways to get assistance using Paradox if you run into snags that you can't figure out yourself.

User Groups

Paradox User Groups exist nationwide. Some even publish helpful newsletters. You can subscribe to some of the newsletters without being a member of the local group. Participating in a User Group is a good way to make contact with other Paradox users of who may have experienced the same problems as you.

CompuServe

Next to hiring a qualified Paradox consultant, CompuServe Information Service is probably the best source of Paradox help available. CompuServe offers an on-line system which allows users to access information on many topics, including Paradox. You can upload and download files and sample scripts, as well as leave messages for other Paradox users and the Borland Paradox Technical Support Department.

To access the Paradox sections of CompuServe, type **GO BORDB** at the CompuServe function prompt. To access CompuServe, you must be a member of CompuServe Information Service. For information on becoming a member, telephone CompuServe at 800-848-8199.

appendix

Notes on Paradox 386, Paradox OS/2 and Paradox SQL

Paradox 386 and Paradox OS/2 are special versions of Paradox designed to run in specific environments. Both versions are functionally equivalent to Paradox 2.0, and do not include the features added to Paradox 3.0. Although they do not include all the Paradox features, such as multitable forms and set queries, covered in this book, you may find them useful for certain applications.

Notes on Paradox SQL are also included in this Appendix.

Paradox 386

Paradox 386 is a version of Paradox which will run only on an 80386 computer. Paradox 386 is different from Paradox 2.0 in these ways:

- Paradox 386 uses a special command set which takes advantage of the 32-bit architecture of an 80386 processor.
- Paradox 386 makes use of up to 16 megabytes of extended (not expanded) memory on a 386 computer.

Why Use Paradox 386?

The differences noted above allow Paradox 386 to process large tables much more quickly than other versions of Paradox. If you are using tables with 30,000 or more records, you can experience quite dramatic performance gains from using Paradox 386. Some users have reported performance gains of up to 500% while running queries or doing other memory-intensive operations.

Paradox 386 will also help in cases when you have problems getting enough memory to run your Paradox application. Because Paradox 386 can use up to 16MB of memory on a 386 computer, you get much more memory for the Paradox workspace. You can change the percentage of memory which Paradox 386 uses for the workspace by using a command-line option, **-kswap n**, when you load the program: n is a number representing the percentage of memory to be used for swapping.

Memory Requirements

In addition to a 386 computer, you need at least 1.5, and preferably 2, megabytes of RAM in your computer. DOS and Paradox 386 take up about 1 megabyte of RAM. The remaining memory is used for the workspace and the procedure-swapping area. To really experience the performance benefits which Paradox 386 can offer, you should have even more memory. (Paradox loves memory.) The more memory you have available, the better performance will be.

Paradox OS/2

Paradox OS/2 is a special version of Paradox which runs under OS/2, instead of under DOS. Paradox OS/2 is the same as Paradox 2.0 with the addition of the SESSION command. The SESSION command is a PAL command which allows you to start a new OS/2 session from a PAL script.

What Paradox OS/2 Offers

There are two benefits to using Paradox OS/2 over using DOS-based Paradox in the Compatibility Box:

- With Paradox OS/2, you can multi-task.

- Paradox OS/2 makes use of extended memory, providing a performance benefit.

Multi-tasking is built into OS/2. Paradox takes advantage of this because of its network capabilities. The same file- and record-locking mechanisms which let you share Paradox tables on a network, allow you to use the same Paradox tables in different OS/2 sessions. This is a nice feature. It allows you to run a long query, or another lengthy operation, in one session while you continue other Paradox work in another session. To be able to run Paradox in multiple sessions, you must use the **-multi** command line option when you start Paradox OS/2.

If Paradox OS/2 is started without *-multi*, the gain in performance experienced by Paradox OS/2 users is often similar to that reported by Paradox 386 users who have the same amount of extended memory available. There are differences, of course, depending on the type of tables and operations in use. In general, though, you can expect similar performance for Paradox OS/2 and Paradox 386 in long operations such as queries and sorts.

System Requirements

Paradox OS/2 will run only on an 80286- or 80386-based computer which is 100% compatible with one of the following computers:

- IBM PS/2 Model 50, 60, or 80
- IBM PC XT 286 or PC AT

In addition, the computer must have at least 3 megabytes of RAM, with the memory above 640K configured as extended, not expanded, memory. The computer must have a hard disk and at least one high-density floppy drive.

You can use Paradox OS/2 on a local area network which supports OS/2 workstations.

Networking with Other Paradox Users

Paradox 386 and Paradox OS/2 users can share Paradox tables with Paradox 2.0 and Paradox 3.0 users on one of the networks supported by Paradox. The file and record locking mechanisms in all of the products is the same. Borland International thus supports the sharing of information between users of Paradox from Version 2.0 on.

Paradox and SQL

With a special version of Paradox, scheduled to be available in 1990, you will be able use Paradox to access information from an SQL database using the Paradox QBE (Query-By-Example) commands which you already know. The following SQL servers will be supported:

- IBM OS/2 Extended Edition 1.1 Database Manager
- Microsoft SQL Server
- ORACLE SQL Server

You will be able to use Paradox SQL to:

- Update and add records to a remote SQL database
- Embed SQL statements in a PAL program and pass it to an SQL server
- Use the tables retrieved from an SQL remote database as you do any local Paradox table.

Paradox Add-On Products

There are several products available which can add capability to your Paradox system. A few of them are listed in this Appendix, along with notes on the purpose of the products, and information on where to obtain them. The information presented is not a recommendation to use the products listed; it is offered only for your convenience and as an example of the type of Paradox add-on products which are now available.

Paradox Script Editors

PlayRight

PlayRight is a text editor specifically designed for use with Paradox. With PlayRight, you can load as many files as can fit in memory and copy or move blocks between files. "ProofWrite," part of the product, formats scripts by automatically indenting lines and standardizing the case of Paradox reserved words. PlayRight is available through:

The Burgiss Group
3332 Eastburn Rd.
Charlotte, NC 28210
(800) 262-8069 for orders

PAL-Edit

PAL-Edit is an editor designed for the PAL programmer. It includes a complete on-line reference system to PAL, including every command and function in Paradox 3.0. PAL-Edit also provides the ability to view tables and their structures from the editor, includes templates to complete commands for you, and special support for procedures. The editor is completely customizable, has unlimited "Undo," allows for multiple scripts in memory at once, and has complete window support. It is available in single-user and network licenses. The PAL Help system is also available as a standalone product.

> Kallista, Inc.
> Suite 504
> 600 South Dearborn St.
> Chicago, IL 60605
> (312) 663-0101

Utilities and Other Programs

ParaLex

ParaLex is a utility which documents your Paradox tables. It creates three "dictionaries." The Data dictionary deals with the structure of your tables. Field names, types, and all validity checks are accounted for. The Table dictionary deals with the family objects associated with your data files. It tells you the number of records per table, record size, shows statistics on all secondary indexes, and so forth. The Password dictionary lists all rights assigned to each field for auxiliary passwords.

There are 12 reports, which can be sent to the printer, screen, or file, included in the system. The reports vary greatly in detail and sort order. This helps point out errors, omissions, and inconsistencies in table design. ParaLex can use any number of tables found in any number of subdirectories. It is totally menu-driven, very easy to use, but includes information useful to even the most demanding developer. ParaLex may be ordered by calling (800) 336-6644. For other questions, contact:

> Alan Zenreich
> Zenreich Systems
> 208 Kinderkamack Rd.
> Oradell, NJ 07649
> (201) 261-3325

Desktop For Paradox

Desktop For Paradox provides over 30 add-in features designed to simplify basic tasks. Many features provide pop-up reference information about your hardware, the state of Paradox, and any tables you are using. Other routines reduce keystrokes and automate repetitive functions. Desktop For Paradox is written entirely in PAL, and all source code is provided. Desktop For Paradox is available through Kallista, Inc. See the section on PAL-Edit above.

P-Dial

P-Dial is a small add-in which will read a telephone number from a designated field and dial that number on your Hayes-compatible modem. After you pick up the phone, you are returned to Paradox. P-Dial supports multiple COM ports, dialing prefixes and suffixes, and has many other options. P-Dial can be obtained from Kallista, Inc. See the section on PAL-Edit above for information.

ParaTrak

ParaTrak is a Paradox procedure-tracking program. It is designed for use by Paradox application developers. With ParaTrak, you can document the relationships between procedures in an application easily. You can get ParaTrak from:

> Financial Modeling Specialists, Inc.
> P.O. Box 1251
> Arlington, VA 22210
> (703) 356-4700

X-TAB

X-TAB lets you create crosstabulated tables from a menu-driven system or by using a special command in your scripts. Crosstabulated tables can be useful for generating reports and graphs. A variety of Numeric and Date groupings are possible with X-TAB. X-TAB is available through Financial Modeling Specialists, Inc. See the section on ParaTrak above for details.

Paradox Viewer for Magellan

Magellan is a tool from Lotus for viewing, searching, gathering, and organizing information in your PC. It is very fast and works with the files you already have. The Paradox Viewer for Magellan lets you scroll through your tables and scripts quickly without having to load Paradox. You can download the Paradox Viewer for Magellan from the LotusB forum on CompuServe.

pTools

pTools is a set of utility programs which aid application development efforts by allowing you to process and document data dictionaries, browse tables, perform queries, and import/export data outside of Paradox. pTools is available from:

CompuMethods Company
P.O. Box 338
Westminster, CA 92684-0338
(714) 893-6838

Paradox
Reserved Words

There are certain words you must avoid when naming Paradox objects because they are already used by Paradox. This Appendix lists Paradox objects by type, along with the reserved words for each group.

Tables

When naming tables, avoid using the names of Paradox's temporary tables, unless you specifically want Paradox to treat your table as a temporary table. You should also avoid using names which Paradox uses for some of its temporary work files.

Temporary Table Names

ANSWER	INSERTED
CHANGED	KEYVIOL
CROSSTAB	LIST
DELETED	PASSWORD
ENTRY	PROBLEMS
FAMILY	STRUCT

Other Table Names To Avoid

Temporary Paradox Files

CHGTEMP	PROBTEMP
DELTEMP	SORTnnnn (where nnnn is a number)
INSTEMP	Zzz*****

DOS Device Names

AUX	LPT3
COM1	NUL
COM2	PRN
CON	ESC
LPT1	Subdirectory name in table's directory
LPT2	

Fields

You should not use *[#]* as a field name. This is reserved by Paradox for the record number field.

Scripts

Naming scripts with a DOS device name can cause problems. Avoid the DOS device names listed in the section above for tables. Also, don't use the names *Init* or *Instant* unless you purposely are using them.

Variables, Array Names, and Procedures

When you name variables and arrays, you cannot use the names of Paradox commands, command keywords, functions, or system variables. These names are all listed below. In addition, you cannot use the name of a Paradox function for one of your own procedures. Paradox functions are preceded by an asterisk in the list.

ACCEPT	COPY
*ACOS	COPYFORM
ADD	COPYFROMARRAY
ALL	COPYREPORT
ARRAY	COPYTOARRAY
*ARRAYSIZE	*COS
*ASC	CREATE
*ASIN	CREATELIB
*ATAN	CROSSTABKEY
*ATAN2	*CSTD
*ATFIRST	*CSUM
*ATLAST	CTRLBACKSPACE
ATTRIBUTE	CTRLBREAK
AUTOLIB	CTRLEND
BACKSPACE	CTRLHOME
*BANDINFO	CTRLLEFT
BEEP	CTRLPGDN
*BLANKDATE	CTRLPGUP
*BLANKNUM	CTRLRIGHT
BLINK	CURSOR
*BOT	*CURSORCHAR
CANCELEDIT	*CURSORLINE
CANVAS	*CVAR
CASE	*DATEVAL
*CAVERAGE	*DAY
*CCOUNT	DEBUG
*CHARWAITING	DEFAULT
CHECK	DEL
CHECKDESCENDING	DELETE
CHECKMARKSTATUS	DELETELINE
CHECKPLUS	*DIRECTORY
*CHR	*DIREXISTS
CLEAR	DITTO
CLEARALL	DOS
CLEARIMAGE	DOSBIG
CLOSE	*DOW
CLOSED	DOWN
*CMAX	DOWNIMAGE
*CMIN	DO__IT!
*CNPV	*DRIVESPACE
COEDIT	*DRIVESTATUS
COEDITKEY	ECHO
*COL	EDIT
*COLNO	EDITKEY

EDITLOG
ELSE
EMPTY
END
ENDFOR
ENDIF
ENDPROC
ENDQUERY
ENDSCAN
ENDSWITCH
ENDTEXT
ENDWHILE
ENTER
EOL
EOS
*EOT
*ERRORCODE
*ERRORMESSAGE
ERRORPROC
*ERRORUSER
ESC
EXAMPLE
EXECPROC
EXECUTE
EXIT
*EXP
*FAMILYRIGHTS
FAST
*FIELD
*FIELDINFO
*FIELDNO
*FIELDRIGHTS
*FIELDSTR
*FIELDTYPE
FIELDVIEW
FILE
*FILESIZE
*FILL
FIRSTSHOW
FOR
*FORM
*FORMAT
FORMKEY
FORMTABLES

FROM
*FV
*GETCHAR
GRAPHKEY
*GRAPHTYPE
GROUPBY
HELP
*HELPMODE
HOME
IF
*IMAGECAVERAGE
*IMAGECCOUNT
*IMAGECMAX
*IMAGECMIN
*IMAGECSUM
*IMAGENO
IMAGERIGHTS
*IMAGETYPE
INDEX
INFOLIB
INS
INSTANTPLAY
INSTANTREPORT
*INT
*INTENSE
*ISASSIGNED
*ISBLANK
*ISBLANKZERO
*ISDIRNAME
*ISEMPTY
*ISENCRYPTED
*ISFIELDVIEW
*ISFILE
*ISFORMVIEW
*ISINSERTMODE
*ISLINKLOCKED
*ISMULTIFORM
*ISMULTIREPORT
*ISPRIVATE
*ISRUNTIME
*ISSHARED
*ISTABLE
*ISVALID
KEYLOOKUP

KEYPRESS
KEYTO
LEFT
*LEN
LIKE
*LINKTYPE
*LN
LOCATE
LOCK
LOCKKEY
LOCKRECORD
*LOCKSTATUS
*LOG
LOOKUP
LOOP
*LOWER
*MATCH
*MAX
*MEMLEFT
MENU
*MENUCHOICE
MESSAGE
*MIN
*MOD
*MONITOR
*MONTH
MOVETO
*MOY
*NETTYPE
NEXT
*NFIELDS
*NIMAGERECORDS
*NIMAGES
*NKEYFIELDS
NOEXT
NOREFRESH
NORESTORE
NORMAL
*NPAGES
*NRECORDS
*NROWS
*NUMVAL
OFF
ON

OPEN
OTHERWISE
*PAGENO
*PAGEWIDTH
PAINTCANVAS
PALMENU
PASSWORD
PATTERN
PGDN
PGUP
*PI
PICKFORM
PICTURE
PLAY
*PMT
*POW
PRINT
PRINTER
*PRINTERSTATUS
PRIVATE
*PRIVDIR
PRIVTABLES
PROC
PROCS
PROMPT
PROTECT
*PV
QUERY
*QUERYORDER
QUIT
QUITLOOP
*RAND
READLIB
READONLY
*RECNO
RECORD
REFRESH
RELEASE
RENAME
REPORT
REPORTTABLES
REQUIRED
REQUIREDCHECK
RESET

*RETRYPERIOD
RETURN
RETVAL
REVERSE
REVERSETAB
RIGHT
ROTATE
*ROUND
*ROW
*ROWNO
RUN
SAVEVARS
SCAN
*SDIR
*SEARCH
SELECT
SETDIR
SETKEY
SETMARGIN
SETMAXSIZE
SETNEGCOLOR
SETPRINTER
SETPRIVDIR
SETQUERYORDER
SETRECORDPOSITION
SETRESTARTCOUNT
SETRETRYPERIOD
SETSWAP
SETUSERNAME
SHOWARRAY
SHOWFILES
SHOWMENU
SHOWTABLES
*SIN
SKIP
SLEEP
SLOW
SORT
*SORTORDER
*SPACES
*SQRT
STEP

*STRVAL
STYLE
*SUBSTR
SUBTRACT
SWITCH
SYNCCURSOR
*SYSCOLOR
*SYSMODE
TAB
*TABLE
*TABLERIGHTS
*TAN
TEXT
THEN
*TIME
TO
*TODAY
*TYPE
TYPEIN
UNDO
UNIQUE
UNLOCK
UNLOCKRECORD
UNPASSWORD
UNTIL
UP
UPDATE
UPIMAGE
*UPPER
*USERNAME
VARS
*VERSION
VERTRULER
VIEW
WAIT
WHILE
*WINDOW
WRITELIB
*YEAR
ZOOM
ZOOMNEXT

Pictures

Picture Examples

Picture	Description
###-##-####	Social Security number. Will fill in hyphens automatically.
###-####	Phone number. No area code. Hyphen filled in automatically.
[(###)]###-####	Phone number. Area code optional. Hyphen filled in automatically.
#[#]/##/##	Date. Slashes filled in automatically.
{1,2,3,4,5,6,7,8,9,10,11,12}/##/##	Date. Checks for valid month.
*?	Letters only. No spaces allowed.
&*?	Letters only. First letter capitalized.
*&	All uppercase letters.
!*	First character capitalized.
!*[{ ,.,(,;,}*{ ,.,(.;.}!,	Capitalizes first letter of every word after period, comma, blank, or parenthesis.
Yes,No	Can press Y, y, N, or n and have word filled in automatically.
{0#,1#,2{0,1,2,3}}: {0,1,2,3,4,5}#:	Time format. Colons filled in automatically.

Sort Orders

ASCII Sort Order

Char	ASCII Code	Char	ASCII Code	Char	ASCII Code
65	A	82	R	105	i
66	B	83	S	106	j
67	C	84	T	107	k
68	D	85	U	108	l
69	E	86	V	109	m
70	F	87	W	110	n
71	G	88	X	111	o
72	H	89	Y	112	p
73	I	90	Z	113	q
74	J	97	a	114	r
75	K	98	b	115	s
76	L	99	c	116	t
77	M	100	d	117	u
78	N	101	e	118	v
79	O	102	f	119	w
80	P	103	g	120	x
81	Q	104	h	121	y

Char	ASCII Code	Char	ASCII Code	Char	ASCII Code
122	z	145	æ	226	Γ
128	Ç	146	Æ	227	π
129	ü	147	ô	228	Σ
130	é	148	ö	229	σ
131	â	149	ò	230	µ
132	ä	150	û	231	τ
133	à	151	ù	232	Φ
134	å	152	ÿ	233	θ
135	ç	153	Ö	234	Ω
136	ê	154	Ü	235	δ
137	ë	160	á	236	∞
138	è	161	í	237	φ
139	ï	162	ó	238	∈
140	î	163	ú	239	∩
141	ì	164	ñ	240	≡
142	Ä	165	Ñ		
143	Å	224	∝		
144	É	225	β		

International Sort Order

Char	ASCII Code	Char	ASCII Code	Char	ASCII Code
97	a	135	ç	69	E
132	ä	67	C	144	É
160	á	128	Ç	102	f
133	à	100	d	70	F
131	â	68	D	103	g
65	A	101	e	71	G
142	Ä	137	ë	104	h
98	b	130	é	72	H
66	B	138	è	105	i
99	c	136	ê	139	ï

Char	ASCII Code	Char	ASCII Code	Char	ASCII Code
161	ı	80	P	152	ÿ
141	ì	113	q	89	Y
140	î	81	Q	122	z
73	I	114	r	90	Z
106	j	82	R	134	à
74	J	115	s	143	À
107	k	225	β	145	æ
75	K	83	S	146	Æ
108	l	116	t	224	∝
76	L	84	T	226	Γ
109	m	117	u	227	π
77	M	129	ü	228	Σ
110	n	163	ú	229	σ
164	ñ	151	ù	230	µ
78	N	150	û	231	τ
165	Ñ	85	U	232	Φ
111	o	154	Ü	233	Θ
148	ö	118	v	234	Ω
162	ó	86	V	235	δ
149	ò	119	w	236	∞
147	ô	87	W	237	φ
79	O	120	x	238	∈
153	ö	88	X	239	∩
112	p	121	y	240	≡

Swedish/Finish and Norwegian/Danish Sort Order

Char	ASCII Code	Char	ASCII Code	Char	ASCII Code
97	a	107	k	120	x
160	á	75	K	88	X
133	à	108	l	121	y
131	â	76	L	152	ÿ
65	A	109	m	89	Y
98	b	77	M	122	z
66	B	110	n	90	Z
99	c	164	ñ	145	æ
135	ç	78	N	146	Æ
67	C	165	Ñ	237	ø
128	Ç	111	o	232	ø
100	d	162	ó	134	å
68	D	149	ò	143	Å
101	e	147	ô	132	ä
137	ë	79	O	142	Ä
130	é	112	p	148	ö
138	è	80	P	153	Ö
136	ê	113	q	129	ü
69	E	81	Q	154	Ü
144	É	114	r	224	∝
102	f	82	R	225	β
70	F	115	s	226	Γ
103	g	83	S	227	π
71	G	116	t	228	Σ
104	h	84	T	229	σ
72	H	117	u	230	µ
105	i	163	ú	231	τ
139	ï	151	ù	233	θ
161	í	150	û	234	Ω
141	ì	85	U	235	δ
140	î	118	v	236	∞
73	I	86	V	238	∈
106	j	119	w	239	∩
74	J	87	W	240	≡

Index